# LIBRARY ISSUES: The Sixties

# LIBRARY ISSUES:
## The Sixties

Edited by

ERIC MOON and KARL NYREN

R. R. BOWKER COMPANY, New York & London 1970

Published by the R. R. Bowker Co. (A XEROX COMPANY)
1180 Avenue of the Americas, New York, N.Y. 10036
c 1970 Xerox Corporation

Library of Congress Card Number: 71–103618
Standard Book Number: 8352–0297–6

Printed and Bound in the United States of America.

# Contents

# Introduction

"Journalism," said Bruce Bliven after he had been at the trade for over 60 years, "is like putting up building blocks which seem to be going up at random, but you look back after 100 years and you see you have been contributing to an edifice. You make people conscious of themselves, of where they stand in relation to the world, of what is possible to be done, and then they do it, with heartbreaking slowness. But the world do move, eventually it moves."*

The journalist in the service of any group is called on to do more than just record and arrange on pages what others do and say, what events occur; when he is doing his job properly, he is creating some part of the world in which he lives.

The decade of the sixties was a turbulent and critical one for librarians, as it was for other professionals. The changes that occurred in that decade are probably irreversible: federal funding; the rollback of the censors; the rise of a different sense of the librarian's mission in society; the slow melting away of racial discrimination; the assertion of the rights of professionals to share in decision-making.

Add to these the surge of new buildings, the sudden spread of school libraries, the commitment to automation, the proliferation of non-print media; the innumerable systems, networks, and cooperative schemes which sprang up to link institutions and in some cases to create wholly new institutions; the beginning of a wave of changes in library education; the shaking of the venerable foundations of associations.

Looking back over *Library Journal* for this decade, the first and most notable fact is that journalistically it was the decade of Eric Moon. Under his skillful and impatient direction, *LJ* abandoned the echoing of platitudes which too often passes for editorial comment and took on the role of an advance guard, searching out and tangling with issues—often long before the main body of librarians were ready to start thinking about them.

It is because of this eagerness to come to grips with important issues that a ten-year compilation of *LJ* editorials provides such a graphic map of the rugged and exciting terrain of the 60's. It is a special kind of history— or rather source material of history—for it is still alive with indignation, or enthusiasm, or disgust, or joy which was felt about issues of the day— reminding us that history is made and lived through by vulnerable, fallible, and live human beings, and it is not to be understood otherwise.

# CHAPTER 1

# Federal Aid:
# Progress & Program

At the very beginning of the decade, the Library Service Act, thought of by many as a temporary measure, made the big breakthrough of federal aid to libraries. By the middle of the decade, the limited concept of aid to rural areas had been expanded and legislation was forged to lend government support to a wide spectrum of library service—in cities and suburbs, in schools, colleges and universities. By 1967, the National Commission on Libraries was created to lay the foundation ideas for the newly accepted fact of large-scale federal involvement in library support. And by the end of the decade, although war expenditures were threatening to bring growth to a halt, there was no denying the fact that libraries had made it on the national scene—and would stay there despite any setbacks.

## LSA'S FUTURE ASSURED
February 15, 1960

The future looks rosy for the Library Service Act. The most confirmed optimists among us could scarcely have hoped for better treatment or predicted a more enthusiastic response than this program for the extension and improvement of rural public library service in the U.S. has been receiving in the past few weeks in Washington.

For 1961 the Department of Health, Education and Welfare has asked the largest appropriation ($7.3 million of an allowable $7.5 million) since the program started. Seven bills have already been introduced into Congress to extend the program for another five years after the expiration of the first Act in 1961. It is not alone the number of bills which is impressive: one of them has 15 co-sponsors and, when Senator Hill, chairman of the Senate Labor and Public Welfare Committee and author of the original Library Services Act, introduced a like measure he carried 53 senators with him as co-sponsors.

The warmth of the response to this program is typified in the remarks of the Hon. Edith Green, Representative from Oregon, which appeared in the *Congressional Record* on January 11, when she introduced her own bill:

"Mr. Speaker, the Rural Library Services Act is not the most extensive or the most costly of the Federal grant-in-aid programs. But this program is surely one of the most rewarding, one of the most encouraging, and one of the most productive of the educational grant programs. The experience of the first 4 years surely augurs well for what can be accomplished in the next half decade, as library doors swing open for more and more of our people."

Some of the great achievements during the first four years of the program were listed by Senator Hill, as reported in the *Record* on January 14. Here are a few only:

"Thirty million rural people now have new or improved public library services available to them as a result of this cooperative State-local-Federal program.

"State appropriations for public library service to rural areas have increased 54 percent since 1956.

"More than five million books and other informational and educational materials have been added to the cultural resources of rural communities.

"State library extension agencies have been able to strengthen their staffs and resources to assist rural communities in improving their library services or establish new services. Some 90 field consultants were added to State agency staffs, an increase of 80 percent over total field staff in 1956."

More libraries, more books, more staff, more funds, and more people served—on its record alone this program is one thing about which we would expect librarians to be unanimous in their support. Not so.

In a mail vote which closed on December 15, the ALA Council revised its position on the Act and approved ALA support of an extension for "another five-year period at not less than the present authorization." But of 166 voting members of the Council only 137 voted in favor of extension. Eighteen did not record a vote, six ruined their votes, and five actually *opposed* extension.

There are clearly still some librarians who are not sold on LSA. We feel sure that others will share our curiosity about the identity of the five who cast negative votes, and their reasons for doing so. It seems unlikely that their votes reflect in any way the opinion of the majority of the members who elected them to the Council. Undoubtedly the bogey of federal usurpation of states' functions is not yet laid low, and probably accounts for some of the opposition. It may be also that, since LSA is so patently a public library measure, there are some in other areas of librarianship who believe that it does not obtain. Nothing could be more shortsighted. Better libraries in any field can ultimately only be of benefit to librarianship as a whole.

*Eric Moon*

## IF YOU'RE MALE OR MARRIED
December 15, 1964

We went over to the Office of Economic Opportunity to talk with William Lynch, who is in charge of recruiting the educational staff for the Job Corps camps, the first of which are scheduled to open in February. The prospect for librarians was better than we had anticipated, and the main drawback to a prospective applicant seems to be sex.

The Job Corps camps, which should number at least 150 in a year, will be small, each planned to train some 200 young men aged 16 to 22 who have dropped out of school and need vocational rehabilitation. They will be staffed by two agencies: the vocational staff will be appointed by some other office, such as the Department of the Interior; the education team, chosen by the Job Corps, will consist of a deputy for education, two instructors, a counselor, and seven "advisors"—volunteers from VISTA.

At the instructor level in each camp, there is a place for the librarian. Mr. Lynch explains that the curriculum for the camps will be unstructured, carefully adapted to the students' intellectual and emotional requirements, which are still an unknown quantity, with much reliance on individualized and programed teaching. According to *Education, U.S.A.*, the camps can also serve as a laboratory for new teaching techniques and materials, and as a training ground for a new generation of professionals devoted to the special needs of the deprived.

Thus the Job Corps is looking for instructors who can establish rapport with these young people. Accordingly, not only certified teachers are invited to apply, but social workers and librarians with 18 credits in education or the behavioral sciences, or with some teaching experience with this age level. The main proviso: that the person be male, or, if female, married. (The merits of a husband-and-wife team are obvious; single women can take heart in the fact that there will soon be women's camps as well.)

Since any curriculum requiring a flexible approach to individual needs, emotional intuitiveness on the part of teachers, and a knowledge of many media requires someone geared to working with the individual, the value of staffing each Job Corps camp with an instructor-librarian is apparent. So would be the creation of a post, on the national level, for a library coordinator. A committee of nine, working with Jane Manthorne, reader's advisor for young adults at the Boston Public Library, has compiled a recreational booklist for the Job Corps libraries, and a permanent post would keep the library program a dynamic, ongoing function. But the opportunity for service does exist, and provides librarians with a splendid challenge to use their particular talents, be they for motivating a young person, finding just the right book, or knowing the many instructional tools needed for a flexible program. For the special task of teaching dropouts who are many years behind the normal curriculum, a training course is provided by the Job Corps. We urge librarians to apply for positions in this most crucial phase of the war on poverty, for an experience that is not only rewarding in itself, but invaluable in view of the emphasis that vocational education will be given in the next few years.

*Evelyn Geller*

## THE BIG PUSH
January 15, 1965

In his article on library progress in 1964, which launched the new year for LIBRARY JOURNAL (Jan. 1, 1965, page 56), Eric Moon, *LJ* editor, noted the great surge of activity in librarianship that the country has witnessed, due notably to the passage of the Library Services and Construction Act. We might say as much for school libraries. Certainly the last five years have seen a decided growth in school library consciousness, not only with the formulation of ALA *Standards for School Library Programs* and the School Library Development Project, but through outside help from the Knapp Foundation, National Library Week, the International Paper Company, and the U.S. Office of Education. Commissioner of Education Francis E. Keppel's article on school libraries, which appeared in the November *McCall's* magazine, is now being distributed by National Library Week, and should provide a powerful impetus to citizen support of the school library movement.

To these efforts comes a boost from the Federal government in the way of new acts that form a remarkable mosaic of legislation. As Commissioner Keppel points out in our lead article, this new source of help does not affect libraries directly, but it is no less significant for that. In the first place, institutes are now provided for librarians, library supervisors, and educational media specialists, promising relief of the acute shortage of trained school librarians. Secondly, the provisions for buying books (excluding textbooks) and other materials promise much for school library collections, since any instructional tool used by more than one class or department is likely to be located in the school library. Third, the NDEA amendments in themselves connote an important shift in educational philosophy, at the national level, from an overemphasis on science to support of English, reading, social sciences—subjects whose value is less directly utilitarian, and which form "the lower limbs of the liberal arts tree." Last, in implementing these ends through an enriched curriculum that meets particular needs with an abundance of materials, the new legislation promotes a philosophy for which the school library has always stood, but which it has often failed to realize.

But, for all the new opportunities, we'd like to voice some doubts. Will the librarian be able to face up to the new opportunities for book selection, or will he fall prey to the newest gimmick or teaching machine, the pushiest advertiser? We wonder, and base our view on a few rather disconcerting instances. One librarian wrote in, rather vaguely, to "the R. R. Bowker

Company," asking for a list of NDEA-approved titles; there was no mention of a particular subject or grade level. Another librarian, reports Melville Beauman of the Baker & Taylor Company, knew what she wanted, but sent out an advance order without consulting her school. She was willing, she said, to "fight the principal" for her ideas. And in confirmation, Eleanor E. Ahlers, school library supervisor for the State of Washington, comments on the use of NDEA funds: "The lists to be checked out come to my office, and the quality of some of the materials that are hurriedly added to libraries is very distressing. Also there are materials going into individual departments with no central listing, which is another disturbing aspect. Now that we have such an opportunity to broaden our libraries in many such areas, it is essential for librarians themselves to be aware of the possibilities."

The crucial point here is that there are, theoretically, no constraints on book purchase, if orders are justified through consultation with teachers and librarians and submitted as parts of state plans. Nor does this mean that the librarian submits himself to some autocratic authority. It is his job to carry his title with some responsibility, and to free himself from the routines which keep him from the central task of book selection. Some of the old NDEA funds were, after all, turned back to the government—a fact that indicates the potential of federal aid for the librarian who has the initiative.

*Evelyn Geller*

## THE HANDS-OFF POLICY CONTINUES
February 15, 1965

For those who feared that increased federal support of education through the expanded National Defense Education Act (NDEA) and other pending legislation would lead to federal control, the word from the Office of Education was reassuring indeed. In talks before the American Book Publishers Council, the American Association of School Librarians at ALA Midwinter, and with us personally, Dr. Marjorie Johnston, director of the OE Instructional Materials Branch, which administers the NDEA, spelled out a strict line of federal aid without federal edict.

Take the provisions for buying materials under the revised Title III, whose few restrictions are extremely scrupulous. Apart from textbooks and consumable items, almost anything goes. The OE will not issue, Dr. Johnston told the ABPC on January 21 and the AASL six days later, a master list of NDEA-approved books. Such a list, she explained, would limit book selection, excluding items needed in one area, including materials not necessary elsewhere, and would, in any case, be obsolescent when published. Moreover, since no item is approvable outside of a specific instructional context, "a book order just won't do." Here the judgment of qualified personnel is the only reliable and flexible guide.

Second, the act is splendidly structured to pass responsibility for curriculum planning—a much more central concern now that the NDEA includes most subjects taught in school—on to the states, and to permit the states themselves to delegate their authority to the districts and schools. The funds for supervisory positions, for example, now doubled from $5 to $10 million, provide for specialists in the subject fields at the state level, to ensure free and effective use of the funds, involve teachers in planning, and help them resist the pressures of overzealous salesmen. The degree to which this authority will be passed to the local schools is left for the states to decide, but the effort to make project planning a grass-roots affair, including not only administrators but teachers and librarians—those who work most closely with students—is encouraged. The projects will be approved by the Title III coordinator in each state, at the state level.

Within the broad framework of the act and regulations, there will be great variation throughout the country and within the states. Although the 50 departments of education are setting priorities (e.g., whether to stress elementary or secondary school improvement, concentrate on a particular subject or teaching medium, or build up the poorer schools first), many states are not sending prior allocations to the districts. "Setting a quota for the schools," Dr. Johnston says, "might cut short planning because of a supposed shortage of funds, or encourage overspending where funds were generous." In brief, the federal government is bending backward to permit utmost autonomy at the state and local levels.

At the same time, the federal mandate, by its very permissiveness, is leaving the field open to competition among the a/v people, the subject specialists, teachers who may opt for large classroom collections, and the librarians. Librarians, included with media people in the category of "related services," have at most an advisory role, and in states or local districts where library staffing and service are weak may be left out of the picture altogether. Though many materials may go into the library, the question of classroom *vs.* library collections is again a local affair.

Since the librarian's role here will depend so much on individual and tactful initiative, we'd like to suggest a few pointers. Prepare your lists of books and other materials, rigidly divided by the eight subjects covered under the act, and be sure to volunteer this information to teachers and principals in staff meetings, individual consultation, or memoranda. A multi-school or district librarian should try to be at each meeting in her area. Use Commissioner Keppel's moral support of school libraries by showing his article, now available in reprint, to other staff. And take comfort in the fact that processing costs, if included as part of the cost of the books, are NDEA-eligible.

At the Midwinter conference, librarians who felt neglected under NDEA were consoling themselves with the promise of the pending education act, with its flat support of school libraries. But even that bill, split up between textbook and school library book allocations, seemed to us to raise its own problems. Perhaps it is only with time, and bolstering of the kind that the President and the Commissioner have given us, that the profession will really come into its own, and derive its deserved support from outside. Meanwhile, the race is to the swift.

*Evelyn Geller*

## A TEACHERS' CORPS—AND PRIVATE EDUCATION
March 15, 1965

Edward Kennedy and Gaylord Nelson have introduced bills in the Senate to attract talented, idealistic young people into teaching through a National Teachers Corps—a program that would permit them to teach in schools in deprived areas with the support of federal funds. The Kennedy version asks the federal government to spend $30 million a year and employ 2500 experienced teachers, either retired or willing to resign their present positions for this venture. Senator Nelson has asked for an expenditure of $40 million a year to recruit 1000 experienced teachers plus 5000 recent college graduates who would be trained by the Corps. Enrollees would serve for two years in deprived-area schools, in much the same way that the Peace Corps now operates. Both bills, says the *New Republic*, "would make manpower available to poor schools at low cost, and manpower not available to these schools at any price." They would draw dedicated people into teaching where they are most needed.

Like the Peace Corps and the domestic Job Corps, this is another singularly imaginative program. Its structuring along the lines of the earlier efforts speaks well, in turn, for the youth who have thrown themselves into unremunerative work with high enthusiasm. Librarians and students in library schools would do well to keep track of the fate of this legislation, which will surely have a place for them.

At the same time, the Teachers Corps, and the Books for Appalachia project which Sargent Shriver has just initiated, set us thinking again about the church-state issue. The Education Act of 1965 has broken rank with previous legislation in the direction of partial support of church schools because it is improbable that the bill would be passed under any other conditions; heretofore, federal aid to schools has been blocked by religious opposition in Congress. Now the bill is being supported as a good thing on which some compromise is necessary. For school librarians particularly it poses uncomfortable questions of conscience. Educators generally want it to pass because it supports education; school librarians because of Title II (which is not poverty-linked) and other provisions which address themselves for the first time to their unique problems. The raising of what the American Civil Liberties Union calls "sticky constitutional issues" might upset the whole applecart. Thus, opposition to the act in the only form in which it is likely to pass becomes, indirectly, an obstacle to the culturally deprived student's learning, and, in some vague way, discrimination against religion.

But the question is more complicated, for it rests not merely on the fear of church control but the role of public education in a democracy. The decline of the public schools in our large cities is due in some measure to increased enrollment in private schools of children whose families wish to avoid *de facto* integration. The city school, caught between the move to the suburbs and the growth of private school enrollment within the metropolis, has been left with totally inadequate funding. (And it is in the cities, as has been repeatedly pointed out, that the school library situation is worst.) The Education Act thus tends to perpetuate a system of "separate but equal" schools that prevents the mingling of cultures on which we have always vaunted ourselves.

Secondly, for all the publicity given to it, the school-aid bill does not provide, in quantity or distribution, the degree of support that is really needed; the revision of the bill in committee, adding to the allocation for antipoverty programs under Title I, attests to this. And so do the new programs suggested by Senators Nelson and Kennedy, and by Sargent Shriver. What they are doing, in effect, is leaving the funding of education—education of the deprived particularly—to volunteer effort and private support, at the same time that the Education Bill pays for books and ser-vices to private schools, going outside its area of *required* obligation.

In the end, then, the question is not just one of principle; it is also a matter of the most urgent expediency. Given a limited outlay of federal funds, which is to come first? The subsidy of private institutions (not pupils, for our public schools are open to all), or the strengthening of our public agencies—including school and public libraries—which have been clamor-ing for help for so long?

*Evelyn Geller*

## SUCH EASY CHARITY
April 15, 1965

With so many federal projects starting up now, one can expect some of them to be mistakes sooner or later; but the government seems to have put its foot in it pretty early in the game. One of the newest and best-publicized antipoverty programs, the Books for Appalachia Project, noted and briefly criticized in last month's *School Library Journal* (pp. 2, 126), may well set school library progress in Kentucky back a good decade.

As described by the Office of Economic Opportunity, this plan calls on parent-teacher orgainizations across the country to launch book drives for the poorer schools in Kentucky, in a program that may eventually spread to all of the 11-state Appalachia region. The plan calls for checking books against a list of several hundred children's titles, and the weeding of the collections by a professional librarian (Jean Moister, working in Berea, Kentucky) before they are sent to the schools.

Controlled as the project seems in theory, librarians who have had long experience with the pathetic results of book drives are worried. They know it is one thing for a citizen to add a sacrificial tone to his spring cleaning by hallowing it in the name of charity; quite another to check his fusty volumes against approved lists or actually go out and buy the books. The first shipments which came in to Kentucky, from Iowa, were of the James Bond-Mickey Spillane ilk, though, the Appalachian Volunteers explain, this was before the list was made available. Even should the program tighten up to restrict donations, the chances are slim that they will permit libraries to be systematically built up with the kind of balance they need. No assembly of discards can make up a collection.

What is worse is the ultimate effect on school libraries of the very assumption that collections can be built through charity drives. The revised NDEA and the Education Act permit new funding of libraries, but allow for alternatives in each case; and librarians are afraid that school administrators, thinking that library needs have been met by these volunteer efforts, will divert the funds intended for library collections into other equipment, or to other schools. It is anticlimactic—after the federal government has for the first time permitted the improvement of the school library situation—that the antipoverty program should itself let this phase of school service slip back to the sporadic, chaotic, and unpredictable efforts of volunteers, however well meaning. And ironic that two government spokesmen—Francis Keppel and Sargent Shriver—should have so little apparent communication with each other.

One reason why such heavy publicity is being given to an effort that makes children's books as easy as toys and old clothes to give away is the fact that so much citizen support is required, that President Johnson wants the entire American community to be involved in the antipoverty campaign—to feel responsible for the well-being of the deprived. This, after all, is what the grass-roots community action programs should be all about, and the Council of the Southern Mountains, the agency behind the Books for Appalachia effort, has certainly made an ingenious pitch for nationwide support.

One wonders, however, what such easy charity can do but appease our own consciences, as we sacrifice objects that we don't need, without spending money, without interrupting our lives, above all by giving as largesse what should belong to others by right. The kind of charity exemplified by the civil rights workers in Mississippi, or the Selma-Montgomery marchers, seems to be limited enough: the province of students, some extremists, a small minority of idealists. We sit back and watch television, smiling approval at our representatives in Mississippi and Alabama, stunned at the murder of our surrogates, satisfied with our *feelings* of concern, carefully avoiding any guilt for the situation.

Can the Books for Appalachia program, a minimal, token, long-distance effort, pass any better for real citizen involvement? There are laws to provide what is being done here in a gush of civic sentimentality; there is a profession that can give these children the books and reading guidance they need if it has the funds and authority. And it violates the spirit of the antipoverty program to think of equal opportunity as a matter of middle-class leavings.

*Evelyn Geller*

## SINGIN' THOSE FEDERAL BLUES
February 15, 1966

In four short months, every school district in this country will have had to "encumber," to use the official word, its share of the $100 million in Title II of the Elementary and Secondary Education Act, and the prospect has everyone, from book manufacturer to librarian, singing the Federal blues. For it seems pretty clear by now that the massive ordering of library materials by June 30 is going to demand an unprecedented mobilization of the book publishing and distribution industry, as well as the school library profession, in an agonizingly short time—on pain of losing Federal benefits.

The library title seems to have a special problem. Titles I and III, not being dependent on state plan approval, have had a head start and are going full blast. They benefit also in being able to hire staff for their programs, and Title III has the special advantage of a year's breather space, with time till 1967 to commit its money. By contrast, Title II administrators are caught short by the complexities of the program. Spending $100 million is not in itself a problem; at a base price of, say, $20,000 for even a midget 5000-volume school library collection (*excluding* equipment and construction), you could buy a bare 5000 collections; Pennsylvania alone is 2000 school libraries short. But the method of distributing money is not so arbitrary. Before a district can order, it must inventory whatever collections it may have, by quantity, quality, and subject. Then it often waits until the state has checked its resources against school library standards and determined "relative need"—i.e., budget—of the district.

The attendant staff and deadline problems are staggering. While some district projects have already won approval and the handling of additional money can be absorbed by existing staff in small districts, there are large metropolitan areas with great Federal budgets and new relationships to work out with private schools, which may number from a third to a half of all the schools in a city. In many areas of the country, school libraries must be started from scratch *en masse*, yet without the atrocities that characterized some National Defense Education Act planning. Right now there is precious little time for such planning, and whatever is accomplished is done after hours by available staff; only state-level administration is funded by Title II.

We think that Title III may have some useful lessons here. With less money to spend (only $75 million), Title III has been moving cautiously but surely, and with a firm sense of direction. The final guidelines give heavy emphasis to planning grants, obviously in recognition of the amount of study of available resources that must be completed before school districts can go ahead on ambitious projects. Most impressive, perhaps, is the strong quality control maintained now: Of the 746 proposals submitted to the USOE in the first round of Title III applications *only 216* were approved; most were sent back with suggestions for revision. So far only 20 percent of this year's allocation has been spent. These precautions have given the Title III program an extraordinary, if not unique, air of accomplishment. But then, it doesn't have a deadline to contend with.

Though we grant that there *is* difference between a basic educational service—the school library—and a supplementary educational service, the establishment of school libraries often will, in fact, be supplemental to existing educational programs, so far behind are school libraries in development. Moreover, librarians are in the midst of redefining even what is "basic" to a school library (*viz.*, the new *ALA Standards for School Library Programs*, now in progress). Last, the Title III proposals described in this issue stress the *same* need for an inventory of basic school library resources and for bibliographical control that is required of Title II planning, but they have time and staff to plan.

We feel, therefore, that consideration should be given to providing funds for administering Title II below the state level. And we believe, certainly, that the schools should be given more leeway in spending funds so that libraries can pace their own growth, rather than face a crash program which is straining the resources of book manufacturers and publishers (who must rush into print with quality titles) and professional leaders. Librarians are trying desperately not to waste funds in this first crucial year of the Education Act. If they push hard enough, it may not yet be too late to make this possible.

*Evelyn Geller*

## THE FIRST $10 MILLION
July 1966

When Paxton Price of the Library Services Branch of the US Office of Education rushed into New York, late in May, to tell publishers about Title II of the Higher Education Act of 1966, his story left us consumed with doubts and fearful that we were about to see another federal grant program dissipated in the wastefulness of last minute spending.

In the supplementary appropriations bill passed by Congress in early May, there was $10 million to finance basic grants to the libraries of institutions of higher education in fiscal 1966. Price explained: USOE would send guidelines and the necessary application forms to more than 2000 institutions by the end of May. To get the basic grant (maximum $5000) the library would have to return the completed application by June 4, with proof that it had increased its budget for library materials in fiscal 1966 by as much as the grant.

This much has already been accomplished by those institutions which have applied. As we write this, the colleges are anxiously awaiting approved grants from Washington, the only problem being that the money must be "obligated" by June 30.

This timing may have been enough to scare off the timid. Many colleges would certainly face pressures to spend leftovers in their regular budget at the same time. Many felt that the resulting rush would produce chaos among suppliers, wasteful rush expenditures by libraries, and a lot of money spent in small grants, with little to show for it. Publishers entered the picture with a great quantity and variety of package deals.

We decided to survey a few local colleges to see what had happened. We approached the task convinced that we'd expose frantic confusion, great outcry against this dissipation of the funds, gross misuse and questionable acquisitions, and a generally ineffective disbursement of $10 million, spread so thin, so fast.

Now we think we were wrong, provided the money comes. Every institution we called had applied for a full $5000 grant. Nearly all were prepared with acquisitions lists long before the appropriations bill was even passed, and had orders ready to mail as soon as they received any portion of the funds requested. Acquisitions departments were mobilized for immediate action. Suppliers were ready to bill libraries on immediate notice.

We found that most of the money was going to be spent for back runs of periodicals, either in full-size reprints or on microfilm ("Stuff we've always needed but never been able to finance out of one budget."). One weak library in a good college was going to buy the LC printed catalogs for the first time, "and save a hell of a lot of cataloging time and money in the deal."

While a couple of larger institutions dismissed $5000 as a "drop in the bucket," almost every librarian saw the grants as a boon to the smaller college library. While they were all irritated by the close timing, no one seemed to think it would be an insoluble problem. Most libraries had sufficient 1966 budget increases to cover the matching provisions of the law without special fund raising.

The librarians of city- and state-supported institutions were used to panic spending: "We've been operating on this kind of crisis basis as long as I can remember. It doesn't make much difference whether the panic-button is pushed in City Hall, Albany, or Washington, we're used to it."

There were other comments: "There hasn't been this much excitement in some of these libraries for years." "This grant will break the log-jam of needs that we've been building for a decade; I'm delighted." "Our administration is really library-conscious now, and the grants will force our budget higher."

To be sure, the 1966 grants are a mixed blessing. There will be unnecessary duplication of resources, as one librarian suggested. The grants are small, to lessen the total effect of a $10 million injection.

Even if you are opposed to this kind of frantic, last-minute bonanza, you have to admit that the response from the colleges, especially the smaller ones, is more than favorable. The basic grant program for fiscal 1966 is already forcing budgets upward, and it has reawakened some pretty tired libraries and librarians. And if you need ammunition to convince a Congressman that he was right to vote for the $10 million, just do as we did, and telephone the nearest dozen college libraries. They'll gladly tell you how effective even this first $5000 will be.

*John Berry*

## THE COMMISSAR AND HIS COHORTS
October 15, 1966

The sudden eruption of the "guidelines" issue in the popular press has subjected the Office of Education and Harold Howe II, US Commissioner of Education, to stringent criticism. In the House Rules Committee, where the 1966 Education Act was held up, partly because of debate on the guide lines, L. Mendel Rivers (D., S.C.) said to Howe: "This man talks like a Communist. That is why some of us who know him call him the Commissar of Education. The President should fire him."

Howe and his colleagues were called "tyrannical" and "insulting," and the guidelines "harsh and exacting." Apparently worried about a recent Gallup poll report, which found that 52 percent of adults in a nationwide survey thought the Administration was pushing integration "too fast" (in 1952, before the Civil Rights Act, "only" 32 percent thought so), the House Judiciary Committee promised to investigate the guidelines right after the November elections; and this promise came just a day after Mike Mansfield, Senate Majority leader, made front pages by saying the guidelines were being pushed too hard. (A day later, in a less publicized statement, Mansfield qualified his criticism, saying progress might be "too slow.")

Unfortunately, there is little discussion in all this debate of what the guidelines specifically say, although comments in Congress and the press relate the issue to the white backlash and adverse reaction to the Black Power movement. It is a sorry confusion, for the race riots and antiwhite sentiment, involving largely those for whom educational reform has come too late, have a somewhat more subtle relationship to the guidelines' efforts to prevent such waste (not to mention civil war) in the future, while the assumption that collective rights can be handed out as rewards for good behavior is ludicrous if not alarmingly racist. Moreover, the guidelines are quite narrowly addressed to elimination of the dual school system, which was outlawed 12 years ago, not to the problem of racial balance in the schools. They are an attempt to flesh out the paper compliances which the 1965 guidelines demanded.

We feel, moreover, that one of the most important issues raised by the guidelines (much more recent than the question of student integration) involves librarians as professionals and educators, not merely as citizens.

This is the question of faculty integration, which is raising a new clamor in the South, and which according to Joseph L. Reed, executive secretary of the Negro Alabama State Teachers Association, is a prime concern of Governor Wallace, since pupil integration, at least in Alabama's urban schools, has already begun. The great demand of the guidelines' interpretation, according to an OE spokesman, is that within each school district, one full-time professional per school should be teaching across racial lines—that is, in a ten-school district, one Negro on a white faculty, one white professional on a Negro faculty, or a proportionate average within the district. This rather modest requirement makes a mockery, we feel, of the statements that the guidelines may be attempts to "enforce integration" rather than "prevent segregation," a rather dubious semantic distinction at best.

It seems to us that librarians, as members of the American Library Association or the National Education Association (both of which have supported integrated membership and meetings), have a particular professional obligation to support integration on the job as well, and to publicize the true intent of the guidelines. For this reason *School Library Journal* has printed part of the statement made by Harold Howe on September 27 to the House Rules Committee, a statement, we feel, that has not been adequately publicized. If you have read it, pass it around, and write your Congressman in support of Office of Education policy. If librarians fail to follow through on the consequences of the legislation they pressured for, they will have proved to be members of lobbies and not professional associations.

*Evelyn Geller*

## WHITHER COOPERATION?
November 15, 1966

The complete amendments to the Elementary and Secondary Education Act (ESEA), just extended for another two years, are not available yet, but a summary in the Office of Education *Legislative Notes* includes a provision for Title II that will doubtless be debated for months to come. The amendment "requires coordination of this title [Title II] with programs funded under the Library Services and Construction Act." According to the tentative wording in the October 19 *Congressional Record,* a Title II state plan should

> provide assurance that, in order to secure the effective and efficient use of Federal funds, there will be appropriate cooperation at both state and local levels between the program carried out under this title with respect to library resources and the program (if any) carried out under the Library Services and Construction Act.

This comes at the same time as the new LSCA amendment, Title III or "interlibrary cooperation," which funds projects that provide policies and objectives for the systematic and effective coordination of the resources of school, public, academic, and special libraries and of special information centers for improved services of a supplementary nature to the special clientele served by each type of library or center . . .

Though the allocation for LSCA Title III has been slashed from its 1967 authorization of $5 million to a pathetic $350,000, and the provisions limited to planning, not operations, these first steps will bring to a head the matter of school and public library cooperation. The issue will doubtless be sharpened by that other item in our alphabet soup of legislation, ESEA Title III, which sponsors "supplementary educational services and centers," and which, even last year, brought those long-standing supplementary educational centers, the public libraries, into new projects with schools.

Though the new guidelines for these titles have yet to be issued, we'd like to raise some questions we hope they will answer. First, how can we avoid the fragmentation of library services to students, so feared by Congress and President Johnson, if the legislation itself is fractured? Should the ESEA amendment have mentioned only LSCA? With high schools demanding depth collections, doesn't Title II of the Higher Education Act warrant attention? Who will decide whether multi-school or cooperative public library-school setups make the best systems? And which funds will pay for this coordination? LSCA Title III has been cut to minimal effectiveness; ESEA II has barely the administrative funds to run its own program; and ESEA III, which *is* coordinative in conception and purpose, is hardly the logical choice, as a segment of the Education Act, to take on the burden of coordinating *all* types of libraries and systems.

Second, who will do the research (e.g., of surveys of LSCA grants, of school *vs.* public library facilities) and will these data yield any meaningful conclusions? The Sept. 1, 1966 *Library Journal* survey of circulation trends showed a heavy drop in juvenile circulation, explained by some to the school libraries bought with Title I and II money; yet some librarians held that better school libraries boosted public library circulation. Can we ever have enough "duplication" for everybody? Are we now going to shunt kids and adolescents to school libraries for "curricular" reading and the public library for "leisure" or "supplementary" services?

Third: Granting all the willingness of young adult, and reference, and college librarians to help students, are we not forgetting that the thrust of the school library today is for *autonomy*—for as broad a range of materials and services as possible in the school library itself? The student is entitled to have the information *on tap*. He has been cheated so far with poor collections and sloppy guidance, pushed by irresponsible and vague assignments to institutions that cannot help in intelligent research. The student should be able to find his books anywhere, but not at the expense of stunting school libraries in which alone he can get the instruction and continuous guidance of school librarians with subject specializations at every stage of research. A harried public librarian, an 8mm film on the *Reader's Guide* in the public library (already in the works) can't begin to do the job.

These questions barely touch the complexity of issues involved in coordination. But when that planning begins, we hope librarians will be thinking concretely in terms of the student's needs and not adopt networks neatly dividing funds among bureaucracies, that make even more rigid the divisions that presently exist.

*Evelyn Geller*

## BALANCING THE COMMISSION
January 1, 1967

The National Advisory Commission on Libraries met for the first time in Washington on November 30. It could not reasonably be expected that anything earthshaking would emerge from the first exploratory gathering of a group of this kind but, in fact, the Commission did take one step which should be warmly applauded by the library profession. It agreed that the body's membership should be brought up to the full complement and forwarded, in mid-December, a list of suggested names to the President for consideration as additional members.

By way of explanation, the Executive Order establishing the Commission "authorized" 20 members. Only 14 members, however, were announced at the time the President set up the Commission. Since that time one further appointment has been made: that of Mrs. George R. Wallace, wife of a Fitchburg industrialist, former member of the Massachusetts Board of Library Commissioners, and a noted benefactress of libraries for many years.

The original imbalance in the Commission's membership, however, remains, and it is to be hoped that the additional names recommended to the President are designed to correct this imbalance, which has greatly—and properly—disturbed many elements in the library profession. The original 14 members—certainly distinguished and variously "expert"—were nevertheless drawn almost exclusively from the worlds of research, systems, and higher education.

Mrs. Wallace's appointment helps to fill one of the more obvious gaps in the Commission's collective background and expertise. The former absence of representation of the state level (of government and library service) was one of the most critical omissions—for several reasons. Among those reasons are the need to find ways to persuade the states to shoulder a larger share of the fiscal support of library service and to noticeably strengthen the state library agencies, which are ill-equipped to handle the vastly increased responsibilities thrust upon them by the federal impetus. But most importantly, it seems clear that no national system or pattern of libraries can be fully successful without the active involvement and cooperation of the states. The presence of a member of a state library board should do something to assure those at the state level that they are not being left out of the Commission's reckoning.

There remain a number of other immensely important areas of library service, each reeking with problems, which demand similar representation. High on the list, surely, must be the larger public libraries which are caught up in the cross-currents of metropolitan crisis. The complexities of the city libraries' problems are ripe for inquiry—and action.

While much of the readership for which city library collections and services have been shaped over the years has moved away to the suburbs, it has been replaced by a new potential readership, hitherto unserved and largely ignored, whose needs will require not only greater effort but substantial changes in collections, methods, and patterns of service.

At the same time, the city libraries are reeling under the geometrically increasing demands upon their reference and research facilities. Many of those suburbanities, whose taxes now go to the support of other libraries, find that their personal (and often corporate) reference and research needs can still only be met by the superior resources of the city library. One scarcely needs to mention, in addition, the pressure from students from all levels of formal education who use the city library as a backstop.

Perhaps the most startling single omission from the Commission's original membership was school library service. Nowhere more than in this area of massive legislative crash programming does the question the President asked when he established the Commission—"Are our Federal efforts to assist libraries intelligently administered, or are they too fragmented among separate programs and agencies?"—seem more relevant.

And finally, there is that problem area that pervades all others and hangs like a threatening ceiling of smog over today's potential and tomorrow's promise: manpower and library education.

Adequate representation of these crucial areas of concern will do much to ease whatever doubts there may be as to whether the Commission is equipped to provide the President with a proper perspective on the nation's varied, but often interrelated library problems.

*Eric Moon*


## LIBRARIES AND TITLE I
January 15, 1967

"The fact that 20 percent of the sample projects set aside funds for library programs, indicates a marked deficiency of librarians and materials in those elementary and secondary schools serving disadvantaged children. Libraries are included in most new elementary school construction, but many older schools, especially those in deprived neighborhoods, have no library and often lack sufficient reading materials.

"While some Title I money is being used in support of libraries, Title II of the act is the primary resource for increasing library services in elementary and secondary schools.

"It is encouraging to note that in most states the bulk of Title II funds is being spent for libraries, but we recognize this as only a beginning. Many school systems are forced to use both Title II funds and those available under Title I to purchase books. The Council urges that in disbursement of Title II library funds, maximum attention be given to the schools serving deprived neighborhoods, and the unique needs and circumstances of disadvantaged children be taken into special account in the selection of materials."

This conclusion, from the report of the National Advisory Council on the Education of Disadvantaged Children, an independent committee appointed by President Johnson to evaluate projects funded under Title I (the "poverty" title) of the Elementary and Secondary Education Act of 1965, highlights one of the most promising outcomes of ESEA—a recognition of the prominence of libraries in the teaching of disadvantaged children. It is also a healthy step away from the obsession with "remedial reading" techniques and extra drill which can reinforce the distaste for reading the "disadvantaged" child already carries with him.

For librarians, it is nothing new to find Title I experiments (such as the one in Pittsburgh, Pennsylvania), where "trade books rather than basal readers are used since they better meet the interests of the children." The Fader experiment with paperbacks, which capitalized on books geared to a noninstitutional market, also confirmed what good librarians have long assumed. It is significant, however, that recognition is becoming prevalent *outside* the profession, particularly in poverty programs.

For this reason especially we'd like to urge the need for better coordination of library projects in poverty areas. New York handled a complicated situation well by creating a position of responsibility for Title I library projects in particular—a post which provides not only supervision by a specialist, but coordinates Title I library services to public and parochial schools. Another large-city supervisor we spoke to, however, seemed to know little outside the area of her immediate concern. When she repeated the common (and justifiable) complaint that Title II buys library materials only—no staff, no facilities—we asked whether Title I had been used for this purpose, only to get this response: "Oh, has Title I been passed yet?"

Certainly not all the faults of coordination lie with the librarian himself. Too often there is lack of communication at the state and local level: one department is simply not informed of another's activities. A Title I project approved by a Title I coordinator may have library quarters specifications that violate state specification, only because the state school library supervisor wasn't consulted. Or, in cases where the library supervisor does have a hand in reviewing a project, he is rushed into letting it pass without making important revisions. One of the saddest situations we heard was described in a project cited with approval by a representative of the Office of Education: A school superintendent, concerned with choosing books for a Title I-funded library, was leafing through publishers' catalogs for guidance on purchases! This pathetic situation could have been averted through appropriate review.

This year will find librarians better equipped to handle their ordering under Title II of ESEA. They will have had a year's experience, a slight improvement in administrative funding below the state level, less of a deadline squeeze, and, in effect, less money to spend (p. 43). It is past time now to look for new potentials under Title I, which *can* support a total library program, and which moreover, is geared to those children who can't buy books, who depend on the library for getting them, and who have been most short-changed in the decade of education "revolution" that has affected, mainly, only the aristocracy of our schools.

*Evelyn Geller*

## HIT THE DECK—RUNNING!
February 15, 1967

The Model Neighborhoods program of the Demonstration Cities Act has just appeared off the bow. The U.S. Department of Housing and Urban Development has released two publications: a mimeographed introduction entitled *Model Neighborhoods Under the Demonstration Cities Act,* and a 51-page *Program Guide* to the same. As far as we can determine, the word "library" occurs only once in the descriptions of performance standards and criteria for participation. The only other possible reference is a listing of the Library Services and Construction Act in a supplement which notes other federal programs which might conceivably be integrated with the Model Neighborhoods program. In short, another major Great Society program of innovation has taken nearly definitive form without librarians participating in its planning.

*Program Guide: Model Neighborhoods in Demonstration Cities* is available from the Superintendent of Documents for 55 cents. If it hasn't come in the mail of its own accord, it should be sent for immediately. A quick skimming of its contents will turn up a number of passages with potential significance for many libraries and librarians. Perhaps the first to take note of is the statement that the program is *not* just a big city program. Congress stipulated that small cities must be included as potential candidates.

Note the following phraseology encountered under various items in Part III, Program Standards: "to improve educational facilities and programs . . . to enhance recreational and cultural opportunities . . . physical improvement (of) facilities, services and amenities . . . provision of high quality, easily accessible educational services to area residents of all ages, in school or out . . . preschool programs . . . adult and basic vocational education . . . both formal and informal educational agencies" (this is where the word "libraries" gets its single mention).

Note the description of financial arrangements: "All grants are to be made to the City Demonstration Agency (which) . . . may in turn contract with other agencies and organizations, whether public or private, to carry out parts of the program with grant funds . . . staff services of such agencies may be contracted for to assist in planning . . . contracts may be entered into with such agencies to carry out various projects. . . ."

There are several other passages which bear underlining and pondering, with thought being given to two implications: librarians who haven't found the way to City Hall had better learn it quickly. Also: these programs are going to call for a lot of involvement of local poor people in their planning and operation. Not many librarians have ever considered such a possibility—yet the pattern of democratic involvement which the community action projects have been pioneering will undoubtedly be the modus vivendi for the model neighborhood.

How do librarians get into this new action in the war on poverty? An obvious first step is for ALA to sit down with Mr. Weaver and his family in Washington and talk to them about the importance of libraries as key components in any neighborhood. It would be good to bring forward some specific ways in which librarians can contribute, some specific examples of activities in which they have gained relevant experience. Housing and Urban Development will be evaluating proposals in the near future; if the idea of library service isn't in their frame of reference, librarians and their representatives will have only themselves to blame.

The other front to move on is the local city government. Few librarians have cultivated a direct relationship with their government officials, as has Joe Sakey of Nashua, New Hampshire (pop. 39,096), who is assigning a librarian full time to legislative reference work—a miniature, but effective "Library of Congress" operation. But besides the initiation of direct contact by local librarians, city officials can be reached in other ways: ALA can certainly help on one very appropriate level by memorializing such groups as the International City Managers Association, and the various state associations to which mayors and city managers belong.

Here's for openers: The project itself will need control and handling of information; library experience in working with trustees, friends, and neighborhood groups can be valuable; technician-trainee programs can be expanded; and soon *any* library will be able to bring to bear the resources of state and national systems.

The time is short—boarding parties away!

*Karl Nyren*

## NO STRINGS ATTACHED
February 15, 1967

"Maybe we are moving to the end of an era—the era of categorical aid. Many voices from many quarters are calling now for general aid instead— some of them the very same voices that once spoke most loudly against it." These were the comments, only mildly ironic, of Associate Commissioner of

Education Wayne O. Reed at a recent seminar held by the National Education Association. If, as he says, we are reaching the "end of an era," its span has been appallingly brief.

Reed's statement comes in response to a variety of protests that have emerged in the past year (see "A View from the Hill," *LJ*, January 15, p. 313; and this issue, p. 827). And since categorical aid, in the form of Vocational Education Act assistance and the National Defense Education Act, has been forthcoming for some time, one may conclude that the opposition is largely to the Elementary and Secondary Education Act of 1965. If President Johnson's 1968 budget goes through, ESEA will command a whopping 42.5 percent of the entire U.S. Office of Education's $4 billion budget. Loath to relinquish any share of autonomy, or their share of this fat purse, education groups have been arguing federal policy with varying degrees of justification. To sum up some charges this year: the federal government has been forcing aid to parochial schools, and it has been forcing integration. It threatens an unholy alliance with business to impose technological innovations on the schools (though schools retain absolute decision-making power on what to buy), and it challenges state authority by approving supplementary education projects the states veto, or turning down proposals OK'd by the states. And finally, it is imposing uniformity on education by sanctioning a national assessment of education, being undertaken by an independent agency.

Though the details of these arguments have still to be discussed in legislative hearings, they seem to forget that with the Education Act Congress wanted a change, and not just more of the same; wanted a new attention to educational priorities determined by long-range planning and national needs, not the demands of pressure groups. For these reasons ESEA is varied in structure to include five target areas, and is based in part on recourse to other than state supervision So, while Title V is aimed at strengthening state departments, Title I money (not control) is passed *directly* to the districts in terms of income and population. Title II, though it allows alternatives, makes school libraries a matter of national emphasis. And Title III is designed to speed up innovation by allowing a loophole, in a few cases, for local districts hamstrung by state control. "We have not thought systematically about how you produce change in our school system," commented one Congressman at the ESEA hearings last summer. "I think that our programs are not always designed to produce change." So far, Title III is still the honey of the Education Act, and, it seems, expanding geometrically, with its $75 million appropriation increased to $135 million this year, and likely to go to $240 million next year.

What the issue boils down to, in short, is whether Congress is going to be allowed to spend its seven percent share of the national education budget in the way it sees fit, or whether it is going to allow that sum to depend entirely on the varying abilities of state and local education agencies, which are often more parochial in orientation and certainly more bound to local political pressures. "Relative need" and "equality" mean different things at the federal and state-local levels; for the latter, it's often not a matter of spending the money where it's needed, but satisfying local politicians and Congressional representatives who may feel their districts are being given short shrift. Even the "relative need" clause of Title II was objected to by some state school library supervisors on these grounds.

If federal control of education is a serious threat, aid with no strings attached poses other dilemmas. When hearings begin on the ESEA in a few weeks, we hope that librarians will remember the Library Services and Construction Act was itself determined by national priorities in the face of abysmal state and local support; that poverty would not have become a national concern (or an important investment for publishers and equipment producers) without federal emphasis; that integration would have remained at a standstill if left to local authorities; and that school libraries would have continued to be neglected had they not been the subject of a "national assessment" by the USOE, and a specific focus of Congressional concern.

*Evelyn Geller*

### IT'S A DATE—DON'T BE LATE
March 1, 1967

"If Heaven drops a date, open your mouth," goes the Chinese proverb. A date was dropped from an earthly—though still lofty—level when, last September, President Johnson appointed a National Advisory Commission on Libraries. The date will not stay long in the air. Time—the relentless, governmental power of gravity which is at work in this case—will pull it quickly to earth.

One-quarter of the short life-span allotted to the Commission has already passed. If there is, as yet, no public indication of the direction of the Commission's thinking about the future of library service in this country, there are ample indications of an encouraging receptivity on the part of the Commission—indications that the Commission *wants* the library profession to open its mouth.

First, the Commission came to New Orleans to meet with ALA leaders during the recent Midwinter meeting. Second, it promised to meet again with the ALA leadership during the San Francisco conference. Third, it announced that librarians, educators, and others will be asked to present written or oral testimony.

The most concrete evidence of receptivity, however, was the President's appointment, at the end of January, of an additional six members to the Commission. This move not only filled many of the gaps in the original make-up of the Commission which we noted in an earlier editorial; it came, without much question, in response to reasoned and reasonable pressure by certain library leaders for a Commission membership which would include persons intimately in touch with some of the unrepresented specific problem areas of library service. The new appointments undoubtedly bring added strength and a more varied perspective to the Commission, and both the President and the original Commission members are to be complimented and thanked for the readiness of their response to the profession's request for a more rounded representation of interests and experience on the Commission.

"A new and potentially powerful agency which may influence both the direction and the dynamics of future library development more than any other group" was how Edwin Castagna, chairman of ALA's Committee on Legislation, described the Commission during the Midwinter ALA meeting. He called upon the profession "to present in unmistakable terms what we believe are the missions of the libraries of the United States." Before the Commission completes its report to the President next November, Castagna said, "we must communicate our convictions about American librarianship."

We share Castagna's estimate of the size and potential succulence of the date the President has dropped. This may be one of the best opportunities librarianship has had or will have to make its voice heard plainly, its needs understood clearly, at a level where some of the dreams about a nationwide system of library service have a chance of being translated into reality. How will the profession respond to Castagna's call to communicate its convictions? Will it open its mouth?

The Commission, as a body, clearly will be able to consult directly only with a minority of the profession. But the future of library service is the concern of everyone engaged in it. Any librarian with constructive ideas or proposals should, it seems to us, grasp the initiative here and transmit them by some route to the Commission—perhaps to individual members of the Commission, or to Commission executive director Mel Ruggles, or through ALA or other national associations, or via the professional press.

*LJ* has already written to a number of librarians working in different fields and various sections of the country to ask them about the problems to which they would like to see the Commission's attention directed; what proposals they have concerning the future of library service; what courses of action they would hope to see recommended by the Commission; what new directions in library legislation—or in the structuring of government agencies which administer legislative programs—seem necessary.

There is, however, no reason why responses should be restricted, either to answers to questions formulated by us or anyone else, or to persons invited to testify or produce ideas, evidence, or proposals. If you have beliefs, convictions, answer Castagna's challenge and present them in "unmistakable terms."

The date is falling fast. Is *your* mouth open?

*Eric Moon*

## A WASHINGTON BRIEFING
November 1, 1967

When some 250 representatives of the publishing world gathered in Washington on September 11–12, they sat for two days of solid briefing—primarily by Office of Education personnel, but with reinforcement from the

National Education Association, the American Council on Education, the National Audiovisual Association, and the Washington Office of ALA. Publishing people, ranging from company brass to "library reps," came to get the word on what they could expect to sell to libraries and schools. Men from the investment community came to see how the bookmen made out. And *LJ*, there to look at them all, found more of interest to librarians than the purported business of the briefing.

Instead of market information, publishers got the message loud and clear that they hadn't been very helpful in creating the new materials called for by the new needs in education, but that they could try some more this year. Publishers were invited to join in setting future policy, but the invitation had the tone of NASA suggesting cooperation from the buggywhip industry. Some rather chilling remarks were made about the imminent demise of both books and publishers, and there were suggestions that the educators themselves might well have to produce their own books and other materials.

But the most significant aspect of the two days was not translatable into facts for the business planner; it was the chance to listen long enough to catch the tone and tenor of education as she is spoken in the capital, and to perceive the dominant themes in the thinking of a vital and purposeful agency which has more than a vague notion of what it wants: an "educational system truly responsive to the needs of society." On the creation of this system, says the educational leadership, depend our chances of solving the big problems: military security, civil rights, and the new industrial revolution.

Though education in toto is next to warmaking in economic importance, accounting for some seven percent of the GNP, only four percent of government spending is for this end, as Ralph Huitt of HEW pointed out. To achieve the aims of OE planners, this outlay will have to be increased in the face of a possible middle class backlash against spending for the disadvantaged, and in the face of such competition for Congressional attention as the aerospace industry's human wave tactics of lobbying. Don White of NAVA (National Audiovisual Association) calculated that, as against the total of 17 lobbyists which the whole education field can muster, "aerospace can put 200 active lobbyists on Capitol Hill in a pinch." And among other financial hazards foreseen by the men who intend to forge the tools, techniques, and personnel that can rescue whole populations from educational disadvantage, is the emergence of other, highly appealing causes: air and water pollution, airline safety, and urban renewal, for example. These, it is feared, can easily take up the slack in any spending power released by the end of the Vietnam war.

"Priorities" was a word that recurred somewhat ominously as one answer to the problem; there may be changes ahead in the way OE funds are distributed, in order to make sure the most important aims are realized. These aims are simply stated for planners in the fields of elementary and secondary education: research and then development of new and better teaching materials and new and better teachers.

Ray Fry and his staffers from the Division of Library Services and Educational Facilities had more comfort for the publishers in their share of the briefing. They cited the national inventory figures for the great shortages of books, declared that home libraries were due for a resurgence, noted that academic libraries were buying more books, and pointed out that even money spent for library buildings had a stimulating effect on book purchasing. If librarians are at all unsatisfied with the tools that publishers and other industrial interests are providing, it isn't showing in Washington or Podunk. On the contrary, librarians have seemed to be more concerned that *they* adapt to the advances of industry; as one consequence, an increasing number of library functions are being performed outside the library community.

Librarians, whether assisting at a quantum increase in "higher" education that is too often inferior, or faced with publics which can't find their way into either the library or society, are quick to roll up their sleeves and fight. But they might well wonder at their lack of the philosophical imperatives which sustain the zeal of the educators of the young.

*Karl Nyren*

## NEW FACES IN WASHINGTON
January 1, 1968

Few agencies in the library world are more important today than the Division of Library Services in the U.S. Office of Education, and few months in the Division's life will be more important than the ones dead ahead in 1968. Struggling with reorganization of its Washington office, and establishment of nine regional positions around the country, the DLS has had little to say for itself in the past year, but its new structure is formally launched in this issue of *LJ* with an article by its director, Ray McNair Fry.

Not in that article, however, is the uncertainty that will surround the operations of the Division in the coming year. Budget cuts throughout the government threaten to hit the Division hard, and undo much of the change wrought by Fry in a year of intensive planning and rounding up of fresh talent. About the only cost-cutting option Fry has is the deferment of the appointment of his full complement of new people—and if he has to do this, all the effort of getting four new branches established in the Division, with consequent upgrading of the top positions in each unit, will have been wasted for the time being at least. Expensive and scarce talent brought to Washington for creative planning and coordination will be spending their time administering grant programs.

The spectre of crippling budget cuts is not the only danger the newly-reorganized Division faces. Around the country there is still suspicion that the decentralization program, which puts nine library specialists out into the field for grant approval and consultative services, will exist as only another layer of bureaucracy, slowing everything down and weakening the authority of the Washington agency at the same time. But this, says Fry, just isn't so. The nine new people out in the field will have full authority and a high level of competency which will be more easily tapped by librarians than if the same specialists were in Washington.

Signs of acceptance are cropping up, however, as librarians realize the caliber of the new field representatives. Bessie Moore, Arkansas library commissioner, was dead against the regionalization until she learned that Arkansas would be handled by S. Janice Kee. Arkansas is now happy about decentralization.

And the new field people—seven of the nine positions have been filled—have other things going for them. In many cases, they are well known and trusted in their regions. Those already on the ground report that they are bringing to their branches of OE the library representation which was generally lacking from offices staffed by elementary, secondary, and vocational education people, and frequently headed by ex-school super-intendents with no particular library expertise.

The nine field people represent a broad spectrum of experience; as administrators, educators, specialists, and consultants, they have been asso-ciated with progressive and significant library activities. And the four new branch heads, whose names are still not officially announced at this writing, will also be impressive for their range and stature.

The decentralization, along with the whole new division structure, deserves a fair trial. If it works as well as Fry hopes, it will bring order to the chaos created by overlapping library legislation. It will have the re-sources of talent to take its place creatively under the policy-making um-brella of the new and permanent agency which is now expected to follow the National Advisory Commission on Libraries—also under the umbrella would be the national libraries and the National Science Foundation, which are outside Office of Education jurisdiction, and badly need coordinating with it.

If Ray Fry's new team can fight off the damaging budget cuts which now threaten them, many good things are in store for 1968: a brand new branch devoted to library education, with emphasis on education in the new technologies; a research program that will be sponsoring studies aimed at the problems that both libraries and the Division will face five years from now, as well as the ones plaguing them today; a built-in, ongoing evaluative process which will give the Division and its programs a steady scrutiny; and a talent pool which can be called on for creative policies, planning, and advice. The new team, according to its director, are "people who think big and can also think together." Every librarian should be concerned that they get the chance to do just this in 1968.

*Karl Nyren*

## THE NEW ESEA AUTHORIZATIONS
January 15, 1968

Well, the agony is over, and the new school aid authorization bill, which has been dragging since spring, finally cleared Congress just before Christmas. Coming hard upon the long-delayed Senate version of the authorization bill, which passed in December after months of haggling, but in a form superior to the House of Representative's speedier version, the compromise measure was detailed too late for inclusion in our News section, and we are taking space here to describe and comment on the final bill.

First the funding. Like authorizations in past years, the amounts allowed are generous but unlikely to be met in the actual appropriations. The two-year bill, negotiated between the House's one-year and the Senate's three-year version, allows about $9.3 billion (about $4.5 billion a year) for fiscal 1969 and 1970. To be more specific: a total authorization of $9,229,-860,644 breaks down into $4,448,184,699 for 1969, and $4,481,675,945 for 1970. The breakdown by Titles is as follows:

Title I (antipoverty programs) allows $2,725,959,699 for fiscal 1969, and $2,862,175,945 for 1970. This is for Part A; a new Part B has been written into Title I which provides for incentive grants, to the tune of $50 million each for fiscal 1969 and 1970, to states that have shown better than average effort.

Title II, which is slated directly for library and other teaching materials, should, if fully funded through appropriations, be getting $162 million in fiscal 1969, and $200 million in fiscal 1970; while Title III will get $512,500,-000 and $550,000,000 for those two years, respectively. The change in Title III will shift 75 percent of the funds to state control in 1969, and 100 percent to the states by fiscal 1970, a notable states'-rights victory which the Senate had sought to delay so that experimental programs would have a better break without conforming to the more traditionally oriented state departments of education. Meanwhile, Title V, which provides for personnel to strengthen state departments of education, was given $80 million for fiscal 1969 and 1970.

A few Titles added on in recent amendments to ESEA are also noteworthy. Title VI, tacked on last year, gives (among other services) grants to the states for providing services to the handicapped: $162.5 million, then $200 million, for 1969 and 1970. Title VII, the new "bilingual programs" amendment, was passed with an authorization of $30 million for 1969 and $40 million for 1970, providing a new source of funds for services to foreign-language-speaking children. A new section in the general ESEA provisions, inserted in the Senate version of the bill and approved in the compromise measure, gives $30 million each year, in 1969 and 1970, for dropout prevention programs. And the Adult Education Act, which was shifted from OEO to Office of Education administration, will get $70 million for 1969, $80 million for 1970.

Although the Senate lost out on retaining federal administration of Title III funds, it is fortunate that its version, which was, in general, more liberal and far-reaching than the House bill, won out through the adoption of certain amendments, and in two other important areas: the integration enforcement provisions, and the recommendations for advance funding. The strength of HEW was seriously threatened in the House version of the bill, whose Fountain Amendment would have kept the government from deferring funds to a school district until after a hearing had been held. The compromise bill dropped the Fountain amendment and accepted Secretary Gardner's letter of assurance of advance notice as acceptable evidence of HEW intent.

And certainly hopeful was the acceptance of the Senate attempt to ease the bottlenecks and crises resulting from the incompatibility of legislative appropriations and school-year deadlines. Written into the authorization bill (as distinct from ESEA itself) as Title IV, is a provision that would allow Congress to make its appropriations a year in advance. To get the show off the road, Congress would in the coming year vote its appropriations for 1969 and 1970 at the same time, enabling school districts to coordinate federal and local budgets. Unfortunately, it comes too late to affect fiscal 1969 (which begins July 1968)—unless the 1969 appropriations can be squeezed into the supplemental appropriations bill to be passed this January or February. To push for a better chance this year, we urge librarians to write their Congressmen recommending inclusion of the 1969 ESEA funding in the pending supplemental appropriations bill.

*Evelyn Geller*

## A TIME FOR REGROUPING
February 15, 1968

Delivering his report in Bal Harbour to the ALA Council, Legislative Committee Chairman Edmon Low characterized the past year as "frustrating." Though the Committee, and particularly the staff of the Washington Office of ALA, have had their hands full, it has been with minor engagements and holding actions. Damage to library budgets from postal increases was held to a minimum; threatened cuts in library program funding of all types were fought; library concerns in the long copyright squabble were put forward; and funding was achieved for the two new fledgling LSCA Titles. With the memory of the great legislative victories of the past still green, 1967 was indeed a year of grueling and disappointing struggle.

About the only new development which Low noted in his report to ALA was the ESEA amendment permitting Congress to appropriate funds a year ahead of time, a principle which could well be incorporated into other legislation for libraries. A future step may be—eventually—general aid to education, with block grants, locally administered, supplanting the categorical aid which has been the pattern so far.

But big new battlefields lie ahead, and the Association cannot begin too early to plan for legislative wars that may pose new and unfamiliar challenges. The report of the National Advisory Commission on Libraries will be before the membership next June in Kansas City. Whatever its recommendations, it will provide the starting line for a long campaign to establish libraries and librarians in a world of communications where powerful forces have already staked out claims.

Long before an ALA Legislative Committee is actively lobbying for or against an actual bill, however, the library presence will have to be established. Statesmanship will be needed to get librarians on the ground in new national planning—the promising new relationship between the ALA International Relations Office and the State Department's Agency for International Development is a model situation. It will be equally important to place formidable spokesmen among those who will draw the plans for the next decade in attacking disadvantage of all types, creating the national information distribution network, and redefining both the status of the individual and democracy itself in the new industrial society which Galbraith has sketched so convincingly.

Age has not always meant maturity in the library profession, and perhaps rarely does anywhere except under the pressure of necessity. But mixed with some embarrassing signs of belated childhood, the signs of growth are visible, both in the activities of the Association and in the broad stream of library activity which it reflects, though not always very faithfully.

The ALA is moving, however slowly, toward gaining for the profession greater control over the education of its members, both professional and technical. It is wrestling with the problems of standards that must be effective and intelligent if librarians are to have the authority to exercise the all-important evaluative function in their own world. The commitment to research is growing, though control over just what research is to be done is imperfect and must be extended, with librarians the sole judges of what research is needed in their field. Along with this, research forces will have to be called in far more often; too many problems, either real or fancied, are still being dealt with by the inordinately expensive and wasteful device of "committee work," which was applauded as usual at the Midwinter meeting in Florida, but all too often turns out to be an unproductive chewing over of semantic jello—witness the PEBCO meeting on "cooperation" reported painfully on page 728 of this issue.

One major wind of change was sensed in Edmon Low's report: discussions are under way to bring Association strength to bear at the state level, where critical weakness exists, but where more important tactical decisions will probably be made in the future as the nation responds to a real, but little-understood urge toward decentralization—a trend which could be a disaster of Balkanization for libraries, or an opportunity for a great creative release of energies.

In all this, no need is greater than that the profession handle its relations with other groups with energy and sensitivity: with educators, legislators, private industry, the varied research community, unions, Friends, trustees, and the largest group of all, people who need libraries.

*Karl Nyren*

## SOPHISTICATED DROPOUTS
February 15, 1968

The January 25 announcement by John W. Gardner that he'd be leaving before March as Secretary of Health, Education, and Welfare is a ghastly comment on the state of educational reform. Gardner came to HEW in mid-1965 after ten years as president of the Carnegie Corporation, in the wake of the Great Society legislation he had helped to plan, and it seemed then he knew its problems and its promise.

He had written in 1960: "Critics are saying that we have lost our devotion to American ideals. They are saying that the individual American has lost his faith, his discipline, and his vitality. They are saying that he is a spoiled, demanding, overfed oaf who cares for nothing but his own comfort and diversion. I don't believe it. But something is wrong."

He had to be disenchanted by 1968. Vietnam may be part of the problem, since Gardner's department was obviously caught in the conflict of priorities that the war is creating, though it is not his complaint. He said just two months ago: "We are in deep trouble as a people. And history is not going to deal kindly with a rich nation that will not tax itself to cure its miseries." Here he was hinting not so much at guns *vs.* butter as at the *malaise* of a country resigned to war—so long as its affluence is not threatened by controls, tax loads, or big budget deficits to maintain welfare programs; a country apparently committed to fighting the "war on poverty" at home with machine guns and tanks. One gleans such gentle lessons in democracy from the bickering, spiteful Congress of the last session, Wilbur Mills' mulish leadership of the House Ways and Means Committee, and the cool reception given the liberal components of Johnson's cautious State of the Union message.

But Johnson, nursed on politics and compromise, and directly responsible to the country, must change, or at least modulate, his tune as he sounds public opinion; whereas Gardner, directing a bureaucratic arm that must function with some continuity and administrative discretion, cannot so easily see-saw on congressional in-fighting or on popular whim, particularly when he is charged with grappling the central—albeit unpopular—issues of civil rights, urban welfare, and equal education. And on these major issues, Gardner faced the same frustrations as his colleagues. Keppel before him tried to integrate Chicago's schools, backed down (or was backed down) before Mayor Daley—and out of the Office of Education; Harold Howe II, who started with fine flair and courage, subsided into strange silence; the Office of Economic Opportunity has encountered a series of explosions and cutbacks since its inception; and even Gardner, this December, had to deliver a "letter of intent" appeasing the Southern clique in the Senate, then lop $594 million off his department budget in a year of spiraling welfare costs.

It is ironic that a national leader should face the same blocks as the individual teacher in bucking the bureaucracy and prejudices of local political and school systems. Having just finished Jonathan Kozol's *Death at an Early Age* (Houghton Mifflin, 1967) and Herbert Kohl's *36 Children* (New American Library, 1967), which recount the experiences of two Harvard-educated teachers in the Boston and New York public schools, we were struck by the parallel. Trying one ploy after another to avoid the dated, condescending textbooks and fulsome paeans to democracy, they brought in their own books, recordings, and slides, and succeeded in teaching the "unteachable." The result: Kozol was dismissed from the Boston school system for having read the wrong poem by Langston Hughes to his class, and for deviating from the fourth-grade curriculum. Kohl faced teachers' disapproval, his own students' disillusionment as they went on to new classes with old prejudices, and decided he had to effect change from outside rather than work alone, and largely in vain, as a teacher.

In the lead article of this issue, which discusses urban education, John Gardner criticizes the "sophisticated dropout" who washes his hands of the Establishment. It is clear that by leaving HEW to study urban problems for the Corporation he once headed, Gardner simply reaffirms his commitment and sense of crisis. But it hardly speaks well for the future of education that this brilliant man should be doing the country more good by working for an independent group than he did as head of a national agency that dispenses more than $13 billion a year.

*Evelyn Geller*

## A STRATEGY FOR CHANGE
April 15, 1968

For librarians who tend to avoid the power plays of the public scene, politics is pretty much a foreign affair, if not anathema as a field of endeavor that threatens to compromise idealism. But this year, which has put Title II of the Elementary and Secondary Education Act on the chopping block along with a number of crucial domestic programs, will require a drastic change in philosophy and in strategy.

Right now in Congress, a subcommittee of the House Appropriations Committee is working out the details of the 1969 Health, Education, and Welfare Department budget, which includes the Office of Education budget and in it the 1969 funding of Title II. According to the present table, *May 12* is the deadline for the House HEW-Labor Appropriations Subcommittee to report its recommendations to the full House Appropriations Committee.

*Which means the time for action is now.* The professional and industry associations which will be affected by the cutback—the American Library

Association, the NEA Department of Audiovisual Instruction, the American Book Publishers Council-American Textbook Publishers Institute, the National Audiovisual Association, and several religious education groups—are informing their membership of the proposed cutbacks and counseling action. The American Association of School Librarians, working through ALA, is also attempting to tell school administrators—many of whom, being involved with the administration of current, 1968, funds *do not know yet of the proposed cutback*—what cutting the guts out of educational materials programs could mean for their district. But these efforts can be effective only if they are buttressed by the hard work of individual librarians working with administrators, teachers, members of the community, and salesmen (as some publishers have already proposed) to restore the Title II funding to at least the $99.2 million level of 1968.

The result will be crucial to the future of Title II, which as been the lifeline of school libraries ever since the Elementary and Secondary Education Act was passed, and to school library development itself. The importance of the program is already obvious from the number of states which report increased local and state support of school libraries at the same time that Title II funds came into the schools. These combined efforts, in fiscal 1966, resulted in a near doubling of per pupil spending on libraries—a trend that enabled school after school to approach national school library standards. They made the "instructional materials center" an everyday term for administrators and curriculum groups. And they helped millions of teachers and children discover what a rich and varied educational program could mean—at a minimum of administrative costs.

Yet if Title II is cut to $46 million, that level can set a precedent for the years to come. Some reports from Washington indicate that the programs cut back (ESEA-II and also NDEA-III) were the ones that could meet with strongest opposition in Congress. This is passing the buck back to you, librarians, educators, publishers, producers, and dealers, to act on or *before May 12.*

For this reason *SLJ* in the March issue devoted considerable editorial and news coverage to the slashing of Title II funds (see *LJ* March 15, pp. 1259 and 1263), and in this issue has given a detailed breakdown of current trends and criticism. The job for you is to take these arguments to the right people; in your own district, work for the candidate supporting a strong education budget; and push, through a mail and wire campaign, for a restoration of the Title II funds by the House of Representatives. Because of the structure and deadline of committee discussions, strategy is crucial here. The Senate, whose corresponding appropriations subcommittee will not meet until after the House hearings have ended, should not be contacted until *after* the House has come to its decisions; NDEA-III should be campaigned for *after* the fate of ESEA-II, the immediate issue, has been determined. If Your Representative is a member of the *House* Labor-HEW Appropriations Subcommittee, write to him; if he is not, write to your own Representative urging him to inform the House subcommittee chairman,

Daniel Flood, of your stand. Above all, see to it that your principal and school administrator, the lay community, and other professional organizations are also involved, so that the reaction is not confined to that of one interest group.

Even more effective would be to organize, through a personal contact with your Representative, a delegation of educators and laymen who would visit him when he is home (most Congressmen return to their communities once a week or every two weeks).

We have not provided a model letter, which would impair the effectiveness of a mail campaign, but we have provided the ammunition on page 1703 of our News section, and in our abstract of the first annual report of the Title II office at USOE (p. 1741). We have included criticism of the education budget; we have listed the estimated results, in dollar terms, in each state, of the proposed cutback; we have reprinted the strong statement of Representative St. Germain (D., R.I.) urging full funding.

In addition to the benefits that have resulted from Title II (they are listed as highlights in the prefatory paragraphs of the Title II abstract on page 69), the ALA Washington Office suggests that the following arguments be included as areas of existing need:

—There are still about 36,000 elementary schools alone that lack libraries;

—The money that in fall 1965 covered a national program when enrollment in elementary and high schools was 43.5 million now has to be stretched to meet the needs of 45.4 million pupils to be served, an increase of about 1.9 million pupils;

—There are still grave shortages in the number of trained personnel to serve teachers and pupils;

—The present 2 percent allowance for local administration, already inadequate to meet the administrative needs of Title II, will be virtually erased from the program if the funds are cut even more;

—Funds are given out so late in the fiscal year that it has been impossible to plan for the judicious spending of money;

—Per pupil expenditures for books and a/v materials are still far below national standards;

—The collections of professional books which are needed by the teaching staff, and which Title II funds could buy, are extremely limited and need to be updated, according to reports from school superintendents.

These needs must be judged not only against Vietnam but against dubious *domestic* priorities that must be reappraised before the educational needs of our students are sloughed off the federal budget. The supersonic transport jet program, for example, totally unnecessary for domestic use, is still getting $251 million (—at a time when Johnson is discouraging foreign travel!); the $440 million Apollo program, the $600 million Air Force Manned Orbiting program, and other lower-priority NASA projects could easily be deferred in part to allow for an education program that doesn't shortchange the next generation.

The current Presidential contest has put new hope into the peace campaign and into our faith in the political process itself. There is a chance, now, to use the democratic machinery to bring fresh air into our educational efforts too. But it will never come about unless you as librarians and educators, adopt the philosophy of political activism that you propound for your own students as future citizens.

*Evelyn Geller*

## WINTER DEADLINE
December 15, 1968

In this uneasy winter and the year ahead, there may be promise in Senator Ralph Yarborough's (D., Tex.) Educational Technology Bill, introduced October 10 and scheduled for reintroduction in the Senate early in January. In the words of the Senator, this draft is intended "to stir comment, open dialogue, and set in motion the thoughts of the American educational community," and it is now time for librarians to express both their interest and some serious reservations.

Originally drafted by Loran C. Twyford, chief of the Bureau of Classroom Communications for the New York State Department of Education, the revised bill asks for a $400 million authorization to fund a variety of a/v programs, mainly in elementary and high schools. It is excellent in providing a comprehensive program of media implementation, including demonstration and experimental projects, straight acquisition of a/v materials and equipment, money to help staff a/v projects, grants to schools and colleges for inservice and preservice training, minor remodeling, state plan administration, and development of "area communications centers." It also opts for a USOE Office of Instructional Technology and a National Advisory Commission on Technology.

For all who know how hard it has been under NDEA-III and ESEA-II to buy materials but not hire the people to put them to use, to buy books but not shelving, to buy a/v materials and then scrounge for essential equipment funds through other acts or local money, the range and scope of the bill are laudable.

Nevertheless, it is phrased in terms of some rather shallow ideas that don't reflect the thinking of modern school librarians and media specialists, and that tend, therefore, to split technology from the curriculum it is supposed to be serving. First, the bill seems hardly influenced by the most important thing that has happened to both librarians and a/v specialists in recent years: the recognition of a unity of purpose so intimate that it led to the cooperative development of the joint DAVI-AASL *Standards for School Media Programs* and the plea that education of print and nonprint media specialists must be unified. At the core of these developments is the thesis that print and nonprint media form a communications continuum in which no medium can be divorced from another, and that all should therefore be administered together. This concept also underlies the recent Committee on Economic Development report *Innovation in Education.*

There are a few subtle but significant ways in which the new bill reveals an innocence of these concepts. First, in definition 4, it excludes library books (though definition 5 may encompass print materials—the wording is too unclear to determine). This in itself might not be a serious detriment if the bill were seen as an expansion and refinement of ESEA-II without cutting into these funds; yet the simple exclusion tends to split the media and encourage separate print and a/v programs, working against the *Standards* concepts endorsed by 31 education groups.

Next, terms like "library" and "media center" are conspicuously absent —except in the provision (sec. 112) prohibiting federal control over choice of library materials. It would seem, however, that if definition 4 allows "any" a/v equipment and materials yet *specifies* "classroom" materials, library and media center materials and equipment should also be specified. Where "computer assisted instruction" and radio and TV are specified, films, film-strips, and discs, etc., should be specified too. Otherwise, this permissive language which nevertheless picks out certain items could siphon funds from individual schools to expensive systems and area communications centers—which indeed, seem more suitably defined as "supplementary centers and services," better left to handling under ESEA Title III. Last, the description of demonstration and training projects could cite as examples programs implementing the new *Standards* in selected schools in each state.

Such minor changes in an otherwise commendable bill should (if we can hope for a larger education budget) help both librarians and a/v specialists in their common efforts. The important thing is for librarians to show their involvement by writing *immediately* for copies of the bill to: Sen. Ralph Yarborough, Educational Technology Bill, Room 460, Old Senate Office Building, Washington, D.C., 20510; discuss it in their schools; and send in suggestions. In this way they can help it to be reintroduced, in Yarborough's own words, as "hopefully, an even wiser and better document" than it is.

*Evelyn Geller*

# CHAPTER 2

# Fighting Words

With the problems of physical survival of libraries as acute as ever, so that thousands of them existed at a base subsistence level, there is no doubt but that many librarians would just as soon not have had to face the painful problems raised by a decade in which demands for personal freedoms mushroomed. But the issue could not be avoided and bitter debate raged over what—if any—role librarians were called on to take.

Similarly, librarians found themselves taking sides on political issues—and on the question of whether this was proper. Throughout the 60's, *LJ* spoke up often and strongly against racism, the Vietnam war, Goldwater for President, and right wingers in general.

## Aspects of Intellectual Freedom

### THE RIGHT TO WRITE
August 1960

The Fiske Report is a disturbing piece of evidence that there are librarians who do not in practice defend "the right to read" as rigorously as the profession preaches it. This is bad enough but we have been growing increasingly aware that many librarians are tolerating restrictions upon an even more basic right. "The right to read" remains an empty slogan, a pious pronouncement, unless authors are free to write, and to publish what they have written.

Three hundred and sixteen years ago the defense of this liberty was memorably laid down by a great poet with failing sight but no lack of vision: "What can be more fair, than when a man . . . publish to the world what his opinion is . . . Christ urged it as wherewith to justify himself, that he preached in public; yet writing is more public than preaching; and more easy to refutation if need be." Three centuries after Milton, many librarians are denied the basic liberty to publish, and too many accept this violation of their rights as individuals in a free world. If librarians are not prepared to fight against censorship of their own words, it is difficult to suppose that they will stand firm as defenders of intellectual freedom when censorship places its grubby paw on the works of others.

One who stood firm against this more personal form of censorship was a library school professor who recently submitted an article to *LJ*. She was informed in writing by her university: "Your article entitled *Librarians as Literature Experts* is disapproved for use under the name of St. John's University *and even under your own name* while you are a member of St. John's University faculty." Since the latter part of this dictum is no longer in effect, and that others may judge the pernicious quality of this censored article, it is published in this issue, together with comments from a number of librarians.

We know of numerous examples where less courage has been displayed in resisting such impositions from above. An ironic instance involved a review of the Fiske Report which appeared in the May 16 issue of the *New Republic*. A footnote said of the author of this review. "Raymond Stringer is an administrator in a large library system; he writes under a pseudonym because his employers insist on clearance before publication." A letter in the following issue of the *New Republic*, signed I. M. Gemel, Washington, D.C., carried a note explaining: "The pseudonym above is used to avoid the complications of clearance with my employer, the Library of Congress."

The irony is underscored in the comment by the pseudonymous Stringer in his review: "Librarians, as a group, are more than usually liberal in their general outlook. But they tend to be timid." The brave Stringer should fear for his glass house: his stone may boomerang.

Anyone who writes or speaks must be willing to accept any consequences arising from the exercise of his freedom, but "prior restraint" is contrary to our concept of individual liberties or legal rights in a free society.

The employers who impose such restrictions upon librarians would do well to heed Milton's advice: "We should be wary . . . what persecution we raise against the labours of public men." But the librarians who accept such restrictions are more to blame, for no man who lives and works in the world of books should need reminding of *Areopagitica's* message: "Give me the liberty to know, to utter, and to argue freely according to conscience, above all liberties." Nor should they have forgotten so soon that the *Library Bill of Rights* advocates "resisting all abridgement of the free access to ideas and *full freedom of expression* that are the tradition and heritage of Americans."

*Eric Moon*

## SPRING BAN
April 15, 1962

In spring our own particular fancy generally turns lightly. But this month's thoughts are a shade weightier than our usual spring ones: A) We are worried, too late, about the fallout that has been promised in April's showers. B) We are worried, not too late, about book censorship.

Last Sunday, feeling more chipper, we went into Riverside Park, a ribbon of green along the Hudson River just a hop away from the treeless street on which we live. Pleased, we looked around us, savoring the new mildness of the afternoon. As we glanced accidentally toward the sky, we had the dark thought about fallout. So we turned our gaze to a teenage couple, side by side on a beat-up bench, reading separate books. Then we had the thought about censorship.

Specifically we thought about a certain fat folder we had left at the office on Friday. It contained a large collection of clippings about various recent bannings and damnings of children's and young people's books. It told, for example, how in California local pressure groups had tried to ban from high school shelves copies of *Catcher in the Rye* and *Of Mice and Men*. It told how in Ohio *1984* was jumped on and, in Texas, Plato (rest his soul) came near to being put away for good. In another part of California a youngster had to take home his copy of *Wonderful Wizard of Oz* because someone called L. Frank Baum a Communist. In Michigan parents attacked *The Scarlet Letter, Drums Along the Mohawk* and *The Good Earth*. And in Levittown, N.Y., a teacher chopped up copies of a racy little textbook called *A History of the United States from the Age of Exploration to 1865* because it made reference to the Colonial custom of "bundling" (two in a bed, with clothes on and a board between).

The list of similar censorings is lengthy and absurd. It would make us laugh, if it were not so tragic. We would pass it off, if it were not so serious.

The problem has become, in fact, so suddenly prominent and widespread that the ALA, at its 1962 Midwinter meeting in Chicago, adopted an official statement to guide librarians and educators in the effort to resist book censorship. The statement lists six principles that schools and libraries would do well to follow (establish a written book selection policy, establish a clearly defined method for handling complaints, etc.), and offers an additional six pointers on what to do "in case of attack." Further, it lists five basic documents (such as the Library Bill of Rights and the School Library Bill of Rights) with which all school and public libraries should be familiar if they would defend the freedom to keep books on their shelves so that all persons might have freedom to read. The ALA statement, titled "How Libraries and Schools Can Resist Censorship," is available from ALA. You should have a copy.

Focusing again on the young couple in the park, we wondered briefly what books *they* were reading. *Tarzan* perhaps? *Tropic of Cancer?* We decided not to ask; we just let them go on reading.

*Ellen Rudin*

## ANOTHER BOSTON?
May 15, 1962

"Now that California has dusted off a little used obscenity law and a book seller has been found guilty in the *Tropic of Cancer* case," said a March 20th editorial in the *Los Angeles Citizen-News,* "we can look forward to Los Angeles becoming another Boston."

The editorial writer appeared not to "look forward" to this prospect with any great delight, and conjured up a vision of "fly-by-night opportunists in the book publishing field hurrying to get their brand of smut banned in California to assure sales to the curious elsewhere in the nation." A Boston ban was for years, he added, "a sure-fire money maker."

To be sure, this editorial writer put his finger on one of the boomerang dangers of censorship—that it has a tendency to promote that which it wishes to suppress. But musing that "condemnation has led to the success of many a shady or less than artistic enterprise," this Los Angeles sage concluded with an incredible and somewhat horrifying suggestion: "We in the news and broadcasting fields could nip this in the bud by refusing to consider a book banning as news."

This writer either believes that the banning of a book is *not* news, or he is advocating the suppression of any news which does not produce a result he considers desirable. In either interpretaton, this is a pretty cynical and degrading suggestion.

Newspapers are the first to yell, and rightly so, when anyone lays a finger on the sacred principle of "freedom of the press." Some of them, however, seem not to understand that freedom of the press is only one aspect of "freedom of the mind," and they overlook the lesson of totalitarian societies. When freedom of the mind or society's other basic freedoms are suppressed, freedom of the press is usually an early victim.

Differences of opinion are to be expected, particularly on a controversial topic like censorship, but we still wince every time we see a newspaper on the side of the forces of censorship and against publishers, authors and librarians who defend the freedom of the printed word. Such newspapers, we can't help feeling, deserve the suppression that would be their ultimate fate if their campaigns were totally successful.

The ALA statement on "How Libraries and Schools Can Resist Censorship" says: "Most attacks come from small groups of people who have little community backing. Time after time the American people have shown that given the facts they will solidly back the responsible exercise of professional freedom by teachers and librarians and that they will insist on protecting their own freedom to read."

Sometimes the voices for freedom are not strong or united enough to be heard above the shrill scream of the censors, but even this state of affairs is better than that the activities of the censorship campaigners be allowed to go into an underground of silence. It is certain that such silence would be interpreted by some as approval.

Let both sides be heard by all means. It will be a sad day if we ever reach the point where books may be banned—or where anything may be banned—without public comment or reaction. Freedom then will be dead—and so perhaps will be the *Los Angeles Citizen-News*.

*Eric Moon*

## CANADA CONSIDERS
February 1, 1963

It was the Fall of 1961 when the fall-out from *Tropic of Cancer* dropped across the border into Canada. The Mounties marched on the Vancouver Public Library, and the Toronto Public Library had to hand over its copies to the Department of National Revenue.

Within a month, a special report had been prepared for the Canadian Library Association, which recommended that the Association, "rather than pass judgment on one particular book, consider the whole matter of intellectual freedom and issue a public statement *as soon as possible*" (our italics).

In December 1961, CLA set up a Committee on Intellectual Freedom with the following terms of reference: "To examine to what extent, if at all, the communication of information, ideas and/or works of the imagination (through the printed media) should be prohibited by law." The announcement in the January 1962 issue of *Canadian Library* indicated that "a statement on Intellectual Freedom . . . is expected [to] be ready by February," and that it would appear in the March 1962 issue of the Association's magazine.

What did appear in that March issue was a reprinting of *The Freedom to Read*, the Westchester statement of the American Library Association and the American Book Publishers Council, and ALA's *Library Bill of Rights*.

To date, over a year since its appointment, no statement has been issued by the CLA Committee on Intellectual Freedom.

Some of the reasons for this delay become apparent on reading an article in the November 1962 issue of *Canadian Library*. It is entitled "A Catholic Librarian Looks at Intellectual Freedom in the Canadian Setting," and is written by Edmond Desrochers, S.J. Father Desrochers is chief librarian at La Maison Bellarmin in Montreal, and a member of the CLA Committee on Intellectual Freedom. He is also first vice president and president-elect of the Canadian Library Association—in short, a powerful voice within the association.

In his article Father Desrochers draws attention to the fact that "about 50 percent of Canadian people are of the Roman Catholic faith." Moreover, he says, in the province of Quebec the great majority of public libraries "are bound to be created, administered, financed, used by communities which are close to if not altogether 100 percent Roman Catholic. Such is part of the Canadian setting, nearly 30 percent of it." Therefore, he says, "a policy for *all* public libraries in Canada must be acceptable to this group. Otherwise would it be a national policy?"

Father Desrochers points out that "in most *public* libraries in Quebec province, the book selection policy is expected to include a 'book rejection,' or let us not be afraid of the term, a 'censorship' of pornography, of Communist literature and propaganda, and of 'Protestant' books. Such is the application of the principles of Catholic philosophy and Catholic librarianship."

Throughout the aricle, Father Desrochers repeats that ALA's Library Bill of Rights needs "some clarification" in various paragraphs (he cites individually all paragraphs from 1 to 4). And he asks also for clarification of individual words like "political" and "religious," and declares that the "ALA next sidesteps . . . the question of the 'moral' view of the writer."

The gist of the article seems to us that a national policy statement on intellectual freedom is not possible, or that at best one can be produced which includes a succession of exceptions to be applied in any area where Roman Catholics may use libraries. Much else Canadian has foundered on the rock of Quebec, or has been pinned there immobile and indefinitely. It would be a pity if intellectual freedom in Canadian library service suffered a similar fate because of the down-the-middle denominational split among Canadian people.

The flaw in Father Desrocher's argument is that a "national" policy has to meet with unanimous approval. Was there ever such a policy—in librarianship or anywhere else? It is perhaps understandable that religious doctrine should supplant professional belief in a library *run by the church for people of one denomination,* and any CLA statement could easily incorporate recognition of this situation for the benefit of Catholic librarians. But surely the Catholic view of censorship should not be imposed on those libraries and librarians serving people of various faiths.

*Eric Moon*


## THE SATISFIED CONSCIENCE
May 15, 1964

We have not always been among the most ardent defenders of the Wilson Standard Catalogs, but we can forget our reservations when we see the *Standard Catalog for High School Libraries* attacked for *including* such books as *The Grapes of Wrath, The Great Gatsby, An American Tragedy,* and *Winesburg, Ohio.*

"Why," asks a recent critic, "do we have to be drowned in profanity and sex?" This notable literateur would have libraries represent some of our major American authors only by their more minor and "harmless" works, such as *The Red Pony* or *The Pearl, The Old Man and the Sea,* or *A Single Pebble.*

That same critic's view of some of our literary landmarks reads as follows: "*The Grapes of Wrath* . . . is sociology but replete with vulgarity. *The Great Gatsby* is about a speak-easy society of infidelity, mistresses, divorce, and murder. *The American Tragedy* . . . involves drunkenness, brothels, running down a little girl, flight, seduction of a girl whom our hero drowns upon pregnancy so he can seduce another. *Winesburg, Ohio* has a group of lonely frustrated people including a peeping Tom minister, shotgun wedding, and homosexuality."

The author of these asinine annotations has the effrontery to add: "We do not go looking for dirt but in these instances, it is forced upon us."

We have become accustomed to the frequent discovery of this illiterate view of literature and this cloistered view of teenage susceptibilities in the columns of certain publications issued by some of the rabid censorship organizations. In such places, these effusions are no longer cause for comment. What is shocking about the views quoted above is that they appeared in a professional library periodical, and were written by a librarian.

The rallying call to librarians with an inclination toward censorship appeared in the *Catholic Library World* in March. The author, Richard J. Hurley, is supervisor of school libraries in Fairfax, Virginia. The philosophy behind the comments above is summed up in the following paragraph, also taken from Mr. Hurley's "Talking Shop" column:

"As librarians and service people, so we pass judgment on what a teacher does in a classroom by refusing to buy books we consider substandard (Note that word in relation to the condemned titles—Ed.) Are we to be 'neutral' in controversies stirred up by these and similar books? Are we men, or mice, or robots? (There are other possibilities, Mr. Hurley—Ed.) As professional people trained in the art of book selection with its very definite criteria (?—Ed.), we must adopt a positive attitude (!—Ed.) because otherwise we can be justly accused of wasting money entrusted to our stewardship. Beyond that, and more important than finances, we are accountable for the values system basic to education. We can buy such marginal and what I would call 'controversial' materials with the understanding that they be used by the teacher who requested them, in his classroom—not to be cataloged or placed on open library shelves. This avoids bad public relations, the hue and cry of censorship and satisfies our own conscience."

The abortive practices suggested by Mr. Hurley may satisfy his conscience, but we sincerely hope they will trouble others. From Fiske on, book selection studies have revealed that self-censorship is a widespread ailment among school librarians, and the Hurley column will undoubtedly offer succor to those who need their weakness reinforced. But let all ask what "values system basic to education" condones or encompasses the imposition of a barrier between growing high school students' minds and some of the greatest works of American fiction of this century.

*Eric Moon*


## COALINGA TO PHILADELPHIA
July 1965

"Gosh, I was proud of Coalinga last Thursday night. And I was proud of the library board." This girlish gushing came from Judy Flander, local newspaper columnist for *The Record,* following a recent censorship explosion in Coalinga, California.

Further along in her column, the bubbling-with-pride Miss Flander declared: "What came out of that [board] meeting was not even what you could call a compromise. It was a sensible, acceptable solution to a real problem."

Well now, what was the uncompromising, sensible, acceptable solution that the library board of the Coalinga District Library adopted? Among other things, it decided that "controversial" books would be "coded for identification by staff and patrons." Books at Coalinga now come in three categories. They are either "controversial and restricted," or "controversial but open shelf," or "open shelf." Classifiers will bemoan the lack of mutual exclusiveness of these classes, but others may discern more fundamental faults in the decision. Some, like us, may see a flagrant violation of the ALA policy on "Labeling Library Materials," which declares that "labeling is an attempt to prejudice the reader, and as such, it is a censor's tool."

We were just contemplating this when along came an article on book selection and censorship in North Carolina public libraries ("They Play It Safe," *LJ,* June 1, pp. 2495–98). The author of that article, Eldon Tamblyn, comments that most librarians in North Carolina "were in complete agreement with the Library Bill of Rights and the Freedom to Read Statement, but less than half of the respondents reported complete agreement with the ALA Statement on Labeling." He says that "this may have been due, in some part, to unfamiliarity with the statement."

We would accept that charitable judgment in the case of some smaller libraries, but it does not detract from the feeling that has been with us for a long time that the ALA labeling policy, of all ALA policies in the intellectual freedom area, has been the least successful in the sense of its general acceptance. It may be unknown in some areas, but it is studiously ignored in many others.

The special conference on intellectual freedom in Washington last January, which was sponsored by ALA's Intellectual Freedom Committee, extended the labeling concept with the declaration by one of its discussion groups that "Segregation of books on a closed shelf because of their ideas, rather than for their physical protection only, is a form of labeling and contrary to the principles of intellectual freedom."

Just as we had re-read this statement in the June issue of the *ALA Bulletin,* in which are published the excellent papers and recommendations of that conference, there came into our hands a recent policy declaration issued by the Office of Work with Adults and Young Adults at the Free Library of Philadelphia, dated May 27, 1965.

This communication notifies "all agencies" of the Free Library that two recently published books, Genet's *The Thief's Journal* and Mailer's *An American Dream,* "are designated for restricted shelving and circulation." The memorandum also notes, "This brings to five the number of works . . . designated for restricted shelving and circulation." In addition to the two above, the "restricted" list includes *Tropic of Cancer* by Henry Miller, *Our Lady of the Flowers* by Jean Genet, and *My Life and Loves* by Frank Harris.

Provision for this kind of restriction at Philadelphia is made under the library's book selection policy, one section of which is headed "Restricted Adult Collections." This section reads, in part:

"Occasionally, the Free Library purchases books which it believes advisable to place on closed shelves, and which for purposes of control should be circulated on a 'pink pass' rather than machine charged. Two types of books are contained in these restricted collections. They are:

"1) Books which are continually stolen or mutilated, e.g., books on automotive mechanics, marriage manuals, etc.

"2) Books likely to be regarded as pornographic by many patrons and which are predominantly unsuitable for persons under 18 years of age. Examples: *Memoirs of a Woman of Pleasure* (Fanny Hill) by John Cleland, and *My Life and Loves* by Frank Harris.

". . . Books in the second category are designated for restriction only by the Office of Work with Adults and Young Adults following administrative discussion. These titles are restricted in all agencies and circulate on 'pink pass' to patrons eighteen years and over. Titles restricted bear notice to that effect when they are placed on order . . . and a circular is sent to all public departments and extension agencies."

This statement raises some interesting questions. There are, for example, the minor but fascinating ones, like why is *Tropic of Cancer* on the restricted list but no other book of Miller's? Doesn't FLP have the others, or is this one simply because it generated a lot of what the computer boys call "noise"? Why, since it appears in the policy statement as an example, isn't *Fanny Hill* on the restricted list? Could it be that Fanny has found no home in the library of the City of Brotherly Love?

But the major question is, how far is this kind of restriction justified? Anyone who saw our June 1 cover, or who heard Emerson Greenaway speak at last year's ALA conference about the *Tropic of Cancer* shindig in Philadelphia, will know that this city has been a warm spot in the censorship war the last few years. One can feel sympathetic about the local situation without being convinced that the library's policies and actions spelled out above are destined to improve the situation.

The phrase in that book selection policy which worries us, however, is "Books *likely to be* regarded as pornographic . . ." (our italics). This sounds like the kind of anticipatory internal censorship through nervousness that the Fiske Report condemned in California school and public libraries.

If this kind of thing happens in one of our great public libraries, whose director is a past president of the American Library Association, do ALA's pronouncements, via the Intellectual Freedom Committee or special conferences designed to backstop the Library Bill of Rights, have any real strength or meaning? Also, is closed shelf segregation of books a form of labeling, as the January intellectual freedom conference indicated?

Whether it is or not, there does appear to be sufficient professional equivocation about "labeling" to justify a reconsideration by ALA of this 14-year-old policy statement. The Association should seriously consider whether it needs reaffirming, strengthening (how do you give it teeth?), or rescinding in the light of present practices.

*Eric Moon*

## "MORE THAN LIP SERVICE"
September 15, 1965

The persistent problem of censorship, difficult as it is in adult book selection policy, bogs down with peculiar stubbornness when it comes to reading for young people. Even the superb Intellectual Freedom Committee conference last ALA midwinter, which had a lot to say about reading on the young adult level, failed to reach any clear answer as to what adult books should be provided without restriction to children. And a special conference on this precise issue, called for at the Midwinter meeting, seems to have been temporarily shelved, at least in part because the whole area of reading for the young adult has been getting "too much" publicity. At a time when school librarians are chastised for backing down on controversial books, and when recent legislation threatens new bans on the acquisition of "dubious" books by young people, it seems appropriate to stand back and see what weapons the youth librarians really have at their disposal.

Let us pass, for this discussion, the question of whether the teen years aren't really the proper time for prurience (*rather* than the twenties or middle age), to look at some administrative aspects of censorship. These were aired quite recently at the University of Wisconsin at a workshop which discussed what the ALA had only contemplated discussing: the question of free book selection in the schools. The workshop tried bravely to cover the field; yet while it served to bring censorship again to the attention of the press, it had precious little to offer that has not been suggested time and time again: the shifting views of what is controversial; the importance of a written book selection policy; the need to stand up to the public.

Where it missed the mark most was in leaving the librarian (and teacher) at the mercy of the school, when it is the principal or administrator himself who may be the ultraconservative, or the community which insists on the final say. And Terrence E. Snowden's remark that the teacher must defer to public opinion or get out of town only brought the discussion back to its troubling beginning.

As for that classic standby, the written book selection policy, Marjorie Fiske in her *Book Selection and Censorship* survey found "little uniformity in what happens to policies after they have been completed"; two thirds of the librarians doubted their value, and used such alternatives (apart from taking books off the shelves or just not ordering) as demands for a written complaint, "discouragement by committee," and reliance on book reviews and approved sources.

Well, what about the book selection tools? Curious about what the librarian can fall back on, we checked the ALA *Basic Book Collection for High Schools* (7th ed., 1963) for a few items, with these results: on James Baldwin, nothing; William Faulkner, nothing; Hemingway, only *The Old Man and the Sea;* Mackinlay Kantor, only *The Voice of Bugle Ann;* Orwell, only *Animal Farm*—not *1984:* Steinbeck, only *The Pearl;* Salinger, nothing. Wilson's *Standard Catalog for High School Libraries* did better, though it was only when we came to the NCTE's *Books for You* and the NAIS' *3000 Books for the Secondary School Library* that *Catcher in the Rye* was mentioned.

It is true that the ALA *Basic Book Collection* lists only 1400 titles, as against the NCTE's 2000-odd, the NAIS' 3000, and Wilson's (with the supplements) approximate 5000. But the issue is hardly quantitative, and it seems to us ironic that librarians who have been recommending *Catcher* for years should have to look for support, in the most questionable cases, anywhere but in the recommended list of their own professional organization.

The American Library Association has been remarkable for its stand on intellectual freedom, yet there seems to be a curious gap between the high zeal of its moral leadership and the reflection of its principles in its own book selection practices, in which one finds, rather than daring or imagination, the stale, well-trodden paths of mediocrity it purports to avoid. In the youth divisions, too, there is a dearth of discussion of practical issues in censorship: ways of "selling" a controversial book, success and failure in applying written selection policies in concrete situations, techniques of confrontation (or evasion), and of creating a climate of confidence in the community. Until the youth librarians obtain this kind of support, neither they nor the ALA, we fear, can claim to give what the IFC conference hoped to provide—"more than lip service" to the principle of the freedom to read.

*Evelyn Geller*

## THOUGHTS AT CHRISTMAS
December 15, 1965

ICY went through 1965 with hardly a murmur, and it is best, perhaps, that it should die thus, in acronymic anonymity; for what could we do but look away from "international cooperation year" as the painful road of our foreign policy permitted no resolution of the principle of peace. Yet at Christmas, a time, we would hope, of peace, and at year's end, a brief examination is warranted of our double vision of the world, as it is, and as it should be, and the manner in which we are to communicate that vision to our youth.

These thoughts were occasioned by the theme of this issue, which is colored by the extraordinary optimism that the success of our domestic policy engenders, and the concurrent rash of isolated yet alarming censorship incidents noted in our news section. If we add to these the threat of the New York Hecht law (reported in September) we gain a picture of a strange and unwarranted assumption of adult infallibility.

Let us examine some cases in detail. In Vestal, N.Y., high school principal Thomas Mullen deferred to the pleas of several Baptist ministers and cancelled a school performance of *Inherit the Wind* because it "caricatured" their beliefs, though his decision was questioned by the local press and members of the school board. In his after-the-fact comment, school board president John Alden took pains to inform students that the controversy itself illustrated freedom of expression in American society. Yet the play which has been substituted, *The Crucible,* is removed and sublimated through time and the dead issue of demonology—safe, as it was when Arthur Miller wrote the play in the heyday of McCarthyism. Nor does it deal at all with the issue, never mentioned, of what *Inherit the Wind* is really about: academic freedom itself, and what the teacher is permitted to teach.

In Waterford, Connecticut, the school board did stand firm against religious pressures, yet a glance at the questionable books (p. 49; *LJ,* p. 5487) leaves us in doubt about their relevance to fundamentalism and the protestors' understanding of their message.

We know the issues behind these incidents, of course. The taxpayer pays the school to communicate what it sees as tradition, and the school must, in Mr. Mullen's words, defer to the mores of the community. Or, if you accept Dr. Max Rafferty's view of book selection, "Just because a thing exists, it is not necessarily incumbent upon the school to serve it up to children any more than a physician is obligated to prescribe arsenic to a patient," you may conclude with him that a book like *Catcher* may be read only by a student "grounded in the wisdom and the culture of the past," and not by others less well equipped.

But the conclusion, somehow, evades the question of the wisdom and culture of the *present,* which, as librarians, we hope to transmit with somewhat less assurance than many of our educators profess. There is no way of predicting just what book will have a given effect. In our sex-pressured society "pornography" may ease teenage prurience enough to avert experimentation; in this uneasy age, Camus may provoke a youth to murder; and in our commercially oriented civilization, TV advertisements and innocuous middle-class comedies can be more damaging to a slum youth than all the readings of Marx.

For in the end, we cannot hope that children and teenagers, caught in the web of our decisions, will easily subscribe to the view of reality as we wish it to exist, no matter how hard we try to wrap them in prophylactic bunting. Did the Vestal students, we ask, accept Mr. Alden's explanation of the controversy, or did they wonder at our own pomposity? Do the young adults, as some YA librarians say, really look away from Vietnam, or are our conclusions projections of our own irresolution or the fact that we never ask them?

This will be a great year for libraries, but as we feed ourselves into the educational establishment, we must not fail to ask ourselves these questions. We are a worried generation, fixed at once on ideals we have failed to accomplish, and on conditions we have learned to live with. If we neglect to convey these dual realities in our literature for young people, we will have betrayed our moral bankruptcy, ruptured the link between generations, and substituted doublethink for the double vision for which, after all, Jesus died.

*Evelyn Geller*

## A SOCIAL EXPERIMENT
March 15, 1966

"Censors will remain necessary until society—in Learned Hand's terms —decides that censorship is no longer necessary. The decision is entirely one for society at large, to be taken by its representatives in the light of the pressures the public exerts upon them." So says Stuart Perry, City Librarian of Wellington, New Zealand, in the Introduction to his book on *The Indecent Publications Tribunal* of that country (*see* review, pp. 1394–95, this issue).

Society has not been able, in any country thus far, to decide unequivocally that "censorship is no longer necessary." Nor have society or its representatives been able to come to grips with the problems of, first, how to define what censorship *is* necessary, and second, how to operate the process of censorship without restricting literary expression or infringing upon the liberties of individuals. Because society remains so far from any lasting or acceptable solutions, it is worth taking a careful look at any new attack upon these intractable problems.

Those who espouse the cause of intellectual freedom usually regard the establishment of an official censorship body as the ultimate anathema. We would, ourselves, find it very difficult to go to bat for the desirability of such a body. Yet, without ignoring the inherent dangers of the procedure, it must be said that New Zealand's *Indecent Publications Tribunal,* which was the result of legislation passed in 1963, has so far considerably *improved* the censorship climate in that country.

The legislation and Tribunal procedure has, for example, rescued librarians, booksellers, and individuals from many of the former uninformed depradations of the Customs Department. Prior to the new legislation, Mr. Perry points out: "The Customs Department was in the habit of making restrictive classifications when it thought fit, in the form of lists circulated to the Collectors and made available to Associated Booksellers and the Library Association; they had, of course, no legal validity, but it required some hardihood to disregard them."

The Tribunal procedure has also made it possible "for the character of a book to be determined without anyone being haled before the Court." Thus, authors, publishers, and others are no longer vulnerable to the kind of persistent legal (and financial) harassment that is possible—that is, indeed, rife—in this country.

But perhaps the most interesting aspect of the New Zealand Tribunal is that it decides not only whether or not a work is "indecent" under the terms of the censorship legislation, but also whether or not circulation of the work should be restricted to certain classes of individuals. While this provision reeks with dangers, the *effect* thus far has been a liberalizing one.

This latter aspect is of particular interest in the US at this time because of a notable change in the censorship climate in recent years. The repeated liberal decisions of the US Supreme Court on censorship matters seem to have persuaded some of the procensorship groups that their efforts to restrict adult reading are doomed to failure in the long run. The main effort today is directed at controlling what reading shall be made available to teenagers. Aware of this trend, ALA's Intellectual Freedom Committee is attempting to arrange a pre-conference meeting at San Francisco in 1967 which, it is hoped, will find some answers to the problem.

Now, what has happened in New Zealand since the Tribunal came into being is that books like *Lolita* and *Another Country,* for example, have not only been declared "not indecent"—and thus, presumably, rescued from further obscenity charges—but the Tribunal has refused to issue an order restricting the circulation of these books to adults. Librarians and booksellers in New Zealand, therefore, are no longer faced with the problem of determining the age of the person who wants to borrow or buy the book in question, nor do they face the possibility of legal action if they make a wrong determination about the customer's age. This, certainly, is an improvement upon the US situation.

We would not like this editorial to be misunderstood. We are *not* arguing for the establishment of a US censorship board. It is our feeling, however, that librarians engaged in the battle for intellectual freedom will defend it best if they are informed about all approaches to the problem of censorship—which cannot be counted on to disappear. The New Zealand experiment deserves study for whatever lessons it may offer to us in our confusion.

*Eric Moon*

## SEX EDUCATION AND THE CENSOR
April 15, 1966

When a mass-circulation magazine like *Look* devotes two features to making sex education in the schools respectable (March 8), a revolution in the teaching of sex seems clearly on its way. Add to this the emphasis on giving our teenagers more than the facts of life, apparent at recent conferences of the Child Study Association and the National Association of Independent Schools, and a new responsibility of the schools emerges—to take on what was formerly left to parents: the teaching of a personal ethic.

This imminent change in education will meet with many conservatisms—including those of school administrators, embarrassed teachers, and the not unnatural reticence of youth—who often, even when given complete freedom of reading by their parents, prefer to peruse their sex treatises under the covers with a flashlight. Whether such exploration takes place in the wake or the absence of formal teaching, an urgent concern of the librarian seems clear: to permit as wide reading as possible as the child or teenager gropes from his first curiosities to the development of individual values. This concern involves not simply books on sex and reproduction, but the encouragement of ease and self-confidence so that the child won't confront a Botticelli nude or a Michelangelo sculpture, or a descriptive or narrative passage, with nothing more than a silly leer.

The list of books prepared by the New Jersey School Library Association when it fought passage of the recent anti-smut bill (*SLJ*, Feb. 1966, p. 54; *LJ*, Feb. 15, p. 1044) illuminates the range of this responsibility, as it cites the curricular areas vulnerable to extremist activity:

LITERATURE: Chaucer, *Complete Works*, any ed.; Dante, *Paradise Lost;* Tom Lea, *Hands of Cantú* (Little, Brown, 1964); John Milton, *Paradise Lost;* any ed.; *Plays of the Restoration and Eighteenth Century*, any ed.

FINE ARTS: Albert E. Elsen, *Rodin* (Museum of Modern Art; Doubleday, 1963); *Horizon Golden Book of the Renaissance* adapted for young readers by Irwin Shapiro (Golden Press, 1962); Ludwig Goldscheider, *Michelangelo* (4th ed. Phaidon, Graphic, 1962); *I, Michelangelo, Sculptor*, ed. Irving and Jean Stone (Doubleday, 1962); H. Jensen, *History of Art* (Prentice-Hall, 1962); Bernadine Kielty, *Masters of Painting* (Doubleday, 1964; o.p.).

ANTHROPOLOGY AND SCIENCE: Robert J. Braidwood, *Prehistoric Man* (5th ed., Chicago Natural History Museum, Oceana, 1961); Heinrich Harrer, *I Come from the Stone Age*, tr. Edward Fitzgerald (Dutton, 1965).

HISTORY AND GEOGRAPHY: Erica Anderson, *World of Albert Schweitzer*

(Harper, 1955), Aaron J. Arickson, ed., *The Peace Corps* (Hill and Wang, 1965); Isaac Asimov, *The Greeks: A Great Adventure* (Houghton Mifflin, 1965); Anthony Birley, *Life in Roman Britain* (Putnam, 1964); Curtis Harnack, *Persian Lambs and Persian Lions* (Holt, 1965); Life's *Picture History of Western Man* (Time, 1951, o.p.).

MYTHOLOGY: *Larousse Encyclopedia of Mythology* (Prometheus, 1959; sale by Putnam).

HEALTH AND SEX EDUCATION: Karl DeSchweinitz, *Growing Up* (4th ed., rev., Macmillan, 1965); Evelyn Duvall, *Why Wait Till Marriage?* (Association Press, 1965; also in approved "special Catholic edition"); Eric W. Johnson, *Love and Sex in Plain Language* (Lippincott, 1965).

PERIODICALS: *Horizon; Natural History; Unesco Courier;* and *National Geographic*.

In its accompanying statement, the NJSLA said: "There is little evidence that a free discussion of sex does any real social damage. There is overwhelming evidence that sexual ignorance brings tragic consequences to countless thousands of our young people each year. . . . [With passage of the bill] the natural curiosity of youth about the meaning and practice of sex behavior would, of necessity, be channeled to back-street information and hard-core pornography."

The hairbreadth escape of New Jersey from the anti-smut bill, just as it lay awaiting the Governor's signature, and the present efforts of New York State's schools and libraries to exempt themselves from the strictures of a similar state bill, which passed because the Intellectual Freedom Committee was sleeping, provide a cautionary tale. And the very sketchy list of books presented here should certainly disabuse any librarian of the notion that his school or children's collection would be exempt from anti-smut legislation. It is likely that the pressure for sex-education reform will increase in the coming year, as will the efforts of extremists encouraged by the recent Supreme Court decision. If this conflict is resolved in favor of the censors, which librarian will be able to call his library safe?

*Evelyn Geller*

## TITILLATION'S A CRIME
April 15, 1966

"With Mr. Justice Fortas still an unknown quantity on censorship issues before the Court, one could wish for the presence and the certitude of Mr. Goldberg's liberalism."

We made this comment in our news review of 1965, referring to the *Fanny Hill,* Ralph Ginzburg, and Edward Mishkin cases which were then under consideration by the US Supreme Court. So many crucial censorship cases have been decided by a 5–4 vote that Goldberg's departure from the court seemed to open the possibility of a sudden change in the censorship climate.

That change has now come about: decisions have been handed down on the three cases. Certainly, Ralph Ginzburg must be wondering whether his life for the next five years may not have been determined by a series of quirks of fate—the death of Adlai Stevenson, LBJ's appointment of Goldberg to the UN Ambassadorship—which had nothing to do directly with *Eros* or the other publications which first brought Ginzburg before the courts. Justice Abe Fortas, who replaced Goldberg on the Court, joined the majority in another narrow 5–4 vote upholding Ginzburg's five-year sentence and $28,000 fine.

For nearly a decade, the Court has adhered to the obscenity test it announced in 1957 in the Roth case: "Whether to the average person, applying contemporary community standards, the dominant theme of the material taken as a whole appeal to prurient interest." The Roth test also required a finding that the material be "patently offensive" and "utterly without redeeming social value."

What most believers in intellectual freedom hoped for, as a result of the Court's deliberations on these three cases, was a clarification of the Roth decision which might do something to forestall the incessant attacks and misunderstandings in lower courts. What we got, instead, was a further clouding of the issue, and the addition of another weapon to the censor's armory.

In the majority opinion on both the Ginzburg and Mishkin cases, Mr. Justice Brennan added, as a new element in the already difficult obscenity equation, the manner in which the material in question is advertised, promoted, or marketed. And he admitted that this factor "may support the determination that the material is obscene *even though in other contexts the material would escape such condemnation*" (our italics).

As Mr. Justice Douglas pointed out in his dissent, this opinion has implications that ripple far out and beyond the publishing world. "This new exception," he said, "condemns an advertising technique as old as history. The advertisements of our best magazines are chock-full of thighs, ankles, calves, bosoms, eyes, and hair, to draw the potential buyers' attention to lotions, tires, food, liquor, clothing, autos, and even insurance policies."

We must agree with Justice Douglas also that "The sexy advertisement neither adds to nor detracts from the quality of the merchandise being offered for sale. And I do not see how it adds to or detracts one whit from the legality of the book being distributed. A book should stand on its own, irrespective of the reasons why it was written or the wiles used in selling it."

This Court decision raises another intriguing issue. Ginzburg, apparently, has been convicted because of the way he advertised and promoted materials he had himself published. But books may be advertised and promoted by many agencies in the book trade—book clubs, booksellers, distributors—in addition to the original publisher.

Does this decision mean that a book, however discreetly announced by the publisher, and regardless of whether it passes the Roth test, may nevertheless be banned if some obsure distributor obtains copies and then promotes them (as some do, even in the pages of the *New York Times Book Review*) through advertisements permeated by what Justice Brennan calls "the leer of the sensualist"?

If this implication is valid—and it certainly is not ruled out by this incredibly jumbled decision—are the book, its author, and its publisher then to be the victims of some other agency's advertising technique and business methods? Even if the case be brought against the advertiser, if the result is that the book is banned, the author and publishers are the financial victims.

As Justice Stewart said in another dissenting opinion: "The Court assumes the power to deny Ralph Ginzburg the protection of the First Amendment because it disapproves of his 'sordid business.' That is a power the Court does not possess."

*Eric Moon*

## THE LIPS WILL MOVE AGAIN
May 15, 1967

Just before the Midwinter 1965 meeting in Washington, D.C., the ALA put on one of its "specials." A high-level, well qualified group of people—including representatives from the ACLU, the National Education Association, the National Council of Teachers of English, and other bodies—met to explore what further steps might be taken to *implement* the Library Bill of Rights. "More Than Lip Service" was the theme of that meeting, and out of it came some of the most specific and concrete recommendations we have seen from such a gathering. Among them were: 1) a full-time legal counsel for ALA; 2) a special dues collection to finance a headquarters-directed intellectual freedom program that was spelled out in some detail; 3) more executive authority for intellectual freedom committees at both national and state levels, so that they could move swiftly and effectively; and, among other proposals, a "similar conference to work toward a consensus on the extent to which access of children to adult materials should be guided."

It is, in a way, a sad commentary on our stance as a profession that the one recommendation of that earlier conference to become a reality thus far is the convening of another conference on "Intellectual Freedom and the Teenager," at San Francisco. Admirable as it may be for the profession continually to stand up in public and *en masse* to discuss the controversial topic of freedom of the mind, these gatherings can have little purpose—other than a vaguely and debatably "educational" function—unless the deliberations are translated into action.

Will the San Francisco conference pay more than lip service to its topic? There are pressing reasons why it should. It is clear that the susceptibilities, real or imagined, of teen years have become the concentrated target of the pressure groups favoring censorship. These groups have not done as well as they hoped with their more generalized attacks which, though they have had nuisance value, have frequently fizzled in the courts, particularly the Supreme Court. In the teenage area, the censorship groups figure, with some justification, they will have more going for them.

First, of course, there is a pervasive nervousness among adults about the supercharged atmosphere of the teenage world: its noise and persistent rock beat; its vigorous insistence on being heard on such explosive issues as civil rights, peace, drugs and what all; and its preference for love (still an obscene concept in many an adult lexicon) rather than war. And even without the teenage surge of demonstrations in recent years, parental nerves have always been close to the skin where "influences" upon their children are concerned.

Another relevant factor is that the courts seem by no means convinced that the Constitution *meant* to leave out any age limitations when it guaranteed civil liberties variously to "citizens," "persons," or "people"—and, incidentally, in the 14th Amendment, to "*all* persons born or naturalized in the United States."

The other potent weapon in the censors' armory is the uncertainty, when the issue is specifically applied to the teenage area, of professions and other groups who have been rigorous defenders of intellectual freedom in the abstract or as an adult matter.

The first order of business at San Francisco, it is clear, will have to be an attempt to determine whether the library profession *believes* in intellectual freedom for teenagers. Assuming—dangerously—that it does, where does the conference go from there?

The concern from this point on, it seems to us, will have to be not so much with the teenager as with his parents, his teachers, his school principal, and the like. It will scarcely be enough for the conference to outline another nice little tactical handbook for the individual librarian or library board to use in future, endless local skirmishes with the many adults who do *not* want teenagers exposed to the world as it appears on the adult shelves of libraries. Will ALA undertake the kind of vigorous campaign which would be necessary to gather the support of the National Congress of Parents and Teachers, the National Education Association, and other such groups for a policy advocating real freedom to read for teenagers in libraries? And will the defense fund proposed at the Washington conference be urged again? It may really be necessary, this time, if we have the courage to draw firm battlelines on the teen reading question.

*Eric Moon*

## HALF A CONFERENCE
September 15, 1967

On June 27, Ervin Gaines, chairman of the Intellectual Freedom Committee, reported to Council the success of the preconference on censorship and the teenager: librarians had agreed that teens should have a free run on the library collection. How that happy confluence of opinion was arrived at is discussed elsewhere in this issue. Here we'd like to comment on the connection between this unanimity, the "evangelical" tone of the conference, and the committee's intent.

A meeting called mainly to gain support for a cause is more commonly termed a rally than a conference, for the latter still has connotations of true consultation and the airing of differences; frankly, we wish the IFC had chosen to use the former term. For rather than any real dialogue, librarians were exposed to a chain of provocative, articulate, yet unanimous opinions—intended to rally them from sluggishness to the cause of intellectual freedom. Not that the intent was reprehensible; the private comments echoed the Fiske report in sorrowful repetition. Yet consensus should have been only half the purpose, the other being a true examination of policies and problems. Instead, the Committee betrayed its own commitment to diversity.

Perhaps the most serious sin of omission was the failure to invite Max Rafferty, the influential state superintendent of education in California, who got his pungent remarks across to a different, and powerful, audience, exemplifying the arguments, force, and indeed seductiveness of the conservative opposition.

What is ironic about the whole situation is that with all this moralizing the librarians got precious little practical support. Stanley Fleishman, noting that the librarians can get into trouble trying to enforce his legal freedom, advised: "Get a good lawyer." Alex Allain stressed that trustees couldn't be relied upon to support the library's policy in handing "harmful" reading matter to teens if a causal connection could be found between reading and antisocial behavior.

What would a real conference on censorship and the teen have studied? At least these questions:

1. What different issues and problems in book selection for teenagers are involved in school and in public libraries? And how are school and public library relations to be affected by such decisions? With these two youth groups cosponsoring the conference, one would have thought this question rated a systematic investigation. The dimensions for the two kinds of libraries are very different: in the public library the problem is simply whether a book important enough to buy, and hence of social significance, should also be allowed to circulate to the teen. In schools, book selection cannot offer the argument of adult demand—books are bought *for* the teen, and under more careful surveillance. So school libraries have often "solved" the censorship problem by evading it, and it is a common enough opinion (among trustees, for example) that "certain" books belong in a public though not a school library. It is easy for a school library to decide a title is not "curriculum-oriented," sometimes shirking its responsibility, sometimes with justification.

Unfortunately, even if it had occurred to the conference planners to touch this matter, there would have been precious little discussion, because so few of the leaders of the school library profession were represented. It was unfortunate, not only because school librarians have become over-obsessed with bread and butter issues to the neglect of crucial matters of principle (or did they know, in this case, they were being conned?), but because they'll be hard put to it to call for higher standards and larger collections if the real diversity of opinion rests in the public library.

2. Whose responsibility is it to determine book selection policy? It's amusing when we're told how a library director has to keep reminding his stuffy YA specialist that anything in the library should circulate to the teenager. But what if the situation is reversed and the director is conservative? Or the hidebound school superintendent insists: "It's ridiculous to arouse the parents that way—why did you put the book on the reading list?" The people are different, but the principle, the bureaucratic structure, the locus of decision-making, the same. Should the conference have addressed itself, rather, to the final arbiters of book selection policy?

3. We deplore the parent's attempt to "weed" a collection for his child's sake, but can we interfere with his effort to control his own child's reading as long as that attempt doesn't encroach on others? The practice of requiring parental consent for free use of the library does encourage censorship and was rightly criticized, but the problem of parental control which it attempts, however clumsily, to grapple with, and the alternative solutions, were never considered. What about the somewhat milder policy of issuing a restricted card to a teen, but only if his parent insists? And: can the library enforce practically its legal invulnerability in circulating anything, telling the parent to police his own child's reading as best he can? Or is it better, after all, to have restricted access to some titles in order to preserve freedom in book selection? In short, what are the policy dimensions?

4. Is there any age at which we can argue censorship, or "protection"—or, how minor is minor? We argue now about the under-18 age group. Do we extend those rights down to age 11? ten? eight? What about the library with the unrestricted card?

5. Last, could the proposed survey of the "effects of reading on behavior" force the library profession to compromise itself on intellectual freedom? The reasons for getting ALA in on a survey to offset a "know-nothing" investigation were pointed out cogently by Peter Jennison of the American Book Publishers Council. Yet, once you have removed the red herring of pornography, the fear of the "effect" of reading on behavior is as old as censorship. Youth librarians—and school librarians particularly—have little to gain from a study of pornography, which does not touch on the books creating *their* problems, while a general study of the practical consequence of reading, for example, *The Autobiography of Malcolm X* could yield some pretty explosive results today.

In planning the conference, the Intellectual Freedom Committee muffed its chance to bring these problems into the open, to define precisely the responsibility of the librarian to the teenager in *operational* terms. Worse yet, it neglected by some unimaginable oversight to explain what an

IFC office at ALA headquarters could really provide in the way of influence as well as moral leadership—in imposing sanctions, negotiating with principals for the retention of librarians, and providing legal support. Was it more interested in gaining support than describing the issues? Concerned with the youth divisions only because of the quasipornographic titles that threaten adult collections? (The books that cause problems for youth librarians, after all, would never reach the courts!) The proverbial sheepishness of youth librarians might diminish if they knew they had support from—or against—the superiors who really determine their actions when it comes to choosing books for kids.

*Evelyn Geller*

## THE USES OF ADVERSITY
October 15, 1968

It is a source of increasing dismay to see how the slogans of individualized learning and independent inquiry manage to sell the library as an administrative construct with complete blindness to its intent: to serve as a battleground where ideas, in their fiercest form, grapple for the minds of young people. It almost seems that, having failed with uniform textbooks to create a uniform product, we're trying now to produce the same (ah, individually paced!) homogeneity through more reading levels, shorter chunks of trade book copy, "tracking," and sugar-coated media, all parroting the identical message. Are our various "prescriptions" (a favorite USOE word) for various students just a different form of processing? Or can we ever see cmmunications media as more than carriers of our own ideologies? If we can't begin to now, the result can only be an irreparable breakdown in the patchy dialogue between educators and students.

These questions are raised with some force by several features in the current *SLJ:* Milton Meltzer's article, which punctures our pious notions that we carry the antidote to the lockstep curriculum, by showing that children's books on controversial subjects often show the same shallowness, bias, and cowardice as our texts; the criticisms, in our Letters and News columns, of racism in that latter-day Newbery winner, *Dr. Dolittle;* and our News story (p. 99) on the threatened police inquest of a school library book on "pot," and its resultant transfer to the teachers' collection.

The three issues vary greatly in substance, but unite in revealing how we fail, whether through the faults of publishers or our own selection practices, to deliver the variety, balance, and honesty we promise in our libraries; and—an ironic concomitant—how we continue to revere the printed word (how else such a sense of affront?). Thus we neglect to teach the simple corollary of our shortcomings: a healthy skepticism of print (or film); which could make the faults of published books case studies in communications, and increase immeasurably the range of controversy we permit in our libraries.

One case of this excellent kind of exploitation was reported recently by John Hendrik Clarke, who teaches a group of Harlem dropouts under a Haryou-Act Program. Taking available texts, with their omissions and distortions of Afro-American history, he sent his students on a quest to the library to check their books against more authentic sources and return with their (considerable) corrections. He had turned a racial slur into an educational opportunity.

This approach, of course, is a pathetic answer when variety itself is missing in published sources, and it is particularly important, during the current wave of educational reform, that we do not content ourselves with "weeding" our collections and substituting one form of benign propaganda (ideology, if you wish) for an earlier, unjust one, covering our tracks in the process. Our children are growing up in a society of the Big Lie, accusation and counter-accusation, the rhetoric of advertising. They are ready, very early, for their most important curricular experience: understanding the "pragmatics" of communications—that is, not merely the content of the media, but the social forces and power groups that spur their creation. It is not too soon, in the elementary school, to begin the approach that Carolyn Leopold argues for eloquently in this issue: teaching students the problems of authority, of corporate authorship, of variant editions in their texts. It is not too soon to expose the faults of the books we have in our collections, even to compare the old and the "expurgated" editions of the Dolittle stories.

This approach, in turn, could prevent the kind of solution that school superintendent Ronald Notley and his "review committee" found to the "pot" book issue. Standing up courageously to the threatened police "book burning," insisting on professional autonomy in book selection, stressing the need for conflicting viewpoints on controversial issues, he still held that the book "tended to instruct" youth in breaking the law. What good did the decision do at that point? It confused a book's content with a school's policy position on drugs, confined argument to palatable limits, assumed that students are not getting stronger enticement from their peers, and acknowledged the school's impotence in arguing with the author. By thus cutting off a crucial area of discussion with youth, and in the process giving the book the same illicit appeal that drugs have, the decision can only have engendered further skepticism of authority and the party line curriculum (rather than of the book's argument itself)—a kind of skepticism that is now creating revolution on the campus.

*Evelyn Geller*

# Book Selection

## BALANCE IN BOOM-TIME
January 1, 1960

Book selection is the most important, most interesting and most difficult of the professional librarian's responsibilities. It is an area of his work where he is surrounded by potential dynamite, labelled with such well-known trade names as "censorship," "pressure groups," and "hobby-horses." The safety goals towards which the librarian must aim through these traps are balance and neutrality. He seldom gets there, and when he does nobody cheers.

Nowhere are these goals harder to achieve than in the section of his bookstock devoted to religion. Numerous and powerful as the problems have been in the past they seem to be increasing.

One of our contributors asks whether the number of best-selling novels with religious themes are indicative of a trend. The publishing output of religious non-fiction seems to indicate not just a trend but a religious revival, a biblical boom. In the five years from 1952 to 1957 the sales of hard-bound religious books (excluding Bibles and hymnals) increased in the United States by 68 percent; religious paperback sales increased in the same period by 169 percent.

A subject breakdown in the *American Library Annual 1959* of the new books published in the United States in 1957 shows that better than 11 per cent were in the field of religion, which led the field by more than 100 titles. The nearest contenders to Religion's 883 new titles were History with 773, Biography with 699, and Science with 697. The question is: what does this do to the librarian's conception of balance in his book selection? It is doubtful whether the shelves of any general library reflect these proportions, and certainly they could not be justified by past circulation statistics. The publishing output, however, must be related in some degree to reader demand and interest, and it seems at least possible that a greater proportion of library book funds will have to be devoted to religious books.

The increasing publishing volume is not the only pressure which keeps the librarian's balance wheel delicately poised. Some denominations are much more diligent than others in seeking out, reading and promoting the literature of their own faith. It is rare, for example, for a new Catholic book to go unnoticed or unasked-for. How does the balance-conscious librarian react to these enthusiasms? Does he resist them as something akin to best-seller pressure? If he does, he is open to a charge against his neutrality. On the other hand, if in an attempt to retain the balance he buys books on another faith which have not been requested and promotes them to ensure their use, he is open to the same charge. And what does he do with some of the minor denominations that, in an attempt to become major ones, inundate the library with a donated deluge of their publications?

There is a further growing trend which may influence the librarian's book selection decisions in the religious field. A note in this issue spotlights the amazing growth of the library of the First Baptist Church in Greensboro, North Carolina, which now has over 3000 volumes, 22 staff, and is open 7 days a week. There are now 500 libraries in the Baptist churches of this State. How will the growth of church libraries on this scale affect the provision of religious books in public, and indeed college, libraries? Will they no longer need to stock more than one or two basic works on a religion or faith for which such adequate provision is made elsewhere? Unless all the churches provided libraries of their own such a decision on the part of the public library could set the balance wheel spinning crazily.

In no other field also is it so difficult to draw a clean line between what is propaganda and what an exposition on the elements of a particular faith or creed. In some subject fields the librarian often cannot do better than seek outside advice; in dealing with religious books this can often be the most dangerous course of action, for almost everyone is partisan.

While the librarian should rejoice at the thought that a section of his stock, hitherto too often neglected, is likely to be much more heavily used, he will probably do well to pray for guidance if he is to retain a balance in this boom-time.

*Eric Moon*

## THE SANCTITY OF BOOK SELECTION
October 1, 1960

A number of larger university libraries have decided in recent months to place blanket orders for university press publications. Why, they have reasoned, go through an expensive process of individual selection and order when in any case they normally acquire something like 90 percent of these publications? The larger discounts received and the considerable saving in staff time are only two of the advantages to be weighed against the small disadvantage of receiving a few books they otherwise would not have purchased.

Similarly, many of the larger public libraries have decided to participate in the plan originally worked out by Emerson Greenaway and the Lippincott Company which has become known as the Greenaway Plan. This plan and its purposes and advantages are described by Mr. Greenaway in this issue of *LJ* (see p. 3387).

If we have a doubt at all about the blanket orders for university press publications, it concerns the real need of some of our university libraries for such a large proportion as they purport to buy. Nobody could fail to recognize the valuable contribution to scholarship made by the university presses. Equally, nobody could fail to recognize that a fair volume of pretentious academic flotsam originates from the same sources. But granted that a university library already buys 90 percent, we see no great additional harm in acquiring the other ten percent if the library saves money and time thereby. There has been no suggestion that the practice is applicable to all college and university libraries, only to those who buy such a large proportion that it is a saving to buy all.

The Greenaway Plan is admirable in its motives, and again, we see no objection to it as applied by the larger public libraries and the larger publishers. If we have any lingering doubt, it is that perhaps all libraries participating are not using it as a method to help them review books themselves before publication, but merely as a way of getting one copy of everything put out by cooperating publishers *cheaply* as well as quickly. How many of these libraries face up to the decision to discard books for which they have already paid, but which they would otherwise not have placed on their shelves?

We have some doubts too about the application of an amended or abbreviated version of this plan for medium-sized or smaller libraries. This implies a degree of pre-selection by publishers which should be undesirable in the eyes of professional librarians.

With this reservation we get near to the fundamental objection of those who have dismissed these book-buying practices as "get-'em-all" methods. Librarians, say the objectors, by employing these methods, are abrogating their prime professional responsibility for book selection. If this were so, we should have to line up with the objectors, for the librarian's responsibility for, and ability in, book selection is surely his raison d'être, the factor which places him apart and makes him a professional. But is it so? We think not. To select when it is unnecessary is as wasteful and as stupid as the performance of any other superfluous task. There is always the danger that something holy can easily become a sacred cow. Those who wage indiscriminate war on behalf of the sanctity of book selection are in danger of precipitating this process.

The Greenaway Plan, says its originator, "is a method to ensure an early receipt of books and should not be confused with book selection." This comment is equally applicable to the blanket order process for university press publications. The confusion exists nevertheless, and we hope that *LJ's* roundup of views in this issue will encourage a little more clarity of thought on the subject.

*Eric Moon*

## REASONABLE PROPORTIONS
January 1, 1961

One of the conditions specified in the new legislation bringing state aid to libraries in Massachusetts is that a city or town, in order to qualify for state aid, must spend a "reasonable" portion of the library's total budget on books and periodicals. It is interesting to speculate on what the Massachusetts Board of Library Commissioners will consider reasonable.

*Costs of Public Library Service in 1959* (ALA, 1960), the latest supplement to *Public Library Service*, suggests, as did the previous supplement in 1956, a distribution of "about two thirds of the total" for salaries, and "about one-fifth of the total" for books and related materials, including rebinding. The ACRL standards advocate that twice as much or more should be spent for salaries as for books and related materials.

The only state standards which are specific on this point, to the best of our knowledge, are Indiana's, which state that "19 percent plus" of a system's annual budget should be allocated to the purchase of books and non-book materials. In passing, it is worth noting that New Hampshire state standards see fit to record that a minimum of 25 percent of the book fund should be spent for children's books, and South Carolina, very conscious of rising acquisition costs, specifies that "in general, the total cost of ordering books should not exceed ten percent of the total amount spent for the purchase of books."

In the light of current practice the cautionary move of South Carolina seems particularly pertinent. Three annual compilations of selected statistics from public library systems have been published by the Office of Education in the past few months. They show the proportions of public library expenditures on salaries and books to be as follows:

| POPULATION RANGE | NO. OF LIBRARIES | % ON SALARIES | % ON BOOKS |
|---|---|---|---|
| 35–49,999 | 102 | 66.6 | 16.7 |
| 50–99,999 | 118 | 68.7 | 15.5 |
| 100,000+ | 110 | 72.1 | 12.4 |

The only generalizations possible from these over-all figures are that: 1) the majority of libraries are not reaching the desirable proportion of 20 percent of the total budget to be spent on books; and 2) the larger a library becomes, the smaller the proportion of its budget it assigns to book expenditure.

A look at the individual figures shows that only 58 of the 330 libraries recorded in these statistics spent 20 percent or better of their 1959 budgets on books and periodicals. Of these, 28 were libraries in the smallest population group (35,000–49,999), 27 were in the middle group, and only 13 of the largest libraries (serving over 100,000 population) reached the 20 percent for books recommended in the ALA standards.

The extremes are even more enlightening. In the smallest group, four libraries spent less than ten percent on books, while seven spent more than a quarter of their budget on books. The over-all range in this group is from Hamtramck, Michigan, which spent 4.2 percent for books and 86.3 for salaries, to Biloxi, Mississippi, way up at the top with a 38.8 percent expenditure on books and 50.2 for salaries.

The picture in the middle population group is about the same, with five libraries spending less than ten percent, and seven spending better than 25 percent on books, and with a total range from 3.2 to 29.8 percent. Here,

Hoboken (N.J.) must set some sort of record with a mammoth 91.8 percent on salaries and only 3.4 on books.

In the largest group, however, only two libraries devoted more than 25 percent of their budgets to books, while 16 spent less than ten percent. These latter include some of the famous names in the library world—Boston, Cleveland, Minneapolis, Newark, Oakland, Providence, etc. Among the giants included in the statistics, the seven systems serving populations over one million, Brooklyn achieved the highest percentage for books (17.6) and Detroit the lowest (7.6).

An odd feature which comes to light in this group is that libraries spending roughly the same proportions of their budgets on salaries show wide variance in the proportions applied to books. Kansas City, Camden (N.J.) and Trenton (N.J.), for example, all spend about 62–65 percent on salaries. But whereas Kansas City spends 26.8 percent on books (the highest in the large library group), Camden spends only 8.5 percent and Trenton 8.2.

The annual statistics published in *College and Research Libraries,* January 1960, illustrate that it is not at all uncommon for university and college libraries to spend 25 percent, a third or half of their budgets, on books. With today's increasing publishing output, surely this is necessary. Yet the trend in public libraries has been consistently in the reverse direction. Year after year, salaries eat up an increasingly larger proportion of the budget, and the allocation for books declines in about the same ratio.

Shouldn't the emphasis in some of our campaigns be shifted a little? The New Jersey Library Association, to cite one example, has passed resolutions at each of its last two conferences on minimum starting salaries for professional librarians. All well and good. But isn't it time for a good strong resolution on book budgets? Five of the largest libraries in New Jersey—Camden, Elizabeth, Jersey City, Newark and Trenton—figure among the group spending less than ten percent of their budgets on books.

Desirable as adequate salaries and top-rate professional librarians may be, this trend must soon be reversed. Whatever the charms or the professional competence of the staff, they will never equal books as a drawing card for libraries.

There are only two possible conclusions from the figures quoted above. Many libraries are either spending too much on staff, or too little on books. In view of the great shortage of professional staff, the former seems the least likely. But the statistics at least hint at a tendency in the larger units to overload the administration at the expense of the bookstock.

*Eric Moon*

## LITERARY HISTORY
February 1, 1962

Once upon a time the novel was an honored and respected literary form. It was reviewed by eminent critics and read by scholar and "general reader" alike. That early lion among librarians, Melvil Dewey, ranked it equal in importance with poetry and the drama, and considerably more important than the Russian language, electrical engineering or astronautics.

As fiction came of age, the number of novels grew at an alarming rate and the demand for them grew even faster. Librarians were faced with one of those inevitable moments when an administrative decision has to be made. It was obviously ridiculous to break up the sequence of the classified shelves with one section of one division of one class which was as large or larger than the rest of the bookstock combined. And since more than half of their readers wanted fiction it would obviously be more convenient to shelve fiction as a thing apart. So librarians made their decision, and fiction was removed from its classified place of honor in "Literature."

In time, the factor of administrative convenience began to fade from the memory, to be replaced by other elements. Fiction slowly came to be treated with as little respect as science books received in the pre-Sputnik era. As the twentieth century wore on, society came more and more to idolize the fact rather than the idea, retrieving information became vastly more important than capturing thought. And in a culture in which everything took on connotations of status, positive or negative, the novel became something of a reverse status symbol.

Around the middle of the century, librarians jumped on the band wagon of survival. Increasingly, they emphasized their educational and informational functions. They pointed with pride whenever their statistics showed an upturn in nonfiction, a decrease in fiction. They allowed patrons to reserve the works of Norman Vincent Peale or Adelle Davis but not those of such practitioners of the degraded art as Carson McCullers or J. D. Salinger. They would send on interloan a "how-to" or a murderer's autobiography but not *Dr. Zhivago* or *Lolita*.

It was in the fifties and sixties that events took the final turn leading to the inevitable demise of the novel. Librarians began to help the circulation statistics along by buying less and less fiction, a trend that could only be seen in the annual reports of some of the larger libraries at first (the historic 1960 report from Pittsburgh, for example, revealed that only three percent of the total book budget had been spent on new adult fiction).

This was happening at a time when fiction was still being read and asked for. But the decline took on momentum, and gradually what little fiction was published was reviewed only by the most severely competent critics—the police, judges, ministers, customs officials, representatives of veteran's organizations. They found that contemporary fiction, almost without exception failed to meet their first criterion—it was not suitable reading for those between the ages of ten and 13.

Librarians, who had for some time shown a preference for morals protection rather than book selection (a tedious task involving judgment and standards), concurred with these able critics, and fiction (other than an occasional leather-bound edition of Twain or Thackeray, which had historical curiosity value) began to disappear from the shelves.

Today, February 1, 1984, we celebrate the death of fiction with a ceremonial burning of the last copy of George Orwell's notorious book to be withdrawn from the largest and oldest American public library. This work survived so long perhaps because it brought fiction dangerously near to fact.

*Eric Moon*

## WASTELAND REVISITED
October 1, 1962

Take one "vast wasteland" (TV). Plant one dead or dying literary form (poetry). For your green thumb use a cast of good actors mostly just below the all-star level. And what have you got?

Not much, you say? At best, another pious failure? Well, you would be wrong. You have not only one of the best hours of viewing—and listening—yet to emanate from the hypnotic box in the living room, but as its aftermath, *the largest mail response to any program ever broadcast on the CBS Television Network.* That italicized bit is a quotation from a letter received from CBS.

August 16 was a date in television history. At 10 o'clock that night, while many were predictably singing along with Mitch or spending an unmentionable hour with the Untouchables, CBS went "worthy" and must have wondered what sort of unpredictable audience they would find with a network program called "Americans: a Portrait in Verses."

It was a kalaidoscopic picture of the American people, from the earthy types of Spoon River to the measured coffee-spoon lives of Prufrock and his drawing-room friends talking of Michelangelo, from Sandburg's sidewalk philosophers to Cummings' "sweet old aunt, etcetera."

Beautifully produced and well read by actors who did not impose themselves on the poetry, it probably had the best team of writers any TV show ever had—Frost, Benet, Emerson, Whitman, Emily Dickinson, Ogden Nash, Marianne Moore, even Allen Ginsberg. Twenty-two American poets in all. But neither the poems nor the poets were identified on the program. The words were left to speak, oh so powerfully and so rightly, for themselves.

At the end of the broadcast, the announcer invited anyone who might be interested to write in for a bibliography of the poems from which selections had been made. So help us, the man used the word "bibliography." No pandering here.

In our defeatist way, we figured that not many people would write (and now confess, with shame, that we did not take a few minutes to send a word or two of praise for those dared). CBS, apparently, also had no great expectations. Hopefully, producer Richard Siemanowski had run off 5,000 copies of the bibliography.

A few days after the broadcast a truck rolled up to the CBS door. A dazed secretary signed for 11 huge bags of mail. At the end of one week— wait for it—Mr. Siemanowski had received 54,600 letters from viewers in every state of the union, praising the hour of poetry and asking for the bibliography. The letter we received from CBS used words and phrases like "incredibly," and "unbelievable reaction," and "completely unexpected."

A special task force will now go through all 54,600 letters in the most extensive analysis of audience mail ever conducted by CBS. The results will be broken down, geographically and otherwise, and made public on completion of the analysis. We hope to pass some of them on later.

This flowering in the wasteland is not all of the story. Now comes an announcement of the first National Poetry Festival ever to be held by an agency of the United States Government. During three days this month (October 22–24) some 40 American poets and writers will be presented at the Library of Congress in a program of talks, readings and panel discussions of poetry. The theme, "Fifty Years of American Poetry"; the occasion to be marked, the 50th anniversary of *Poetry* Magazine, founded in Chicago in 1912 by Harriet Monroe.

And, just for good measure, the Pennsylvania State Library has announced that it will also commemorate *Poetry* Magazine's anniversary with an exhibit to run through October and November. This exhibit will mark, in addition, the opening of the library's collection of nonmusical records (many of them poetry) which will be made available to public libraries throughout the state.

Who says poetry is dead? On this evidence, it would seem that, unlike the old soldier, it refuses even to fade away. But one question remains. If all this activity on the verse front presages a revival of interest in poetry, are the library shelves ready to cope with it? Or are there still too many where it is hopeless to expect to find anything more exciting than a tattered collected Longfellow or Whittier?

Sir Herbert Read said, in a *Wilson Library Bulletin* symposium on poetry and book selection (January 1962): "I believe that if a special room for poetry were to be established in every public library, the whole situation for poetry would change." We don't ask this much, but a couple or three shelves of well selected poetry would certainly help.

*Eric Moon*

## OUTSPOKEN NEWCOMER
June 15, 1963

Dwight Macdonald and the editors of a little magazine called *The Sixties* have not been alone, only prominent, among those who have for long decried the absence of serious, critical reviewing in most of our magazines and newspapers. For them, and for librarians and others who are tired of the milk-and-water reviewing diet supplied by some of our stately sources, there is good news.

One of the brightest torches lit during the long darkness of the New York newspaper strike was *The New York Review of Books*. The first, undated, "special" issue indicated that the editors' hope was to "suggest however imperfectly, some of the qualities which a responsible literary journal should have and to discover whether there is, in America, not only the need for such a review, but the demand for one."

When nothing followed that first issue for several months we began to assume, sadly, that *The New York Review of Books* had been just another of those hopeful cries in the newspaper-less night, and that one experimental shot had been enough to sink those idealistic editorial expectations. Then May brought forth another issue, still undated, still "special," but very welcome for all that.

Even more welcome is the news that the response to the first attempt was encouraging enough to persuade the editors and publishers that "there may be sufficient demand in America to support a literary review of this sort." So, it is announced, the plunge will be taken. Beginning in September, *The Review* will be published twice monthly, and in future issues it will review "not only important works of fiction, poetry, history and politics, but significant scientific books, books published abroad, interesting scholarly works and, from time to time, text books, especially those used in the elementary and secondary grades." The same intellectual quality will be maintained, the editors declare, and they "will continue to assume that the serious discussion of important books is itself an indispensable literary activity."

Now, not everyone agrees that *The Review* is manna from heaven. We heard Virgilia Peterson, for example, at a book and author luncheon during National Library Week, decrying this vicious new thing which even attacked such elegant sacred cows as Updike and Salinger. But whether or not one agrees with *The Review*'s opinions, nobody can deny that the book reviewing field is a place where there is room for an outspoken newcomer. And when it can bring together in one issue such contributors as Edmund Wilson, Allen Tate, Arthur Schlesinger, Jr., Stephen Spender, F. W. Dupe, Truman Capote, Robert Hielbroner, Richard Wilbur, Alfred Kazin, Lionel Abel and Kenneth Burke (to name less than half the cast of the second issue), those opinions are worth more than a passing glance.

Louis Untermeyer expresses our feeling very well in one of the many letters *The Review* received as a result of its first issue: "It is the first—and a welcome first—attempt to raise reviewing in America to an intelligent level." Like many of the other correspondents he found the new publication the first thing on this side of the Atlantic comparable with London's *Times Literary Supplement*.

We were pleased to see two librarians, Emerson Greenaway and Stuart Sherman, among those who applauded the first issue and had their letters printed. It is to be hoped that librarians will respond with something more substantial than letters, however, now that *The Review* has decided to publish regularly. No book selector should be without this new aid, and because it is a venture which we believe deserves the solid support of libraries, for once we unashamedly advertise on this editorial page. An annual subscription to *The New York Review of Books* costs $6. Send it to 250 West 57th St., New York 19, N.Y.

*Eric Moon*

## MRS. KENNEDY'S LIBRARY
October 1, 1963

One of the strangest instances of metamorphosis since Kafka is that of the new White House Library. Assembled because Mrs. Kennedy wanted "a library of books central to the understanding of the American national experience," it is now being described as "a working reference library for the present President and all the Presidents to come as well as for their families, cabinet officers, and White House advisors" (*New York Times,* August 16).

Having looked over the list once and noted its partially repository character, one goes back to it for a second look from a different angle, shivers, and wonders about quite different aspects; wonders just what "a working reference library" is—or should be in the Presidential context (can it be much less than the Library of Congress?); how good any library can be that approaches every subject from one national point of view; whether we want to foster a worldwide image of the American President chewing on an American cornstalk, smiling a contemplative American smile, looking neither to the East nor to the West, neither to the North nor to the South—nor, God forbid, *out,* but deep into the all-American navel where presumably he will find the wisdom to lead his people through all the follies of earth on to the beautiful pastures of heaven.

A dismal image this, and one that should be shattered before it sets. People of every nation read the *New York Times;* many of them must be puzzled by a collection of books presented as "a working reference library for the American President" that contains no works of most of the great minds down the ages nor contemporary works that are vital to an understanding of the present multiple revolution that engulfs the world.

*We* understand that the President's use of the library will be selective, that he isn't going to depend on information about events (even those that pertain to the American national experience) filtered exclusively through American minds and expressed in the American idiom in a kind of endless murmur of Americans talking to themselves.

*We* know that he isn't going to spend his working hours shooting Red Indians with Kit Carson, occupying California with Fremont, roping, throwing and branding with the American cowboy, hanging a friend and winning a schoolmarm with *The Virginian,* heeding *The Call of the Wild* with Jack London, sorrowing or rejoicing with *Little Women,* stringing along with Mr.

Dooley or Uncle Remus, reivewing *Architecture and Town Planning in Colonial Connecticut* or life on *The Sod-House Frontier;* that he isn't going to take time out for happy hours with American folklore, American folk song, American folk art, American interior design, American silver, American glass, the American circus, American showboats, etcetera, etcetera, etcetera; that if he refers to Schumpeter—admitted to the library one supposes because of his "Americanization"—he will also sneak a look at Keynes and possibly at Alec Nove, and on through all the corridors of world thought, past and contemporary. We know all this but will the rest of the world? Won't others reflect on this "working reference library for the American President" with a twinge (or more) of apprehension?

And so our wonderings become a question: Instead of indulging in a kind of highflown pomposity about a collection of American books, however fine it may be, wouldn't it be better if this library in the present Presidency and through all the Presidencies to come be known simply as Mrs. Kennedy's Library? Or, since it may be a good deal more and somewhat less than she expected, being a bit light on creative American thought of the last two decades, as the Messrs. Babb, Powell, Towner, Lacy, Rogers, Barrett, Duffy Library in the White House? The hopeful understanding being that the President will browse in it at will, and that someday, becoming a bit impatient with the premium it sets on death, boldly invite some living poets and novelists in.

*Margaret Cooley*

## ARIUS THROUGH DIATHERMY
December 15, 1963

When librarian Jones and librarian Smith first heard that a new encyclopedia was being published, in stages, over a period of about a year, several volumes already were off the press and the publisher had begun a heavy advertising campaign. The salesmen who visited librarian Jones and librarian Smith described a very attractive prepublication discount, and showed samples of the first few published volumes. Jones examined the samples, liked them, but felt he must wait until all the volumes were off the press and reviewed in toto before he could decide whether or not to buy. Smith examined the samples, liked them, and, despite the fact that the concluding volumes would not be published for another six months, he bought the set.

To buy or not to buy? That is the question, which we ask seriously. Tradition, habit—call it what you will—tells the librarian to wait and examine the whole book before purchase. Nevertheless some librarians do buy the parts of an encyclopedia or similar reference work before the whole is completed. Are they mistaken to do so?

The waiters argue validly against early purchase, on grounds that there is good chance a finished product won't live up to its promising start. Granting (but doubting) this possibility, what motivates the librarian who actually buys the partial book?

A number of things might prompt him. First, his interest in the work has been aroused through publisher's promotion. Second, teachers have heard about the book in the same way, and parents also, and they have come to him with inquiries about it, so that already there is user interest and user demand. Then too, the encyclopedia—partial though it may be—is more up to date than any similar work on his reference shelves; the information now is fresher than it ever will be, so why wait six months to put it to use? Finally, if the librarian is any kind of idealist, he reasons that his purchase represents an initial return for the publisher, enabling him to continue production; furthermore, if the first volumes do prove unsatisfactory in use, maybe he can tell the publisher about it in time for subsequent volumes to be improved.

Our mythical gambler buys the partial book with all these presumed considerations in mind. But how about the real-life gamblers—you, yourself? Have you bought reference books that are being published piecemeal over a period of months or even years? If not, why not; if yes, what prompted you and, having done so, do you regret the purchase? Are we tangling with a sacred cow, a "professional" habit, or are there good reasons for the delayed-purchase tactic?

A specific example of the kind of book we are talking about is the projected 20-volume all-new *Encyclopedia International;* a review (or preview) of the first five volumes appears in this issue of *LJ* (*see* page 64). The final volumes will not be completed until spring of 1964 although the publisher already is publicizing the set widely. Our reviewers, while recommending these first five volumes guardedly, nevertheless advise that "librarians wait for a review of the complete set before purchase." We are not so sure we agree with them, and we wonder how you feel about the matter.

Perhaps you already have heard of this particular work. If not, you will know something about it after having read the review. How many of you already have bought the first volumes? How many of you would consider buying on the basis of the review, despite the reviewers' cautious recommendation? Your answers will open up discussion on a point that needs airing.

*Ellen Rudin*

## ON THE SHELF
January 15, 1964

Many years ago, first in a relatively small branch library, then in a large central library, we conducted some experiments in what we then called "saturation buying." We compiled lists of all the works of a number of classic or contemporary authors which we knew to be in demand, then checked the *shelves* (not the catalog) to see how many were there. More often than not the outstanding titles were not present.

We then bought a predetermined number of copies of each missing title and placed them on the shelves on a recorded day. Several weeks later we checked the shelves again, and once more multiple copies were purchased of each missing title. This process was continued until the point was reached where a specific title began to "show" pretty consistently on the shelf. At that point we took a count of the number of copies in stock.

The documentation on this little project has long since disappeared, but we remember clearly that with more than 40 copies of some Hemingway titles in stock (in a branch library serving some 25,000 people) it was difficult to find *on the shelf* a copy, for example, of *For Whom the Bell Tolls*.

The thinking behind these ancient experiments went something like this:

1) There are a number of absolutely basic, standard works which the reader might justifiably expect to be *readily* available in any library worth the name.

2) There are a number of readers who do not automatically "ask the librarian" when they do not find on the shelf the book they want. How many leave the library regularly disappointed because *the* book is not there?

3) Most librarians would agree that the emphasis in their collections, and the priority in their book expenditures, should be in favor of the books that last rather than the passing froth of today or yesterday. While it may be justifiable to send to the Rental Collection, or keep on a long reserve list, the reader who wants *The Three Sirens* or some such, the reader who wants a copy of *Hamlet* ought to have better-than-even chance of finding one when he wants it.

4) Probably the weakest tooth in that old saw, "the right book for the right reader at the right time," is the last one. The man who wants his *Hamlet* now is not enchanted by the response that "it's in the catalog" when he does not find it on the shelf.

So, long ago, we set out to discover what it takes in quantity to give the reader who wants quality a reasonable chance of getting it when he wants it.

Our memory of these experiments was stirred by the list, compiled by Caroline Hieber, of books which the college-bound student should have or should be reading (see pp. 185–87). How often, we wondered would the eager student in search of one or other of these mostly standard titles be disappointed when he visited his local public library?

Are librarians still prone to be satisfied with copies recorded in the catalog or shelf-list, or do they check their shelves regularly enough to know that some items are never there? Do copies slumber in reserve stacks while empty spaces adorn the open shelves? Are we so busy buying the "new" titles that we too rarely go back and check our shelf representation of the "old" ones?

Well, we like answers, even to our own questions. We selected 20 titles from the fiction and nonfiction works listed by Miss Hieber and checked the shelves of eight New York and New Jersey public libraries, varying in size from the gigantic city library to the medium-sized suburban library.

We chose titles which we thought most librarians would agree were basic stock items, and our choice was justified by the fact that nearly all the titles were "in stock" in nearly all the libraries we visited. We also chose titles which were all available in paperback. This, we thought, gave the libraries an extra advantage, since some of the eager readers would have bought their own copies, thus lessening pressure on the library, and also the library that needed to duplicate fairly heavily in order to satisfy demand for these titles *could* do so, without wrecking the book fund, by buying extra paperback editions.

What did we find? Were the books generally "on the shelf"? Space does not permit elaboration here, but the results were quite interesting in their variety. While seven out of eight could produce *Sister Carrie,* only four had *Vanity Fair* on the shelf, and none could supply *Lord of the Flies*—and three didn't have a Milton in sight! For more, as the serial writers say, see next installment (next issue).

*Eric Moon*

*Ed. note: The results of the survey appeared February 1, 1964 in an article titled* The View from the Front (*pp. 570–74*).

## POINTS FOR THE BUDGET
February 1, 1964

The figure 18 may recur often in the budget requests of librarians this year. The table in the January 20 issue of *Publishers' Weekly,* shows that the price index for hardcover trade books rose 18 points in the past year—the largest increase in any one year since the indexes of book prices were first compiled at the end of the forties. Over this whole period, prices have increased by 82.4 percent, and another year at the 1963 rate of increase would result in book prices having doubled in about a decade and a half.

Prices are not the only factor which may leave library book budgets reeling. The January 20 PW also reveals that the total American title output in 1963 increased by 18 percent (that magic number again) over the previous year, from 21,904 to 25,784 titles.

There are, of course, many variables which affect these increases in book prices and title output, and certainly not all libraries will be affected as seriously as the total figures suggest. But the large or specialized library which collects fairly comprehensively within certain subject fields must surely feel the pinch.

With the price index rising 16 points and the title output up 31 percent in the business book field, the library with a business department obviously cannot buy the same representation of the output without a considerable budget increase. Similarly, the science field shows a title output increase of 26 percent and prices up 17 points on the index.

The large increases are not all in such special fields. Presumably the general college and public libraries, as well as high school libraries, will notice the 20 percent title increase and prices up by 20 points in the field of literature.

Add to these price and title output increases the considerable rise in the use of libraries in recent years, and libraries appear to have a ready-made and solid case for a substantial hike in their book budgets. There have been steady, indeed notable, increases in book appropriations for libraries. For example, *The Bowker Annual, 1963* reported public library book budgets up 27 percent between 1959 and 1961, and college and university book budgets up by 44 percent. But there is also evidence that libraries are still not managing to keep pace with the pressures from prices, output, and use. A recent article by Henry Drennan of the Library Services Branch (*LJ*, Jan. 1, pp. 67–70) showed a steady decline in the share of metropolitan public library budgets which is spent for books, and a decline also in the funds expended per capita, "when adjusted for rising book prices."

Should the necessary large book budget increases fail to materialize, what then? The first and most obvious result is that the selection process will have to become much more rigorous. But this may be as much problem as solution. Selection is itself an expensive process in terms of staff time (usually the time of the most expensive staff), and the more money that is poured into staff costs the more likely it becomes that the share of the total budget which is allocated to books will continue its steady decline. Perhaps an evaluation of the selection process in libraries is in order. Need it be as expensive or individual as it usually is? Does cooperation offer any answers here?

And if libraries select more rigidly, where will the emphasis be? In our article in this issue (*see* pp. 570–74) we try to lend some support to our belief that most libraries are already unable to duplicate titles of obvious worth in sufficient numbers. Will the butter now be spread even thinner? Or will more librarians have the courage to face the "demand" problem and the increasing supply problem, and put up a stouter resistance to the mounting tide of new and more expensive, and often ephemeral, titles?

*Eric Moon*

## BLUE CHIP BOOK SELECTION
June 15, 1964

Book reviewing and book selection are, in many ways, similar processes. In both activities, for example, the greatest problems are posed by what is usually called "creative literature." Only a little thought is required to understand why this should be so.

A book in a subject field, such as biology or economics, can be measured in several fairly concrete ways—by the scope of its content, its academic level, its relationship to other books in that subject field. But against what does one measure the worth of a new novel, or a new collection of poems? Here, the decision is influenced by personal taste, by reading and educational background, by whatever feel or instinct one may have for literature. The sheer chanciness of this process results in a kind of ultra-conservatism among most librarians, and most reviewers. Being unsure, they avoid judgments or decisions altogether.

The net result is a very unfortunate one for the new creative writer. Either the review medium ignores his work entirely or the reviewer produces a totally "neutral" review which leaves the reader without even an opinion to match against his own uncertainty. If the reader of the review is a librarian, a further result is that the new creative work is largely ignored (i.e. not bought).

Libraries have taken on a multitude of responsibilities in this century (some of them pretty extraneous), and some librarians always seem to be looking for new fields to conquer. But there is one responsibility—or obligation—which many librarians have seriously neglected. As Dan Lacy, Managing Director of the American Book Publishers Council (and an ex-librarian), puts it: "The slight increases or even decreases in the publishing of serious fiction and poetry reflect the fact that libraries simply do not buy extensively in these fields, and especially not in poetry. Libraries know that they are an essential part of the educational process, and they have a deep sense of commitment to that process, ready to invest their time, their labors, and their acquisition funds to its service. Libraries rarely realize they have an equally essential role in the unfolding of creative literature. New poets and new novelists have little chance to be bought, or more important, to be read except as librarians buy their works and bring them to readers."

In a fascinating article in the May 1964 issue of the *PLA Bulletin* (Pennsylvania Library Association), Mr. Lacy shows that, while publishing volume in fields like science, sociology, and economics, has increased since 1950 by 200 or 300 percent, the increase in publishing of serious fiction or new poetry has been negligible. Much of the blame for this situation, he says, must be laid at the door of librarians, for "For the most part, the pattern of publishing is simply a reflection of the pattern of library purchasing."

Mr. Lacy continues: "Some new poets and novelists are gifted; most are not; a few are very good indeed; once in a while, one is great. To publish them requires a substantial amount of money and the psychology of an optimistic bettor at the fifty-dollar window. Librarians are likely to approach the same writers with the psychology of a Vermont banker investing the funds of widows and orphans. The doctrine of many book selection manuals and library school courses is that libraries should buy only the blue chips of poetry anthologies and the collected works of standard poets, and avoid the reckless investment of dollars in new works. In the probably sound turn from providing mysteries and romances to serving students and inquirers, some libraries seem to have developed a puritanical attitude toward fiction as a somewhat frivolous part of their services, to be countenanced only when it is 'nonfiction' fiction ('tells you about life in the Middle Ages') or when the author is safely recognized or when the work itself is enshrined as 'literature' in the 800's."

Dan Lacy also talks about a survey a couple of years ago of "well-supported urban libraries," the results of which showed that "the larger major urban libraries buy about one new novel in seven. The typical large library buys annually 15 to 25 volumes of poetry, almost entirely anthologies and collected works of standard poets. . . . The publisher of a new manual on bridge or a cram book for civil service examination will have the library market going for him; the publisher of a new poet's work simply won't."

It is Mr. Lacy's final paragraph, however, which should be read at all book selection gatherings and in library school courses:

"There is no librarian, confronted with a new, shy, and hesitant inquirer, uncertain of his needs, who will not warmly and gladly devote time to his service, hoping that here may be one who in time will be a reader for whom the librarian has been able to open doors to a new world. I should like to bespeak a similar warmth and hospitality to the new novelist or new poet, who stands on your doorstep, with his work shyly and tentatively in hand. *It costs less to buy a new writer than to work with a new reader.* As with the new reader, one will more often than not be disappointed. Most new writers fail, as most new users become discouraged. But here and there comes the genuine burst of discovery in which you will have a part. It can be a wonderful experience for both writer and reader, and for the librarian who has brought them together."

*Eric Moon*

## FICTION CONSENSUS
October 15, 1965

The demise of the novel has been predicted for years, but the old soldier refuses to die. The prophets of doom have been most vocal in the post–World War II years, yet the judgments on the fiction of this period still range to the extremes. "A lean, lean 20 years," says *Newsweek's* Richard Gilman. "Easily the richest period in the history of the American novel," says Gore Vidal.

These assessments are the ends of a rainbow of opinion which appeared in a fascinating special issue of *Book Week* for September 26 (*see LJ*, Oct. 1, p. 4030). *Book Week* polled 200 prominent authors, critics, and editors to see if it could find a prevailing pattern to critical estimates of postwar fiction. Which of the 10,000-odd works of fiction produced during this period, *Book Week* asked the select 200, "were most artful, most truthful, most memorable," which most likely to survive? And which writers had created the most substantial body of work during the two decades.

As *Book Week* candidly acknowledged, "Such a critical consensus may prove little; it simply tabulates opinions." History may reach other and different conclusions but, as *Book Week* claims, it "will not be uninterested in what the contemporary judgment was."

Everyone tends to check such lists against his own opinions and prejudices, and we are no exception. We found Bellow, at the top of the distinguished authors list and with four novels in the "best 20," considerably overrated. And Katherine Anne Porter, although a superb shortstory writer, seemed scarcely to deserve inclusion for the creaking *Ship of Fools*, her only production during the period under review. But there were pleasures in the selections, too—notably the high ranking given that scintillating craftsman Nabokov, and the inclusion of John Hawkes, perhaps the least-known novelist of real merit in America.

In the list of the 20 best books (chosen in the order of frequency cited) we found delight in the first three—Ellison's *Invisible Man*, *Lolita*, and *Catcher in the Rye*—and, given the cushion of hindsight, like to feel that we would have picked all three at the top of our own list. But if the inclusion of four Bellow novels was extravagant, the exclusion of Carson McCullers and James Baldwin entirely seemed unjust.

Personal opinions aside, what will libraries make of this critical consensus? Will some be persuaded by so much critical weight that some of those "dangerous" books of these dangerous times, which have been excluded from library shelves for a variety of unconvincing reasons, should be given public exposure after all?

What of the 22 percent of those libraries we surveyed a few years ago (*see "Problem Fiction," LJ*, Feb. 1, '62, pp. 484-96) which, perhaps persuaded by such comments as Kirkus' "literary pornography," exclude *Lolita*? Will they even consider the possibility that this later critical judgment may be right, and their earlier one wrong? Will the critics' choice of Burroughs' terrifying *Naked Lunch* as among the best 20 have any influence on the considerable number of public libraries which did not buy it?

The other question which has to be asked is: *should* such collections of critical opinion have any bearing on the book selection process? The replies we have had from librarians to a number of surveys in this area would seem to argue a positive reply to that question. We have been told many times that "literary merit" is a major factor in the selection decision, but contemporary judgments on literary merit seem often to be so varying as to be only a matter of opinion. Here, in the *Book Week* survey, is literary merit assessed by a fairly large body of literate people with critical experience, operating in this case with some benefit of time and hindsight? Are these judgments not as valid, or more valid than those made by librarians and reviewers on publication day?

"The reviews," again, ranked consistently high among the reasons given by librarians in our own surveys for selection or rejection of certain books.

Here, in the *Book Week* survey are the considered judgments of 200 of the most prominent reviewers in the country. The reasons given before by many librarians who rejected *Lolita* and such, if those reasons included "literary merit" and "the reviews," would now seem to justify a sharp about-face.

We'd be glad to hear from any public library which has *all* the books listed in the two *Book Week* tabulations. Any takers?

*Eric Moon*

## PAST THE MIDDLE RANGE
November 15, 1965

An off-beat booklist came our way a week back, via, indirectly, that Bible of the supermarkets. In a full-page ad in the New York *Times* October 22, it ran a list of 55 book titles, announcing to parents: "If your child hasn't read at least 20 of these books, *Family Circle* says he's not ready for college."

So who's *Family Circle?* In this case, Frank Jennings, educational consultant to the New World Foundation, editor-at-large for *Saturday Review,* and author of the widely acclaimed *This Is Reading,* who, in July, had written on vacation reading for the college bound, with recommendations on which the list was based. The items come from divers bibliographies and crop up regularly on the College Entrance Examination Board exams. Here they are:

*The Way of All Flesh* (Butler), *Fathers and Sons* (Turgenev), *Of Human Bondage* (Maugham), *Look Homeward, Angel* (Wolfe), *Jane Eyre* (Brontë), *Winesburg, Ohio* (Anderson), *The Stranger* (Camus), *Cry, the Beloved Country* (Paton), *A Passage to India* (Forster), *Man's Fate* (Malraux), *Benito Cereno* (Melville), *Lord Jim* (Conrad), *Notes from the Underground* (Dostoevski), *Bread and Wine* (Silone), *The Ides of March* (Wilder), *I, Claudius* (Graves), *Hadrian's Memoirs* (Yourcenar), *Peter Abelard* (Waddell), Samuel Pepys' *Diary, A Journal of the Plague Year* (Defoe), *Seven Pillars of Wisdom* (T. E. Lawrence), *Twelve Against the Gods* (Bolitho), *Death Be Not Proud* (Gunther), *Lord of the Flies* (Golding), *Animal Farm* (Orwell), *Green Mansions* (Hudson), *Dead Souls* (Gogol), *The Uses of the Past* (Muller), *The Romans* (Barrow), *The Greeks* (Kitto), Thomas Mann's *Joseph* tetralogy, *War and Peace* Tolstoy), *The Leopard* (Lampedusa), *The Persian Wars* (Herodotus), *The Peloponnesian Wars* (Thucidydes), *Anabasis* (Xenophon), the *Iliad* and *Odyssey, The Greek Way* (Edith Hamilton), *The Crusades* (Henry Treece), *The England of Elizabeth* (Rowse), *The American Character* (D. W. Brogan), *The Uprooted* (Handlin), *Marco Polo's Travels, Gulliver's Travels* (Swift), *Don Quixote* (Cervantes), *The Divine Comedy* (Dante), *Paradise Lost* (Milton), *Science and Human Values* (Bronowski), *The Sleep Walkers* (Koestler), *The Nature of the Universe* (Hoyle), *Knowledge and Wonder* (Weisskopf), *The Search* (Snow), *The Story of Language* (Mario Pei), and *The Tyranny of Words* (Stuart Chase).

It is an ingenious assortment, as much for what it excludes as what it cites, for there is, between *Winesburg, Ohio* and the Joseph stories, quite a gap to be filled. Wolfe, insatiable adolescent, is there, though Eliot, who with Auden articulated the *angst* of a whole generation, seems already dated. There is not, interestingly, a single volume of contemporary poetry here, though present-day renderings of other times abound. Other literary pleasures too obvious to mention are bypassed (from Chaucer through Faulkner); though why include Xenophon and also Homer, then leave out the *Oresteia,* or list 19th-Century Russian literature over the French, by which it was influenced, and omit altogether Marx, Darwin, Frazer, and Freud, formers of 20th-Century culture?

It is a list, then, that provokes rather than limits selection, touching a few borders and omitting the vast middle ground of high school reading; one sees in it again the marvelous diversity of high school literature today. The probabilities are that most high school libraries would have the minimal 20 titles, but we'd like to know more: How many librarians can claim to have all 55 titles for the student who comes into the library hunting them up? Or 50? Or 45? And how many "standard" or "basic" lists will you have had to use to get them?

*Evelyn Geller*

## LIGHT ON THE NEGLECTED
January 1, 1966

Our latest book selection survey (*see* pp. 57–64) included one of our pet questions. We asked respondents to try to uncover a worthwhile book which might have been passed over by a number of libraries.

A few people objected to the question. They couldn't possibly know, they said, what the majority of libraries might or might not buy. The complaint was valid, but we recognized that we were asking for unscientific guesses. If our respondents chose wrongly—that is, picked books that *weren't* being overlooked—it would do no harm. But if just one of them turned up a "sleeper," it would be a real service to libraries which had missed it.

Last March, Robert Franklin noted, in the Toledo's Public Library's *Tee-Pee,* that it is standard procedure at his library (it should be at *all*) to check any recommended lists of books. It's an effective way, he said, to close gaps, but it doesn't answer the question: "Why doesn't TPL have the good ones as soon as any comparable library?"

The answer to that question is perhaps that book selection is a very human and very fallible process—which is what makes the constant checking necessary. Librarians aren't the only people who miss "the good ones";

so do critics, review media, and publishers (how many are the tales of the masterpiece rejected by a dozen publishers!).

The trouble is that so many of the annual lists emphasize the obvious. They keep the spotlight firmly on many of the books which need it least. We were trying to focus just a little of that light on a few books that might have been consigned to perpetual shade.

Not long after our survey had gone out, we discovered that *Holiday* magazine was publishing in its December issue a list of "the most unfairly neglected books," and that this would be an annual *Holiday* feature. Our belief in this kind of approach was strengthened when *Holiday's* first list included *The Olive Field* by Ralph Bates, one of our favorite novels of all time, but one we haven't seen or heard of for years. Check stock on that one.

*Eric Moon*

## CAUGHT IN THE DRAFT
February 15, 1966

"One temptation that should be resisted is that of buttressing unduly our views on the use of force—regarding the draft board as the antagonist, and trying to win as the debater wins. If the objector can clarify his reasons for rejecting violence, and present them clearly, his sincerity will carry him where argument would fail." This bit of tactical advice is quoted from the *Handbook for Conscientious Objectors*, a 110-page paperback published at 50 cents by the Central Committee for Conscientious Objectors at 2006 Walnut St., Philadelphia. A secret best-seller, the *Handbook* is now in its eighth edition which was published in November, 1965. Since the first edition more than 50,000 copies of the little book have been distributed, without any professional marketing, distribution, or advertising.

The *Handbook* is not a plea to draft-age men to become CO's; it is predicated on the assumption that the man who has a copy and is reading it, has already decided to try for noncombatant status when he is drafted, but that he is ignorant of his legal rights, and doesn't know how to go about it. The book offers step-by-step tactical and legal advice to the man facing induction who is conscientiously opposed to the use of force.

Another current best-seller is Arco's *Practice for the Armed Forces Tests*, cited as the "most stolen book" in a recent "Books for Young Adults" review (*see* p. 1086). Like the *Handbook, Practice* . . . doesn't urge men to join the armed forces. Instead, it gives them guidance to help them achieve greater success when they are inducted and face the seemingly endless batteries of tests so familiar to anyone who has served in the US military.

In other words, neither of these manuals really represents a point of view, except by implication. One is addressed to those who want to get into the armed forces and succeed at it. The other is aimed at that embattled minority who are variously labelled as cowards, vietniks, yellow-bellies, and traitors—those who do not want to become soldiers. Both audiences are a part of the library public.

When we first heard about the *Handbook*, we were curious as to how it might fare in libraries. We decided to try to find out, and spent a day on the telephone to 15 libraries in various parts of the US. A sample that small is not scientific; indeed, it is not sufficiently broad to allow generalizations with any assurance of validity. Furthermore, our method may have provided some inaccurate answers. We telephoned, as a patron might, and asked if the library had either, or both, of the books. About all the librarian could do was quickly check the card catalog, although either book might have been in some vertical file, or elsewhere. Anyway, we got the same answer that a patron would probably get if he telephoned to ask for the two books.

The evening before the calls were made we mentioned the idea to a nonlibrary friend. He reacted as follows: "Come off it—you really believe your own propaganda!" "What do you mean?" we asked. "Listen!" he said, "Nobody would look for that kind of stuff in a library. Libraries just don't have all the information that you keep telling me they should. I wouldn't expect that thing to be in our library." He was partly right, partly wrong.

The public libraries of East Orange, New Jersey; Philadelphia; New Haven; Chicago; Glendale, California; and Flint, Michigan, own both the Arco manual and the *Handbook*. Those of New York (NYPL); Newark, New Jersey; Baltimore (Enoch Pratt); Oakland, California; New Orleans; Fort Worth, Texas; Burlington, Vermont; and Concord, New Hampshire own only *Practice for the Armed Forces Tests*. The library in Falls Church, Virginia reported that it had neither publication. Six libraries have the *Handbook*, 14 have *Practice* . . ., one has neither.

There was, among these 15, no regional pattern that we could discern. Size of the library, its public, budget, or collections, didn't seem to matter. The library's proximity to military bases, colleges, or potential draftees or objectors, was not a factor.

A few of the libraries gave reasons for not having either Arco's book or the *Handbook*. One said, "We used to buy the Arco title, but it was missing so much that we gave up." About the *Handbook*, a librarian said: "We don't think it would be appropriate to spend public funds for that!" Another said, "I've never heard of it. If we just had a review or something, we would probably get it." Seven of the nine without the *Handbook* said there was no demand for it, and nearly all pointed out that it was not reviewed, advertised, nor well-known.

In short, it is fairly clear to us that there is no fear of the *Handbook*, despite the unpopularity of the position of the conscentious objector. Libraries didn't have it because they didn't know about it, or because, unsure of their own selection judgment, they were waiting for a review. Since the first edition of the *Handbook* was published in 1952, it is unlikely that reviews will be forthcoming now.

This small sampling, of course, is inconclusive, but it yields food for thought. If librarians are going to live up to the propaganda that our friend mentioned, then they ought to know how to find out about fugitive material such as the *Handbook*. It has received newspaper and television coverage in recent months, and we got a copy with no trouble at all. Certainly a specialist in information should be able to find it.

Beyond that it seems to us that the heavy reliance upon demand as a selection criteria is putting undue limitations on library collections. If librarians haven't heard of the *Handbook,* then it is unlikely that their patrons will know about it. It is equally unlikely that a young man will announce to the librarian that he wants to become a conscientious objector and would like information. If he comes to the library at all, he will probably appreciate finding the material he wants by anonymously searching the card catalog.

Finally, we do have some nagging doubts regarding the subject matter of the two books. Obviously, in this small sample anyway, libraries are quick to provide material presenting an acceptable view, or goal; but they are not so quick to give advice that is unacceptable to the majority. In our view, as information specialists, they should provide equal access to both.

*John Berry*

## DISSENT AND THE "CHILDREN'S" STIGMA
March 15, 1966

Not quite six years ago, a young library science teacher at St. John's University in Jamaica, N.Y., took librarians to task as "literature experts," with special regard to quality vs. usefulness in book selection in the *Fiction Catalog*. Finding in that volume nine single- or double-starred items by Bess Streeter Aldrich, only one with that distinction for Faulkner and two for Hemingway, she charged: "When our two most important living authors combined are considered one third as valuable as Bess Streeter Aldrich, we are hardly on our way to earning recognition as literary critics." The article appeared in the August 1960 *LJ*; and the young lady lost her job.

St. John's University has since gone on to greater notorieties, and Dorothy Broderick to better things—with no retreat from her original pungency and honesty, which we need hardly say is a special virtue in the children's field.

Just how rare that virtue is has become apparent to us in the last few months, since Miss Broderick reviewed *The Elementary School Library Collection,* commending it, among other things, for its selection policy, its a/v collection, and its effort to supply a new tool. But she did fix her eye stubbornly on some failures to carry out that purpose: the rich streak of cataloging errors, the volume's dubious value as a book catalog (presumably the justification for its format), and its padding with titles of questionable quality.

For this detailed examination Miss Broderick has gotten a lot of secret admiration and open hysteria. The admiration, for her "temerity," comes out in private discussion; the hysteria in charges of "betrayal," "poor timing in terms of school library development," and of all things lack of specialization—emotional, quasipolitical considerations that are bolstered with commendations of the very features which Miss Broderick praised. What a contrast to the adult and disciplined discussion that followed her piece on the *Fiction Catalog* years ago!

In her review Miss Broderick was concerned about the collection both as a selection tool and for what it purported to be besides. There are limitations in any booklist that you pick up, and the ALA for that reason holds that each "standard selection tool," no matter how reputable, be reviewed, for every title, in the light of particular needs, a consideration that is especially important in the elementary school. The *Elementary School Library Collection's* Selection Policy acknowledges the importance of the school librarian, but to adapt and update *"this"* collection. And its statement that the list should "make it possible for a school librarian to put a program of service into action promptly and effectively when a new school library is opened" easily lends itself to abuse. Here's one example, a memo from a New Jersey principal:

> You will receive in the near future, a copy of the Elementary School Library Collection. . . . This is a basic list of books for Elementary Libraries and is the one we will be using for our guide in building the elementary library collections. May I suggest you use this as a buying guide and check each title you order.

The procedure, which is being used for book purchase under NDEA and even PTA funds, and for libraries that have already been started, illustrates the dangers inherent in a list that suggests itself as definitive. It is one reason, perhaps, why a librarian at the midwinter conference expressed the hope that the American Association of School Librarians would come out with a statement on booklists.

For many librarians who were hoping for another selection tool, probably in paperback, and for library school professors, the book catalog format seems an expensive redundancy. When you consider that this format is inaccurate unless it represents the collection, its value is clearly diminished by every book it doesn't include—and each of its titles the school doesn't hold. Sloppy cataloging is another source of chagrin, while the computer mistakes are startling: that *machine infernelle* even muffed preparing the tables for the article by Miss Gaver. The title count for the supplement, for example, was cited as 1600 in the *Pennsylvania Library Association Bulletin,* but changed to 1100—almost 50 percent off—after a hand count, in time for its reprint in *School Library Journal.* Miss Gaver has acknowledged these errors graciously, and one certainly cannot blame the advisory and selection committees for every last error of detail (though *someone* might have picked up the pieces, for a professional $20 list); but this is no reason to discount the errors that occur.

It is this task that Miss Broderick has assumed—hardly a cataloging of "trivia," but an invaluable professional service, for few others would have raised these questions or are likely to discuss them. However important school library development may be, we have also a responsibility for open and mature criticism. For years Miss Broderick has exercised this responsibility, removing therewith much of the stigma often attached to children's work. We hope that her contribution is well appreciated—especially by those who wouldn't stand up to be counted.

*Evelyn Geller*

## DEWEY PROPORTIONS
June 1, 1966

How do the subject proportions of a library's total circulating book-stock relate to the subject proportions of its current acquisitions? Obviously they are not *exactly* the same. Some areas of the bookstock clearly turn over faster than others, some wearing out sooner (fiction?), others needing more frequent weeding (sci-tech?). But *how* different are the current acquisitions and total stock proportions?

These questions were raised in our mind by one of those nuggets of information that *The Tee-Pee*, Robert Franklin's jottings from the Toledo Public Library, offers from time to time. In the March 16 issue, Franklin gave the proportions, by Dewey classes, of the adult circulating book stock at his main library and at a typical Toledo branch library.

As a matter of interest, *LJ* compared the Toledo percentages with our adult book review coverage for the first three months of 1966. The comparisons are not precisely accurate, since *LJ* does not arrange its reviews by Dewey, but a little judicious grouping of our own subject categories gets us fairly close. The Toledo and *LJ* percentages, then, compare as follows (you will note that the *LJ* percentages miss 100 percent by 2.6: that's the percentage of reviews in January through March that were grouped under the heading "Reference," and we have not tried to distribute these):

Dewey 000: Toledo main, 0.5 percent; Toledo branch, 0.2 percent; *LJ* reviews, 2.1 percent (this is mostly reviews of library science items in "Professional Reading").

100–200: Main, 7 percent; branch, 4.2 percent; *LJ*, 8.3 percent.

300: Main, 9 percent; branch, 6 percent; *LJ*, 16.3 percent.

400: Main, 1 percent; branch, 0.4 percent; *LJ*, 0.3 percent.

500–600: Main, 16.5 percent; branch, 13.1 percent; *LJ*, 7.8 percent.

700: Main, 8 percent; branch, 7.4 percent; *LJ*, 10.5 percent.

800: Main, 12 percent; branch, 7.2 percent; *LJ*, 10 percent.

900 (History, Travel, *and* Biography): Main, 22 percent; branch, 18.9 percent; *LJ*, 20.1 percent.

FICTION: Main, 24 percent; branch, 42.6 percent; *LJ*, 22 percent.

It is immediately apparent from these figures that the greatest disparities between the Toledo holdings and the current *LJ* reviews are in the

300's (social sciences) and the 500's and 600's (science and technology). In the former, the *LJ* review percentage is almost double that of the Toledo holdings; in sci-tech, the reverse is true. Apart from these two major areas, where the discrepancies bother our review staff—are we over-reviewing in social sciences and under-reviewing in sci-tech (even for public libraries)? —we wonder whether the comparison tells us anything valid.

Can other libraries—public, college, high school—provide similar percentage breakdowns, not just for total stock but *for annual acquisitions?* How do *they* compare with our review coverage? We'd like to know because, obviously, we'd like to feel that we are reviewing (within limitations) what most of our subscribers most want to hear about.

*Eric Moon*

## WILD BLUEBERRIES
October 1, 1966

Cherished among writers is the venerable shell game of proving that one plus one equals three, and that old and worn things are really fresher and more durable than the new things with which they are currently being replaced. The *New Yorker* did it recently with covered bridges, matching them in Vermont against crass steel structures and bringing Currier and Ives home in the lead once again. It would be a nice exercise to do the same for the *New Yorker*.

But since this is the issue in which we celebrate the fall flood of books from our publishers, it is tempting to take books themselves for a turn at the old shell game, and prove that these archaic artifacts are young and vigorous and perennially blooming.

Of course, we all know they are on the skids. Whenever librarians and educators gather at their dark rites in Illinois or Idaho, and one rises to utter the word "book" the assembled congregation responds with a voice of thunder, "AND OTHER MATERIALS!" With the quiet firmness which characterizes those removing embarrassing evidences of a predecessor's gaucherie, we have been eliminating from the language, not only the word "book" but its Mediterranean relatives beginning with lib- and bibl-; replacing them with "information," "teaching machine," and especially, "resources."

Could it be that the book is now beginning to undergo the withdrawal from the profane world that has already occurred to the bow and arrow, the legitimate theatre, the film, and the poem? Prostitutes to utility, these elder phenomena at last found themselves largely unemployed and forced to fall back on earlier and sounder trades; society laid them off and they returned to obscure domestic service.

It may well be true that in the past several hundred years we have harnessed the book to too many tasks which have had no relation to its singular genius, and have unwittingly hastened its demise; our "nonbooks" have certainly caused more than a twinge of guilt in recent years. Could it be that this singular genius, like that of poetry itself, like the flavor of wild blueberries, can be expanded by cultivation only at the price of dissolution? It has often been suspected that there is a finite amount to love, or courage, or goodness in the world, or in a man; for that matter, or even in his noblest works; as compensation for the near-emptiness of the glass we have the sense of inestimable value that endows the last few drops of the wine.

So when books today seem to recapture the primitive and volcanic function of their ancestors, which was to create storms and sunlight in the human heart, we fear them anew, and build lead shields of critical respectability around them, but we don't burn them any more.

Books have been feared, and with reason, for they knock everlastingly at our locked doors and puzzle at the knots that bind the consciousness of man. Today, however, there is a difference; for perhaps the first time we are afraid that the book itself is mortal and finite and in need of shelter.

Evidence of all this is rampant in this issue of *LJ*, in which Jason Epstein, vice president of Random House, describes the curious antics of our nine old high priests as they protect the book by flapping broken-winged away from the nest like so many maternal and balding partridges—meanwhile stomping on a vulgarian. A writer, Jean Stafford, details her perennial intoxication with the making of books, bringing home to us once again just how difficult it is to bring a book to birth and how much rejoicing is in order when the infant is healthy. Robert Franklin, director of the Toledo Public Library, pleads against that strange form of bookicide achieved by buying one copy of a title when as many as a hundred are needed; and Daniel Melcher, president of Bowker, bends himself to a humble task something like taking in washing in order that the book may keep up its working life a bit longer.

Perhaps the only way to win this shell game, considering the odds, and prove that the book, like the covered bridge, may yet prevail, is to turn to the extensive fall foliage of new books on the pages of this issue. There we find Malamud, Updike, Lowell, Nabokov, and O'Hara among a sizable clutch of writers who have not yet gone to work producing audio-visual materials. The publishers are indeed still using this quaint form of "resource" to deal with such diverse matters as God, the Middle Ages, Presidential assassination, poverty, music and, by golly, there's a book on barns and covered bridges!

*Karl Nyren*

## 100 MILES AN HOUR IN THE FOG
February 1, 1967

As we go to press with our spring announcement issue, listing some 3000 books about to be published, the climate in which we live is winter. Snow tires and heating crises are a way of life; fog lies along the river roads and we are getting used to the danger of driving through it. So too are we weathering and travelling through the larger winter; since the brief thaw of victory and peace 20 years ago, we have grown accustomed to peering through the fogs that lie across our course. Our vision is obscured, but we cannot stop driving.

A fair proportion—perhaps ten percent—of the new books bear the stamp of our uncertainties. That means some 300 titles—fiction as well as nonfiction—dealing with Vietnam, crime, race problems, delinquency, conservation, education, sex, politics, and other areas about which we, as citizens, have a responsibility to know, as publishers or librarians a mission to make available to the general public, and as individuals a standing dare to contemplate. Ten years ago the same percentage of books was devoted to similar problem areas—but book production has nearly doubled. In this one area of book selection, librarians must consider not 150 but 300 titles about to be published, pick the most important, and find the funds to buy for their readers a fair sampling of significant reading. Simple arithmetic indicates that if only 200 of these titles should be acquired for a community, ten copies of each title, each circulating 20 times, would enable a small group of 8000 readers to read five books apiece in the year when they are most applicable and most worth reading. The book bill, at five dollars a volume, would be $10,000 for this one item in the book budget. We are producing books, but a missing link in distribution has to be forged before we can truly say we are "publishing" them—getting them to the public. And this public is supposed to mark an intelligent X on a ballot in 1968.

To the fairly large number of Americans who have some share in the making of our decisions, from the man who only votes to the man in the White House, the 300 titles offer help in exploring the questions: How shall the world change? How shall our government change? How shall man change himself?

A future historian, analyzing our new crop of 1967 books, might well wonder to see so little surface hysteria among a people whose situation was that of passengers in a car doing 100 miles an hour in the fog, with a driver over whom they have no control—beyond taking away his license after the accident. The future historian might well instead compare our behavior to that of the well trained astronaut, who, finding his craft yawing wildly, abstains from reaction until he can think ahead of the ship's gyrations by several steps. And if there is a future historian, the flattering description will have been partly true, and the American reader will have fulfilled the quietly heroic role which his publishers seem to have in mind for him.

Today's headliners among the fiction offerings show an even more international trend than did a similar list of ten years ago. But in 1956, it may be remembered, Graham Greene set his *Quiet American* in Saigon: comment that year was either miffed at the criticism of Americans or intrigued at Greene's picture of an innocent at the wheel of history. The scene will be re-explored this Spring by Daniel Ford, Andrew Tully, and Robin Moore.

Nonfiction, of course, is concentrating heavily on the war. But any list of titles which deal either directly with Vietnam, or with its geographical and ideological hinterlands, resounds with a hollow and rhythmic return to the theme of China.

The terms of our national discussion are set forth in this area and in many others by the titles of our new books; the syntax which we will select to compose these terms into statements of our intent as a people must be worked out rapidly. Millions of Americans should be reading—now—the books and articles which suggest the permutations by which the terms can be combined and finally simplified into the marking of an X in a little box on the next presidential ballot.

One can predict that the review media will substantially upgrade the visibility of the 300 titles; something like 25 percent of the books they will choose to review will be in the categories of serious topical nonfiction and fiction.

For it is a problem of vision finally, and we can be grateful for good lights as we hurtle on at a hundred miles an hour in the fog that lies along the rivers of the world: the Yellow River, the Vistula, the Mekong, the Potomac, and the Pedernales.

*Karl Nyren*

### SATISFACTION POINT
May 15, 1968

How many public library branches throughout the country possess 40 or more copies of *Who's Afraid of Virginia Woolf?* Or 50 copies of *Manchild in the Promised Land?* Perhaps the more significant question is: How many librarians believe that this number of copies—of these and a great many other books—may be necessary?

George Moreland's article in this issue on the recent Montgomery County Libraries' paperback experiment (pp. 1975–79) reveals once again the enormous chasm that yawns between library book selection practices and actual reader needs. Taking a national average, the Montgomery County Libraries are fairly affluent, and certainly, they are better stocked than many public libraries we have seen. Yet, the branch librarians involved in this project must have learned a great deal about the inadequacies of their libraries' holdings.

To take the two examples with which this editorial begins, the three branches for which statistics are given in Mr. Moreland's article held, at the beginning of the experiment, five, two, and two copies, respectively, of the Albee book. At the end of the project they had 45, 32, and 42. In the case of Claude Brown's book (a book of enormous relevance in today's troubled society), the holdings rose from four, two, and two copies to 51, 56, and 17. And the library with 56 copies still had not reached "satisfaction point"— this being defined as "the number of copies needed to guarantee that *at least one copy* would be in each branch at all times." Another among the many staggering discrepancies between practice and need is illustrated by Arthur Miller's *The Crucible:* the Davis Library, which had *no* copies at the beginning of the project, wound up with 30, and had still not reached satisfaction point.

The Montgomery County experiment was prompted, in part, by an earlier user survey which had revealed that the greatest cause of dissatisfaction among library patrons was that they could never find the books they wanted *on the shelves.* They might in most cases have been able to determine that the books were in stock but, as we have said before, we never knew a reader who wanted a book and left the library enchanted with having found a catalog entry for it.

We are not suggesting that every library should try to reach "satisfaction point" for every ephemeral best-seller published, but there are a great many books of lasting worth and quality that the library user ought reasonably to expect to find available on the shelves at most times.

Libraries spend altogether too much time on the initial selection and acquisition of a book and altogether too little on bookstock control thereafter. Much more active and continuous shelf scrutiny is necessary to determine whether a book, once bought, is ever really *available.* The storekeeper, who sells a product for profit, knows that it isn't enough just to put it on the shelf initially; he must make sure that it is continually available while there are customers for it. The profit for the librarian in being as diligent about his shelf stock is greater reader satisfaction—and the consequent possibility of broader patron support.

A determined attack also needs to be made on the too-common library goal of acquiring the largest possible number of *titles.* This disease is most prevalent in the larger research libraries—where there is *some* justification for it—but it pervades even the smallest institutions. The result of this policy is satisfaction of the more esoteric demands and an escalating level of failure on the titles needed by the largest number of patrons.

Thirdly—and this may be the most acceptable of these observations— most library book budgets need to be not just increased but tripled or quadrupled before there can be much hope of reaching any very general satisfaction point. Even with increase of this magnitude, the goal could still not be achieved without more realistic economic practices. It would be possible to avoid the escalation of staff costs which we insist must accompany much larger book budgets—IF more of these book funds were spent for heavy duplication (rather than more and more titles) IF more of the heavy demand were soaked up through the purchase of paperback copies— and IF librarians didn't insist on undermining the economic gains that paperbacks make possible by then adding the heavy costs of elaborate cataloging, processing, and record keeping.

Book selection will never reach satisfaction point until we give as much emphasis to the word "quantity" as we do to that more pious word "quality."

*Eric Moon*

# Book Awards

## HOW BEST?
March 15, 1962

The suspense is over: the word is out: Elizabeth Speare has won the Newbery medal for *The Bronze Bow* and Marcia Brown has won the Caldecott for *Once a Mouse*. We doff our cap to these two deserving ladies, and to their publishers and to everyone who had anything to do with these books, including the postmen who carried the manuscripts.

We doff our cap also to all children's book publishers, who in 1961 turned out 1,513 new books from which the Newbery-Caldecott jury had to choose.

A future for the two winning books is now assured; but what is happening to the other 1,511 books? Well, we know that three of them are runners up for the Newbery and three for the Caldecott, so we don't have to wonder about those six. Others have won or will win similar, though perhaps less heralded, awards for their content or design. Some are being judged "notable," some have already found a place on recommended booklists and some, probably because they deserve to be (but not always), are being utterly ignored. The greater part will wind up on library bookshelves, and of this great number an inevitable percentage will die this year, the bulk will be circulated until reader interest wanes or they are superseded, and a very few (who can say which?) will live forever as children's classics.

Precisely because no one can say which, we, as profferers of books to children, are obliged to place before them as much of the total treasure as we know exists. They, not we, will separate the dross from the gold. We may point out the pearls, of course, but that is all.

The concept of best is not unknown to children, especially in these days, and it is one we would do well to de-emphasize, for the child who grows up on a diet of only best will not learn to enjoy something that is merely good.

Surely the good, and even the middling, have something to offer and they deserve their due. We once overheard a conversation between a young student of the violin and her musical father: "Daddy, who is the best violinist?" "There are a lot of great ones—Oistrakh, Stern, Menuhin, Szigeti, Elman, Francescatti, Heifitz, Kreisler, Milstein . . ." "I know, but who is the greatest?" "They are all greatest."

This is not unlike the story of the wise rabbi who had been called to settle a violent argument between two men. The rabbi listened to one and said, "You are right." He listened to the other and said again, "You are right." A bystander cried out, "But, rabbi, they can't both be right." And to him the rabbi replied, "You are right."

This is not to say that there are not standards by which to judge a book great, but only to suggest that there can be twenty and thirty more books equally, or nearly equally, great.

Every year a committee of distinguished couturiers selects the world's ten best dressed women. Perhaps you live next door to a woman whose clothes and manner of dress you very much admire. Her name has never appeared on that list, nor will it ever, nor does it matter. Your neighbor has never been called "best dressed," but the fact remains that she is.

What is true of clothing is true of ice cream and authors. There is the story of the boy who asks his girl, "What is your favorite ice cream?" "Yes," she answers. Or the one about the critic who was asked, "Who is your favorite author?" Said he, "Bellow, Capote, Baldwin, McCullers, West, Kazantzakis, Fast, Remarque, Hemingway, DeVries, Huxley, Waugh, Gary, Dickens, Kafka, Twain, Proust, Saroyan, Dos Passos, Hesse, Woolf, Marquand, Shakespeare and Charles Schulz. Now if you've got a couple of hours, ask me what is my favorite book. I can think of about 200." So can children.

*The Bronze Bow* is an exciting story, superbly handled by a talented writer. Yet there are children who will not like it, just as there are those who will. The striking design and illustration of *Once a Mouse* will stir response in some children and none at all in others.

Books, many books, are our pleasure, not just the best ones. We know a man who each year reads only one book and each year states, "This is the best book I have read all year." Indeed, it may even have been a National Book Award winner. But, ah, what else this man is missing!

*Ellen Rudin*

## NOTABILITY AND PERMANENCE
March 15, 1964

It is again that time of year when critics and librarians and committees and juries climb high trees, scan the previous year's literary landscape, and then crawl far out on a precarious limb to reach down and pull from the already fast-growing weeds of ephemera their choice of another year's flowers. Transplanted into the current year, watered and nurtured by press releases and awards ceremonies, these rescued flowers, the gambling gardeners hope, will radiate their beauty and influence at least another season. And the most optimistic among the rescuers may even hope that omniscience will have led them to a perennial or two, or even (wildest hope of all) to an immortal.

ALA's list of "Notable Books of 1963" appears on pages 1204–06 of this issue. Although publishing a list of this kind is at any time like flying a target, there is little percentage in shooting, either at the selections or the omissions. The range is too short for accuracy. But it is interesting to cogitate over the meaning of that word "notable."

A press release accompanying the list describes it as a "selection of outstanding books particularly worthy of the attention of American adult readers published during 1963." If one is charitable enough to overlook the construction of that sentence, it can be judged a conservative and reasonable statement of purpose. Certainly, most of the books listed are worthy of attention.

The release also quotes Fern Long, president of ALA's Adult Services Division, who says: "These books were selected for their contribution to literature and general knowledge—sincerity of presentation, perception of present-day problems and values of literary excellence, and informational validity."

This is a heady soufflé of selection criteria, but perhaps it does throw some light on the interpretation of "notable." While the contributions to our literary heritage are not too obviously apparent, there are clear examples of the weight given to such factors as perception about present day problems, informational validity, and "contributions to general knowledge." Many of the listed titles are clearly "books for today." This does not mean that they are not important, only that their notability may fade relatively soon.

*The Censors and the Schools*, for example, is not a particularly notable book in any long-term sense. It is an adequate piece of reporting on the *current* state-of-the-art of textbook censorship, and one must doubt that the book would even have been considered did the problem not sit so squarely on our own doorsteps. Jessica Mitford's lively encounter with *The American Way of Death* is, again, surely a very current piece of muck-raking reporting. And the current importance attached to such subjects as conservation, Latin America, and depressed areas may well account for the presence of a number of other titles on the ALA list.

Our own definition of "notable" would tie in with our annual hope to see included more titles with the promise of permanence, but we do recognize that one man's guess is as good as the next about what is likely to resist the abrasion of the years. We are also quite sure that *no* prophet is going to be able to uncover 50 books with this built-in permanence from the publications of *any* one year.

Others will probably share our initial shock at finding only two works of American fiction included in the "notable" list. Not trusting memory we checked back over the year's output, but with our definition of "notable" rather than ALA's in mind we could not find too much more on which we'd like to gamble or for which we would argue strongly.

Pursuing our thoughts about notability and permanence we looked back *ten* years—at the Notable Books of 1953. Without checking on what had been left out, if we had been a member of the committee which chose that list, we would not now be too unhappy about most of the inclusions. A good number of those 1953 books *have* lasted well, and some look like lasting much longer.

Much of the fiction in the 1953 list, however, has faded pretty badly, and few titles, with the towering exception of *The Adventures of Augie*

*March,* seem particularly "notable" today. How many, for example, remember Jefferson Young's *A Good Man,* described as "a memorable first novel"? How notable today does Vern Sneider's *A Pail of Oysters* seem?

So perhaps, after all, the ALA committee's policy is sound, if not exciting. Play it safe, avoid the experimental and the possibly creative, pick today's winners and let some other prophet look after tomorrow. Even so, we can't get away from the feeling that a committee which chose Sartre's *Saint Genet* and described it as an "exhaustive examination of France's most provocative writer-dramatist" might have had the courage to risk including *Our Lady of the Flowers* by that same "provocative writer-dramatist." Who'd like to bet that it won't last longer than, say, the last title on the ALA list, *The Edge of the Storm?*

*Eric Moon*

## THE NOTABLES
March 15, 1967

Of the making of lists by librarians, there is no end, nor would we have it so. But of all the lists which they perpetrate in response to whatever hiccup in the genetic code it is that sets them off from their fellows, ALA's "Notable Books" (p. 1102) is surely the most enjoyable to ponder.

The relationship of librarians to books is not always clear. It is, therefore, a pleasure to see a committee of librarians called annually to stand and deliver in terms of excellence—to select the books most worthy of consideration by libraries from all the staggering output of American presses.

The bravery of this committee is appalling, for if librarians are slow to commit themselves on an issue, they are generous with their attention to any clearcut stand taken by their fellows. Each of the 60 titles—and the 30,000 left out—offers itself as a potential boomerang at the collective head of the committee.

Of even more interest than the individual titles is the list itself, which presents a kind of collective Rohrshach, not just of the committee, but of the library profession which it represents at a moment in time.

First, one notes that this year there are ten fiction choices, leaving 50 nonfiction, including poetry. The committee's release says there are five of the latter, but a count shows six—a mournful little comment on the low visibility of poetry in libraries as in the American culture.

Next, one notes that this is indeed a big year for Doubleday, with nine choices, closely followed by Harper, Random House, Viking, and Farrar Straus. In 1966, five university presses made the list, but none did in 1967. One is bemused by significances here for the sudden radiance of commercial publishing, or the lamentable falling off of academic presses, or even an inexplicable sea-change in the dark heart of librarianship.

But most intriguing of all are the results when we consider the list as a microcosmic library, and imagine a classification scheme to suit it. The scheme could be simpler than even the primitive Reader Interest arrangement, which is based on the notion that readers enter a library thinking, "I want a book on 'family living' or on 'hobbies' or on 'travel.'" And they may, for all we know.

Let's suppose, however, that our readers enter the microcosmic library most conscious of emotional needs which need satisfaction, ego ideals in need of bolstering, and ravaged faiths in need of repair. Now let's arrange the books on the list to reflect our judgment of the relative importunacy of these needs.

Dominant groupings appear immediately in our collection of 60 books. Most numerous by far are those which offer the joys of contemplation and retrospection to the sedentary mind—fully one third of the list. From *The Hours of Ann of Cleves* to the years of Colette's *Earthly Paradise,* and Jon and Rumer Godden's *Two Under the Indian Sun,* this little library basks in an autumnal glow.

But on the next shelf we find sustenance for the more serious mood, when enjoyment is to be tempered by self-improvement. This is naturally only half as large a selection, but it offers such good works as Oldenbourg on the Crusades and Maurois on Balzac. This is an even better shelf than the first for the decoration of coffee tables.

The third shelf, with another one-sixth of the list, is rigorous, and will appeal only to the mind that is well rested or in need of stocking against an imminent cocktail party with annoyingly bright companions. Here we find Fletcher's *Situation Ethics,* Altizer's *Radical Theology,* and Lorenz's *On Aggression.* At the end of this shelf is a small section marked "View With Alarm"; here a few of one's worst suspicions of his fellows are fed by Ralph Nader on the automobile and Donald Carr on water pollution.

Our poetry will be shelved with the first large group; it is generally hoary rather than hairy, as poetry can be, and most of the authors are aged or dead. Here one can read Warren, Roethke, Moore, and Graves, and enjoy the echoes of anthologies used in Contemp. Amer. Lit. I. Artistic excitement needs no more space in this library than in most; deviant desires will have to make do with Barth's *Giles Goat-Boy,* Malamud's *The Fixer,* and Albee's *A Delicate Balance.*

This little library, and larger ones in its image, should have no trouble getting widespread support. Even the CIA would probably contribute to the building fund.

*Karl Nyren*

# Paperbacks

### "WHEN IS A PAPERBACK NOT A PAPERBACK?"
January 15, 1961

This riddle was posed by author Diana Pullein-Thompson, writing last October in the British book-trade magazine *The Bookseller*. If you are like us, you like answers to your riddles. Miss Pullein-Thompson supplies one— "When it is bought by a public library."

The article seeks to extend the battleground on which the "public lending right" campaign is being fought by British authors, and to draw attention to what is described as a "lamentable practice"—the binding of paperbacks in hard covers for public libraries. Concerning this practice of turning "a perishable paperback into a crypto-hardback which will survive at least 80 readers," Miss Pullein-Thompson asks: "Is it legal?" Consistently, she provides her own answer—"Nobody seems to know at present. Certainly it is not ethical. But the libraries seem to have ignored that aspect in their efforts to get something on the cheap."

The article calls for clarification of the legal position. The author's own view is that "it seems unlikely that the hardback binding of paperbacks constitutes an actual breach of copyright, although, surely, the large-scale binding of paperbacks with the deliberate purpose of substituting them for hardcover editions infringes the license granted by the hardcover publisher to the paperback reprint publisher."

The London *Times* let off a discreet editorial blast against the authors and publishers who opposed this library practice of binding paperbacks, and the discussion rages yet in the pages of the *Bookseller*. The *Times* editorial drew a reply from R. W. David, president of the (British) Publishers Association, in which he declared categorically that the commercial rebinding of a paperback for resale to libraries *is* an infringement of the original publisher's rights, since usually the license he grants to the reprint house only allows the latter to publish in paperback form. "If the original publisher's exclusive right to publish in hard covers cannot be legally protected (and there is every evidence that it can)," says Mr. David, "the consequences must be that in self-defense authors and publishers will postpone the granting of paperback rights for a much longer period after first publication; and who will be the gainer by that?"

Libraries in this country have not adopted the practice of binding paperbacks on the same scale as in Britain, but it seems that if they move in this direction they must be prepared for retaliation. Curiously enough although most of the verbal outbursts have come from hardback publishers and authors in Britain, the first positive move to prevent the wholesale rebinding of paperbacks has come from a paperback publisher.

*Liaison,* the British Library Association's news-sheet, reported in November that Penguin Books has announced a new condition to be imposed upon the sale of all their books, forbidding them to be "lent, rebound, hired out or otherwise disposed of in a multilated condition or in any unauthorized cover by way of trade." The Library Association, says *Liaison,* is taking legal opinion on the effect of this upon libraries.

It seems to us a somewhat elastic interpretation to describe binding a paperback as "publishing" in hard covers. What is the library to do about preserving the title published originally, and perhaps only, in paperback form? Why should it be more unethical to bind a paperback than to bind a periodical?

The recent developments in Britain pose a number of problems and possibilities which may well have to be considered by American librarians as paperbacks grow in importance and infiltrate increasingly into our libraries.

*Eric Moon*

## VICE OR VIRTUE?
April 15, 1961

"Poetry doesn't need poets' recommendations," said Randall Jarrell in his acceptance speech during the presentation of the National Book Awards in New York last month. "And perhaps it is a mistake to keep telling people that poetry is a good thing after all, one they really ought to like better; tell them that about money, even, and they will finally start thinking that there's something wrong with it. Perhaps instead of recommending poetry as a virtue, poets should warn you against it as a vice, an old drug like love or dreams. We say that virtue is its own reward, but we all *know* that vice is its own reward—know it too well ever to say so."

Mr. Jarrell's thoughts about poetry and persuasion are perhaps applicable to books in general. Have librarians, and others who care deeply for books, stressed too heavily that books are educational, reading cultural, and that only an informed society can survive today? This may be the right kind of persuasion to exercise upon authorities; the right road towards official support, government grants, institutional recognition. But surely it is the wrong approach to the individual reader, or more important, the unconverted reader.

To reach him we must take the book off its pedestal and convince him that reading is as hypnotic as television, as exciting as a World Series game, as sinfully enjoyable as smoking in bed. The 20th Century advertiser knows, and exploits, the fact that most people, like Oscar Wilde, "can resist everything except temptation." Does library publicity for books exhibit the same awareness?

In a National Library Week editorial in the *Saturday Review* last year, Howard Mumford Jones suggested that "librarians might be more successful in their campaign to hold the line on reading if their professional training included more excitement about the insides of books and less technological lore about what to do with the book as an object in space." The man who makes converts is the man who is not only convinced, but is excited about his convictions. Excitement is infectious; conviction, without it, often tedious.

The paperback is one recent phenomenon which has demonstrated hope that the book can continue to hold its own against magazine and newspaper reading, against television, the movies and a hundred other "easy" roads to information sugared with entertainment. William Nichols, editor of *This Week* magazine, pointed out at the National Book Awards that "nearly one million paperbacks are sold in the United States every day . . . over 50 percent more than the newsstand sales of ALL the leading national magazines combined."

Perhaps one reason why the paperback has made so many converts to book reading is that it seems less formidable, less obviously virtuous, Mr. Jarrell might say, than the hard cover book. It can be treated casually, like an old friend rather than an influential guest. You need not feel guilty about turning down a leaf, scribbling in a margin, stuffing it unceremoniously into a coat pocket. Certainly the covers of paperbacks have exploited Mr. Jarrell's philosophy—there is more appeal to vice than virtue in many of them. But for all that, a rack of bright paperbacks presents a more tempting sight to the nondedicated bibliophile than a shelf of library-bound volumes.

Might we not be more successful with a campaign for reading, not for "a more informed America" but for a "more relaxed America." Let's not be too compulsive about it all. Take the duty out of reading and put the fun back into it. We might well place above our desks the text from Howells: "The book which you read from a sense of duty, or because for any reason you must, does not commonly make friends with you."

*Eric Moon*

## PAPERBACKS—FOR SALE?
May 15, 1964

In one of the many articles on libraries which appeared in large, general circulation magazines during National Library Week, there appeared, again, a suggestion which has been made many times by many people. It is interesting that it should continue to be made because, as far as we know, despite years of plugging, the idea has never met with any positive or enthusiastic response.

Writing in the April issue of *Atlantic,* author and historian Oscar Handlin says: "The library will strengthen its demand for support by clarifying its own function and by retooling for the job new conditions have created . . . It ought to be flexible, adaptive and experimental in the way it plays its role."

One way the library might move in this direction, Handlin says, is by easing the problem of duplication of titles "by laying in a stock of paper-backs *for sale* to those readers who do not wish to wait for titles in heavy demand. It could thus relieve the pressure on much-used volumes, nurture the book-buying habit, and still have popular titles available for those who wished only to borrow them."

We italicize "for sale" in that paragraph because this is the oft-repeated idea which has always landed with a dull thud in library circles.

School libraries provide most, if not all, of the exceptions. A good many of them have retooled in the way Handlin suggests, and have hurdled limited book budgets by meeting "excess" demands through the sale of paperbacks. A survey in 1962 led the editors of *School Management Magazine* to the conclusion that the principal "and the librarian are the most frequent initiators of the idea of installing a paperback bookstore." Also, half the schools surveyed had installed their paperback bookstores in, and as a part of, the school library.

But public libraries have been totally unresponsive to the idea. Indeed, they have been somewhat unresponsive to the paperback "revolution" in general. Jay Tower, of New American Library, commented: "Public libraries, of all the groups directly concerned with books, are the least friendly to paperbacks" (*LJ*, Jan. 15, '63, pp. 265–7).

The last time we asked public libraries what, if anything, they had done or considered doing about selling paperbacks, we had a fairly typical response. Some libraries didn't answer that question at all, six said they had never considered the idea, and three others said they had considered and decided against it. Strangely, two of the three which had at least given the idea some thought were large libraries in New York and Baltimore. The negative decision in these cases was not at all surprising, since with all the paperback outlets already available in these cities, there perhaps isn't much of a gap which the library needs to fill.

But what of the community where the outlets for paperbacks may be few (or none) and of poor quality? Could the public library not render a valuable service there, by selling better paperback titles? Might the library not reap rewards, in hard cash and good public relations, by so doing?

There are several reasons why the time may be ripe for public librarians to reconsider this question. As one public librarian pointed out recently, "The public library can, in a sense, be considered an outgrowth of an economy of scarcity: the borrowing of reading materials obviously has some relation to the inability of the general population to own them. In conditions of affluence, ownership of certain types of reading materials might make more economic sense than loaning them, both for the individual and the community." And Senator Humphrey's recent proposal of a free paperback book program similar to the School Lunch program (*see* p. 2128, this issue) illustrates his perception of the value of book *ownership* as a stimulus to the reading habit.

There is another factor which suggests the need for reconsideration by libraries. A recent article in *Publishers' Weekly* (April 13, '64, pp. 29–30) warns of the growing resistance of retailers to the "paperback flood." With more than 26,000 titles in print in paperback, and more than 300 new titles flowing from the presses each month, this is scarcely surprising. But what are the implications of this drawing in of horns by the retailers?

In the many communities where the book outlets are already meager, it is certainly too optimistic to expect that most of these outlets will select the *best* material from the flood. Should the cream of the paperback crop then, simply because of the absence of hard covers, not be available at all in those communities? Where lies the responsibility of the public library? If it cannot afford to add these books to its permanent stock, why should it not make them available for sale?

*Eric Moon*

### A BOOK BY ANY OTHER NAME . . .
September 15, 1966

While librarians, the past few years, have been eagerly hopping aboard a number of late-model bandwagons, variously bedecked with automation, book catalog, or poverty program flags, one gigantic vehicle has rolled noiselessly past many a library door, picking up and perhaps drawing away an unknown number of library uses but apparently invisible to the librarian-eye. We refer, of course, to what one respondent to our recent survey on declining public library circulation (*LJ*, Sept. 1) called "the ubiquitous paperback."

Judging from reports heard at two major sessions during the recent ALA conference in New York, the much-heralded paperback revolution seems to have largely passed libraries by. It is beyond the bounds of probability that the sale and reading of literally millions of books in paperback form has had no effect on library use. But whatever the impact has been, it has been little influenced, other than negatively, by the practices of many public libraries.

A fairly large-scale survey on the use of paperbacks in public libraries—conducted by the School & Library Promotion and Marketing Committee of the American Book Publishers Council and the Public Library Association of ALA—turned up some findings which Victor I. Bumagin, chairman of the ABPC Committee, aptly described as "rather stunning."

For example, 44 percent of the 2000-odd librarians who responded to the survey said that their libraries did not use or buy paperbacks—and the majority put forth as their principal reason that paperbacks were "not suitable."

Of those who do buy paperbacks and know how much they spend on them, 40 percent lavish less than $200 a year on the purchase of paperbacks, and 20 percent spend less than $50 a year. Very few libraries spend more than five percent of their total annual book budget on paperbacks; most spend less than two percent.

The survey results also raise a number of questions about the ways in which paperbacks are being used by those libraries which have found them "suitable." For example, nearly nine out of ten librarians said that the demand for paperbacks in quantity arises primarily from assignments in local schools. This demand comes mostly from secondary school students, from adult education students, and to some extent, from college students. This being so, the paperback might appear to have remedial potential in dealing with that much bemoaned "student problem."

But what kind of paperbacks do libraries actually buy? According to Aaron Rabinowitz of A & A Distributors, in answer to a queston during the ALA conference, his firm has been watching library sales of paperbacks closely. Said Rabinowitz: "We can almost predict that 90 percent of the library orders wil be made up of teenage romances and teenage adventure stories, a few currently popular works of fiction." Libraries, he added, order "very, very little of the broad spectrum of good fiction and nonfiction actually available in paperback."

Another good example of library discrimination against the paperback (and the paperback reader) is the lending period. More than half of the survey respondents said that they kept circulation records for paperbacks, and 85 percent of these restricted the lending period to one week or less. It is doubtful whether a one-week loan period for all books is common in many libraries today. What kind of sense does this restriction make? A book is a book is a book. It may look smaller in paperback form, but it takes just as long to read—perhaps longer, since the type is usually smaller, the margins narrower.

Finally, very few libraries, even among those which have decided to make use of paperbacks, seem prepared to take advantage of the paperback's greatest asset—its cheapness. Sixty-two percent of those who replied to the survey said that they *completely cataloged* paperbacks received by the library. Estimates of cataloging and processing costs still very madly, but even if one takes a very conservative figure, it seems close to economic idiocy to spend $1.50 cataloging a 50-cent item.

Much of this response suggests that to some librarians the paperback is some very curious new medium of communication, terribly difficult to handle and way off beyond the microfiche and the magnetic tape in its exotic qualities. May we suggest a slogan to be hung over every librarian's desk—and to be digested by the occupant of the chair below: "The Paperback is a *Book*."

*Eric Moon*

# Political Topics

## MINUTEMAN RECRUITER
April 1, 1962

One of the strangest groups yet spawned in the current surge of the radical right is a loosely knit federation of guerrilla bands, who have armed themselves to resist a Russian invasion," said *Newsweek* in its issue of December 4, 1961. "The leader of this implausible group is Robert DePugh (38) of Norborne, Mo., a member of the Birch Society and owner of a veterinary-drugs firm."

The "implausible group" to which *Newsweek* refers is the Minutemen (the California group prefer the spelling Minute Men). They were organized two years ago, according to *Time*, "by ten Midwestern duck hunters." DePugh was chosen leader and established his headquarters in Independence, Mo., not far from his Norborne home.

Robert Bolivar DePugh is the son of a former Deputy Sheriff in Kansas City, an ex-Signal Corps radar-man, and ran for Congress several years ago, although he admits "I wasn't a serious candidate." His estimates of Minutemen membership have been reported variously as anywhere between 12,000 and 25,000, but law enforcement authorities have put the figure at only a few hundred, mostly in southern Illinois and southern California.

One figure that has been consistently reported, however, is DePugh's dream of a three million membership by 1963. The Missouri guerrilla, who says his membership consists of "well-educated, quiet, responsible people," clearly has faith in the organization's recruitment activities. In a recent network television program, DePugh gave an indication of the way in which the Minutemen discover new prospects.

A Brinkley-less Chet Huntley brought together on NBC on February 16 what he called "A Gathering of the American Right." Present was Robert Bolivar DePugh, and this is part of what he had to say about the Minutemen's procedure for gathering new members:

"Now we had been in existence about, oh I'd say six or eight months. We had tried to keep our identity on (*sic*) our existence very secret. One night I received a phone call, right out of the clear blue sky, from a man who told me that he was a member of a similar group in the Kansas City area and that he knew about us. And they knew pretty much who we were. And they had pretty well decided what we thought and what we stood for. Well, I was amazed. You see, we were rank amateurs at this thing—and I thought our security was pretty good. And we wondered and wondered for a long time, how this other group found out about us.

"Well, finally, later on, when we'd become more or less affiliated, we learned that one of our members worked in the Kansas City public library and kept track of every person who checked out a book relating to guerrilla warfare activities. And if you go back to the library looking for that material you'll get tagged pretty quick."

This claim may, of course, be pure fiction. This may be simply another attempt by the far right to undermine confidence in the public library as an arsenal of freedom. But it is difficult to believe DePugh or his Minutemen capable of such subtlety.

True or false, the charge is a damaging one to be made against a public library in the glaring light of network television. A librarian, in our view, like other people, is entitled to any political or other opinions he likes. But he is *not* entitled to use his job to support underground political activities.

When an individual cannot use a public library without the fear that his reading activities will be reported—either to authority or to some crackpot organization like the Minutemen—we move dangerously close to totalitarian practices. The implications are frightening.

An investigation at the library in question seems clearly called for. The staff itself should welcome the extraction of the maggot (if there be one) from the apple.

*Eric Moon*

## MAN-IN-THE-STREET
September 1, 1963

The test ban treaty has been signed and perhaps will already have been ratified by the Senate by the time this editorial appears in print. But we are concerned with the process of democratic decision which preceded ratification, and since there will surely be other crises, other moments in history when the same process will occur, perhaps these thoughts have pertinence for the future as well as for the recent past.

On the day the announcement came that agreement had finally been reached by Russia, Britain and the US, a television reporter in New York took his microphone and went out to ask "the man-in-the-street" how he felt about the treaty. Watching those interviews was a somber experience. Six men- (and women) in-the-street in a row said, in effect, that they hadn't heard anything about a treaty, hadn't been reading the newspapers lately, had no views on the subject.

For the next several weeks, as Dean Rusk and Averill Harriman and others tried to convince Congressional committees that sanity and hope should both be preserved, even with Russia's help, one heard Senator after Republican Senator being firmly noncommital. Most frequently they indicated an unwillingness to declare a position until they had had more time to elicit the views of their constituents.

Well, we heard the views (or nonviews) of some of those constituents in the heart of our greatest metropolis, and we wondered what they might have been had that television reporter taken his microphone to other parts of the country which are less well served by the media of communication and information. We could not feel sanguine about the possibilities.

What has all this to do with libraries? Libraries are an important part of the informational and educational processes, if we are to believe the propaganda, and much has been written about the role of libraries in adult education. But how many of our public libraries, in the weeks of negotiation in Moscow, made a serious attempt to focus local public attention on the issues at stake? How many dismantled their nice displays of summer reading or best gardening books, and pushed to the forefront materials on the crucial subject of the life or death of the world?

Perhaps many did. We'd like to think so. Perhaps the problem, in any case, is not the library user but the kind of man-in-the-street that libraries don't reach. If this be so, those interviews and the later statements by Senators whose views are determined by a sort of Gallup poll of their constituents make it terribly clear that libraries must greatly increase their efforts to reach that uninformed man-in-the-street. Apparently, the world is in his hands—we dare not let him drop it.

*Eric Moon*

## A CLEAR CHOICE
October 15, 1964

"It will become, I suspect, harder and harder to be both a Goldwater Republican and a friend of the library." This comment was made by Dr. Robert A. Dentler of the Institute of Urban Affairs, Teachers College, Columbia University, in a paper delivered to the Westchester Library Association conference last May.

Dr. Dentler raised what he called "five outrageous questions about suburban libraries." He expressed the belief "that suburban libraries, like most other public library systems, will come for the remainder of this century to require increasingly massive state and federal aid in order to adapt to changing conditions." His implication, clearly, was that if Senator Goldwater becomes President such aid is not likely to be forthcoming.

This set us to examining the political record. As far as the major political parties are concerned the recorded evidence reveals no great chasm. In 1960 the platforms of both parties included a good word for libraries. The Republican platform said: "Toward the goal of fullest educational opportunity for every American, we pledge. . . . Support of efforts to make adequate library facilities available to all our citizens." The Democrats, in their 1960 platform, pledged "further Federal support . . . for libraries." If the Democratic statement is rather less equivocal than the Republican, let us not quibble about that—equivocation in platform writing is a fact of life. In their 1964 platforms the parties still remained somewhat in harmony—neither one even mentioned libraries. But there has been strong bipartisan support for most library legislation in Congress in recent years, and we must assume that it is still there.

So we have to get beyond the parties to the individuals who are running for President and Vice President (remember, Dr. Dentler's comment refers specifically to Goldwater Republicans!).

Let's take a look at the record of the four candidates on a few specific pieces of legislation of vast importance to libraries, and on which there were roll-call votes.

The Library Services and Construction Act of 1964 was passed by a vote of 89–7 in the Senate; clearly, it received support from a very large majority of both parties. But not, as Senator Humphrey's campaign chorus has it, from Senator Goldwater. He was one of the seven dissenters. Senator Humphrey, who in 1960 had been a sponsor of the bill to extend the old Library Services Act, voted for LSCA in 1964. Representative Miller did not vote when the House passed LSCA, but according to the *Congressional Record* of January 21, 1964, he was recorded by the clerk as paired against the bill. President Johnson, of course, was in no position to vote, but when he signed the legislation on February 11, he said: "There are few Acts of Congress which I sign with more pleasure, and certainly more hope, than this new Library Services and Construction Act. . . . The library is the best training ground for enlightenment that rational man has ever conceived."

The Higher Education Facilities Act passed the House in 1963 by a vote of 107–56. Again, Representative Miller did not vote, but this time he announced for the bill. In the Senate, Humphrey voted for the measure which received strong bipartisan support, passing by 60–19. Senator Goldwater was not only one of the 19 against the bill, but he also submitted an amendment which would have eliminated $900 million in grants for academic facilities. He was still, thankfully, in the minority, and his amendment was heavily defeated.

The National Defense Education Act was first passed in 1958. In the Senate both Johnson and Humphrey voted for it. In the House, again Miller did not vote. Senator Goldwater, of course, voted against it, but he then launched into a curiously inconsistent record on NDEA in the years to follow. In 1961, when a bill to extend the NDEA (as well as the impacted areas education program) passed the Senate by 80–7, Goldwater voted for it. Two years later he was back to his original position, and on October 8, 1963 did not vote, but was paired against a bill authorizing new grants for vocational education, a three-year extension of NDEA, and federal aid to impacted areas.

Finally, the Economic Opportunity Act. This is by no means library legislation, but there is no doubt, in Dr. Dentler's words, that *it* can help libraries "adapt to changing conditions." President Johnson's position on this war on poverty hardly needs to be mentioned. In the Senate, Humphrey voted for the legislation; Goldwater flew in specially from Arizona to vote against it. And in the House, Miller not only voted against it, but supported a motion by Virginia's Howard Smith which, had it been successful, would have killed the bill.

One could add much more, but on these four crucial pieces of legislation, each of which has, or can have, a vital impact on library service in this country, the position of at least three of the four candidates is crystal clear. President Johnson and Senator Humphrey have demonstrated, time and again, in words and actions, their support for library services and their awareness that the kind of progress which is urgently needed is only possible with greater aid from both federal and state sources. Senator Goldwater certainly has no record to indicate support for library legislation, and he has demonstrated, time and again, in words and actions, that he is opposed to all forms of federal aid to education, including libraries. Representative Miller's position is the cloudiest of the four. The *Congressional Quarterly* recently said: "Miller has voted consistently against federal aid to secondary education. His record on federal aid to higher education is mixed." We can only add that his record on library legislation is almost nonexistent.

Magazines of many other professions have taken political positions at election time, but no library periodical, to our knowledge, has done so. We propose to make a dent in what we regard as a lamentable record of unnecessary neutrality.

Let it be clear that the choice between the two major parties as such is no concern of ours here. Both parties, as we have said, have strongly supported legislation affecting libraries, and in the election of individual Congressmen and Senators there are too many factors, including local ones, influencing the librarian-citizen's vote to make generalities on a party basis valid. Perhaps our publication—in this issue—of a lead article by a Republican Congressman will make it the more obvious that we are not waving any particular party banner.

The Presidential election is another matter. Even if one discounts all other issues, many of which are of frightening concern to all of us as individuals, we feel that we have a strong responsibility to speak out on an election in which the candidates offer us "a clear choice" on the future direction and health of library service in the United States. On these grounds alone, this magazine must declare for President Johnson and Senator Humphrey, because we do believe, with Dr. Dentler, that libraries will require "increasingly massive federal and state aid" and that they must "adapt to changing conditions" if they are to fulfill their proper role in society. If Senator Goldwater becomes President, we cannot feel sanguine that these things are likely to happen.

*Eric Moon*

## END OF THE STORY
December 15, 1964

"Your silly damn cover didn't make a bit of difference!" our friend shouted into the telephone on Wednesday morning, November 4, 1964. He may have been right. Difference or not, our first editorial endorsement of a presidential candidate in the October 15 *LJ*, brought more letters and reaction than any recent position we have taken. An editor is always pleased by response, pro or con, but unlike Wyman Jones in our last issue we are more surprised when there is response than when it is absent. So we were pleasantly surprised when we received nearly 40 letters and a variety of other communications about that one editorial, even though they represent only about one tenth of one percent of our readers.

If this beginning suggests that we are about to rehash our position, or gleefully tell you that we were right, relax, we do not intend either.

Because so many, after giving us their own "editorials" on the election, expressed interest in the response to our editorial, we will offer here a brief tally of the raw data (and some of it was pretty raw): 60 percent of those who wrote were against the editorial, the remaining 40 percent for it, plus one writer who remained uncommitted. Among the "antis" there were three basic opinions: they favored Goldwater, they were against federal aid, or they opposed professional journals "dabbling in politics." We will discuss the last of these later in this editorial.

There were a half dozen cancellations, several humorous comments, and some rather violent reactions for and against the cover on the issue (a gold-framed portrait of Goldwater). The cover controversy was a standoff with equal numbers against both cover and contents, for both, or against one and for the other.

We were told by supporters of both candidates that our stand should have embraced issues beyond the library. We agree that there were other, far more important issues involved in the election, but we took those which impinged directly on librarianship as the proper province of this periodical. Goldwater people called it "selfish" and "promoting pork barrels," while Johnson fans said peace, prosperity (or poverty), and extremism were more important. Others said the editorial was trying to "brainwash the profession" or "tell us how to think."

More than half of these letters were carried in our "Reader's Voice" sections in the issues of November 1 and 15. The following excerpts present some additional views (please note the scholarly level of both thought and language):

"Trying to brainwash some idiots, such as you are one of, in the library profession does not go . . ."

"[You] have finally gone too far in your side splitting activity of telling librarians what dumb clucks they are."

About the cover they said: "You can't judge a periodical's editorial policy by its cover," or "What the hell was that for!"

One southerner said: "The state would like us to be part of a regional library system but we prefer our independence." Another put it this way: "The federal government is sticking into everything, so they can control the votes, the projects . . . while they get rich . . . I am shocked at many magazines and newspapers backing the Johnson Administration . . . Have they become 'Pink' or 'Red' again?"

Librarians, like all citizens, have every right to oppose federal aid, a presidential candidate, or an editorial. They are entitled to hold and articulate a political position. They are not on such firm ground in our view, in demanding, as one irate conferee did at the recent Southwestern LA meeting (see *LJ*, Nov. 15, p. 4490), that professional journals, organizations, or librarians remain neutral and not be allowed to voice a political position.

We do not propose to re-argue our often stated position against the political neutrality of librarians. John F. Kennedy's charge to teachers, "Every citizen holds office," is equally valid for librarians. There is no need to document the statements of our leaders or the activities of our national association that are political. Instead we will quote an editorial by Rinehart S. Potts from the November 1964, *Bulletin* of the Special Libraries Council of Philadelphia and Vicinity:

". . . the present editor believes it would have been highly inconsistent for *LJ not* to have spoken out. That journal, and every other one I know in the field, and the great majority of leaders in the profession have firmly favored Federal aid to libraries and education. . . . It would have been pussy-footing not to have opposed a political candidate who rejects that principle. Those who oppose Federal programs are, or should be, just as consistent in supporting him. Our objectivity and neutrality in selecting and making knowledge available cannot and should not mean that we hold our beliefs in a vacuum. I do firmly applaud those—on both sides—who do something about their beliefs by supporting candidates who will advance them."

*John Berry*

## ESCALATION AND LIBRARIANS
January 15, 1966

When the first session of the 89th Congress failed to appropriate funds to implement the Medical Libraries Assistance Act and the library programs under the Higher Education Act of 1965 it was widely interpreted as a mere oversight due to the rush for adjournment. The profession seemed to accept it as a foregone conclusion that an early supplementary appropriation would correct this legislative oversight. This view was even widely espoused in Washington and the Office of Education began to plan for Title II of HEA even without funds.

We have no real evidence that the appropriation won't be forthcoming soon, but complacency seems dangerous in the light of recent events. William McChesney Martin and the Board of Governors of the Federal Reserve System have decided to raise the cost of borrowing money, including the cost of government borrowing. On the heels of that decision President Johnson held cabinet-level discussions on the Vietnam war and told the nation it would cost more in 1966. The cost of the war might even necessitate a cut in domestic spending. It would be a bitter pill if libraries and education were again forced to take a back seat, if the war in Southeast Asia forced a truce in all those domestic wars: against poverty, against illiteracy, against inadequate schools and libraries. Our affluent society may be able to support both foreign and domestic wars, but there is no assurance that it is willing; some signs suggest that it is not.

This poses a serious question for the profession as an organized lobby with legislative goals. Resistance to the view that Vietnam should come first in the budget may very possibly be interpreted as self-seeking and unpatriotic. Any pressure from educators and librarians to get the authorized millions of dollars for their stillborn programs could be politically inexpedient in the face of the foreign crisis. In that age-old economic battle between guns and butter, guns usually seem to win.

The individual librarian, back home, will face a similar dilemma. He will find many of his patrons increasingly impatient with views that urge alternatives to the official US foreign policy, alternatives to continued US involvement in the Vietnam war. In some places the trouble has already begun. A New Jersey librarian was denounced because he displayed a poster urging participation in the Washington march against the war. A well-known Connecticut author of juveniles was threatened with violence when he offered transportation to that march.

If the professional association's lobbying for more federal library support is misinterpreted as unpatriotic and meets with congressional hostility, a similar hostility may develop toward the local library when its traditional open door to all opinions welcomes material opposing the government's position on Vietnam. The local librarian may find hostility among his trustees, may be threatened with budget cuts if he forces the issue and demands that all sides of the Vietnam issue get shelf space. There was a great public and political outcry against Rutgers, the State University of New Jersey, when its president and board refused to fire Professor Genovese because he publicly stated his opposition to the war. Budgetary vengeance against Rutgers was demanded.

On the other side there is a growing anti-war literature. Its opinions vary from moderate pleas for negotiation to demands for out-and-out US withdrawal. The library, along with other democratic forums (remember the sit-ins, teach-ins, protests at universities), will thus be faced with assaults from both sides—not only by those who want their peace views represented, but also by strong voices, from Congress, from City Halls, from newspapers, which are already equating dissent with treason.

Librarianship has weathered similar storms before, sometimes with courageous resistance, sometimes with meek retreat. The profession has no business taking sides on foreign policy even though its individual members will and should. Even if it remains neutral on Vietnam, however, its organized lobby for library support at the national level, and its local defense of the freedom to read may lead to public and political accusations, to the misinterpretation that librarians are unpatriotic. In the face of mounting pressure for a national consensus on Vietnam, librarianship and the local librarian may be denounced and labeled by those who see only one side to the debate. How they respond to this challenge can either strengthen or destroy the profession's traditional stands for better library service and freedom of expression.

*John Berry*

## VOICES ON VIETNAM?
October 15, 1967

Dissent—or more particularly, the lack of adequate representation of dissenting voices in library collections—has often been a topic of discussion in these pages. But what of librarians themselves? As citizens concerned with social issues they seem unable or unwilling to escape from anonymity; as dissenters they are scarcely visible.

True, a few did turn out to demonstrate when Maxwell Taylor spoke during the ALA Conference in San Francisco this summer, though the librarian few were well outnumbered by the peacefully passionate youth of the Bay Area.

As the U.S. government's Vietnam "policy" malingers on, taking those defensive bombs ever nearer the China border, ruining the land from which a peasant people draws its meager sustenance, alienating our friends abroad as well as heating up even our cooler cold-war opponents, the indignation and protest at home begins more and more noticeably to swell.

The voices of opposition to the Administration's nebulous policies come from an incredible number of directions. Demonstrations have been held and statements made by churchmen, civil rights groups, teachers, housewives, veterans, writers, businessmen, the academic world (faculty and students alike), and a host of others. Sadly and strikingly absent thus far among the voices of dissent have been representatives of major segments of the book world of America—publishers, booksellers, and librarians.

We have noticed before when public protests have been made—even in areas closely related to library interests, such as censorship—that while the names of writers, publishers, editors, illustrators, and photographers can be counted on to appear in support of such statements, the names of librarians have stood out only because of their rarity. Among the possible reasons for this phenomenon are:

First, that because librarians properly assert that the library is neutral ground—in the sense that it represents (or should represent) *all* sides of public issues—the conclusion has been drawn that librarians themselves are all neutral, and they are therefore rarely asked to participate in public protest.

Second, that librarians really do *not* care, that their concern with social, political, and international issues is less than that of other members of society or members of other professions.

We are not prepared to accept the latter grim conclusion, nor to believe—if the first of the assumptions above has any validity—that the anonymity of librarians among the voices of dissent need continue.

This matter came up a week or two ago when we heard that a group of prominent publishers was preparing a statement opposing the Administration's policies on Vietnam. They intended gathering the names (and financial support) of several hundred individual people in the publishing and book trade fraternity. Why, we asked, not make this a united front on the part of the book world? Librarians and publishers may have had their disagreements on other matters, but the public and private sectors might well find some common ground in this conflict. Why not ask librarians too?

How many are there, we were asked, who are prepared to put their names—and their cash (perhaps $10–$15 a head to finance a full-page ad in the *New York Times*)—on the line? We said we didn't know, but we imagined there were quite a few, and that we were prepared to find out more precisely. This editorial's purpose is to do just that.

The statement being prepared by our publisher friends will be a broad one, appealing to President Johnson to stop the bombing of North Vietnam and to start serious and purposeful negotiations for an end to the conflict. The statement is, in essence, an attempt to add to the chorus of other responsible citizens from the worlds of business, the professions, and the arts, the voices of those men and women of the book world who can no longer tolerate in silence the Government's apparent conclusion that the Vietnam conflict will yield only to military "solutions."

Any librarian who is prepared to support and sign such a statement is asked to send his name and address to the editor of *Library Journal*. As soon as it is completed, a copy of the statement will be forwarded to all respondents, so that they may see it before making a final commitment.

*Eric Moon*

## HOMAGE TO KING
May 15, 1968

A month has now passed since the assassination of Martin Luther King, Jr., and it will be a brutal irony, now that the first shock has subsided, if the goal that he symbolized is, like so many past tragedies, forgotten as our institutions return to business as usual.

It was a good sign of the deepening national consciousness that a sense of collective guilt did pervade the nation in the first few days after the murder. In its more vulgar manifestations it took the form of fear of riots—a sense, in part, that these were a natural, if unhappy, aftermath of the assassination; on a more sophisticated level, it amounted to the recognition that the slaying was a symptom of our national malaise. But amnesia is strong in this country, and we are likely to forget what has been stressed to us again and again by our government, hammered home by the National Advisory

Commission on Civil Disorders, and thrown in the faces of the white community by the civil rights and black power movements—that the problems of black education and civil reform are our central national problem and must be our main priority.

Fine words, these. But how well are libraries translating these demands into programs of action? We think a fairly simple answer rests in a check of their short- and long-range plans in three critical areas: employment, "market research," and the bringing of racial issues—and alternatives to their solution—to public attention.

Employment is the first key, as a means of increasing community contact, promoting integration, and proving intention, for the black community needs jobs first, words later. At present, Mayor's councils and youth boards across the country are working, with the encouragement of the government, to create job programs for teenagers during the summer months. Business groups and civic organizations like the American Jewish Congress have pledged themselves to finding a given number of jobs and urge this as a personal responsibility. How many jobs have the libraries pledged, or explored? (A list of library work opportunities by Walter Curley appeared in the January 1966 *SLJ* and January 15, 1966, *LJ*, and another is available from Pauline Winnick, public library specialist in services to children and young adults, Library Services Division, U.S. Office of Education, Washington D.C. 20202, if you send a stamped, self-addressed envelope.)

The second obvious area is that of community involvement, in increasing concern in education, particularly as local schools continue to ignore the behests of social leaders for programs involving entire families, and to oppose such plans as decentralization. With some few exceptions, public libraries have retained the same insularity—held less accountable than the schools, yet really more to blame, for what function does the public library have except to serve its neighborhood? Those who wring their hands over declining circulation statistics would do well to take another look at Lowell Martin's third, invaluable Deiches Report, *Baltimore Reaches Out*, which disclosed that 80 percent of the nonelementary school graduates, "nonreaders," read some newspaper regularly, so that the motive power (for self-improvement or concern about children's programs) is there, if the relevance is. The job of the library is to determine the latter—a matter of research, not philosophy.

Moreover, if it is true, as Ralph Conant argues in the current (May 15) issue of *Library Journal*, that the black community will eventually take over the metropolitan public libraries as they take over the cities, the question is, essentially, whether the library will simply look away, or whether it will foster the inevitable black revolution through the creation of a willing partnership. Right now, even with the shortage of Negro librarians, possibilities exist in the creation of black advisory boards to further liaisons between the library and community, spell out the neighborhoods' needs in programming, convey their wishes about book selection.

Third, it seems to us crucial that libraries in both slum and suburb open themselves up this summer as arenas for discussion of the problems of prejudice, slums, civil rights, black power, and political alternatives in resolving these issues, spanning the entire spectrum of opinion. These programs can be carried out starting in the children's room. How long, after all, can libraries go on with their bookie stamps and vacation reading, tallying up the summer circulation statistics, *without* having discussions and book talks about what children learn every day at home, at school, and through the media? Why shouldn't the children's books treating these issues sensitively (see *We Build Together,* reviewed on page 59, our reviews, and other bibliographies), and those dealing with Negro contributions to our culture, be used not only to build the black child's self-image, but to sensitize the children of suburbia? Why can't "white" and "black" branches hold joint programs or visit each other, just as the schools, as in Detroit, have inter-visitations?

On the teenage level, with the possibility of student planned programs, with a vast range of literature to choose from, the potential is even richer. There are numerous books in our popular literature, lists published or cited in this and other magazines, as well as an exceptionally useful list of books and audiovisual materials which just came across our desk as we were writing this editorial—William Loren Katz' *Teacher's Guide to American Negro History,* published by Quadrangle Books (Chicago) for $2.25 in paper, $5.50 clothbound. The book, a kind of running bibliography, has use for school and public library programs far beyond what its title suggests. Its main purpose is to show teachers, through trade books, films (commercial and educational), filmstrips, recordings, pamphlets, etc., how to integrate Negro history into the teaching of American history, but its chapters on contemporary affairs bring you right up to the present civil rights and Black Muslim movements. For a library program which wants to connect a book with a motive, it is enormously useful.

In addition, libraries would want to consider having teens discuss (or read parts of) Kenneth Clark's *The Negro Protest* (see Grace Mims' bibliography, *SLJ,* March 1967, *LJ,* March 15, 1967) which contrasts, through taped interviews, the philosophies of James Baldwin, King, and Malcolm X, also using King's works and the recent Stokely Carmichael–Charles Hamilton *Black Power: the Politics of Liberation in America.* Or use, in juxtaposition, the recordings of King's *I Have a Dream,* put out by 20th Century Fox Records, and Malcolm X reading *Malcolm Speaking, Ballet or Bullet?* ($4.98, prepaid, from the National Memorial African Bookstore, 101 W. 125th Street, N.Y.C.). Use the Gordon Parks film, *A Choice of Weapons.* These are just beginnings.

We can't claim it will be easy. In areas where anti-white sentiment is strong, and where the library is short on black professional staff, it is probably best even for the hippest librarian to bring a Negro friend, work with black community groups, and above all have the youth in the black community help plan, preview, organize, and publicize. But the risks are no more than any agency involved in the civil rights struggle has to take, and the white community has in its favor now the *challenge* of the black movements to bring the white population in as allies in the civil rights movement.

The suggestions spelled out here represent the least that libraries can do in response to the crises delineated in the Urban Commission's report, and in homage to King. Not only because of civic responsibility, but because the library's role as disseminator of our intellectual and social dialectic, in all its communicable forms, has peculiar relevance to what Martin Luther King stood for: the possibility of a dialogue between the races, and the power of ideas, and rhetoric, as alternatives to violence, to improve society.

*Evelyn Geller*

### THE GATHERING STORM
September 15, 1968

This past June, at the Annual Conference of the American Library Association, a small but violent storm developed, and its waves have been spreading; a counter wave is also rising, and it gets a strong statement in our Viewpoint column in this issue (p. 3105). The storm has risen over the question of whether librarians, acting in concert through their national organization, should discuss social issues.

In a quiet time (when have we had one?) this would seem to be a pretty bland issue. But this is no quiet time, and the question is no simple one. Regardless of its wording, this is no question of discussing, but of taking a critical stance toward the government and the establishment—in relation to the war and the slums.

Librarians, like many of their fellow Americans, are sheltered by this establishment and this government. They may chafe at their lot, but they are fed and housed and protected against harm as are few people in this world, and as Negroes and migrant workers are not in this country. We who are thus protected would like other people in the world to be comfortable too, especially if they are about to throw firebombs at us when they become discommoded.

It is difficult not to have a role in a revolution. In both Russia and France, sympathy led many of the aristocracy and the growing bourgeoisie to open the gates to a revolution which was to sweep them away as well as the more obvious benefactors of the old regime. The revolutions growing up around us, like those old ones, will not be appeased by token sympathy and understanding and even help; once the tide of rising expectations begins to run it cannot be turned back except at a frightful cost in repression, and relatively few Americans can support that.

One could say that this is a question which one decides for himself. But when was any important question so decided? There is a group decision, and then one finds himself with either the majority or the minority. One important result of a group decision by librarians could be the guidelines for who is to be served and how well, by libraries. Great computerized information systems are being developed on the one hand for industry; while on the other hand a few librarians are going out on the streets to tell stories to children—the allocation of resources is itself a value judgment.

Librarians have not seriously thought about alternatives in foreign and domestic policy—at least not in public—until Kansas City. A serious debate has been opened at last, however, and it will affect the librarian deeply whether he participates or not. Participation looks likely; already the California Library Association has moved toward forming a group to concern itself with social responsibilities, and other associations may follow.

The terms of debate will be bitter, as one can see already. One member protested in Kansas City that he wouldn't pay dues to an association that opposed the war in Vietnam; and Ervin Gaines, one of the more courageous members of the profession, and past chairman of the Intellectual Freedom Committee, also condemned the move—or more specifically, its "spurious haste." Serious discussion is already going on in one major metropolitan library system to the end of turning over one library agency to a Negro community group, and sharp lines of controversy are emerging around this move.

If we add to the picture the number of small but determined initiatives being taken by individual library agencies and at least one library school so far, the number of librarians committing themselves to service to the disadvantaged, and hence almost necessarily committing themselves to a collision course with the present allocation of national priorities, is growing more impressive each day.

By next June, and the next Annual Conference of the American Library Association, the elections will have come and gone; irrevocable decisions will have been made without this profession ponderously getting itself into position to make its thinking known on the issues and establish the order of priorities for the efforts of its members and their institutions.

There is clearly a need for grass roots grappling with the big questions raised at Kansas City, and it is to be hoped that associations of librarians at all levels take it on themselves to thrash out their own attitudes toward the role of the profession and the Association, and to bring their conclusions, however late this time, to Atlantic City.

*Karl Nyren*

## CAUCUS AND ROUND TABLE
October 1, 1968

The American Library Association is not the only national organization which is being urged by an active membership group to exhibit a greater concern over current social problems and issues. The efforts in Kansas City of those who sought an ALA Round Table on the Social Responsibility of Libraries were mirrored by the activities of a group within the American

Political Science Association (APSA) at that organization's convention early in September.

The APSA activist group, the Caucus for a New Political Science, was, in fact, more immediately successful than the Round Table proponents were in Kansas City; the Caucus persuaded APSA's Council to change the Association's constitution—and by a resounding vote of 16 to two.

Like ALA, the American Political Science Association is insistent about its nonpartisanship and declares that "it will not support political parties or candidates" and "will not commit its members on questions of public policy." But APSA's constitution now includes the statement that "the association nonetheless actively encourages, in its membership and its journal, research in and concern for significant contemporary political and social problems, however controversial and subject to partisan discourse in the community at large these may be."

According to the *New York Times* (September 5), what sharpened this issue of broadening the area for debate within APSA was the avoidance by the association in its panel discussions at the 1967 convention of such subjects as "Vietnam, urban problems, riots, and the New Left." The parallel is not exact, but this sounds very close to Kenneth Duchac's plea at the ALA convention for "an outlet for expression of libraries' and librarians' concerns on such issues as race, violence, war and peace, inequality of justice and opportunity." APSA's Caucus has recommended that the organization's 1969 panel discussions be concerned with the subject of "Prospects for Revolution in America."

There are other parallels between the APSA Caucus and the ALA Round Table proponents. For example, the political scientists are debating whether the Caucus should publish its own journal—"with association financial encouragement"—or whether the *American Political Science Review* will open its pages for discussion of current issues. One of the first things discussed at the ALA convention during a rump session of Round Table supporters was whether the proposed Social Responsibility group should have its own publication. Better by far, in our opinion, for the supporters of this movement to make full use of the national library periodicals already in existence. Some of these periodicals, at least, are actively interested in promoting the wider discussion of social issues that the Round Table proponents want.

It is interesting to speculate whether one other parallel between the Caucus and the Round Table may yet emerge. At its September convention, the APSA Council voted to move the association's 1970 convention from Chicago to San Francisco. The APSA Council gave no reason for the move, but the Caucus wants the APSA membership to go on record with the view that Chicago is not open to public discussion and that no association convention should be held there while Mayor Richard Daley holds office.

The American Political Science Association is not the first or only national organization to take such action since the debacle of the Democratic Convention in Chicago. A similar move was made recently by the

American Psychological Association—a decision which prompted a telegram from Richard Nixon, of all people, who urged reconsideration of the decision, since "what happened in Chicago might have happened in any great city in America."

Will the Round Table on the Social Responsibility of Libraries, if and when it comes into being (perhaps at the Midwinter ALA meeting in January?), urge similar action upon the ALA Council? At present, the 1970 Midwinter meeting of ALA is scheduled for Chicago. There does appear to be some support among the ALA membership for a move of this kind—*LJ* has already received a number of letters urging such action (we have advised these correspondents to write directly to the ALA President). A protest of this kind might be particularly effective coming from ALA, a Chicago-based organization. Maybe the new Round Table won't see it that way, but we would regard it, certainly, as a socially responsible move.

*Eric Moon*

## NIXON'S THE ONE
September 1, 1968

A few weeks before the election we received a letter from Maurice D. Walsh, Jr., administrator of the Jefferson Parish Library in Louisiana. By way of background, Mr. Walsh is the gentleman who, in 1964 (*LJ*, November 15, 1964, p. 4490), tried to persuade the Southwestern Library Association to pass a vote of censure on the R. R. Bowker Company because of *LJ's* editorial endorsement of the Johnson-Humphrey ticket in that year's election (*LJ*, October 15, 1964, pp. 3926–27).

Quoting that editorial in his letter, Walsh asked: "Does *LJ* again 'propose to make a dent in . . . a lamentable record of unnecessary neutrality'? Will the two unendorsed presidential candidates' pictures share a cover or will they be honored in separate issues?"

We thanked Mr. Walsh for reminding us that 1968 was an election year and informed him that *LJ* was desperately neutral about the available crop of candidates. We had considered, we said, a cover supporting either Snoopy or Pat Paulsen, but had concluded that one of them was a shade weak on law and order and the other a little unclear about his foreign relations policies.

Now, however, it's all over, and such levity must be abandoned. Nixon is the one, and one cannot but reflect on what this portends for libraries in the next four or eight years. Not much of the writing on the wall, of course, is clear enough for anyone to read with any certainty yet, but it is apparent that many of those who have carefully nurtured the growth of that frail plant, federal support of library services, would feel more secure if Humphrey were due to move into the White House in January rather than Nixon.

Whatever his propensities, however, Nixon faces great difficulties. He comes into office with no real mandate from the people and, as contrasted with Eisenhower's massive popularity, with a burden of widespread distrust. And although the next Congress appears to be more conservative than the last, it remains a Democratic Congress. Whether or not a real chasm opens up between the new President and Congress seems likely to depend largely upon the quality and acceptability (to both parties) of Nixon's cabinet appointments. One has to hope that the choice of Agnew for Vice President is not an indicator in this regard, and that rumors of such as Max Rafferty for Education Commissioner are merely the products of considerable pessimism.

In the Congress itself, if the loss of Lister Hill is serious, the departure of Wayne Morse may be more so. Perhaps because of his maverick status and his lack of narrow loyalties, he carried great weight—with *both* sides— in matters concerning education. Some men who can talk convincingly across the party barriers will be urgently needed in the new Congress. With ESEA up for renewal next year, and LSCA the year after, the fate of two strong pillars of the library legislation structure will be up for early decision.

One cause for nervousness is that Nixon's position on federal support for libraries is not yet very clear in its specifics. In a statement he sent to ALA just before the election he promised that "a Nixon administration will move decisively to rescue our library programs from their bureaucratic doldrums and to reassert the proper federal role in library services assistance." Mr. Nixon's statement, which is reproduced in full on page 4461 of this issue, is abundantly clear about what he means by "bureaucratic doldrums," if not about what he sees as "the proper federal role." While many librarians would agree with much of his criticism of the handling of library programs at the federal level, however, they would want him to know that these bureaucratic doldrums of recent years have done much more for library service than the doldrums of federal neglect which preceded them.

The report of the National Advisory Commission on Libraries seems now to have a doubtful future, but Mr. Nixon's proposal to establish an Advisory Committee on Libraries may not be too far from the permanent Commission on libraries which was recommended in the Knight Commission's report. If there is to be substantial restructuring of library legislation—and this seems likely—the advice of such a body will be necessary to provide some hedge against new kinds of chaos.

"A modern, progressive library system is a vital national asset," Mr. Nixon declares, and his statement to ALA is evidence that the President-elect and his advisers have given some thought to the problems of libraries. We must hope that his thinking encompasses the proposition that a vital national asset needs and deserves vital national support.

*Eric Moon*

# Discrimination

## THE SILENT SUBJECT
December 15, 1960

It is common knowledge in the library profession that segregation is not something that happens only in schools and lunchcounters; that it happens in libraries too. It is common knowledge that libraries have closed their doors and their bookstocks, not because they were short of funds or readers, but because certain members of the public with the "wrong" pigmentation wanted to read.

All of which goes to prove that word of mouth is a pretty effective medium of communication, for any librarian looking at our library periodicals over the past five or six years would find it difficult to divine that libraries were involved in such problems, or even that a "segregation" problem existed.

Segregation and integration are two words which appear not to have crept into *Library Literature,* but there are two headings which seem to relate to the subject. They are "Negro and the library," and "Public libraries —services to Negroes." In the seven issues of *Library Literature* for 1959–60 we found no single item from a library periodical indexed under either heading, though there was a short news item about black and white rabbits from *Publishers' Weekly,* and an editorial in *America.* There were, of course, plenty of entries under "Services to students," "Services to business and industry," and "Services to senior citizens," but services to Negroes yielded nothing except some library school theses. The 1958 *Library Literature* also revealed seven library school theses touching the subject and a few articles in *South African Libraries.* But we had to delve back as far as 1955 before we discovered any treatment of the subject in an American library periodical. An article on "Library Service in Mississippi," by Dorothy McAllister appeared in the March 1, 1955 issue of *LJ,* and an editorial feature entitled "No Segregation Here," appeared in the November 15 issue of *Junior Libraries* the same year.

After these years of vacuum it is encouraging to see at least two of our library periodicals becoming aware that segregation is a social menace that inflicts itself upon libraries as well as other institutions. Even reporting without comment what has been happening recently in Danville, Petersburg, and other places is an improvement. Even the bland, benign and tentative discussion of segregation in the September editorial in the *Wilson Library Bulletin* is a big step forward. But something more is needed, and we welcome the forthright and honest statement by Rice Estes in this issue (p. 4418). We hope that it will be the beginning of a much wider expression of opinion on a situation which is improving, if at all, desperately slowly, a situation of which the profession can hardly be proud.

With Mr. Estes we challenge the assumption of the editor of the *Wilson Library Bulletin* that "ALA's record is that of an organization opposed to segregation, and *as effective against it as its structure permits.*" Even if he is right, doesn't the opening sentence of ALA's *Goals for Action* state: "The American Library Association recognizes its obligation as an organization devoted to the service of our society *to adapt its program of action* to the changing needs and problems with which our nation contends"? If the structure doesn't permit action, then it should be changed. Here is one goal that demands action.

We recognize that ALA's Federal Legislative Policy states that libraries "have direct responsibilities in making good books . . . available in quantity to all Americans of all ages, races, creeds and circumstance." But why does the Library Bill of Rights feel that it is more important to condemn the exclusion of "any book . . . because of the race of nationality, or the political or religious views of the writer," than to condemn the exclusion of any *reader* for the same reasons?

Even the admirable *Newsletter on Intellectual Freedom* skirts the subject of segregation in favor of Mrs. Granahan, the Postmaster General, Lolita and Lady Chatterley. These are interesting subjects, we admit, but since when did intellectual freedom involve the book but not the reader? Is it any more an infringement of intellectual freedom or an application of censorship to keep one book out of a library than to bar the door to hundreds of people?

Why does ALA need to set up yet another committee to study the question of civil rights when it already has an Intellectual Freedom Committee? And why the stand announced by President Benjamin Powell at Montreal that the Association "cannot and does not attempt to intrude upon local jurisdiction." What constitutes "intrusion"? And how long does a question remain "local"? This is an issue which affects thousands of would-be library users in perhaps a third of the country. In any case, even at a local level the profession has been more demonstrative when someone has tried to keep a book out of a library than when a reader has been excluded.

We would agree that ALA's attitude toward segregation is clear. We do not agree that it is positive enough, nor that it is voiced either frequently enough or at the most appropriate times. And we are not convinced that an attitude is enough to offer. Some Southern librarians are opposed to segregation and are working, as John Wakeman says, "with all deliberate speed" to end it. But we are equally sure that there are some Southern librarians who are not going to stick their necks out on this issue because they can expect no visible or concrete means of support from the rest of the profession.

How many segregated libraries are there today? How many public libraries are there where Negro readers are still not allowed to borrow under any circumstances? In 1955, Dorothy McAllister, in the article referred to above, found that of 50 Mississippi communities providing public library service only 12 provided that service for Negroes, and apparently all these

12 served Negroes through separate branches or rooms, thus cutting off Negro readers from the main central book collection. The other article previously referred to, "No Segregation Here," revealed that two-thirds of the Negro population of 13 states were entirely without library service in 1953. It requires an elastic definition of "local" to cover this situation.

There has been improvement. But the recent eruptions at Danville and Petersburg illustrate that there is still much to be done before public libraries are free in the most important sense of the word. So long as there remains one place where any reader is denied the right to read and borrow freely from a public library, it is not enough for the profession to stand upon an attitude. The individual reader, and the librarian who is fired for fighting for the rights of that reader will not find an attitude very comforting.

What actions should be taken to support the attitude? Mr. Estes suggests several approaches. One we particularly like is that ALA might urge trustees of libraries in the South which have desegrated to use their persuasive powers upon the trustees of those libraries which have not made this elementary advance. The local chapters of ALA could certainly be asked to bring more pressure to bear in protesting the closing of libraries.

Most urgent, in our opinion, is the need for the profession to find some way to give legal as well as moral support to librarians—and if need be, groups of citizens—who at present fight alone to keep libraries open and free. How actively does the profession support other bodies involved in the struggle for civil liberties when libraries and library readers are involved? It is considered unprofessional to associate with "dangerous" bodies like ACLU or NAACP?

The world today is full of deterrents: don't we have any? What about federal and state aid to libraries? Is it reasonable that federal funds made available under the Library Services Act should be apportioned to libraries whose services are not available to *all* the people who wish to use them?

We feel sure that there are many avenues of persuasive action which have been left unexplored. ALA, as Mr. Estes points out, has done some great things. But we cannot be satisfied while there are great things left undone, and the profession should lend all possible aid to the cause of "free" libraries.

*Eric Moon*


## A SURVEY OF SEGREGATION
March 15, 1961

The silent barrier seems to have been well and truly broken, and now at least, we can see the size of the bigger barrier behind it.

The discussion of segregation in libraries in our December 15 editorial resulted in a heartening response from *LJ* readers. A selection of their letters appeared in our February 15 issue, and copies of many of these were sent by the writers to various officers of ALA. All the correspondence we received, without exception, called for stronger and more positive action and leadership by ALA in this area.

It must be said that ALA has answered the challenge initially with a prompt and firm response that deserves the plaudits of the membership, and indeed, the profession as a whole. The statement adopted for inclusion in the Library Bill of Rights is clear and unequivocal (*LJ*, Mar. 1, p. 955), but almost as encouraging as the statement itself was the recognition that, despite the delicacy of the situation, the Association *had* to take a stand. "The risks, whatever they may be," declared Civil Liberties Committee Chairman Herman Fussler, "*must* be accepted by the Association."

What is the next step? The ball now seems to be firmly in the hands of the Intellectual Freedom Committee. The committee will find no shortage of suggestions for future action; whether it will be able to follow any of them is more debatable.

At present, the committee appears to labor under two significant disadvantages. The first is that it has power only to *recommend* action. The recommendatory process is slow and cumbersome and this one, of all ALA committees, needs to be able to move into action quickly when the situation demands it. It is equally important that it should not be in such a position that it can only take or recommend action *after* trouble breaks out, as in the recent Danville case. It should have executive authority to proceed with a continuing campaign of cooperation with other "freedom" organizations and to work steadily with and through local Intellectual Freedom committees in a program of peaceful persuasion towards integration.

The committee's second problem is that it does not yet have as much information as it should have. It should know—precisely—which libraries are still segregated, which libraries claim to be but still practice variations of discrimination, and which libraries have managed to integrate quietly in recent years.

Dorothy Bendix, of the Drexel Library School, one of those whose views were featured in our February 15 issue, suggested that "funds should be sought for a study of: a) the current status of free access to knowledge in Southern public libraries; b) the factors responsible for the successful transition from segregated to integrated libraries in some Southern communities." This latter information is perhaps the most vital of all.

William Eshelman, in a thoughtful editorial in the January *California Librarian*, has recommended similar action. He says: "ALA should sponsor or conduct a survey of libraries in the South to define the problem: how many libraries have quietly integrated? How many remain segregated?" Mr. Eshelman goes further, and suggests that some of the States, and not only the Southern ones, might examine their own houses to see whether they are in order. "Perhaps," he says apropos of California, "we need another Fiske survey, to study this aspect of library service, under the auspices of CLA."

The Intellectual Freedom Committee has *some* information on the present progress towards integration of libraries, and its chairman, Archie McNeal, has incorporated the available facts in an article which will be published in a subsequent issue of *LJ* (probably in June). But the committee itself would, we feel sure, agree with us that more information is needed and that a full-scale survey is needed to provide it.

There are librarians available and anxious to carry out a survey of this kind. Some have already volunteered. Only the funds are needed, and the requirements here do not appear to be of insuperable magnitude. Surely, *here* is a worthwhile project for the Council on Library Resources, one which is at least as important as the kind of charging machines libraries should use. The CLR financiers, the Ford Foundation, whose declared objective is "to advance human welfare," might well see this as an advance toward what William McPeak, a Ford Foundation vice president, recently called "the ideal library of the future."

*Eric Moon*

### INTERNAL INTEGRATION
June 1, 1961

The statement in this issue by Archie McNeal is, to the best of our knowledge, the first public indication that ALA's Intellectual Freedom Committee has been interesting itself for some time in the problems of integration of libraries in addition to its more widely known concern with censorship matters as they affect libraries.

We are pleased that the statement recently incorporated into the Library Bill of Rights (*see LJ*, Mar. 1, p. 955 and Mar. 15, p. 1110) should have clarified the responsibilities of the Intellectual Freedom Committee in this area, if only because it may enable the committee to pursue its evident interest in the problems of integrating libraries with increased vigor.

Dr. McNeal's article gives some indication of the committee's present state of knowledge concerning the progress that has been made towards integration of libraries. We feel sure that he would agree with us that the committee needs much more information than it now has, and we know that Dr. McNeal is in favor of a survey designed to gather such information, as suggested in our March 15 editorial.

We do not wish to make large claims, for fear of further reprisals from Mr. Fussler (*see LJ*, May 1, p. 1706). But we think it is undeniable that since at least two of our library periodicals have been focusing the spotlight during the last year on a hitherto submerged subject, many members of the profession are more aware, and in some instances, aware for the first time, that a great many libraries are faced with segregation problems.

We would like to take this opportunity to compliment the editor of the *Wilson Library Bulletin* for taking what seems, now that he has done it, the obvious and reasonable further step of gathering opinions and ideas on the subject from some prominent Negro members of the library profession (*Wilson Library Bulletin*, May 1961, pp. 707–710). There are more hard facts and good sense in these contributions than in almost anything else which has appeared on segregation in library literature.

There are those who say: "We know the problem exists, but what can

ALA or the profession do about it that has not already been done?" The four short articles in the *Wilson Library Bulletin* provide suggestions galore. We are particularly pleased that two of the contributors should have endorsed our previously expressed opinion (for which we have been much criticized) that there should be investigation of the use of federal funds to make sure that they are not being used to support library services which practice discrimination.

This is one issue on which we have had some difference of opinion with the *Wilson Library Bulletin.* Some readers seem to have made much of the division between *LJ* and WLB on the subject of segregation of libraries. Let it be said now that, except in one or two matters of detail, there is no basic difference between us; in all the essentials we are absolutely in accord.

It would be nice to record that such unity existed throughout the library profession, but it would not be true. If there is anyone not yet convinced of how far we have to go, he should read the contribution by Mrs. Virginia Lacy Jones to the *Wilson Library Bulletin* symposium referred to above. Not only do we have segregated libraries—we have segregated library associations too.

When the dean of a library school is refused membership in her own state library association, it is hard to believe that there can be any other reason than racial discrimination *within the profession.* Perhaps even before we can hope to be very effective in removing discriminatory practices from our libraries, we shall have to set our own internal house in order.

*Eric Moon*

## ON EDITORIALS
August 1961

A number of librarians have been dismayed in recent months by our handling of the issue of segregation in libraries and within the professional ranks. *LJ*, we have been told, has been unnecessarily harsh in its criticism of an association which has repeatedly made abundantly clear its position on this and other freedoms.

Let us say here—for the record—that we believe in ALA's sincerity in this matter and that we are enthusiastic members and supporters of an association which has done a great deal for libraries and librarians in this country and around the world. But pride and devotion do not imply that we should wear blinkers. We *are* convinced of the association's strength of conviction and moral purpose, but we are not alone in sometimes doubting whether ALA is clear about the ways in which these beliefs can be translated into the kind of leadership that is urgently required.

It is all too easy for a large organization to become so enmeshed in procedural and constitutional problems that it reaches the point where the rule book governs the association rather than the reverse. A recent example was the terribly negative editorial in the June *ALA Bulletin,* which claimed that those who have been asking more of ALA in this matter are "a small but vocal element of the membership."

We do not believe that those who truly want "Libraries for All"—a phrase which involves more than just as conference theme—are a small minority of the association. But we were much more disturbed that the first editorial on segregation problems in the official journal should devote itself entirely to the negative aspects. "It is a necessary task," said the *Bulletin*, "to point out why the ALA is not doing and cannot now do some of the things demanded of it."

This editorial demanded an answer, and to date there have been several, but none better than one which came from outside the profession. An editorial entitled "Free Access to Libraries" appeared in the June 24 issue of the Toledo *Blade*. It said, in part:

"The sentiment expressed (in the amendment to the Library Bill of Rights) is commendable, but the difficult question is how it can be more effectively translated into action. To those who would like to see the association 'crusade' the answer has been made that by nature and structure the association 'exists to further the development of libraries, not to regulate the manner in which they are operated.'

"By this, those who speak for the association certainly do not, we think, mean to suggest that the 'development' of libraries is a matter confined to their physical expansion and the perfection of their techniques. They know that a library cannot develop its full potential if it is arbitrarily limited by segregation in the patrons it can serve any more than if it is limited by censorship in the books it can make available. They simply mean, if we understand correctly, that a voluntary association of librarians cannot impose by edict its views on state and locally controlled libraries.

"But while this may be true, it still does not follow that the librarians, assembled as a profession, must content themselves with resolutions and otherwise passively accept the practice of libraries in this respect where they exist, most especially in the South.

"The association, of course, can strive constantly to set the best example possible in the conduct of its own affairs and in the operation of any programs with which it may be connected. But above all, it seems to us, it can exercise a large degree of leadership by encouraging a steady exchange of views among it members, a continuing study and reporting of the most feasible means and methods leading to desegregation, and by offering the backing of the profession in those local situations where its members are trying, or would like to try, to move ahead in this area."

We quote this *Blade* editorial at length because we believe it represents the feelings of more than a "small, vocal element" in the profession itself. Eli Oboler, librarian of Idaho State College, has reiterated what we feel to be a basic point in the latest issue of the *ALA Bulletin* for July–August: "If ALA 'was not designed to do and by its present nature and structure cannot do' those things which its membership want it to do as relates to segregation, then the major and urgent and vital task for the Association now is to change the nature and structure of ALA to conform to its membership's wishes."

The recommendations made by the Intellectual Freedom Committee during the conference are evidence that this committee, at least, believes that more should and *can* be done by ALA. The committee deserves praise for its positive approach, and it has now given the Council a challenge to find the consititutional and procedural avenues which will make these recommendations courses of action.

Many members present at the conference shared the satisfaction expressed by Mrs. Annette Hauge over the report of the Intellectual Freedom Committee, and also her feeling that it would have been a pity if we had not been *told* what the committee had proposed. Had this information not been forthcoming, it would have been hard to detect the relevance of the conference theme, "Libraries for All."

*Eric Moon*

### SELECTIVE FREEDOM FIGHTERS
December 1, 1961

In August, four books—variously alleged to be indecent and subversive—were removed from the shelves of high school libraries in Savannah, Georgia (*LJ*, Oct. 15, pp. 3618–20). As a sequel to this incident, the Georgia Library Association took a stand against censorship during its conference at Jekyll Island in October.

The name of the meeting place conjures up interesting associations. Dr. Jekyll was a man, if we remember correctly, who was conscious of the duality, the mixed good and evil, in his own nature. Hence, Mr. Hyde.

The Georgia Library Association, on the recommendation of its Committee on Intellectual Freedom, addressed an appeal to the Chatham County grand jurors to protect their libraries from "witch hunts," and urged caution in library censorship.

Libraries should not respond to pressure groups or individuals, said the association. Careful evaluation of books was urged to prevent removal on the basis of a phrase taken out of context. And the association agreed to strengthen its code of standards on book selection policy in order to aid librarians in resisting demands for suppression of books.

All this is very laudable, and entirely in line with ALA policies. But the Mr. Hyde aspect of the Georgia Library Association was also in evidence at this meeting. The theme of the conference was "Intellectual Freedom for Libraries," but according to our reporter on the scene, no Negro librarians were present—for the simple reason that Negro librarians are not allowed to join the association.

One man who had the temerity to blast segregation before this meeting was author Harry Golden. When he revealed that he had just spoken to the NAACP before coming to the library meeting, a Georgia Congresswoman,

Iris Blitch, walked out of the meeting with the comment: "He is free to talk and I am free to leave." True, but would that librarians—all of them—had the freedom not just to leave but also to attend.

*Eric Moon*

## WHO'S OUT OF STEP?

March 1, 1962

A bouquet to the ALA Council for their refusal to rubber-stamp the highly dubious statement offered them by the Executive Board during the Midwinter meeting in Chicago (pp. 904–908, this issue).

The statement, which was in essence an attempted answer to the Intellectual Freedom Committee's call for action to eliminate discrimination from *within* the ranks of the association, hedged and hemmed and hawed to the point where the few positive things in it were buried under a garbage heap of reservations, evasions and doubtful suppositions.

Certainly everyone present must have felt some sympathy for those on the Executive Board who had the task of compiling this statement. There is no doubt that it is far easier to tear apart something of this kind than to put it together. But precisely because the subject at hand was so explosively and so humanly charged with such a variety of emotions and conflicting interests, the Council did well to throw the statement back and ask the Executive Board to think again—hard.

If there is cause for congratulations on the result, there is less to be jubilant about in the discussion which led to that result. This seldom got down to brass tacks—and the ground was covered with them.

For example, we were told of three ALA chapters which technically "meet the requirements for chapter status" but which have no Negro members "at the present time." Nobody asked which these three chapters were, although we do know they were southern chapters. Nobody asked how come they had no Negro members.

*Are* the only obstacles those which, according to the Executive Board statement, derive from "state laws and local ordinances which prevent fully integrated chapter meetings?" Or are the Negro librarians *kept* out? We find it inconceivable, in the light of present Negro militancy, that no Negro librarian has *tested* the possibility of joining one of these chapters. Would they be prevented from doing so by the fact that they couldn't attend an integrated meeting in the state? Has any Negro librarian tried? If so, with what result? We don't pretend to know the answers, but the questions seem worth asking if the Intellectual Freedom Committee's recommendation concerning chapter status (and its rejection by the Board) are to be discussed in terms of reality rather than theory.

An even more curious factor about the discussion was that with so many research-conscious people present, nobody made any attempt to uncover the primary sources. What led up to the "drastic" recommendations of the Intellectual Freedom Committee, which led in turn to a statement from the Executive Board that brought charges from Council members of "weasel words," "cynicism," and "intellectual dishonesty"?

If we sensed the feeling of the Council correctly, it was that the majority wanted a much stronger statement, but one which did not involve punitive action. If we *are* correct, then the Intellectual Freedom Committee recommendations—which certainly imply punitive action—and the Executive Board statement—which didn't envisage action of any kind—were both pretty much out of step.

Is the Intellectual Freedom Committee a bunch of wildly impractical radicals? Did such as the Misses Boaz and Gilman, and Messrs. Downs, Ellsworth, Hudson, Kipp, Lacy, McNeal, Martin, Merritt and Moore, tear their recommendations off the tops of their heads, without thought or knowledge of the situation they were trying to correct? Or were they prompted to propose such drastic action by equally drastic complaints from certain sections of the membership?

Also, during the discussion, Evelyn Levy of the Enoch Pratt Library complained about the lack of documentation of the reasons why the Executive Board reached such confused conclusions.

It may be this absence of fact about the sequence of events, and the absence also of any attempt to uncover those facts, that led the discussion into such involved, devious and inconclusive directions.

It might be well, when this matter is brought back at the Miami Beach conference, if the two proposals of the Intellectual Freedom Committee (and the Executive Board's views on them) could be dealt with separately. The two matters dealt with are not perhaps equally practical or desirable, and it would be a pity to see both discarded because one is not feasible.

We go on record as supporting the view of the Intellectual Freedom Committee that state associations which do not operate properly in accordance with ALA policies should not remain as chapters of the parent body. And it does not much matter what their printed constitutions say: it is their actions which count. We do not accept the view that action of this kind means that individual librarians will be forced out of ALA. Even if the chapter loses its status within the national association, the individual member is still left with a choice. He can belong both to the state and the national associations, or to one or the other. This is the choice which faces librarians in Alabama and Georgia at the present time, since these state associations are not chapters of ALA.

Again, nobody asked whether ALA had proportionately more members or less in these two states than in the three which have chapters but have no Negro members. Perhaps figures will be available at Miami.

The fear was expressed that, if ALA removed some state associations from chapter status, some individual members would be forced to leave ALA or lose their jobs. Those who use this argument should be reminded of the teachers in Louisiana, who were directed by the state's attorney general last year to resign from the National Education Association. They were told that they were violating a state law that bars teachers from membership in any organization advocating integration. The NEA had gone on record as "pledging continued support of the US Supreme Court decision on school desegregation." The Louisiana teachers who belonged to NEA (only a quarter, incidentally, of those who belong to the state education association) stood firm, were helped by the national association, and the attorney general's threats were withdrawn.

The other recommendation by the Intellectual Freedom Committee, which would bar any library practicing discrimination from institutional membership in ALA is another matter. We do not think this could be effectively implemented, and it could hamper the efforts of those librarians who are working towards quiet desgregation of some libraries in the South. Here is the place for the Executive Board to replace action with a statement of belief, directed towards the authorities of libraries where discrimination is still practiced. But the statement must be much less equivocal than the Chicago effort.

*Eric Moon*

## THE STUDENT PROBLEM STRIKES
February 15, 1963

"The purpose of the public library is to serve those mature adults who use it for their personal needs, entertainment or for business reasons." This statement, according to *The Gazette and Daily*, of York, Pennsylvania, was made by Katharine Shorey, chief librarian of the Martin Memorial Library, which is the York City and County Library.

The occasion was the banning, on January 2, of junior and senior high school students' use of reference works and reading room facilities at the Martin Memorial Library. Under this ruling students are only allowed to borrow books for home use.

Thus the student problem, which is rightly receiving national attention by librarians this year, came home to roost for Miss Shorey and the Martin Library. Within a matter of days students were picketing the library, the library was making more headlines and editorial pages than perhaps it has known in its history (and not only locally—newspapers in Philadelphia and in the state capital, Harrisburg, gave the story wide coverage), the State Library was involved and so was $72,000 in state aid, and Miss Shorey was criticized by neighboring librarians and blasted by school officials.

State Librarian Ralph Blasingame, Jr., commented: "This is probably the first time the library has had a real impact on the community. Up to now the city took the library for granted. This was a real shock but if handled constructively it could be a good thing for the library."

The matter does not seem to have been handled "constructively" at the outset, or at least the initial decision to impose the ban on students appears to have been taken rather casually. On January 3, George Whiteley, Jr., chairman of the Martin Library's board, told the local newspaper that the action was taken after he and Miss Shorey had discussed the matter. He added that he would "probably" inform other board members of the decision, but said that he did not know when they would meet.

Apart from her philosophy that the public library's purpose is to serve "mature adults," Miss Shorey gave other reasons for the ban. They went something like this:

Improved curricula in county school districts had led to a greater demand for reference materials by students. This imposed a heavy workload and overcrowding on the library. The library was now serving about 1,500 students daily, and had to hire eight part-time employees during the past two years to help accommodate them. In addition to the 13 full-time and eight part-time staff members, the library also had to employ a special person to keep order among the students.

According to the Philadelphia *Bulletin,* Miss Shorey also claimed that "some of the overcrowding is due to boys and girls who come here not to study, but to have dates. They have been making a social club out of the library . . . The young people come in here to enjoy themselves. They have been milling around and making noise. We have been forced to put some of them out. Some of them go out with Indian war whoops. Many young people come in here just to see how far they can go in making you mad. They love to see how far they can go."

A particular complaint concerned the student demand for and use of periodicals for assignments. Said *The Gazette and Daily:* "When the student selects five or six periodicals from the periodical index, the librarian must then get the magazines from the basement where they are kept in packages and tied in bundles. The librarian must untie the bundle, remove the magazine and then tie the bundle again. Miss Shorey said the student then might find he can use only one or two of the periodicals and will select five or six more from the index. The whole process is repeated again."

The students do not alone seem to be at fault here. There is at least cause to wonder whether the library's methods are quite as efficient as they should be. One city school district librarian pointed out that many public libraries actually bind their back volumes of periodicals and thus eliminate a certain amount of tying and untying of bundles.

Reaction from school officials was critical and immediate, though the ban does seem to have made a few of them think of possibilities which might have been considered earlier. Dr. John C. Alcorn, city schools superintendent, declared that one local high school library might now remain open at night, and also said that high school principals had been told to have their teachers evaluate assignments to determine which are necessary and which a matter of "tradition" only.

Miss Shorey was asked whether she thought it proper to ban students, since the York School district makes a yearly donation to the public library. "They may give us $100 now and then," she replied.

However, school board president Dale K. Gemmill, noted that last year the school district granted the public library $1,500 for the purchase of children's books, and also includes $7,500 in its budget for the salary of the children's librarian, although this latter amount is completely reimbursable from the state. A later newspaper report said that the county commissioners donated $2,500 to Martin Memorial Library in 1961, and York School district gave the library $3,500 and $1,500 during the same year.

Reactions among neighboring librarians were also largely critical. While sympathizing with Miss Shorey's problems, neither Daniel H. Healey of the Harrisburg Public Library nor Esther Flory of the Lancaster Public Library was prepared to accept that the public library exists to serve the "mature adult" only. Both these librarians and Mrs. Mabel Wolcott of the Hanover Public Library felt that by accepting funds from local school districts and county commissioners the public library was obligated to serve students.

The question of state aid also became quickly involved in the dispute. Rep. John R. Gailey, Jr., Democratic assemblyman of the first district in York, said he thought open access to the library by all segments of the public should be one of the conditions of state aid. The Martin Memorial Library recently received $5,000 in state aid, 1962 being the first year of such appropriations under Pennsylvania's new library legislation, which was passed in 1961.

State Librarian Ralph Blasingame visited the Martin Library on January 4 for a personal look at the situation. Subsequently the newspapers revealed that the library faced the potential loss of $72,000 in state aid as a result of the suspension of reference service to students. But, said Blasingame before returning to the capital, Miss Shorey had assured him that "this curtailment is temporary."

Blasingame gave no indication of what immediate action, if any, the state might take, but he did say:

"Municipal and school authorities must concern themselves with the problem existing here. The time has come to work out a partnership agreement which is mutually acceptable. A cooperative agreement between the schools and the Martin Memorial Library must be worked out until all concerned can develop adequate resources to meet these increased demands."

The Board of Directors of the Martin Memorial Library finally met on Thursday, January 10 to consider the explosive situation they had on their hands. They were in closed session for two and a half hours, but prior to the meeting Miss Shorey read a prepared statement directed to county high school principals, in which she referred to the situation as a "triangular affair" involving principally the library, county school administrators and the students.

The announced results of the Board meeting were, first, a decision to arrange a meeting on Monday, January 14 between the Board and the City and County School superintendents to discuss the situation further. Secondly, it was decided to set up a student reference desk in the old children's wing of the library. There was, however, no mention of a date for such a service to begin, nor was it stated whether this was a temporary measure or a permanent one.

The joint meeting of the public library board and school representatives on January 14 proposed three areas in which their future efforts would be concentrated.

The first of these would be a mutual working agreement to be set up by an advisory council to coordinate the use of the public library by students. It was not made clear what the representation on the advisory council would be.

The second, and by the far the most interesting result of the York fracas, was a proposal of a three-year plan to bring all the York County school libraries up to ALA standards.

And thirdly, the joint meeting announced, assignments by teachers would be checked to see that they could be backed by adequate resources either in the public or school libraries. Again, it was not said who would do the checking.

We publish this story, not because there is anything particularly new or unusual involved, but because it is one case history of where the "student problem"—a matter of national rather than local concern—can lead us if it is not handled thoughtfully. The most disturbing fact in the York situation is that it was only *after* the ban was imposed and all the criticism erupted that anyone—librarians, teachers, school and library board officials—talked of getting together and considering what is so clearly their joint problem.

There have been many attempts by public librarians to obtain the cooperation of local teachers, particularly in the matter of assignments, and some examples of mild cooperation between school and public librarians. But all too rarely have there been serious joint efforts by library boards and school boards to cope with the problems of library service to students on a higher policy level.

And there is one other body of people who have not been consulted often enough in an attempt to find solutions—the students themselves. We close this report with some sound commonsense remarks from a very good editorial in *The Gazette and Daily*:

"No doubt the decision by library authorities last week to limit the services they will render young people to the loaning of books, and to refuse them access to reference works or to the reading rooms, came as the result of a long series of pressures. But to blame the students, or their teachers, for these pressures is hardly helpful. The library is in the field of education; it is part of the general system of education in York County; it is therefore obliged, as we see it, to seek a solution that will advance the possibilities of education for us all, something that the limitations now in force upon students obviously will not do.

"The problem appears to us one that can best be approached cooperatively. The schools of the county, public and private, and the library, ought to work out an understanding as to the function of the Martin Library in the education system. And when we say the schools of the county, we mean administrators, teachers, librarians—and also the students. In our opinion a great deal of the present difficulty might have been avoided by enlisting, long ago, the participation of the students in deciding what the Martin Library can and cannot do and in establishing regulations for library behavior which would have been formulated in part and enforced in part by the students themselves."

*Eric Moon*

## QUESTIONING A QUESTION—AND SOME OF THE ANSWERS
July 1963

Last fall, we said on this editorial page: "Our vote for the most improved state library association periodical in the country would be awarded unhesitatingly to *The Bay State Librarian,* the quarterly bulletin of the Massachusetts Library Association." The issues of *The Bay State Librarian* which have appeared since that comment was made have given us no reason to revise our opinion. We think editor John N. Berry III has done a fine job—BUT . . . we do question the wisdom and the tactics of an editorial which appeared in the April 1963 issue of the Massachusetts magazine.

Mr. Berry named in that editorial eleven libraries, all located in the south, which had recently received awards under the Dorothy Canfield Fisher Library Award Program, which is administered by the Book-of-the-Month Club, with the advice of the American Library Association. The editorial was headed "A Question," and Mr. Berry's question, in essence, was "Are these libraries segregated?"

In answer to his inquiry, said Mr. Berry, the Southern Regional Council* had stated: "Our files show no record of desgregation at any of the libraries cited in your letter. We assume, therefore, that they are still segregated."

The editorial concluded: "We violently oppose any award to strengthen institutions which maintain a system of service that in any way separates one citizen from another in his use of books. We ask the question in the sincere hope that every library and system involved can and will truthfully answer with a resounding 'no!' to separation, segregation, and unequal library service. Can we expect a reply?"

Mr. Berry's editorial, it seems to us, raises not *a* question, but several. First, there is the basic question as to whether the Canfield Fisher awards— or any other awards—are going to strengthen segregated libraries? If they

---

* *The Southern Regional Council, according to* Encyclopedia of Associations *(3rd ed., Gale Research Co., 1961) was founded in 1918, has 80 members and a staff of 18. Located in Atlanta, Georgia, it consists of "leaders in education, religion, business, labor and the professions interested in improving race relations in the south." It "provides community relations consultation and field services when requested by official and private agencies, distributes pamphlets dealing with desegregation of various public facilities, and fosters elimination of barriers to Negro registration and voting." It issues a publication entitled* New South *eleven times a year.*

are, there are the further questions, why are they and who is responsible? And, Mr. Berry, there is another question of a different kind. Is it responsible editorial practice to ask a question, loaded with dynamite as this one is, without first making an attempt to check the facts with the individual libraries involved, with the state library agencies or with ALA? All of these seem likely to be better informed than the Southern Regional Council, which has such a wide sphere of operations that it can scarcely be expected to have very specific knowledge about library services.

Mr. Berry's basic question was, of course, perfectly valid. The professional press has an obligation to probe issues, even sensitive ones, and a duty to examine constantly the actions of the profession and see that they bear some relation to the purity of some of our official pronouncements. Like Mr. Berry, we oppose (not "violently" perhaps, but certainly firmly) the presentation of awards to libraries operating segregated services, particularly when ALA, whose policies are now clear in this area, is involved in such awards. But this does not condone accusation without evidence—and to ask a question in print without first trying for the answer amounts to about the same thing.

We decided to pursue the matter further, and in order to gather the necessary facts:

1) Wrote to all the libraries named in *The Bay State Librarian* editorial and sent them a copy of the editorial;

2) In some cases where the individual libraries did not immediately reply, wrote also to the state library extension agencies concerned;

3) Asked the Book-of-the-Month Club for a copy of the application form and conditions governing the Canfield Fisher Library Awards;

4) Informed Mr. Berry of our actions.

Ten of the 11 libraries answered our inquiry, and we had letters from three state library agencies. Only in one case did we not get a reply, either from the individual library named in the original editorial or from the state library agency.

The reactions to Mr. Berry's editorial method, to nobody's surprise, were almost unanimously unfavorable. The most fiery reply, appropriately, came from Ray Peppers, librarian of the Beaufort (S.C.) County Library, which won the biggest of all the Canfield Fisher Awards. Mr. Peppers said he would answer the question if it were asked in "the normal way" (he did answer ours), but to Mr. Berry he said: "I'll be damned if I'll answer your editorial question."

Mrs. Leola F. Miller, librarian of the Rolla (Mo.) Free Public Library commented: "The *principle* of 'assuming' a fact without any evidence is something I deplore." Mrs. Evelyn Griffith, librarian of the North Arkansas Regional Library, resented "the tarnish that this editorial would like to spread over [her library's] selection" for the award.

The chairman of the library board, Mrs. James D. Bruton, replied for the Plant City (Fla.) Public Library: "Unfortunately racial strife will continue so long as people, expecting the worst, act on someone's assumption instead of facts. We in the South have become accustomed to the prejudiced and misleading editorials which continue to appear in too many publications, written without basis of fact by editors far removed from the scene. I never expected this practice to extend to library journals, however."

Elaine von Oesen, extension services librarian at the North Carolina State Library, to whom we wrote after receiving no initial reply from the librarian of the Henderson County Public Library (she was on vacation, said Miss von Oesen, and we did later hear from Henderson librarian Mary Kent Seagle), declared herself "appalled at the editorial" in *The Bay State Librarian.*

In sharp contrast to most of these comments was the reply from Richard K. Burns, director of the Falls Church (Va.) Public Library. He sent Mr. Berry three interesting pages, and to us, the following observations:

"We regret that we should be accused without being asked or investigated. The writer of the editorial was, of course, careless and wrong. It appears that he was looking for an argument. For my part, however, I'm not too unhappy about it. Although erroneous in its facts, the editorial does ask a serious question, and asks it seriously. I prefer this to the countless editorials which are spineless in spirit, based on empty ideals, and achieve only their pointless effect, which appear again and again in our professional journals. I can respect *The Bay State Librarian* for, if nothing else, its own admission that public libraries are far from realizing their professed ideals. Inaccuracy is bad, but meaningless pap is worse."

Mr. Berry was criticized on another score in a letter he received from Eleanor A. Ferguson, Executive Secretary of ALA's Public Library Association, who asked: "Why were the Wicomico County Free Library, Salisbury, Maryland, and the Marshall County Free Library, Lewisburg, Tennessee, omitted? They seem as likely to have segregated policies as some of those you do mention. Come on now, if we're going to do research, let's do it thoroughly, and not use biased samples!"

And what did Mr. Berry have to say in response to our questioning of his editorial judgment? It's perhaps only fair, after printing so much criticism of him, to quote him at some length:

It is my contention that any such award, involving as it does the American Library Association, must expect the scrutiny of the profession, and its recipients should respond as freely to inquiries as several have done in this case. The truth, in print, will provide a unique and gratifying statement opposing segregation. If the question were asked privately, and only the segregated replies were published, their spirited denial would have been lost.

The question was asked editorially with the full intention that it would be answered editorially, regardless of the results. It is my conviction that asking libraries, many in the deep south, to respond to this question will serve one of two purposes. If they respond with the resounding "No!" to segregation that the editorial expects and desires, then we have an impressive collection of documentary evidence, from southern libraries, to publicize a fact in which the profession should take pride. We know that this is an award strengthening equal, integrated service. It publicizes a group of libraries with the courage and willingness to publicly deny segregation. We can then give the award, and the receiving libraries, all the publicity and commendation they deserve.

On the other hand, if there are among the eleven libraries, some which do segregate, then we have forced the exposition of this practice, and at the same time discovered a flaw in the selection of recipients for the award. It is my sincere hope that only the first of these purposes may be served in this case . . .

Now, what about the facts on segregation or integration at these 11 award-winning libraries? Seven denied unequivocally that they were segregated:

*Beaufort (S.C.) County Library:* "Each facility of the Beaufort County Library serves any Beaufort County resident who presents himself."

*Falls Church (Va.) Public Library:* "This library has never done other than serve our readers without regard to race, creed, sex, age or any other discriminatory principle. When this library opened its new quarters in 1958, the USIA wrote a feature story on the library and its program. The story has been carried throughout the world in many languages. It is significant that in the photographs accompanying the story, Negroes and whites appear together, both children and adults. It is also significant that one of the earliest members of our local Friends organization, and a most effective supporter of our program, is a Negro. It is significant that in the block where the library is located, property and homes on both sides of the street are owned by Negroes. It is significant that the public schools in this city were totally integrated years ago without incident or protest." (Much more from Falls Church, but read *The Bay State Librarian*).

*Rolla (Mo.) Free Public Library:* "There has never been any segregation in this library." The librarian included as documentary evidence a 1958 newspaper photograph showing both black and white citizens using the library.

*Keyser-Mineral (W.Va.) County Library:* ". . . since its inception as a WPA Library in 1937, has never practiced any form of racial segregation."

*Plant City (Fla.) Public Library:* "Our community is 25 percent Negro and as I write from a desk in our library," said the library board chairman, "I see in the reading room almost as many Negro patrons as white ones, and they have been coming ever since the library first opened its doors for service, and without incident! We have yet to receive the first complaint." Mrs. Bruton also gave, for good measure, the name and address of a local Negro citizen to whom Mr. Berry could write, since he appeared "to need confirmation."

*Killgore Memorial Library, Dumas, Texas:* Sent a copy of the criteria for the Canfield Fisher Awards, and observed: "I understand this to mean that the libraries must be desegregated—ours is."

*Henderson County (N.C.) Public Library:* "It serves all races and has for over ten years," said Elaine von Oesen, extension services librarian at the North Carolina State Library.

Mrs. Elizabeth D. Moore, director of the *Oconee Regional Library, Dublin, Georgia,* said: "I assure you that our governing officials, our library board and our library staff members are striving diligently to provide adequate free library service to every citizen who lives within the four counties served by the Oconee Regional Library. Specific materials and services are available to everyone. No citizen has been refused any material or any library service requested." The same kind of reply came from Lucile Nix, chief library consultant in the State Department of Education. But at least a query must remain here. One of the branches of the Oconee Regional Library is listed in the *American Library Directory,* 23rd edition, as "Negro." The data listed in this directory are based on replies received from the libraries.

The question—Mr. Berry's and ours—was evaded by the *North Arkansas Regional Library.* In a testy letter which returned some fire in the direction of Massachusetts libraries, regional librarian Mrs. Evelyn Griffith merely pointed out "that there are few Negroes living in the northern third of Arkansas and none at all in the mountainous six-county section which makes up our region." She did not state what the library's policy might be should a Negro decide to move to the mountains.

And the question was even more fully evaded by the *Carnegie Library, Eufaula, Alabama,* which did not reply at all—to us nor, as far as we know, to Mr. Berry. Nor did we receive a reply from the Alabama Public Library Service, the state agency.

Finally, from one library, the *Jackson Parish Library, Jonesboro, Louisiana,* came an admission of segregated service. Said librarian M. E. Wright, Jr.: "The Jackson Parish (county) Library is designed for the use of all citizens. The same staff—trained bookmobile librarian and clerk-driver—operate two bookmobiles, one of which is devoted exclusively to the service for Negroes, with a collection selected to appeal to their interest and informational needs. It should be emphasized that any book in the library's collection is available to any reader, since if it is not at the outlet point where he makes his request, it is obtained and sent to him . . . By action of the library board, Negroes do not use the one branch of the parish system, but every attempt is made to give equal service. The pattern of service in Jackson Parish does not deny the Negro the use of any library materials, and it brings close to his door the books which are appealing and useful to him . . ."

It is clear from this last reply that, however one feels about the methods used, Mr. Berry has uncovered a situation which needs further examination. No. 7 among the criteria listed by the Book-of-the-Month Club for the Dorothy Canfield Fisher Awards reads: "The library shall provide equal service to all, regardless of race, creed or nationality." Undoubtedly, those who still adhere to the *"separate* but equal" doctrine would claim that they are meeting this condition, but we feel sure that this is not in keeping with the spirit of the award. Certainly the "separate but equal" doctrine is not in keeping with present ALA policies, and since ALA is finally responsible for the selection of the winners ALA should ensure that the criteria are *fully* met.

The state library agencies in each state are also responsible in no small measure for the way in which these awards are distributed. Elaine von Oesen, in her letter to *LJ*, drew attention to the Book-of-the-Month Club criteria for the Awards, and added: "Not only must the library state, in applying, that it meets the criteria; but the state library agency in each state must endorse each application. *The Bay State Librarian* editorial not only censures these public libraries, it censures the state library agencies in those states. You may remember that Mississippi disqualified itself for an Award."

Miss von Oesen is quite right. The individual libraries are not alone to blame: in fact, the major responsibility rests with the state library agencies. ALA's Eleanor Ferguson claims that "the Committee appointed by the Public Library Association looks closely at the evidence submitted about each library," but she adds: "If neither the library nor the State Agency can be trusted to abide by the criterion [of equal service to all], then indeed it is 'difficult to obtain incontrovertible evidence'." The evidence here presented would suggest that Mississippi's example in withdrawing as ineligible might have been followed by at least one other state—and maybe more. It also suggests that the committee from the Public Library Association will have to look even more closely at the submitted evidence.

*Eric Moon*


## TWO KINDS OF ACCESS
August 1963

After some six months of study, International Research Associates, Inc. of New York brought in their report on *Access to Public Libraries,* and presented it to the membership of the American Library Association during the Chicago conference in July. It was the one item which electrified the conference with controversy.

Twice during the week, the study came up for discussion, first at a meeting of the Library Administration Division, later at a general membership meeting. On both occasions the presentations were followed by lengthy and sometimes acrimonious discussion. This was not totally surprising: nobody could seriously have expected that a study designed to reveal the explosive facts of discrimination in libraries would be greeted with universal joy. But few would have forecast that the most violent and vociferous objections would come from the representatives of such large city libraries as Detroit, Philadelphia and Washington, D.C.

The principal objections were raised against a part of the study which dealt with branch library provision in predominantly black and predomi-

nantly white neighborhoods in ten cities, six in the South and four in the
North. The methodology was questioned, and one speaker accused the
surveyors of a "gross misrepresentation of the data."

After only a cursory examination of the report itself we feel that some
of the doubts and questions raised at the LAD meeting may have some
validity, but we do not propose to dwell on these altercations here because
hasty judgments on the report at this stage would be both inadvisable and
unconstructive. But comment on the manner of presentation of the study is
called for.

ALA's uncommon desire to speed information to its membership on our
professional part in the central concern of our society at this time, is both
understandable and commendable. As Harold Tucker, chairman of the ALA
Advisory Committee on the Study noted, ever since the Cleveland conference in 1961, when the study of freedom of access to libraries was recommended, "there has been a mounting urgency . . . to get a realistic look at
the existing picture."

But speed sometimes enacts its own penalties. Perhaps time would not
have cured the pedestrian and pedantic presentations by the Project staff,
but it could have been reliably predicted that the discussion which followed
would be disastrous, based as it was on such scanty information. Scarcely
anyone present had seen a copy of the full report; the only documents
widely available were an innocuous five-page summary of "Highlights of the
Findings" and a press release, the very selectivity of which made it like a
hand-grenade with the pin already withdrawn. It was, indeed, this latter
item that created the big bang. Altogether too late in the discussions came
Emerson Greenaway's terribly pertinent comment that we had two problems of access here: first, access to libraries, and second, access to the
report.

Let us here pass on to all who were not present at the conference the
recommendation of Virginia Lacy Jones, dean of the Atlanta Library School,
which was greeted with loud applause, that "we accept this report with
open minds." She added, "If some of the facts shock us, we've been broad
enough to seek them out, let's be broad enough to look at them objectively."

The subject of this report is a matter of immense professional concern,
and the report itself seems certain to have some kind of impact on the place
of libraries in our society. But we have not reached the end of the line on
this study.

Having called for the facts, ALA must now decide whether they tell
substantially the whole story, or whether they present a kind of selective
truth which is in itself a distortion and which needs interpretation to bend it
back to accuracy and a correct perspective. Then, and then only, will the
Association be in a position to decide on the next step.

The report is being rushed into print, and copies will be available from
ALA by August 19. In the remaining months of 1963, it is to be hoped that
all members of the profession will give this document most careful and
dispassionate consideration. *LJ* intends to present a full discussion of the

report before the end of the year. It will surely be on the agenda for discussion at ALA's Midwinter meeting next January, and this time we hope the discussion will be an informed one.

*Eric Moon*

## THE PROCESS OF DILUTION
December 15, 1963

An article on "Segregated Libraries" by Rice Estes—the first of its kind in library literature for at least several years—appeared in *Library Journal* in the December 15, 1960 issue. It was clear from the letters we received that the article had opened many eyes, and that there were many librarians who had previously been unaware that discriminatory practices were as deeply rooted in libraries as they were in schools and other public institutions.

Immediately following the Estes article there began the demands for a survey which would elicit some of the *facts* about discrimination in libraries, since this lack of knowledge, some people claimed, was what made it difficult for the library profession to take appropriate action in this area. Within a few months came an editorial in the *California Librarian* by William Eshelman, a letter in *LJ* (February 15, 1961) from Dorothy Bendix, later to be one of the sponsors of the Access Study, and an editorial in this journal (March 15, 1961), whose publishers also became one of the principal sponsors of the Access Study. Here was the real beginning. Promptly after the *LJ* editorial, Archie McNeal, chairman of ALA's Intellectual Freedom Committee, expressed interest in our proposal, and the wheels began to turn.

We record this chronology for one reason only: to make it quite clear that we were in favor of a study from the beginning, if only to remove "lack of facts" from the scene as an excuse for inaction. Our publishers backed our words with financial support for the Study, despite some reservations about the outline proposed for survey. If we now join the ranks of the critics of the report, we do so as clearly interested and involved parties.

It is worth noting that all these early advocates of a fact-finding study urged a survey of *Southern* libraries, where it was clear that direct discrimination was most prevalent and stringent. The objective was not to apportion blame but to find out more, in Dorothy Bendix's words, about "the factors responsible for the successful transition from segregated to integrated libraries in some Southern communities." This, our March 15, 1961 editorial commented, "is perhaps the most vital [information] of all." The thought was that if enough information could be compiled about the ways in which some Southern communities had been able successfully to integrate their libraries, this evidence might be used diplomatically to persuade still reluctant Southern librarians, library boards, and other authorities that similar progress was possible in their communities too.

As the Access Study began to emerge from idea to concrete proposal, it became obvious that ALA did not intend to pursue this reasonably clear and manageable goal. The very term "access" was the beginning of the process of dilution (like so much that was to follow, and like the phraseology of the report of the Access Study, the term had many connotations): the real purpose, it seemed, had to be camouflaged in some kind of research neutralism and respectability. The proposal finally approved by the ALA Executive Board expressed concern "about the Negro and the restrictions still imposed on him in certain areas," but added, "the problem is not limited to one minority group or to one geographical area."

In a sense this was true, but it was also an avoidance of another truth, that the most acute and obvious problem was precisely the restrictions placed upon the Negro reader in particular, and particularly in one geographical area. Nevertheless, diplomacy quickly prevailed over common sense, and we found ourselves faced with a study involving all 50 states and bringing under the research umbrella a variety of digressions such as restrictions upon students, variations in regional resources, etc. It is almost a wonder that ALA did not include some aspects of censorship, which restricts "access" as surely as some of the other factors with which the Study was burdened.

As it was, we already seemed to have on our hands a study blown up to nearly the proportions of the Public Library Inquiry—and the vast, nebulous territory of this newly "defined" inquiry had to be covered for little more than carfare, some $35,000 to $40,000. Then, having found International Research Associates, Inc. to bite off this impossible task, ALA demonstrated a commendable but rare urgency and asked that the job be done as quickly as possible. In barely more than six months the job was "done," the report issued, and the tumult began.

Given the dilution of purpose and the spread in scope of the study, the limited financial resources, a tight deadline, plus the survey team's (later to be revealed) obvious unfamiliarity with library service and practice, it is little wonder that the final result is as disappointing and dismal as it is. The fault lies not nearly entirely with INRA.

Many specific criticisms of the report have been made by the contributors to our symposium, and we do not intend to repeat any of those here. We intend to concentrate only on an aspect of imbalance in the report which stems perhaps from the original shying away from the focal problem.

With the wave of Negro protest expanding rapidly northward in this past eventful year, it seems that the surveyors decided, or were persuaded, to jump on this bandwagon, to prove, at all costs, that discrimination is not a someplace thing, it is everywhere. This scarcely needed proving, but in their attempt to do so the surveyors have eliminated the shadings and have given the spotlight a sharp 180-degree spin to leave it focussed on the places where, if discrimination does exist in library service, it certainly is not as strenuous or adamant or extreme as in some places on the other side of the arc.

The emphases and attitudes in this report vary subtly but considerably, and nowhere more so than in the methods of study and reporting of the Southern situation as opposed to that in the ten selected cities. While protecting the anonymity of Southern libraries, the surveyors erect a signpost prominently pointing toward Washington, D.C., Detroit, Philadelphia, *et al.* While concentrating properly on the services and resources of the main library when studying Southern libraries, the researchers omit all mention of the main library when making their peculiar assessment of de facto discrimination in library service further North. And while sending in interviewers to back up and verify questionnaire findings in the South, Detroit and others get their treatment on the basis of statistics only.

This is not to claim that all is roses and purity north of that famous line, only to insist that the treatment of the libraries surveyed should be as fair and equal as one hopes the services of all libraries might be when discriminatory practices are finally stamped out. Thus, when the surveyors point out with some deliberation that Philadelphia has more branches in "white" tracts than in "black" ones, they surely invoke the obligation to point out that Philadelphia's "black" tract branches contain more volumes than those in the "white" tracts. But there is no need to delve further into the absurdities of the survey team's methods of evaluating branch provision—which bring to mind a delightful little book published some years ago, entitled *How to Lie with Statistics*—for even the Advisory Committee, in its guarded way, seems to have written off this piece of the report.

If the report is suspiciously invalid in this section, it gives hints of being quite as inaccurate on the South. Here, we see the difference in attitude. While rooting for malpractice in the North, determined to find it whether it is there or no, the surveyors have done their best to present the Southern situation in a kindly light. No one objects to sympathetic reporting of course, providing it is done within the bounds of reasonable accuracy. But is it?

In an appendix, the report provides a "List of Integrated Public Libraries," all located in "the eleven states of the Confederacy." Now admittedly, the report also defines its terms—in a footnote—as follows: "The term 'integrated' is used in this listing to indicate library systems in which the main library is accessible to members of all races. Many of these libraries, however, are not *fully* integrated in the sense that they provide more restricted services for one group of the population than for another."

The surveyors are not kidding! But they don't indicate in any way which of those libraries on the list impose some of the most unpleasant restrictions or perpetrate various indignities on their Negro readers. There in the appendix, proudly listed as "integrated," are Albany, Georgia, Montgomery, Alabama, and Danville, Virginia, where various forms of insidious maneuvering like so-called vertical or horizontal "integration" are still in force to remind Negro readers that they use these libraries on sufferance. Footnote or no, the use of the word "integrated" to describe these situations is laughable.

The information upon which this list is based, says the report, was "received from regional informants in the South, visits to the South by interviewers from INRA-New York, and a wide variety of research studies, journals, magazines, and newspapers." Did anyone, we wonder, ask *Negroes* in these communities whether they regarded such libraries as integrated?

The thoroughness of the research may be illustrated by a couple of other comparisons between this bald listing in the Access Study and the evidence in another recent study titled *Integration in Public Library Service in Thirteen Southern States, 1954–1962.* This latter is a master's thesis completed at the School of Library Service, Atlanta University in August 1963: its evidence was collected also by a combination of questionnaires, correspondence, interviews and a literature search.

Two libraries listed as "integrated" in the Access Study are those of Lafayette, Louisiana, and Concord, North Carolina. Of these, the Atlanta study records:

1) "The city of Lafayette supports a library system composed of seven branches and the main library. The branches are still operated on a segregated basis. Six of the seven are operated for use of white patrons and one provides service for Negroes. *The Main library does not offer fully integrated service for Negroes.* A Negro reader must be in high school before he is permitted the use of the main library facilities."

2) "No change in the policy of serving Negroes at the Concord Public Library . . . has been made by the library board. The arrangement which permits Negroes to secure circulating materials from the main library through a segregated branch is still the general rule. A few Negroes have been permitted the use of the reference room. This is an exception to the general rule of the library, and it is not generally known by the Negroes that this can be done. *The library board has maintained that library cards are not to be issued to Negroes at the main library.*" (Our italics in both the above items—*Ed.*)

These are just a couple of samples, but perhaps they are sufficient to demonstrate our point. The report is suspect in its "findings" as regards both North and South, and even more suspect in the contrasting tenor of its presentation of those "findings" in the two cases.

What, then, should the next step be? Ralph Shaw, in this issue, suggests that ALA should: a) reject the INRA report; and b) set in motion "studies that would be meaningful and helpful." Drastic as this sounds, we see little alternative.

One of the original proposals on the Access Study was that, after completion of the survey, there should be "A conference on 'access to libraries' involving *lay* persons as well as library personnel. The purpose of such a conference would be to discuss information gathered, to make recommendations for improvement, and to define problems for further study . . ." These may very well be listed in the wrong order: first we surely need to look at those "problems for further study"—particularly at some of the problems raised by this study, and how to avoid a similar disaster in any future attempts to seek out the real story of discrimination in libraries.

*Eric Moon*

### READING THE LESSONS
February 15, 1964

Where stands the Access Study now? Is it only a dead and disgraced document? Did it, even in failure, serve any discernible purpose?

A brief account of the latest chapter in this sorry story appears in this issue (pp. 814–816). A number of views on the Access Study appeared in our December 15 issue. We wish to repeat none of that here, only to examine the record and see what, if anything, we have learned.

Most of the lessons, it seems, are incidental to the central concerns and original objectives. First, and perhaps most significantly, the review and evaluation by the LAD Board is in some ways a more historic document than the report it is evaluating. Seldom has such stringent criticism of ALA policies and procedures, or such an openly honest exposure of widespread bumbling, been made by an ALA committee.

The message that ALA is not equipped to dive into controversial social (or even professional) issues reverberated through other statements at the recent Midwinter meeting. Said President Wagman: "The fact is that we exert more power for good or ill than we realize. A good hard look at how that influence is exercised is in order." Ralph Esterquest, in another report, underlined "the fact that our Association does not have a clear-cut policy about policies."

We learned things too about the state of our professional art: it is shakier than we knew. After all the standards, all the definitions of goals and needs, suddenly we are told by the LAD Board that library "administrators are *struggling* to find the right way" in the "complex" matter of branch library location and service. Poor INRA! How could they expect to understand what we have failed to learn in more than a century of public library service?

The rejection of the section of the Access Study which dealt with branch library provision has surely taught us that the Association can be prevented from accepting the doubtful too easily if only a few influential members will shout loud and long enough. But do we not need to learn also that easy acceptance is dangerous, even if there be no line of past presidents banging at the door?

Of course there was no demonstration from the South about other sections of the Access Study. Southern librarians were scarcely likely to *protest* that the report was slanted in their favor (though not perhaps to their advantage). But one important Southern librarian told us that the librarians in her state are still laughing at the rosy dream presented in the INRA report. On what basis, then, other than lack of recriminations, did the

LAD Board "particularly commend" those sections dealing with integration of libraries in the South?

What we *most* need to learn is what forces operate, and in what ways, to so sidetrack an investigation from its original, central purpose. *All* who pressed in the beginning for a study in this area—and we believe this includes the ALA Intellectual Freedom Committee—wanted a study that would teach us something about the process of integration of libraries, particularly in the South because there it was both most difficult to achieve and most obvious that it could be done. Yet somehow, when the ALA wheels began to turn, they took us ever further from this objective.

Since the LAD Board particularly commends the section of the Access Study which pretends to delve into this area, perhaps LAD will spell out, for the benefit of simpler souls, and with the admirable clarity of their most recent report, just what constructive lessons were learned from this commendable effort. And LAD might add some notes on how, equipped with this solid, new information, ALA proposes to capitalize on it in pushing forward toward the goal of free access to public libraries everywhere.

If there is much that is sad and depressing in the Access Study story, we do not believe that it should be written off as a complete loss. It has opened many doors of inquiry and suggested several soft spots in our professional knowledge. If some of the areas of further study suggested by the LAD Board's report are pursued, we may expose much more than the Access Study could ever have uncovered. For example, the suggestion that patterns of discrimination in employment and promotion of minority group members in libraries should be studied is an excellent and tenable objective. This might be even more explosive than the Access Study. That's not a reason for not doing it, only for doing it better.

*Eric Moon*

## PROBLEMS OF CONSISTENCY
August 1964

For several years now the American Library Association has been firming up its position on questions of racial discrimination. It has reached the point where its policies, as recorded in print, are sure and unequivocal. Few professional associations have placed themselves more clearly on the record.

But a policy statement, however admirable in its wording or intent—in the area of discrimination no less than in others such as book selection and censorship—lacks conviction unless the actions that follow it are also unequivocal and consistent with the policy.

Ralph Esterquest expounded at St. Louis on some of the problems of unraveling the tortuous tangle of ALA policies, and perhaps it is understandable that ALA has failed to follow through or fully understand the wider implications of some of these policies. The spirited debate, and the motion which was passed with solid insistence at St. Louis (p. 2920–21), arose from one of these rivers of inconsistency between policy and practice.

Four state library associations—those of Alabama, Georgia, Louisiana, and Mississippi—are now excluded from chapter status in ALA, largely because of their refusal (or inability) to admit Negro librarians to membership. In effect, ALA has refused "recognition" to these state library associations until such time as they bring their policies into line with ALA's. It seemed a clear-cut sort of decision, but there were ramifications which had not yet surfaced.

What, for example, is involved in "recognition"? In practice, ALA appeared to be curiously out of step with its stated policy. Was it not some kind of "recognition" for an ALA officer or staff member to speak, in his official capacity, at a meeting of one of these disbarred state associations?

It is not too surprising that this kind of inconsistency can be overlooked. Seen from a position of relative noninvolvement, the argument appears to be at best theoretical, at worst doctrinaire. But for some it is no theoretical matter, as Elonnie Josey and some others pointed out in St. Louis. As an ALA member and a professional librarian, does he not have a crystal-clear right to object when the annual meeting of the state library association to which he may not belong (by virtue of his color) is honored by the presence, say, of the president of his own national professional association?

This was the fundamental issue which the motion at St. Louis sought to clarify. And so the decision was taken. Henceforth, no ALA officer or staff member, in his official capacity, will be permitted to attend or address the meetings of those state associations whose racial policies do not conform with those of the national body.

There are, of course, inevitable losses in a decision of this kind, but they are more than compensated by the gain in meaning and force of ALA policies already on the record. The new ALA president, Edwin Castagna, very rightly pointed out that the motion was not vindictive but corrective. Nevertheless, there was some who found it harsh or extreme, and perhaps others who didn't understand why it was necessary.

The uncertain may take some reassurance from the fact that the White House announced a remarkably similar position less than a week after the St. Louis ALA conference. On July 9, according to the *New York Times,* "The White House made it clear that the administration would not expect Government officials to speak before segregated audiences."

"Would not expect" is, of course, far less explicit than the wording of the ALA resolution. White House press secretary George Reedy was asked whether any directive or order had been issued. He ducked the question but insisted that "the whole policy is against racial discrimination and it has been stated so many times by the President and high officials of the Cabinet that there is no doubt of it now."

It is deceptively easy to assume the absence of doubt, but words and statements will never be free from the tinge of doubt unless actions parallel the words so closely that there are no shadowy variations of interpretation between them.

ALA has necessarily, like society and government, had to grope somewhat toward the point where its actions are as consistent as its intentions. But it has probably never taken a firmer stride toward authoritative definition and implementation of its words than it took in St. Louis. We have come a long way from our tentative murmurings in this area only a few years ago.

*Eric Moon*

## MOVEMENT IN MOBILE
June 1, 1965

We have just returned from Alabama, where we attended, witnessed, and participated in a historic meeting of the library association of that state. What made the occasion historic was that it was the first "integrated" conference of the Alabama Library Association. Significant also is the fact that the meeting did not have to be held on a college campus: it took place in the downtown heart of Mobile at the Admiral Semmes Hotel and Motor Hotel.

There were Negro librarians present at just about all the meetings during this conference. There was, to be sure, not too much open mingling of the races, but we spoke to some of the 15 or 20 Negro librarians who were, for the first time, present at an annual conference of their state library association, and we found them generally pleased with the conference atmosphere. They said they had been very courteously received and that they were having no problems, either with the hotel or the conference generally.

How had it come about? Robert Severance, president of the Alabama Library Association, a man of imposing calm, good manners, and good humor, revealed some of the background at the annual business meeting. The most significant achievement of the Executive Council of the Association during the past year, he said, was something they had *not* done. In previous years, apparently, the Executive Council has instructed the Membership Committee not to accept applications from Negroes for membership in the Alabama Library Association, since the Association could not grant them full membership privileges—including the right to attend meetings and conferences. The passing of the Civil Rights Act, said Mr. Severance, had removed the accommodation hurdle, so this year the Executive Council had passed on no such instruction to the Membership Committee. The presence of a dozen or so Negro librarians at the meeting at which this announcement was made was gratifying testimony to the effectiveness of this "nonaction." Quite as gratifying was the loud applause which greeted Mr. Severance's statement.

If anyone does not share our estimate of the significance of this breakthrough in the Alabama Library Association, or our respect for Mr. Severance and others who have made it possible, let him remember an event which was taking place at the same time, not too far away in Haynesville, Alabama. There, after a virulent racist diatribe by defense counsel Matt Murphy, Jr.—a Klansman defending a Klansman in the case of the murder of civil rights worker Mrs. Viola Gregg Liuzzo—an all-white jury added another chapter of frustration to the long history of the search for justice in Southern law courts.

The Alabama Library Association has not been a chapter of the American Library Association since 1955. It seems clear that this long decade in the professional wilderness is finally coming to an end for Alabama, but the news is that the state association does not intend to apply for ALA chapter status immediately—although it is now obviously in a position to do so.

The Executive Council seems to feel that the integration of the association is achievement enough for one year, that they have pushed hard enough, and that to rub the salty matter of ALA chapter status into the wounds of those who accept the present decision grudgingly if at all, would be one abrasive step too far along a very difficult road. They are perhaps right, and in any case, the people involved are more important than the technicalities.

We heard, at the Midwinter meeting of the American Library Association, that the Georgia Library Association had admitted a Negro librarian, Mr. E. J. Josey, to membership. How broad the welcome mat is in Georgia we do not yet know, but at least the door appears to be open. The Louisiana Library Association has applied for chapter status, which seems to indicate that things are happening there also. And we have even had one letter from Mississippi which indicated that the library association of that state had been integrated.

Some of this is, of course, unconfirmed, but there are enough ripples to convince us, despite our concern over what happened on a related issue at the ALA Membership meeting during the Midwinter conference, that now is not perhaps the time to push harder on the chapter question. We hope that the matter will be allowed to rest at the Detroit conference. There are other issues a-plenty, but this one, happily, seems to be near its end.

*Eric Moon*

## DISCRIMINATION AT DETROIT
August 1965

There have been some who, since our June 1 Alabama editorial, have assumed—some with sorrow, others with satisfaction—that we are no longer so hot on the integration issue as we once were. If we now express misgivings about the latest ALA move in this area—the Oboler motion, at the Detroit conference, on institutional membership (*see* p. 3188, this issue)—

we shall probably strengthen those sorrows or satisfactions. Well, no matter, we have never believed that rigidity and strength were synonymous.

The ALA chapter issue always seemed to us a simple and clear one. It was tangible, logical, and could be enforced. It made no sense for an association which had policies, a constitution, and bylaws which all argued for open membership (regardless of race, religion, etc.) to accept within its family circle—as a chapter—another and separate association whose policies or practices denied this basic philosophy.

The Oboler motion on institutional membership is nothing like so simple, nor perhaps so defensible. This one deals with the membership policies and practices of ALA, not those of any other association. And in fact, if it is finally adopted by ALA, the Oboler motion would actually *reverse* the association's long-standing open-door policy.

The ALA bylaws have it that "*Any* person, library, or other organization interested in library service and librarianship may become a member." The only stipulation is that they pay their dues. Now, for the first time, we are being asked to accept a revision of that bylaw to read "any person, library, etc. *except* . . ." Whenever you start talking about exceptions, it is wise to consider whether this does not open the door to other or future exceptions.

Many other questions and implications are raised by this resolution. Institutional membership is only one of several categories of ALA membership. If institutions which practice or advocate discrimination are to be excluded, why not also individuals who do so? The answer, presumably, is that it is easier and more practical to deal with institutions than with individuals. But is it? Shall only those institutions be excluded which are foolish enough, after the passage of the Civil Rights Act, still to have some clearly discriminatory statute or regulation on their books? The civil rights movement has long since passed the point where it draws a distinction between legal segregation and de facto segregation. How then determine the degrees of subtle discrimination by various institutions? Is the answer what amounts to a loyalty oath for institutions, acknowledging compliance with this particular ALA policy? If so, could not the same procedure be applied in the case of individuals? Does the association want to get into the whole sticky area of loyalty oaths at all? For what other ALA policies might we expect compliance from either institutions or individuals?

For example, ALA has a position and policies on censorship which are quite as strong and quite as clear as those on civil rights. Should libraries which practice censorship also be excommunicated? *That* would make a dent in the institutional membership. Would ALA be able to measure or discern censorship any more or less effectively within an institution (or by an individual) than it can establish or prove discriminatory practices? Is the library which fills its shelves with segregationist books (and none in favor of integration) any less discriminatory than the library which bars the door to Negroes?

This is not an easy editorial to write. All our emotions pull in the direction of the Detroit resolution, but our reason warns against acting without much thought of where actions lead, even by implication. Laws or regulations or policies which are sentimentally fine but which cannot be implemented undermine rather than strengthen the purpose of the body which passes them. "The law is an ass," Charles Dickens once said, and he surely had in mind the often insupportable 19th Century laws that the British authorities were charged to enforce. We should not like to see ALA's increasingly commendable position in civil rights and civil liberties weakened by asininities.

This Detroit resolution demands intensive and wide discussion, and we hope that this editorial will incite a little of it. Whatever can be done to eliminate discrimination by libraries, we are for, but we are not at all sure that discrimination in ALA membership is the way to bring it about. May there be much hard thinking by the ALA membership, at all levels, between now and the New York conference in 1966.

*Eric Moon*

## TOKENISM AT THE TOP?
October 1, 1965

The library profession is under fire—again. The charge, again, discrimination. The victims this time, scarcely to be called a minority group, are women.

The charge was made by Miriam Y. Holden in May at the Washington Convention of the National's Women's Party. Mrs. Holden's address was titled "Discriminatory Practices in the Recruiting of Women for Leading Positions in the Profession of Librarian." It has been published in the August 23 issue of the *Antiquarian Bookman*.

Says Mrs. Holden: "Although women now represent upwards of 90 percent of the profession of librarian, they are represented *in the extreme minority* (our italics) at the top in the few rare jobs that carry highest pay and status."

She also forecasts that "As more attractive salaries and career opportunities open in the future, more men will enter the field to take over those middle-level jobs now filled by women librarians. Thus, fully qualified women in library work now face the plain prospect of being relegated to the lowest and middle-range of salaries and status in a profession which they actually dominate by numbers." There is, charges Mrs. Holden, "only tokenism at the top."

To support her case, Mrs. Holden quotes some rather old statistics from a 1950 *Library Journal* study which revealed: 1) that in ten of the largest library systems in the country, only six percent of the professional librarians were men, yet this six percent held roughly 50 percent of the jobs at the main library "where there are the best chances for advancement as well as professional recognition from beyond the library system itself"; and 2) that

84 percent of the head librarians of the largest college libraries in the country were men.

On the face of it, Mrs. Holden seems to have a strong case. For example, among the 46 large public libraries for which the Enoch Pratt Free Library issues annual salary statistics, there are only seven which are directed by women.

But then we started looking at some of the other seats of power and prestige in the library profession, and the picture began to look less black and white (male and female). The presidents-elect of both the American and British Library Associations, for example, are women. The president of Special Libraries Association is a woman.

With the surge of federal funds for library services and construction, it seems to us that among those who wield immense and growing power and influence are the state librarians and state library extension heads, and the state school library supervisors.

So what is the picture at the state level? More than 60 percent of the state librarians or heads of state extension departments are women. Among the state school library supervisors, there are only six men.

The library schools, we are sometimes told, are in a position to shape the profession of the future. Of the deans of the accredited library schools, nearly one third are women.

ALA itself is surely one of the most potent forces in librarianship today. There, Mrs. Holden could surely find small cause for complaint. The Deputy Executive Director is a woman. The executive secretaries of no less than eight of the divisions are from the distaff side. The Publishing Department, the *Booklist*, the Office for Recruiting, and the immensely influential Washington Office are all headed by women. Four of the eight members elected to the Executive Board by and from the ALA Council are women. Of the new members elected to the ALA Council this year, 15 of 24 are women. A majority of the members of the highly important Legislative Committee are women.

And finally, among the national library periodicals—which are thought by some to have some influence upon professional opinion—no less than seven have women as chief editors: the *Wilson Library Bulletin, School Library Journal, Special Libraries, Top of the News, Catholic Library World, Library Resources and Technical Services,* and the *LC Information Bulletin.*

We are not brave—or foolish—enough to take sides on *this* issue. But we do feel that Mrs. Holden might make a more convincing case if she brought her statistical ammunition up to date. We present these statistical fragments of our own only to show that her case is not so selectively simple.

*Eric Moon*

## ACCESS AND THE SUPREME COURT
April 1, 1966

Access to libraries has been high on the agenda and the conscience of the library profession, consistently, for a number of years. In its latest attempt to grapple with the problem, the ALA Council made a difficult decision—so difficult that it left uneasy even those who agreed with it—against closing the membership doors to those institutions which are still guilty of discrimination.

Only a few weeks after that Midwinter meeting, it became abundantly clear that decisions on access to libraries are not easy no matter at what level they are taken. A much higher body with somewhat more authority than the American Library Association—the United States Supreme Court—has divided five-to-four on the case of five Negro "stand-in" demonstrators who tried in 1964 to integrate the Clinton (La.) Public Library.

There was a measure of satisfaction in the Supreme Court decision for those who had argued, during the ALA Midwinter debate, that the law of the land could better take care of discrimination in libraries than could ALA with any further statements or constitutional amendments. Certainly, the latest decision of the Court appears to establish that Negroes may not be ejected from public libraries simply because they are Negroes.

But the unfortunate narrowness of the Court's decison may possibly herald the testing, again and again in various states, of even this clear-cut issue. If this happens, those who oppose racial discrimination in libraries may be subjected to the same continuing, tedious, expensive legal battle that has plagued and harassed the opponents of censorship. In this kind of situation, one wins only the immediate battle, never quite the war.

If that's not enough of a wet blanket of gloom to throw over a significant milestone decision, let us conjecture a little about some other problems that may be in store for libraries as a result of the views expressed by the dissenting minority on the Court—Justices Harlan, Clark, Stewart, and, most notably, Black.

These four held not only that the Clinton case involved no racial discrimination, but that the state has a right to put people out of its libraries if it wants to. Taking off from this shaky foundation in logic, Justice Hugo Black saw the majority view as a "threat" to "public buildings such as libraries" and concluded that "The states are thus paralyzed with reference to control of their libraries for library purposes."

We are inclined to agree with the *Washington Post* that Justice Black's is a somewhat "spongy premise" and that he has inflated the issue out of all proportion. But some libraries may well have cause to share the Justice's fears.

The Supreme Court decision, in this particular case, was a clear ruling against discrimination in access to libraries on *racial* grounds. If the majority of the Court disagrees with Justice Black on this specific issue, however, does it also disagree that the state has a right to put people out of libraries for *any* reason?

Whenever the profession had discussed access, it has always been in terms of discrimination on grounds of race, religion, or personal beliefs (though ALA's "Access Study" did, sketchily, concern itself with other kinds of limitations). Do the comments of the court's dissenters not now raise the issue of discrimination on grounds other than the usual big three? What of discrimination on grounds of age (the student "problem") or of residence (the non-resident issue)?

Is there not cause to believe that students might demonstrate—successfully—against some of the restrictions which have been placed upon their access to libraries? Could not nonresidents argue that they had a right of *free* access to libraries receiving generous support from state and federal funds to which their taxes had contributed?

It begins to appear that the line between an administrative decision on services to readers and discrimination against readers is becoming as hazy as the line that has never been adequately defined between book selection and censorship. We do not share Justice Black's view of this as a "threat" to libraries, but see it as another opportunity to clarify our objectives. If it makes us think—and do—more about solving the problems of access by all people to all libraries, perhaps we should welcome what some will only dismiss as a new parcel of problems which we should avoid until they are insuperable.

*Eric Moon*

# Tongue in Cheek

**TO BEGIN WITH . . .**
January 1, 1965

We haven't done this for years, but even an editorial page perhaps should relax on that desperate day after New Year's Eve. The offerings below are selective, miscellaneous, personal, and varying in their seriousness. But how else should New Year's resolutions be?

Resolution, like charity, begins at home, so we start with ourselves, but with the hope that some other library periodical editors might like to join us in resolving . . .

• To view with suspicion any article which carries in its title or first few paragraphs the words "challenge" or "image."

• Not to publish any more of those "how I run my library good" articles (we are indebted to Ralph Shaw for the phrase).

• Not to endorse a presidential candidate in 1965.

• To encourage every contributor to match every footnote referring to the wisdom of our professional patriarchs with one idea or thought of his own.

  • Never to publicly disclaim editorial responsibility for the views of the magazine's contributors, no matter how much we might disagree with them.

For library administrators, we offer the following sampling of suggested resolutions:

  • To substitute the phrase "the library problem" for "the student problem," wherever it may occur.

  • To consider, when presented with an idea by a younger and still idealistic member of the staff, not "is it practicable?" but "is it desirable?" and "how can it be done?"

  • To give a swift kick to any staff member who appears to regard personal service to any member of the public (student or not) as "spoon-feeding."

  • Not to plunge into automation, or any new system, gimmick, or piece of equipment, without being quite sure what the system or equipment is for, what its limitations are, and whether it will do even half of what its promoters say it will do.

A good year's beginning for book selectors might be to resolve:

  • To consider, first why the library *should* have a particular book, and not begin by searching for reasons to *exclude* it.

  • Never to buy a book on the strength of one review alone, even if that review appears in *LJ*.

  • And conversely, never to decide against buying a book simply because the *Booklist* failed to review, approve, or notice it.

  • To examine their shelves a little more often, rather than just checking the catalog or shelflist.

Certainly, the New Year is a time when conference planners, looking toward the new convention season, might resolve:

  • Never to have more speakers on the platform than there are people in the first six rows of the audience.

  • Never to plan four meetings if one will suffice to exhaust any material of possible interest—and to consider seriously whether even that one is imperative every year.

  • To remember that exhibitors pay for conventions and appreciate the small reward of seeing an occasional librarian sometime during the week.

Library school teachers might experiment with resolving:

  • To rewrite the lecture which has served nobly for more than a decade.

  • Not to expect students to read more in one week than they (the teachers) have read in six months.

  • To remember that a bored, uninspired student has a very good chance of becoming a bored, uninspired librarian.

For librarians everywhere, here are a couple of thoughts which may just be worthy of some kind of resolution:

  • If you have become so "busy" with administrative matters or participation in professional activities that you no longer have time to read a book occasionally, to ask what you can delegate, pass on to someone else, or drop, so that you can start being a librarian again.

• To spare a moment from all the "explosions" (population, publishing, etc.) and ask yourself why so many people are still *not* using the library—and to give at least a passing thought to the possibility that it may not be entirely due to their lack of interest but due, in some part, to lack of performance on the part of the library.

And finally, to all our readers with a point of view, why not resolve to let us hear from you at least once in 1965? We ask not for agreement, nor yet, necessarily, for controversy, just for a sound.

*Eric Moon*

## FOR UNSUNG HEROES: *LJ* AWARDS
December 15, 1965

As soon as the New Year turns the corner, the award season will be upon us with its annual abundance. The discovered and the deserving will be lauded in the professonal press and will take home cash or a certificate "suitable for framing," or both, after the ALA or SLA or other festivities. They need no recognition here—indeed, our crystal ball is not bright enough to tempt us to predict who they will be.

But every profession has its unsung heroes, its unique but un-epochal events, which receive neither official recognition nor warm applause from colleagues. Warmed by the gift promotion weeks that precede Christmas, we are prompted to make our own small offering to those who, while they deserve to escape obscurity, will almost surely not receive association accolades. *LJ* offers the following awards for "unusual accomplishment" in the library year of 1965:

THE ELMER GANTRY LIBRARY EVANGELISM AWARD—to Lawrence Clark Powell for urging librarians to "embrace tithing" and then announcing his retirement from the profession.

THE SALINGER-MOYERS MANAGED NEWS AWARD—to the Georgia Library Association for announcing publicly that E. J. Josey had been accepted as a member of GLA before telling Mr. Josey.

THE FIRE PREVENTION AWARD—to the United States Information Service for closing down its libraries in Indonesia.

THE CLOSING THE BARN DOOR AWARD—to the Ohio Legislature for raising the salary of the Ohio State Librarian a year and a half after that position was vacated.

THE COMPRESSED HOT AIR AWARD—to the International Federation for Documentation for cramming more than 180 oral presentations of technical papers into a five-day conference.

THE IF YOU CAN'T FIGHT 'EM AWARD—to Eric Moon for his editorial stand against the Oboler motion which would require institutional members of ALA to integrate, and for his defense of "caveats" in *LJ* reviews.

THE INDIAN GIVER AWARD—to the 89th Congress for passing into law both the Medical Libraries Assistance Act and Title II of the Higher Education Act, and then refusing to appropriate any funds to implement either measure.

THE FIFTH AMENDMENT AWARD—to the Conservative Library Association, whose membership list is a guarded secret.

THE DON QUIXOTE BRONZE WINDMILL AWARD—to Frances Clarke Sayers for her attack on Walt Disney in the *Los Angeles Times*.

THE MEDICARE AWARD FOR SOCIALIZED MENTAL HEALTH—to the New York Academy of Medicine for urging President Johnson to put the FBI on the trail of those who produce "salacious literature."

THE EXHIBITS ROUND TABLE EMMY AWARD—to Emerson Greenaway, best actor of the year, for his "realistic" portrayal of a familiar library administrator in the ERT show at the ALA Conference.

THE ROUNDED LIBRARY IMAGE AWARD—jointly to the Detroit bartender who said, "We're sure gonna miss you librarians," and to the Detroit cabby who described librarians as "really intelligent . . . swell joes."

A DECENT LITERATURE CITATION—to the Playboy Foundation for its announced plans to support a study of the effects of smut on readers.

THE INFORMATION EXPLOSION OR THUD (?) AWARD—to Dr. Aziz S. Atiya who brought back "ten tons of books" for the University of Utah from his "book-collecting and research tour of the Arab world."

THE KEEP 'EM GUESSING AWARD—to Grove Press for publishing a "clean" book, Mack Thomas's *Gumbo*.

HEADLINE NEWS OF THE YEAR AWARD—to Special Libraries Association for its *Objectives and Standards for Special Libraries* which notes, among other equally startling revelations, that "The special library serves all who have appropriate need of its services."

THE TRUE CONFESSIONS AWARD—to Jesse Shera for announcing that he had retired from the presidency of "the most impotent organization" he had ever known (the American Association of Library Schools).

THE PRACTICAL PROBLEMS IN COMMUNICATION AWARD—to Rutgers Library School for setting up a Bureau of Information Sciences Research headed by Ralph Shaw, who is in Hawaii.

THE REMAINDER OF THE YEAR AWARD—to the deservedly obscure publisher of *None Dare Call It Treason*.

*John Berry*

## NOTABLES OF 1967
December 15, 1967

Among family, friends, and neighbors, Christmas is the season for giving. On the professional front the season for beneficence comes later. The avalanche of association accolades begins to rumble in the early Spring, reaching full crescendo in the midsummer of ALA's content.

A couple of years ago, *LJ*, eager to give while the Christmas spirit was upon us, decided not to allow accomplishment to sit out the long, cold, winter months unrecognized. This year, there have again been so many Significant Achievements that we feel they demand recognition before the year is dead. Priority has once again been given to those whose achievements, while in our opinion certainly "notable" (to borrow an association term), will predictably be passed over by our professional organizations. We offer, therefore, the following awards for unusual accomplishments in the library year of 1967:

THE GIGO ("Garbage In, Garbage Out") AWARD to Farmingdale (N.Y.) Public Library trustee Carl Gorton, for his unique information retrieval breakthrough; he made, he said, a midnight search of the library's garbage cans, as "the only way I can get access to the library's files."

THE UGLY AMERICAN AWARD to the Mayor of Roswell, New Mexico, who said of the local librarian: "He's not an American citizen and he wears that beard. And he's a Buddhist. If you understand that, you understand the type of person he is."

THE ORDER OF THE BIRD to the Association of Assistant Librarians, which organized a beauty contest to choose a Miss Library World as its contribution to the 1967 British National Library Week.

THE TAKE OFF WITH BOOKS (Children's Book Week slogan) AWARD to the prisoners at Erie County Jail, Buffalo, New York, who used library books to jam open their cell doors during a protest sit-in.

THE CLEAN OLD MAN AWARD to Bill Katz, editor of *LJ*'s Magazines column, who recommended the *Realist* to "the reader who is a witness to the basic goodness and humor of man."

THE HIPPIE-AT-HEART AWARD to Foster Mohrhardt, president of the American Library Association, for his support of the Library Love-In recommended by the Manpower Conference in San Francisco.

THE REBEL WITHOUT A CAUSE AWARD to Mary Gaver, past president of ALA, who proposed a minimum starting salary of $8500 for professional librarians but received no support from the profession.

THE DEDICATION TO POVERTY AWARD to the Public Library Association, which adopted $7000 as a "standard" for beginning professional salaries in public libraries.

THE WILT CHAMBERLAIN AWARD, for creating opportunities for long, thin librarians, to William Dix of Princeton University Library, who is building an auxiliary storage library with stacks eight feet high and aisles .22 inches wide.

THE NO MAN'S LAND AWARD to Robert B. Palmer, the first male librarian to be appointed to Barnard College in its 78-year history.

THE BROAD VIEW AWARD to the Harvard Library Committee, which announced this year that Radcliffe girls will, for the first time, be allowed to use Harvard's Lamont Library.

THE C. NORTHCOTE PARKINSON ADMINISTRATOR'S AWARD to Elizabeth Morton, who proposed that on her retirement as Executive Director of the Canadian Library Association, *two* executive directors be appointed to succeed her.

THE OLDEST PROFESSIONAL IMAGE AWARD to Professor Ralph Black of the State University College, Geneseo, New York, who said: "I've always felt that Fanny Hill would make the ideal librarian. She certainly knew her skills, had her clients' interests at heart, and was anxious to try new methods."

THE SIGMUND FREUD LIBRARY EDUCATION AWARD to Howard Clayton, director of the State University College Library, Brockport, New York, who conducted a three-month, HEA grant-aided effort to discover what personality maladjustments were to be found among graduate students of library science.

THE PLANNED PARENTHOOD AWARD to the Isabel Babson Memorial Library, Gloucester, Massachusetts, for its book review program designed to help parents "direct and influence the character of their babies by pre- and post-natal reading."

THE MADISON AVENUE EDUCATOR AWARD to Jesse Shera who, asked why he wouldn't recognize a four-year undergraduate program for librarians, replied, "It's not how long you make it; it's how you make it long."

*Eric Moon*

# CHAPTER 3

# The State
# of the Art

Like everyone else, the librarian can dwell with passion and at great length on questions related to the nuts and bolts of his calling, and, not unsurprisingly, this is reflected in *LJ*'s editorial pages. Traditionally averse to library literature of the "How I Run My Library Good" school, *LJ* in the sixties was no more averse than the average librarian to taking part in a good argument about the running of libraries. Thus it spoke out on statistics, cataloging, reference work, book preservation, cooperation, and book processing. It commented on standards, the new media, acquisitions, and—at length—on library literature.

## General

### AN EXCEPTION IN EXPANSION
June 1, 1960

Under the neat headline "Great Oaks and Little Acorns," the *Stanford Library Bulletin*, April 8, 1960, presented statistics for the past ten years which, it is said, "show strikingly the expansion of library activity during this period." Certainly all the figures quoted illustrate great expansion of the Stanford University Libraries themselves—volumes cataloged during the year have increased by 21 percent, serial titles by 85 percent, expenditure is up by 126 percent, staff increased by 42 percent (most of it nonprofessional), and the hourly attendance at the libraries is higher by 41 percent.

So far it is a healthy story. But expansion in library *activity*? One figure down at the tail-end of the statistical table does not quite match up with this statement or with the rest of the picture. Circulation from the university libraries at Stanford has gone *down* in a ten-year period by ten percent, and at the Main Library it has gone down by as much as 22 percent. Circulation is not everything: we have said so ourselves, and have heard it said on numerous occasions, and with fine scorn, by reference and university librarians in particular. It may, however, be fairly considered one small sign of "library activity."

The exception in this story of expansion was so startling that we turned the page, expecting to find a simple and logical explanation. What has happened? Does the increase in attendance indicate that the libraries are so attractive that the students do all their reading there? Are there an increasing number of categories of books that students are not allowed to borrow for home reading? There is clearly some kind of a changing pattern in library usage here. The figures explain no such niceties, but the paradox invites inquiry.

*Eric Moon*

## SCIENCE AND THE HUMANITIES
July 1960

"It is reasonable to believe that a library should look to the opinions of the users, rather than to comparisons with other libraries, for judgments of its value." This is the opening sentence of a most interesting annual report for 1959–60 by Donald Coney, Librarian of the University of California, Berkeley. We agree that the belief is reasonable enough but doubt that the practice it suggests is applied by libraries as often as it should be.

"In their own research activities, in the direction of the research of graduate students working for advanced degrees, and in the conduct of their upper division and graduate courses," says Mr. Coney in his report, "the faculty members of the University are in a unique position to gauge the depth and quality of the Library's research collections." The report comments also that the evaluations provided by a questionnaire to the faculty "do not generally surprise." They are none the less interesting, particularly in view of the many attacks upon contemporary American education for its lack of emphasis and achievement in scientific and technological fields.

The emphasis, the highest degree of excellence, in *this* university library, is shown by the faculty's answers to Mr. Coney's questionnaire to be in the *sciences*.

Rated for its value insofar as general department use is concerned, the Berkeley collection proved to be strong in all areas. But while 80 percent found it excellent or more than adequate in the biological sciences, only 55 percent gave it a similar rating in the humanities, and only 46 percent in the arts. When the collections were assessed on the basis of their quality and depth in supporting faculty members' own research fields, the picture was much the same, with biological and physical sciences rating highest, and the humanities and the arts placing lowest. In the latter two fields, rating of less than adequate or poor were recorded by 23 percent and 26 percent respectively of the scholars queried.

A request that faculty members name also the library housing the best collection, in their specialties, with which they had ever worked, presented a picture of the Berkeley collections from yet another angle. Once again the biological and physical sciences ranked highest, "and the percentage of scholars queried who thought the Berkeley collections the best they had ever used decreased successively in the social sciences, the arts, and the humanities."

Mr. Coney outlines convincingly the reasons for this apparent lack of balance. He says: "The use of old, rare, and frequently unique source materials in advanced research in the arts and humanities, coupled with Berkeley's relative youth and immaturity among large research libraries, explains the relative inferiority of the research collections in these fields."

We found Mr. Coney's report the most absorbing to cross our desk for many months, and would like to see other instances of libraries measuring the worth of their collections in the eyes of their users.

C. P. Snow's comments on the "two cultures" and the no man's land which appears to exist between the scientists and the "intellectuals" suggests another avenue which might be explored by one of our university libraries. How much use is made of the arts and humanities collections by faculty members specializing in the sciences? Do professors of English and music and languages make any use of the science collections? Or *are* there two worlds, two tightly sealed little units, operating in complete unawareness of each other? And if so, is there anything the library can do to bridge the gap effectively? Is it not possible that the fragmentation of university collections into specialist departments, necessitated by the immense growth of the universities and their book collections, encourages the widening of the gap?

*Eric Moon*

## NEGLECTED SOURCES
July 1961

What does it cost to catalog and process a book? When a book has been lost by a reader, how much does it cost to replace it? How much cheaper is it to repair a book than to rebind it?

News bulletins and annual reports of individual libraries rarely make absorbing or exciting reading, but enough of them contain some useful up-to-date piece of information to make a general scanning worth the time of most administrators. Answers to questions such as those above—admittedly based on particular situations—are often more likely to be found in these "fugitive" sources than elsewhere.

A bulletin which is consistently both attractive and informative is *News Notes* from the Edmonton (Canada) Public Library. The March 1961 issue, for example, includes a preliminary study of the cost of purchasing, cataloging and processing a book. The study, which included everything except cost of machinery and depreciation, shows that at Edmonton the average cost per book (for purchasing, cataloging and processing, including supplies) went down from $1.31 in 1960 to $1.04 during a two-week test period in January this year. The drop is attributed partly to improved physical organization, better equipment, and the replacement of accession numbers by copy numbers. But the most interesting factor is that the library recently discontinued simplified cataloging "in favor of full form cataloging such as is done at the Library of Congress and the National Library of Canada."

Edmonton is not the only Canadian library to produce evidence of a growing cost consciousness. Another library which has been studying its processes and costs with some care is the Toronto Public Library. Its latest annual report for 1960, *Reading in Toronto,* includes the following average cost figures: to bind a book, $3.50; to repair a book, $1.40; to apply a plastic jacket, 15 cents.

"When fines or charges are calculated on long-overdue or lost books, the shocked sobered patron often remarks: 'It would be cheaper for me to buy the book myself.' True—for the individual, not for the library!" This comment appears in the April 1961 issue of *Rodgers Library Notes* from the New Mexico Highlands University in Las Vegas. A table is presented which shows that it costs about 2½ times the purchase price to replace a lost book—in the example given, $9.50 to replace a $4 book.

Student and nonresident pressures are two of the most important problems of public libraries today. An article in the Boston Public Library's *Schedules and Notes,* May 1961, reports that the studies by a New York management survey firm revealed that 60 percent of the users of the library's Periodicals Room were students. The staff of the library estimates that on a year-round basis the true percentage would be nearer 75 percent. Another table shows how the balance between resident and nonresident use has swung during the past five years at Boston. Forty-six percent of the Periodical Room users in 1956 were nonresidents; by 1960, the percentage had risen to 55, leaving the tax-paying residents well in the minority.

These figures from individual libraries are not perhaps very conclusive, but a carefully assembled collection of the results of such local studies would certainly reveal patterns and trends, and the facts would be helpful to all libraries facing similar problems.

Perhaps a card service should be started which would abstract this kind of data and note sources—a sort of "Facts on File" of librarianship. Perhaps this is a job for *LJ* or one of the other national periodicals, although most of them have too many obligations already. Or perhaps all that is needed is an expansion of *Public Library Abstracts,* which is already partially doing the job of collecting data of the kind we have mentioned. To be fully effective, the scope of this publication would have to be considerably widened, and certainly beyond public library horizons only.

*Eric Moon*

## CONFUSION AND CONVICTION
July 1962

We have written before in this column of Mr. John Ciardi, poet and controversial columnist of the *Saturday Review*. He is an anger-making man—in a sense like a beautiful woman, not easy to live with but hard to ignore—and sometimes we have taken the bait he has offered, and have bitten with fury. But we do now urge librarians to read his "Manner of Speaking" column in the June 2 issue of *SR*.

"May it not be," says Ciardi there, "that we have made too much of conviction as an ultimate goal? Show me a man who is not confused and I will show you a man who has not been thinking. He will be a man who has not asked enough questions.

"He will, in fact, incline to think that the reason for asking questions is to answer them. Is it? May it not be the greater merit of questions that they lead not to answers but to new questions, and the new questions to others, and they to others yet?"

Conviction, Ciardi argues, "is possible only in a world more primitive than ours can be perceived to be. A man can achieve a simple gnomic conviction only by ignoring the radical describers of his environment, or by hating them as convinced men have hated, say, Darwin and Freud as agents of some devil."

Leo Rosten touched on the same thought in our June 1 issue, when he referred to the men who have shaped our civilization, or most that is worth having in it, as those men "who resist the crippling effects of conventional education—who confront the known as if it is new."

One of the terrible dangers in our society, and in its educational processes, is that the *fact* too often seems to be elevated above the *idea*. People are being trained to look for answers rather than being taught how to ask questions. The speed reader lifts only the "pertinent facts" from the skimmed page. And the true limitation of the teaching machine is that it can only ask questions to which there are deliverable answers. (Suppose someone questions the question—what can the machine do about that?)

In our libraries, is the same trend not becoming dangerously apparent? The librarian experienced in book selection knows the perils of certainty. Back of him is the theory that he must or should provide alternatives. In front of him is the pressure of those certain men of the right and the left, and those with *convictions* about what is good and what is moral and what is right. But perhaps, after all, the areas of controversy are those that present the least danger, since here there is often an instinctive compensation, a provision of variety as the best defense against pressure from any direction.

May the greater danger not lie in the direction of the greater certainties? In our library services the accent falls ever heavier on words like "information," "source material," "reference." There is a growing and not always discerning preference for nonfiction over fiction. These are not *necessarily* nasty words or roads to perdition, but if we follow them too far or too devoutly we may well find ourselves running—and perhaps leading our readers, especially the young ones—always in the same direction toward the confirmable rather than the doubt-creating.

The telephone book, Mortimer Adler once said, is full of facts but it doesn't contain a single idea. It's a useful reference book, but is it essentially as *useful* a book as Hamlet, a play full of confusions, a play which poses more questions than it offers answers, a play which is endlessly fascinating because it is never the same?

Only the unreflective, says Ciardi, "always have their fast answers ready." And a better poet, Yeats, once said: "The best lack all conviction, while the worst/Are full of passionate intensity."

Libraries are not only places where fast answers may be found, and those who serve the young might perform their greatest service if only, to use Ciardi's words, they can "teach the sad young of this mealy generation the courage of their confusions."

*Eric Moon*

## SMALLNESS IS THE BIG PROBLEM
January 1, 1963

This issue begins the New Year with a collection of views on the major problems which face library service in this country (*see* "Diagnosis," pp. 39–50). Only a few of our respondents mentioned what seems to us the really gigantic problem—the awful waste and futility of the very small public library trying to operate alone.

Some attention is now being focussed on this target—other than the Library Services Act, which has done most to help. ALA's Small Libraries Project is on the road, armed with a shelf-full of pamphlets. And the Dorothy Canfield Fisher awards, once a single award, now reach out to reward and inspire small libraries in 48 of the 50 states.

But how many librarians *yet* realize how crucial is the problem to be solved? It was demonstrated again for us recently when we received from the New Hampshire State Library the annual statistics for the public libraries of that state for 1961.

Only ten libraries in New Hampshire serve communities with a population over 10,000, and only three of these serve over 20,000. Book expenditures of these "larger" libraries range from a high of $20,416 to a low of $2,574.

Fifty-seven libraries (in 51 communities) serve between 2,000 and 10,000. Here, the book expenditures range from $5,725 to $35. Just over half these libraries spend less than $1,000 a year for books—and one place, Swanzey, has *three* libraries whose *total* book expenditure is $728.

The vast majority of the libraries in the state serve populations below

2,000. In this range there are 160 libraries in 154 communities. The highest book expenditure is $2,291, and at the other end two libraries show *no book fund at all.* Only 12 libraries spend more than $1,000 a year on books, while 120 spend less than $500, half of those spend less than $200, and half of those again spend less than $100.

The annual statistics list another 27 communities which have "no public library, or inactive libraries." This raises the question: "At what point does a library become qualified for the *inactive* list?"

Among those recorded in the presumably active list are two, for example, which show no book funds at all. One has a *total* expenditure of $15, the other $10. One has an annual circulation of 288, the other records no circulation but has a book stock of 943 (acquired by gift?). Opening hours of these two "libraries" are recorded graphically as "anytime."

Is library service even remotely possible under these conditions? Professional staff are obviously out of the question. The bookstock in some of these libraries, with so little annual replenishment, *must* be stagnant. Reference collections cannot be contemplated.

We are all familiar by now with the pronouncements by National Library Week or the Library Services Branch that x-many people have no public libraries or are inadequately served. But these large figures are like water on a duck's back—they don't really touch us. We need perhaps to direct more public attention to the worst individual cases, be more specific, blow up the black spots.

A report some months ago asked: "Are Maine's Libraries in Focus?" The answer is, of course not. Nor are New Hampshire's. Nor are those multitudes of small libraries in some other states.

Hannis Smith, state librarian of Minnesota, warned some months ago that the writing was on the wall for small libraries (*LJ*, Oct. 15, '62, p. 3632), and commented: "The average newsstand of paperback books holds a better collection of general reading interest" than many of them. The typical small library, he said, "has never in its history offered any real range of library services, and never could, standing alone."

The release from the Book-of-the-Month Club on the Dorothy Canfield Fisher awards talks of the simultaneous presentation of the awards in 48 states as dramatizing "one of the most pressing problems of the American library system, the almost universal need of small libraries for more private and public financial support." It needs all the dramatization possible, and the efforts of the Book-of-the Month Club do not go unappreciated. But we wish they had not used the phrase, "the American library system." We have no system—despite Mr. Bryan's words—and shall not have until a thousand small communities are persuaded that library service in their present shoestring isolation is just not feasible.

*Eric Moon*

ZEAL AND APATHY

March 1, 1963

Our first issue of this year began with a long feature titled "Diagnosis." This was a collection of views and opinions on some of the major problems facing the library profession. Subsequent reaction indicates that many found the contributions interesting and perhaps, in some cases, valuable. We had two hopes for the feature: first, that at least one of the many "remedies" offered might lead to some kind of action intended to cure or relieve the ills described; and second, that other librarians and readers of this magazine, realizing that our 27 contributors had made only a beginning in uncovering and discussing the sources of our professional headaches, might be encouraged to come forward with their own "diagnoses."

The first of these two hopes turned out not to be completely pious. One, at least, of the contributions to "Diagnosis" has led an ALA committee to investigate the feasibility of the ideas put forward and the possibility of action.

The other hope could only have been born of incurable optimism on our part. Scarcely any among our thousands of subscribers has been persuaded to respond, to challenge the ideas propounded by our original contributors, or to offer their own solutions, criticisms or ideas. We should have known better than to expect it, for we have faced and have tried to battle with the sheer apathy of much of our readership for three years now. We are glad now to find that the president of the American Library Association finds this apathy as hard to take as we do.

At this stage, we should perhaps indulge in a little confession and admit that the idea for the "diagnosis" feature was stolen. It really originated with ALA President James E. Bryan who, before he took office, asked some 500 ALA members for their suggestions "as to matters of paramount importance to the profession" and "on matters of importance concerning the organization and functioning of ALA."

The action, we thought, was a splendid example of thoughtful, democratic leadership. On later discovering that President Bryan was somewhat disenchanted with the response he received, we decided to pursue the idea in the hope that publication of a number of ideas might produce others.

At the Midwinter meeting of ALA, President Bryan gave a brief account of his own survey, and in a forthright address, produced his version of "the number one problem of the profession and the association." It is, he said, *apathy*.

Mr. Bryan received only about a 50 percent return to his questionnaire, and it is a sad reflection on the 50 percent who did not reply that they will not respond even when called upon for advice and help by the president of their professional association. Said Mr. Bryan: "I am given to understand that 50 percent is a very high return, but since the list was prepared with a thoughtful randomness, if there is such a thing, one can't help but be impressed that interest and disinterest are pretty well balanced and that zeal and apathy pretty well cancel each other out."

Of apathy, he added: "This is the hardest kind of problem to deal with, the greatest difficulty to overcome. And how librarians can be apathetic at a time such as this is difficult to see. Because this is a time when there is the greatest need for interest in, and use of library materials. I can understand disagreement with current library practice and current association policies and procedures—but I have great difficulty in understanding disinterest and apathy. Ours is a service profession, and service minded people have no business to be apathetic."

President Bryan was realistic enough to admit that the solution to this problem is not easy, and to say that it isn't anything the ALA Council or Executive Board can do much about. It is something "we will all have to work at . . . for if we don't work on it, it will work on us." So all of you, the *un*apathetic, out there, have a job to do, a kind of recruiting *inside* the profession. There are dormant people all around you.

Just as we were writing this editorial, a report arrived of the second annual convention of the Society of Puerto Rican Librarians. At the meeting, outgoing president Antonio Matos commented: "As members, it is our duty to keep ourselves informed . . . to point out to the leaders of this Association the goals that are to be met and the activities that should be carried out in order to obtain them." Mr. Bryan, on the strength of his talk at Midwinter, would, we feel sure, agree.

*Eric Moon*

## AROUSED THOUGH RETIRED
January 1, 1964

In our introduction to the "Forecast" which precedes this editorial we mention a refreshing note of self-criticism which appears in the reports from some of the states. For example, the Michigan State Librarian says that, too often, our problems "are cited as a cloak to our own inertia and intellectual bankruptcy."

We have observed, with some interest, that while much of the library literature appears to be a parade of self-testimonials, some of the most pungent criticism of professional inaction often surfaces in the pages of newsletters and other publications of state libraries or state library agencies.

Perhaps the reasons are not too difficult to discern. State agency staff work with other libraries and librarians more than do most members of the profession. They frequently have to conduct legislative and other battles on behalf of other libraries and librarians, both at state and federal levels. They must sometimes wish there were more solid support behind them.

Apart from the Forecast, one newsletter, *News for Public Libraries,* published by the South Carolina State Library Board, brought these thoughts to mind. This publication regularly carries an Ann Landers-type column, headed "Your Problems, by Anne Library."

As in the newspaper variety of the Lonelyhearts species, the letters often seem to be manufactured or solicited—but no matter, providing they serve their purpose of igniting discussion, thought, self-examination. We reproduce here a part of one which may well do just that. Signed "Aroused Though Retired," it appeared in the November issue of the S.C. newsletter.

". . . What struck me in last week's sessions of the SCLA and in conversations with librarians attending the meeting was the readiness to lay the blame for inadequate services and support at the door of strangers. The enemy of library progress was variously identified with the Legislature, the county delegation, an indifferent public, and, I hesitate to mention, the requirements for participation in the State and Federal grant programs. I am convinced that the 'enemy' is closer at hand.

"In the Public Library Section meeting, the minutes of the 1962 meeting reported an enthusiastic session in which a campaign for a real increase in State Aid was endorsed, but in the report made by your Legislative Chairman, there was no indication that anything had been done to achieve this objective. Indeed, the subject was not even mentioned. Now, it would be hard to lay this failure at the door of the Legislature!

"At lunch one librarian mourned that her library had gone as far as it could on local funds, but when another at the table suggested the possibility of a regional combination of counties in an area for service, she recoiled from the idea in shocked surprise . . .

"An old friend came to me for help in locating a reference librarian; I knew of none, but when I suggested the possibility of sponsoring one of the SLB scholarship candidates, her answer was that she preferred someone for the job with less than full professional training because they 'usually stayed longer'! Alas, the poor public!

"One gentleman who is looking forward to retirement in a few years was firm in his determination to engage the library in no projects—'After me,' he said, 'They can do what they want to. In the meantime, we are going to just mark time!' Mark time? Rather downhill! . . .

"And from bits and hints from many sources, I gather that the South Carolina program suffers from the lethargy of many librarians who prefer a comfortable rut to the mental strain of examining what they are doing and re-planning to achieve efficiency and economy in operation."

Anne Library briefly acknowledges that the point made by Aroused Though Retired "is well taken," and comments: "Before we can wage a successful campaign for library progress, we must be sure that the 'enemy within' has been subdued and that our front is united."

Let us not give the impression that self-criticism is a cure-all. It is only a first step in the revitalization process, but it is a vitally necessary one if the many plans being made at state level throughout the country are to be translated into programs of progress and action at local levels. As Aroused

Though Retired says: "How can you move forward unless you can see where you are going?"

*Eric Moon*

## THE LOST WEEKEND
November 1, 1964

If memory serves us correctly, it was at the 1959 conference of the Canadian Library Association that we heard a witty, provocative speech by a Canadian scholar, Dr. F. M. Salter. Somewhere in the course of his remarks he told the librarians in his audience what he, as a user, expected in the way of library service. One of his expectations, we remember, jolted a number of people: it was that libraries be open around the clock. He was, said Dr. Salter, as likely to want to use a library for some specific purpose at three o'clock some morning as at three in the afternoon. Apparently he didn't sleep too well.

Last fall we escorted a large contingent of British librarians around libraries on the eastern seaboard. One of the factors which most impressed these visitors (and this time, because the interval is shorter, we know our memory is correct) was the extensive opening hours of American university libraries.

These rambles down memory lane were prompted by a tabulation we received the other day from the District of Columbia Public Library. It recorded the results of a recent survey of public library opening hours on Sundays and on Saturdays during the summer months. The libraries surveyed are among the largest in the country, but it is obvious that even in the nation's larger cities the hours of public library service on weekends are not on the whole very generous, particularly during the summer.

To summarize a few of the results, only ten of the 28 city systems surveyed open their main libraries on Sunday, and none of these is open for more than five hours. In the summer months, the number drops to three out of 28—Milwaukee, New York, and Louisville. Quite a few of the others had at one time opened on Sundays but have since abandoned the practice.

The Saturday hours were more of a shock. Three of these large city systems close down their main libraries all day Saturday throughout the summer, and three more are open for only half the day, either morning or afternoon. The extremes in Saturday service are illustrated by New York and Los Angeles at one end, and Cleveland, Queens, and Buffalo at the other. Los Angeles keeps its main library (and some branches) open from 10 A.M. to 9 P.M., year-round. New York goes one better, with its central circulation department and main reading room open from 9 A.M. to 10 P.M., year-round. Cleveland, Queens, and Buffalo, on the other hand, close down not only their main libraries but all their branches on Saturdays throughout the summer. Of the three, only Queens gives any indication that this situation is somewhat less than desirable; in the "Comments" column, Queens notes that the "objective for 1965 is to secure funds to provide year-round Saturday service in the new Central Library, presently under construction, and in larger branches."

In general, the comments by libraries indicate three principal reasons for not opening on Sundays or for restricting Saturday hours of service: 1) budgetary strain; 2) personnel shortages or difficulties; and 3) lack of use or demand.

On the latter point there are some curious conflicts or contrasts in the answers. While some libraries say that they discontinued Sunday opening because of "lack of demand" or because "use fell off" or "use did not justify expense," Louisville comments "Very busy on Sunday—Students," and Philadelphia declares that "throughout the academic year weekend attendance leads Monday–Friday attendance." Perhaps what one sees in this "Comments" column are not just different policies but different attitudes. Louisville seems to find student use sufficient justification for Sunday opening. Chicago, which stopped Sunday opening 15 years ago, says "When open, the use, for the most part, were students and the usual 'sitters'." And Portland, which also discontinued Sunday opening, comments "Use relatively low—mostly students."

No one underestimates the problems posed by weekend opening of libraries—or indeed by any extension of service hours. But some libraries, clearly, have overcome them, perhaps because they have given more weight to the positive factor of service than to the negative hurdles of cost and staff convenience. It is noteworthy, for example, that Cleveland, whose library system has the highest per capita expenditure of any of the libraries in this survey, complains that weekend service is "expensive" and is one of the three cities where there is no library agency open from Friday evening until Monday morning during the summer months.

When Walter Brahm drew some comparisons recently between the public library and the post office (*LJ*, September 1, pp. 3093–98), one respondent, Mr. W. A. Wilkinson, pointed out that "a few obvious characteristics were missing," and asked: "I wonder whether librarians, in emulating the post office as 'one of the greatest communication services the world has ever known,' would want to adopt them. If so, they would want to . . . provide no service from 5:00 P.M. Friday until 8:00 A.M. Monday." Apparently, you need wonder no longer, Mr. Wilkinson!

*Eric Moon*

## THE STATE OF THE STATES
March 1, 1966

Job description: Developing library collections; providing legal and financial advice to boards of trustees, library administrators, etc., administration (including establishing policies and procedures, resolving personnel problems, etc.); starting library systems and demonstration projects; giving advice on library buildings and remodeling facilities; public relations and publicity; planning and conducting conferences, workshops, training programs; conducting surveys. Desirable also: some specialized knowledge or experience of a particular type of library or library work. Responsibilities to be on a statewide or regional basis.

The assignments above emerge from answers to a recent survey by Marie Ann Long of the Library Research Center at the University of Illinois. They describe, perhaps in a composite way, *The State Library Consultant at Work*, which is the title of Miss Long's devastating report issued by the Illinois State Library.

What kind of person do you require for a job like this? How much, and what kind of experience should he have? And what do you pay him?

The answers to those questions, as indicated by the facts which this report brings together, are, to put it mildly, disturbing. You pay such a paragon of wisdom and experience somewhere between $6000 and $8000. That, at least, is where 47 percent of the state library consultants lie in the salary range—and some are even below that. Maybe the fact that you don't always get such paragons of wisdom and experience as the job description would indicate is, in some measure, attributable to such salaries. At any rate, one of every five state library consultants came to his job with no professional experience at all.

Library development at this point in time is more explosive and loaded with potential than ever before. What the business world calls "the rate of change of change" (or ROCOC, because one must use an acronym nowadays) has stepped up alarmingly. Librarianship, even its most passionate advocates must admit, has not, historically, been accustomed to the kind of overwhelming growth or opportunities which are now being thrust upon it.

The new pressure has opened up weaknesses, and while many of these weaknesses have been around for a long time, some of them didn't matter too much because they were not located at the points of greatest pressure. There has, however, been a fairly sudden and quite vast realignment of the power lines in librarianship, and Miss Long's survey highlights one important and exposed weak point that has been much discussed in bars and smaller rooms at conventions but largely ignored in public meetings and in print.

Historically, the state level has not been one of the most significant landmarks on the library scene. State governments contributed a miserable share of library income, and federal aid, until a decade ago, was still pretty much a vision. The best qualified, most influential, and best paid librarians were concentrated in the larger universities and city libraries, and certainly much of what power and money and influence there was in librarianship rested with those institutions and their administrators and governing bodies.

Now, however, the federal floodgates have opened and the dams that must control and distribute much of the emerging power are the state library agencies. It is at these points today that more can be done to reshape (or wreck) the future of librarianship than anywhere else in the profession.

Anyone who looks at the state library scene, in general (and, please, we *know* there are notable and highly encouraging exceptions), must be frightened by the inadequacy of that part of the nationwide library structure. Here is where librarianship should be accumulating the brightest minds, the greatest experience, the most dynamic leadership, the largest and most varied pool of specialized knowledge and ability, particularly including some of the profession's best political know-how.

Librarianship dare not leave so much of its potential for the future hanging from some of its weakest links; it must, if necessary, reinforce them by transferring strength from other more secure parts of the chain. If Miss Long's report brings up for public discussion a matter of concern that has been too long avoided—perhaps because it is difficult to talk about without personalities entering the discussion—it will have performed an important and much needed service.

*Eric Moon*

## NUMERICAL NEWS
May 1, 1966

Statistics are news in numbers. Like most neat, simple statements, this one needs qualification. This wise user or reader of statistics will regard them as news headlines rather than news proper, knowing full well that the headline scanner who never reads the background story predictably winds up with a much over-simplified, if not distorted, view of the world. This wise one knows also that statistical news, like news in other forms, can be managed; it's the selection that counts.

One package of the library statistics that makes a fair amount of news—judging from the number of media and the variety of forms in which it appears each year—is the table presenting the numerical facts of life in those larger university libraries which hold membership in the Association of Research Libraries.

It is undeniably an interesting tabulation, scanned as fervently in academe as the racing sheet in public library reading rooms. Who has moved up in the ratings? Does UCLA continue to climb? (Yes, it does.) Does Texas still spend as much on books as any three other universities? (Yes, it does.)

Just as big numbers make big headlines, this list impresses mostly by virtue of the size of the numbers. Of the 64 libraries in the version of the list we were examining, 36 are in the volume-millionaire bracket, and another dozen are only a year or two from that status target. This, clearly, is an elite group (it's the selection that counts). But a problem arises when this kind

of selection gets widely distributed and noticed: it is too easy for the uninformed to gather the impression that Brobdignag is the world. The average
member of society rarely sees such a carefully selected, balancing view of
the Lilliput of the library world.

However much the large libraries in the ARL listing may claim to be
hurting under the pressures arising from human, creative, and technological
fertility, the figures will still look plump and comfortable to the layman or
legislator who does not understand the pressures or their effect upon libraries.

At about the time we were examining these ARL statistics, there came
to our desk another tabulation of annual statistics. They cover the same
period as the ARL figures and are issued by the Oregon State Library. The
*Directory of Oregon Libraries* is concerned, of course, with all libraries in
the state, but we took a particular look at the bookstock and staffing figures
for college and university libraries. Our conclusion is that these numbers are
as headline-worthy as ARL's, but one can bet that they will receive far less
attention. (We are not, let it be understood, "picking on" Oregon. Its statistical story may be no better or no worse than any other state's, for all we
know. But we just happened to catch the Oregon figures when this editorial
was brewing, and they will do splendidly as an example of our point.)

A few details: Of the 34 academic libraries in Oregon (we excluded one
new one for which no figures were given, and the Dental and Medical
School figures which were included in the University of Oregon statistics),
nearly half (16 libraries) have less than 20,000 volumes. Seven of these,
indeed, have less than 10,000 volumes. Even this does not convey how low
the figures can go: one library has only 1,878 volumes, another only 775!

The staffing picture revealed by the Oregon statistics is not much
brighter. Only 14 of the 34 libraries have more than two professional staff.
Twelve libraries have one or less.

Like other professions and groups, librarianship uses statistics often as
propaganda (i.e., news selected or "managed" for a purpose). The cause
which we hope the statistics will help is better library development, more
substantial public support. The ARL statistics represent, at least approximately, the 60-odd best supported academic institutions. Why not issue (a
job for ALA?), at the same time each year, another tabulation showing the
situation in the 60 most abysmally supported academic libraries in the
country? The one thing that can compete in news value with bigness is
dramatic contrast.

The massive aggregate figures in the *National Inventory of Library
Needs* are useful as background propaganda, but they do not, in our view,
have the impact of the careful, and smaller, selection of specific examples.
What better way to illustrate how far we have to go than to show as
examples some of the libraries which have scarcely begun?

*Eric Moon*

RESEARCH IN BIRDLAND
March 15, 1968

"The state of the library art is for the birds." The words are those of one of the library profession's most honored heretics, Verner W. Clapp, speaking at a recent meeting in New York.

The former president of the Council on Library Resources, some might think, has perhaps been in a better position during the past decade to do something about changing the state of the art than almost anyone else in the profession. His surprising verdict, however, "at the end of 11 years, $10 million, and 413 grants, contracts, and projects," is that "the work of CLR has brought about a great many improvements in processes, procedures, and tools . . . but, on the whole, the state of the art is just about where it was when we started."

CLR's ten million dollars, he indicated, have had a less pervasive impact on libraries than have such broader developments as air conditioning, slab construction of buildings, and photo-offset lithography. And the Xerox 914, Clapp added, "has done more for the improvement of library service than anything else I have mentioned."

CLR came into being in the same month, in 1956, as the Library Services Act. "Which," Clapp asked, "has had the most effect on library service?" The CLR program and federal library legislation "have had the same premises and objectives and have followed an almost parallel course—but the introduction of national governmental support for libraries has been among the great movements of our time."

Some soothsayers in our business, after gazing into their crystal balls, have pronounced that technological developments will be among the major influences in improving library services of the future. Clapp, to our surprise—and perhaps to yours—declared that "the state of the library art is not really advanced by technical improvements. It only seems to be advanced." These changes—"from goose-quill to typewriter to photostat to Xerox to LDX"—are all absorbed gradually, almost unconsciously, "but we wind up doing essentially the same things—perhaps faster," Clapp said.

The fundamental point in the former CLR president's speech seemed to be that the library profession must learn to discriminate more (and perhaps adjust the balance of its thinking) between "the apparatus" and "performance"—by which latter term, we think, Clapp meant "service." As the machines, and the men who can run them, take over more and more of the mechanics of librarianship, "librarians will be left with the exclusive duty of giving service." It is in this area—service—that libraries still seem to be doing the same old things, that the state of the art has not advanced along with the march of technology.

Clapp went on to issue a number of warnings which are beginning to sound familiar but which are still ignored or scoffed at in some quarters. Unless present services are modified and extended, libraries will be left behind. They may be able to survive just by being traditional and hoping to grow larger with federal fertilization, but Clapp doubted it—and so do we. There are already signs that cost may become a troublesome factor, he noted, and indications of growing competition for the available dollars. Unless libraries find better answers to present service gaps and what Clapp described as "a great information void" at the local level, they may begin to find the sources of fiscal supply drying up. Libraries, said Clapp, "don't even know how to get to the ordinary person."

There is, as Clapp observed, plenty of research money now available to the library profession—so much that CLR's millions have now become a drop in the bucket. The former CLR president indicated, however, that it is not always spent very wisely: too much of it goes on "bootless inquiries that just wind up in the data slot when they are finished." Certainly, the library field seems to have been, in Clapp's words, "surveyed to death." He cited numerous studies in progress or just completed, such as the 17 done for the National Advisory Commission on Libraries. And then he asked: "What in the hell are we going to do with all this information?" And "what do we want to know?"

Our feeling is, if Clapp's analysis of the state of the art is accurate, that perhaps more of the research money and effort should be put to solving those service problems and gaps, and rather less should be devoted to tinkering with "the apparatus." CLR, itself, could do more to give a lead in this direction.

*Eric Moon*

# Cataloging and Classification

## WHO CARES ABOUT THE CODE?
May 1, 1961

We may as well confess at the outset—be it heresy or no—that we find it difficult to get very passionate or excited about cataloging theory. We have worked in, and organized, cataloging departments, but these interludes do not remain in our memory as among the creative highspots of library life.

This confession of weakness is made because we suspect that there are many noncataloger librarians whose disinterest has enabled them to remain blissfully unaware of the smoke signals arising from the inner conclaves of catalogers heatedly discussing ALA's draft catalog code. This draft represents more than ten years' work by Seymour Lubetzky, more than the thousands of words in print and across the conference tables—it portends a potential upheaval of mammoth proportions in the years ahead.

The two lead articles in this issue touch on some of the critical considerations, and we would endorse most heartily Mr. Watkins' insistence that the code revision "is of concern to *all* librarians and particularly to librarians in service departments who interpret the catalog to users of the library." Catalogs are not *for* catalogers, though there are too many which appear to have been conceived in that image. Many catalogers would do a better job if they were required to spend more time in public departments and become aware of the deficiencies of their end product. And many catalogs would be better if the librarians in the public departments showed more concern over them, and could spell out in catalog-educated terms to the boys in the back room what their needs are in helping the public.

The core of the argument over the code revision—though there are many other areas of disagreement—seems to be whether the new code should, on the one hand, provide a rigid set of rules designed to cover every possible contingency, or on the other, a set of what Mr. Lubetzky has called "unifying principles." The main opposition to the Lubetzky draft comes from "a school of thought which maintains that economy in cataloging requires a code of rules which could be exercised without the exercise of judgment by the cataloger" ("Development of Cataloging Rules," by Seymour Lubetzky, in *Library Trends,* October 1953).

This slight overstatement gets to the heart of the matter. On all the evidence we have seen of the results of individual catalogers' judgment, we should have to join forces with those who believe that the joint causes of economy and uniformity might best be served by keeping to the minimum the degree of dependence upon such judgment.

Mr. Dewton's list of cataloging samples—what one librarian has called "a chamber of horrors"—does much to strengthen this belief (pp. 1726–29). If this list of "howlers" represents the work of professional catalogers in some of our largest and most respected academic and research libraries, the possibilities in lesser institutions present unlimited scope for a fertile imagination.

The financial aspects alone dictate that no revision should ignore the "here and now." In an age of library cooperation and interlibrary loan, no individual library's catalog is an island. At the heart of cataloging cooperation sits the Library of Congress; anything which could conceivably play havoc with its present card distribution and its printed catalogs must, at the very least, be considered with great vigilance by all members of the profession.

It is all very well to talk about the "modern needs of catalogers," but the needs of the public and of the librarians who serve them must be the first consideration. All librarians should care about the code, and consider with more than passive interest the possible effects of what Mr. Lubetzky has characterized as "the change from formalism to functionalism."

*Eric Moon*

## FORWARD OR BACKWARD?

May 15, 1966

"A challenge—The Index to the 17th edition is its most radical departure from earlier editions; as said by its editor it is unique. It is challenging and it is likely to be challenged. But so was the whole of Dewey's first edition, and others after it. Other innovations, the Standard Subdivisions and the Area Table are not challenging; the Area Table is not an innovation except in DC. But these innovations and the expansion and clearing up of the tables are satisfying. The Index may provoke, but the 17th edition as a whole carries on the pick up and drive of the 16th. The Index after all does not affect the improvement, the expansion and updating of the tables. This is one of the must editions. The choice is to go forward with it, or backwards without it."

The above words are those of John Metcalfe, director of Australia's first postgraduate school of librarianship at the Univeristy of New South Wales, and noted classification authority. They appear as the last paragraph in his new pamphlet, *Dewey's Decimal Classification, 17th Edition: An Appraisal* (Sydney: James Bennett, 1965).

We read this pamphlet, with some surprise, not too long after returning from the Midwinter meeting of the American Library Association in Chicago in January. We say surprise because it was at that Midwinter meeting that we first began to be aware of the hostility among the cataloging and classification fraternity toward the 17th edition.

Since then we have attended other meetings where that hostility has been naked and powerful. In fact, when we read aloud the Metcalfe paragraph above, at a meeting of technical services librarians in New York, there were some present whose reactions were what one might expect if one read aloud from *Last Exit to Brooklyn* at a Wednesday afternoon housewives' tea party.

We have heard some of the specific criticisms and rumblings. Some unhappiness is created by the amount of relocation (and the cost of it) necessitated by the 17th edition. But this is not a new problem; it has occurred edition after edition. As the Editor's introduction points out (p. 46), the DC Editorial Policy Committee has concluded "that a reasonable amount of continuing change is not only desirable but inevitable." The question remains whether the amount in Dewey 17 is "reasonable."

Others complain that the greater stress on hierarchy implies even longer numbers. This, too, is no new complaint where the DC is concerned; though some of the examples offered since the appearance of Dewey 17 *are* horrific. For example, a book entitled *Tentacles of Power* (World, 1965), a book about Jimmy Hoffa, now rates the number 331.88113883240924! We appreciate that Hoffa is something special and that he has incited superlatives (of various kinds) before, but this is ridiculous. However, we have always felt that classifiers, had they the will, could chop such theoretical nonsense down to size without creating future chaos in the collection or the catalog.

It is, however, the Index to Dewey 17 which has most "provoked." But what is it about the Index that upsets so many so much. Certainly, it is imperfect, and certainly it is reasonable to argue for something nearer to perfection. But imperfection is nothing new in a Dewey index.

The Editor claims that the Index "is *limited*, because exhaustiveness would be confusing and, if it could be kept up to date, would make the tables unnecessary; it is *coordinated with the tables*, serving as a guide to them, not a substitute for them." The Index, in fact, has been cut by more than 36 percent since the last edition, from 1003 pages to 637.

Is the main impact of the revamped Index, then, as the Editor implies and Metcalfe states: that "the classifier is forced into the tables, to find and understand a classification, which is an avowed intention"? And is *this* the root cause of the discontent? If so, it seems that, even after decades of teaching that one must classify from the tables, we have some sort of implied confession that practical catalogers have relied much more heavily on the Index than has been openly admitted.

We'd be interested to hear from a few classifiers and teachers of classification just what is so horrific about Dewey 17 and, in particular, its Index. And we have no doubt that the DC Editorial Policy Committee would welcome such information, too. If we get some replies (not more than 500 words per contributor) in nonjargon English, understandable to those whose lives are not spent contemplating classification theory, we'll be glad to print them.

*Eric Moon*

# Reference

## FUTURE DIRECTIONS IN REFERENCE SERVICE
April 15, 1960

"What is reference work?" asks one of the contributors to this issue. It is a good question. What indeed is a reference library? Harvard University Library and the New York Public Library would seem to qualify within any reasonable definition. But what sort of definition does it take to include the dark alcove grandiosely announced as "reference department" in the small street-corner branch library?

In this standard-saturated world it is a curious anomaly that reference work, which so many librarians regard as the highest form of library science, should remain the most ill-defined and poorly recorded area of our work and service. Such slender evidence as we do have of the impact of public reference libraries is not particularly encouraging.

Nearly two decades ago Lionel McColvin declared that reference service was the outstanding failure of British librarianship. In quieter terms the Public Library Inquiry, ten years later, delivered much the same verdict on American reference library service. Its nationwide survey revealed "that for many people their library had little significance as a source of information. Their answers indicated that it just did not occur to them to go there for such purposes."

At the beginning of this new decade Lawrence S. Thompson, in the January 1960 issue of *Library Trends,* appropriately crystal-gazes into the future and sees the day "when research libraries will have their millions of titles and public library systems their tens of millions of books. Title or volume count will mean little. The best libraries will be those which base their claims to excellence not on quality but on the completeness of their reference collections. . . ." For many libraries Mr. Thompson's day is far off and difficult even to see without a stronger lens, perhaps hope-rose tinted. Today the comments of McColvin and the Public Library Inquiry, however, seem almost as valid as when they were made.

We have delivered before the platitude that cooperation is the keyword for library service today and tomorrow, and unashamedly repeat it, for nowhere is it more true than in the field of reference provision. Only a tiny proportion of our public libraries can ever hope to be able to afford the collection in great depth and the specialized staff necessary for anything more than rudimentary reference service.

Los Angeles Public Library, in a recent survey on student use of its libraries, discovered that 25 percent of the student requests for information at branch libraries went unanswered. What would be the percentage of unsatisfied requests if other than student demands were taken into consideration? And if this is the position in a large city with the resources of the Los Angeles Public Library, how much worse is the situation in the small town or rural area with very much more limited resources?

The developments in the Nassau Library System, described in this issue, are perhaps an encouraging step in the right direction, towards cooperative reference provision. The subject specialization between cooperating libraries and the interloan features in the Nassau system are also indications of a break with the tradition of one large, static central collection to serve an area. Certainly developments of this kind will be necessary if smaller communities in more rural areas are ever to receive adequate reference service.

Where great reference libraries do exist, they no longer serve a single city or university, and it is no longer reasonable that they should be supported by a single city or university. The Boston Public Library drew attention to this point recently when it announced that payment by non-residents for circulation service did not solve its problem, which was an overload by non-residents on the reference library service. Even the great libraries need assistance to cope with the surging demand for information, and a wide basis of support—regional, state or federal.

*Eric Moon*

## REFERENCE VAGARIES
April 15, 1964

When we wrote to the president of ALA's Reference Services Division, asking for suggestions for this annual reference issue of *LJ*, we were mildly surprised to find an article on interlibrary loan among the proposals. Then, as this issue was in preparation, there arrived on our desk a copy of the January *Library Trends*, devoted to "Current Trends in Reference Services." There, large as life again, was an article on inter-library loan and, this time, roundly described in the title as "A Reference Service."

Lest our surprise surprise anyone, let it be clear that we do not in any way minimize the importance of interlibrary loan. We agree absolutely with Mr. Reynolds (*see* p. 1692–94) that it is a key element in library service, deserves greater emphasis while our library resources are so unevenly distributed, and should be bounded by far fewer restrictions. But we *are* curious as to why Mr. Reynolds, the *Library Trends* editors, and others regard interlibrary loan so adamantly as a *reference* service.

True, the interlibrary loan procedure is often handled by reference librarians in the larger libraries. True, it often involves evaluation at some stage, and some bibliographical checking or searching. But these factors alone do not make it a reference service. In any sized library evaluation of a subject request and some bibliographical checking must certainly be performed sometimes by other than reference librarians.

By its very name and nature, interlibrary *loan* seems to us a circulation function or service. And perhaps it should be, for several reasons. In the majority of libraries (i.e. except the large libraries, which are most often on the receiving end), interlibrary loan *has* to be handled by other than reference staff, because there are no such animals in sight. ALA's reference survey, published in 1961, demonstrated that, even among medium-sized libraries, only 37.4 percent have a full-time professional working in reference.

Beyond the valuation or decision process—whether or not a book *should* be borrowed (and this is a place where some liberalization is due)— much of the interlibrary loan process is routine. If we believe we can teach students to make good use of basic bibliographical tools, why can we not use intelligent nonprofessionals to do the same? Reference service has been, in general, the most undervalued, the most ill-defined, and the least well staffed of all library operations. It cannot afford to be overloaded with functions which can as easily, and as well, be performed by others.

There is another reference/interlibrary loan matter that has always mildly troubled us. Why do so many libraries discriminate against their own readers? Restrictions against borrowing a "reference" book from Library X may be quite severe (so far as its own patrons are concerned). Yet Library X will cheerfully send on interlibrary loan, 50 miles away to Library Y, the book it has refused to allow one of its own patrons to take 300 yards down the road to his home. In the next county or state, the reader who uses

Library Y happily marches away to home and hearth with the book belonging to Library X under his arm. It works in reverse too. No logic, but it has been going on for more than half a century.

But the whole field is full of vagaries. We have tended, as in many other instances, to build artificial barriers. We have adopted as our unsung definition of a reference book, the book which must be used in the library building. But the odds are that a majority of the books taken home from libraries, in these days of student pressure, are used also for reference purposes.

In fact, librarians, particularly in branch libraries and small libraries generally, more often find their answers to reference questions in "circulating" books than in "reference" books. They have to, because so many of them have so few books set aside for use in the library only (i.e. reference books). The fact that neither books nor questions can so easily be categorized is, of course, one of the best arguments for subject departmentalization in larger libraries, because even they cannot answer all the questions from the books set aside for "reference."

If there is a point to these musings, it is that point which Samuel Rothstein and others have so often stressed—that reference service, more desperately than any other area of librarianship, urgently needs reappraisal, evaluation, definition and measurement. If it wasn't clear before, it should be plain, in the second half of the twentieth century, that reference service is the most vitally important of all library services.

*Eric Moon*

## THE UNRESERVED BOOK
May 15, 1965

"Who is bold enough to throw textbooks to the dogs, and lead his class through the recesses of a library?" challenged Justin Winsor in the March 1878 issue of *LJ*.

Rooting around in Melvil Dewey's shortlived *Library Notes* we found a brief piece entitled "Restricted Reference Books," which, in our opinion, is related to Winsor's question. It was unsigned, in the December 1887 issue, and for all we know might have been written by the Great Man himself:

". . . a new vice developed itself. Sum students in their zeal for lerning wanted it all; and, as books wer on open shelves where each helpt himself, we soon found that the books most wanted often disappeared. Usually they were hidden behind other books on open shelves . . ."

The author (Dewey or a disciple?) goes on to detail a system for "Restricted Reference Books" identical to the Reserve Book system still in use in many colleges, even down to the "long slip," 7.5 x 25$^{cm}$, still offered in library supply catalogs. We don't know, but it is our guess that this was the beginning of the reserve book system. If it was a Dewey innovation, our shining image of the "father of modern American librarianship" is slightly tarnished.

How does the Winsor challenge relate to the "Restricted Reference Book?"

The most recent documentation of the implications of Winsor's question is provided by Patrick Barkey in the March issue of *College and Research Libraries* (*see* "Patterns of Student Use of a College Library," pp. 115–18).

In one college, according to Barkey's study, 63 percent of the students borrowed no books at all from the closed-stack library during a 30-day period. The grade point average for the entire student body was 2.45 while students who borrowed *no* books achieved a passing 2.30. Among those earning a "B" or "B—" (2.5 to 3.0) average, 56 percent didn't borrow a book.

These findings are not entirely new. Harvie Branscomb, in his *Teaching With Books* (1940), told us that students ". . . do not use the library's books because in a great deal of their work they do not have to . . ." and John Weatherford, in a 1961 *CRL* study concluded that, "Generally, independence in reading went unrewarded by grades."

Despite this evidence, and more, the anguished cry is that student pressure on academic libraries is too great, and getting worse. One answer to one aspect of this pressure has been the "reserved book system." Aside from being a nifty pedagogic crutch for tired and aging faculty, it relieves undergraduate demand for the rest of the book collection. The professor, intimidated by student resistance to textbook purchases, and secure because he can "reserve" the material he knows and require that it be read, can thus keep the students from going beyond him in the rest of the collection and will gladly reserve massive numbers of titles in multiple copies at great expense to the institution and to the library. Henry Wriston, in his *Academic Procession,* says it best, ". . . the reserve shelf, instead of facilitating use of books, was often, in actual practice, a barrier to their effective employment. Many students never touched any other books; the catalogue, the reference works; bibliographical aides of every kind were all neglected."

Many academic librarians tell us they have no business in the classroom, that such an intrusion violates sacred concepts of "academic freedom." We hope they will reread Branscomb and Wriston, both of whom invaded that forbidden realm. They might even be convinced, as we are, that there are really two "student problems." One is the increasing pressure on academic libraries from undergraduates. It gets all the publicity.

The other "student problem," most recently rediscovered by Barkey, suggests, on the contrary, that students are *not* using the library. In the long run it is probably more serious. To solve it academic librarians will have to accept some responsibility for the instructional program in their institutions. One way might be to restore that quaint tradition whereby they were duty bound to inculcate the library habit in undergraduates. Another would be to re-declare Henry Wriston's "30-year war" on the reserve book and the other barriers which not only allow but encourage a bookless bachelor's degree.

By engaging in these two crusades the academic librarian might create a "real" problem of student use of the library.

*John Berry*

# Library Building

## TEAMWORK IN BUILDING
December 1, 1960

As usual, our annual architectural issue includes no more than a selection of the new building stories received, and those we received or solicited represented only a fraction of the multitude of new libraries being built in all parts of the country. If any trends are discernible in this welter of bricks, glass and concrete, the most obvious are that California appears to be building more new libraries than any half-dozen other states, and that building of new college and university libraries is moving into very high gear to cope with the swelling invasion of books and students.

The latter perhaps accounts for the unusual fact of two new books on college and university library architecture simultaneously in preparation. Earlier this year, Ralph Ellsworth, Director of the University of Colorado Libraries, announced that he was beginning a book which would lay some stress on the written program compiled during the planning stages. This he described as "one of the areas of library building planning that is in most need of critical analysis."

Later, Keyes Metcalf revealed that he would be busy for the next four years preparing a book on college, university and research libraries with the assistance of a grant made by the Council on Library Resources to the Association of College and Research Libraries and the Association of Research Libraries. One of the interesting aspects of this venture was the appeal Dr. Metcalf made (*see LJ*, July, p. 2502, 4) for librarians to send him frank comments on blunders in library architecture that have come to their attention. We liked particularly the fact that this appeal was directed, not only to those who have been involved in planning, but to library staff at all levels. As Dr. Metcalf points out, those who have not been responsible for the mistakes may be more outspoken in their criticism.

Staff participation should not, of course, be restricted to grousing and criticism after the event. John Henderson, Los Angeles County Librarian, stressed at a building clinic held recently in Pasadena, the need for staff consultation in the planning process, involving, in addition to the professional staff, the pages, clerks, janitors, and others who may often be more aware of detailed and specific needs or deficiencies than those responsible for the administration.

Much of librarianship is teamwork, but this is probably nowhere more true than in the planning of a library building. The basic core of a building team, according to Martin Van Buren, Interior Planning Consultant, of Charlotte, North Carolina "is comprised of three members: 1) The Government Authority, whose primary duties are legal, appointive, and financial; 2) The Librarian, who is generally the coordinator (or, you might say, the moderator of the Planning Team) . . .; 3) The Architect, whose duties include advice on site selection, preparation of initial size and cost requirements . . ." Mr. Van Buren mentions two other members who can contribute invaluably to the success of the building. One is the Library Building Consultant, "generally an expert thoroughly versed in both library practice and in architectural procedures; thus he offers an experienced liaison between the librarian, who perhaps has never before faced a building project, and the architect, who may possess a limited background in the architectural needs peculiar to library function and operation." Last, but not least, Mr. Van Buren naturally adds, is the Interior Planning Consultant. Like Ralph Ellsworth, Mr. Van Buren also emphasizes the importance of the written program, describing it as "that vital outline which is the basic key to a successful library."

These comments, and much more practical help and common-sense advice, appear in *Guidelines for Library Planners*, edited by Keith Doms and Howard Rovelstad (ALA 1960, $3.75). This consists of proceedings of the Library Buildings and Equipment Institute held at the University of Maryland in June, 1959, together with two papers on "To remodel or not to remodel" presented at the Washington ALA Conference. We particularly like the comment of architect J. Russell Bailey: "If the staff is not working efficiently because of building handicaps, then money is being poorly used. 'It's not the heat; it's the humidity,' we say in Washington. In libraries it's not the building cost; it's the staff cost."

*Eric Moon*


## BRANCHES—MORE OR LESS?
December 1, 1964

The Standard in 1956: "Community libraries and bookmobile stops should be provided at intervals so that every school-age child is able to reach a library outlet alone." (*Public Library Service*, ALA)

The Changing Scene in 1962: "The same sort of effort, now belatedly under way to persuade many small independent public libraries to join regional systems, should be matched by active discouragement of any more branch libraries too small and too weak to do more than distribute books." (Joseph L. Wheeler and Herbert Goldhor, *Practical Administration of Public Libraries*)

A Forecast in 1964: "[The] revolution in private transportation . . . does away with the need for multitudes of costly small branches of public libraries where service potential is relatively low. Many towns and cities where libraries face an inheritance of . . . decentralization could provide more adequate library service at more reasonable costs with a proper central library building which employs a bookmobile to supplement private and public transportation." (Kenneth Shaffer, "Library Building Needs in Massachusetts," in *The Bay State Librarian*, July 1964)

The philosophy of public library service—if we interpret it correctly from this selection of library literature—has undergone radical revision during the past eight years especially in regard to the provision of branch library services. The population explosion and the transportation revolution have been responsible for much of the changing pattern. No longer is it necessary nor even financially feasible to build a network of small "within walking distance" facilities as called for in the Standards of 1956. Service areas are now measured in terms of driving time, and in such branch programs as Milwaukee's (described in this issue, pp. 4737–39), building plans now provide for fewer but larger, stronger branches.

Wheeler and Goldhor, in their study of the general library scene, also note the strengthening of branches and the distinction between mere book distributing depots and *library service* branches. "If branches are fewer each can be larger; and with parking difficult at most central libraries, branches play a larger part than ever in the city-wide service pattern. Librarians are taking a new look at the place and function of branches."

Quite a different look at branches is taken by another librarian who sets his sights on one specific, well-established, and older section of the country. Mr. Shaffer places the responsibility for more adequate service squarely on the shoulders of the central library but points out the need for a "proper" library building and bookmobile service to supplement this type of centralized operation.

Obviously many central libraries are unequal to the challenge of providing more "adequate service" because of the limitations of their own physical facilities. Larger buildings, requiring strategically located sites, with sufficient provision for parking, will be essential in this pattern of centralized library service. It is obvious also that metropolitan libraries planning such expansion will incur tremendously high building and site costs.

Two main public libraries which have faced the problems of enlarging and relocating their buildings are St. Petersburg (pp. 4714–16) and Plainview–Old Bethpage, N.Y. (pp. 4724–26). St. Petersburg moved out of the downtown area but close to bus routes and with parking space for about 130 cars. Plainview remained in a shopping center, but in order to acquire a desirable location spent over half as much for its site as for its building.

One leading library spokesman and a specialist in the field of the small public library has already voiced the hope that the federal funds which will become available under the Library Services and Construction Act will not be poured into the building of small branches, proliferating the already staggering number of inadequate library facilities throughout the land. Rather, says this expert, let the monies be channeled into the improvement of the larger—and also inadequate—libraries which must meet the pressures of a burgeoning population.

Under LSCA, complete statewide planning of library facilities is now possible. The challenge to the states is great. The awarding of construction grants will require the wisdom of ten Solomons.

As editorial "sidewalk superintendents" of library construction, we shall watch with increased interest the new buildings of the next few years. It should be a period of dramatic and dynamic growth.

*Shirley Havens*

# Problems of
# Preservation

### PAPER FOR POSTERITY
November 1, 1960

A one-day conference was held in Washington, D.C., in September at which some 40 librarians and archivists, book publishers and printers, paper makers and chemists, discussed the subject of durable book paper. Sponsored by the Virginia State Library and ALA, the conference was prompted by the development of sample specifications for a permanent book paper by W. J. Barrow, Document Restorer at the Virginia State Library, whose research has been backed by Council on Library Resources grants.

The present position is that most books printed in the first half of this century are already brittle and may be no more than a microfilm memory in the 21st century. As a result of Mr. Barrow's researches, two commercial book papers have been produced "in a medium price range" which should last for 400 years, and one important producer of book paper, the S. D. Warren Company, has changed over the chemistry of all its papers (at no advance in price) to add old-fashioned permanence to present day printability.

This is news that all librarians will surely welcome, but—without undermining the significance or value of Mr. Barrow's project—it represents no more than the first small step forward. Some fundamental and difficult questions remain to be solved.

How many publishers will use these, or other permanent book papers, in the books they publish? It cannot be assumed, because a permanent paper has been made available, that it will automatically be adopted for use by all. If a good paper can be produced cheaply, it is certain that someone will produce a less-good paper more cheaply, and equally certain that some publishers, anxious to keep book prices down, will use the cheaper and less permanent paper for some of their books, just as they now use groundwood paper for their cheapest reprints.

Which books *should* be printed on permanent paper? There are a number of librarians whose categorical answer would be "everything." Representative of this point of view was Mr. Harwell's comment at this conference that "the third rate and the fifth rate is the material of research value in the future." With the publishing output and the space problems of libraries both increasing at a prodigal rate, we find this position less and less defensible. How can one justify the permanent preservation of Spillane and the third-grade arithmetic textbook, the girlie magazine and the horror comic? Or *every* edition of Poe's stories or Longfellow's poems?

But even if one accepts that one copy of all or any of these should be embalmed somewhere for the benefit of the desperate thesis-writer of tomorrow, what then? Is the publisher to print one copy on permanent paper for deposit in the Library of Congress? Or two, three or four, so that Berkeley and Harvard and Chicago can have copies in case LC should become the victim of natural or man-made disaster? Or are we to demand that *all* third-grade textbooks be printed on permanent paper?

One publisher at the conference, Curtis Benjamin, president of Mc-Graw-Hill, suggested that publishers were already attempting as best they could to determine *which* books and periodicals deserved the better paper. Leaving such decisions to the publishers didn't seem to meet with much approval among librarians, but the librarians themselves have so far come forward with no suggestion other than all-inclusive preservation. Those who adopt an adamant stand for "all" often end with the alternative of "nothing at all."

This conference concluded with a recommendation that ALA take the initiative in forming a committee representing various elements of the book world to pursue a number of problems concerning the development and use of better book papers. Perhaps the librarians on this committee should concentrate *their* main efforts towards the solution of *what* should be preserved. The method and techniques might be easier to visualize if the job can be brought down to realistic proportions.

*Eric Moon*

## TO RESCUE THE BOOKS
March 15, 1965

It all started when William J. Barrow reported that the deterioration of paper in modern books was proceeding more rapidly than most of us had suspected, that the causes of this decay were different than we had thought, and that the process could be slowed by a combination of chemical treatment and cold storage. The period since Barrow's first study was completed in 1959 has been marked by the accumulation of evidence that this problem of book preservation, beyond its scientific and technical ramifications, is one that may affect, in a complex and vital way, the very structure of US librarianship.

Thus, the recent ARL report, "The Preservation of Deteriorating Books: An Examination of the Problem with Recommendations for a Solution" (*see* p. 1272 ff.), may turn out to be one of the important documents of 20th Century US librarianship.

Consider, for example, the report's recommendation for: ". . . a federally supported central agency that will assure the physical preservaton for as long as possible of at least one example of every deteriorating record, and that will make copies of these records readily available to any library . . ."

Imagine every major research library in the US ". . . obligating themselves not to dispose of any cataloged book, or organized group of books, from their collections, without first ascertaining whether or not an example as good as their own, or better, is already preserved." If no example has yet been deposited in the central agency for preservation, then the library will deposit the example from its collections.

Include in this super-collection all titles currently in any US research library, "all significant new books published in the US," and "foreign materials acquired under programs such as PL 480 and the Farmington Plan."

Envisage the availability to any library of positive microform copies, or full-size copies of all these titles, at the cost of the copy, or free of charge on loan.

And think how easy it will be to find a given title in the collection through the *National Union Catalog* after it has added a serial number to every entry, so that the new central preservation agency can just list serial numbers for its holdings.

Finally, calculate the savings to overburdened US research libraries, when the federal government relieves them of this great cost of preservation.

Such is the utopia recommended in the report of the ARL Committee on the Preservation of Research Library Materials, prepared by Gordon Williams under a grant from the Council on Library Resources. It is an impressive document, one that should keep ARL, and all librarians, busy lobbying for some time.

It may keep them arguing too. We will be interested in the reaction to the report's assertion that it would be less costly to physically preserve and store a collection of two million original volumes, microfilming only the two percent the report indicates would be required for use, than it would cost to microfilm all two million and discard the original books. (This estimate includes a cost of $1,620,405 for a building.)

Someone will surely be upset at the decision in the report to include all the titles now in research collections, rather than to select from those collections only the titles worthy of preservation. The report says: "Assuming, as we must assume, that the research library collections have been selected with some care, it seems clear that any wholesale re-selection for preservation would not be economically justified."

Others will take issue with the supporting evidence for this decision, which contends that in order to make weeding of a research collection economically justifiable "about three and a half percent of the books examined would have to be discarded . . ."

Certainly there will be hot debate over the recommendation that a central, single library facility is needed, rather than financial support to allow existing libraries to carry on their own preservation programs.

There will be other points of issue, but none detract from the urgency of the problem or the importance of the ARL report.

When we were in the public library, we always downgraded the "custodial" side of being a librarian, in favor of services, circulation, and professionalism. There is a pleasant irony in the fact that a national program for research libraries may develop from a consideration of that old custodial problem, the preservation of books. The ARL report offers a "grand design" for this purpose; it ought to be read.

*John Berry*

# Cooperation

### AN AID TO COOPERATION?
February 1, 1960

"Togetherness" is an ugly word with generally pleasant connotations which has come into vogue quite recently. In library circles, under its synonym "cooperation," it has been in vogue considerably longer. The ever-increasing deluge of publications, widening subject areas and reader demand, have forced librarians to an active awareness of the truth of the too-often quoted phrase, "no man is an island."

Through cooperation British librarians are now well along the road towards realizing their dream of making at least one copy of every book published available to any reader, no matter where he may live. The national scheme of subject specialization which came into force a year ago is a natural progression from the several regional schemes which have developed during the past ten years in Britain.

In our "Readers' Voice" column (*LJ*, Dec. 1, '59, p. 3650) E. T. Bryant, Borough Librarian of Widnes, points out that the publication since 1950 of the *British National Bibliography* has been a great help in the development of these cooperative schemes. We would go further. It is our belief that without a current classified list such as the *B.N.B.* most of these subject specialization schemes would not have started. Agreement between libraries as to what books came within their allotted subject areas would have been difficult, if not impossible, to achieve without the existence of some central classified list which all could be persuaded to accept.

There may be many reasons why cooperative purchase and subject specialization schemes do not exist in the United States on a similar scale, but a major factor must have been the absence of a basic tool like the *B.N.B.* It is remarkable that the home of Melvil Dewey should for so long have been almost alone among the great nations in not having a current national bibliography based on the Dewey classification.

This omission will be remedied with the publication of the *American Book Publishing Record.* This monthly publication will be a cumulation of the listings appearing in the *Publishers Weekly* "Weekly Record," and each issue will be a classified and indexed record of the U.S. book output of the month past. The first issue will be dated "for the month ending February 1, 1960."

The *American Book Publishing Record* may be useful to librarians in many ways, but its greatest contribution to library service in America could be to act as a spur towards the creation of state or regional subject specialization schemes which could bring us nearer that hackneyed, but still unachieved ideal, of getting the right book to the right reader at the right time.

*Eric Moon*

## SERVICE OR LIP SERVICE?
May 15, 1961

"In summary, the library system of America today presents numerous types of agencies, each performing a service to a different clientele. We find that the majority are deficient in all categories—resources, physical plant, and personnel. We find that all types of institutions give thorough and complete lip service to the idea of cooperation, whether in the development of systems or in the coordination of resources, but with few exceptions, no true patterns of cooperation have developed. It would seem that many librarians are anxious to perpetuate their isolation."

This is just one example of the kind of straight talking which appears in *The Sixties and After,* a special report for the Federal Relations Committee written by John Eastlick and recently published by ALA. This brief survey of the present status and needs of libraries in the United States supplies ammunition for those who campaign for the support and betterment of libraries, a variety of personal and controversial opinions, and some certain jolts for the unduly complacent.

The Eastlick Report advocates, so far as public libraries are concerned, much stronger control by state library agencies which would encourage the elimination of unnecessary institutions, the combining of institutions into systems and the development of natural library systems unhampered by political lines. The problems are also recognized: "To accomplish this kind of directed cooperation will require the highest democratic statesmanship on the part of the state librarian and the state library agency staff. It involves problems inherent in the democratic philosophy of local versus state authority."

There is no doubt in our mind that cooperation is the key that can open many of the doors which bar off the corridors of progress in library service. But the *ideal* of cooperation is not enough. As this report says: "The ideal of cooperation between institutions needs to become a reality. Schools, school libraries, public libraries, college and university libraries, special libraries within a city or region, all need to define and observe their responsibilities."

The translation of the ideal into reality demands a wider vision, a flexibility, and a generosity of spirit that are not yet universal qualities among either librarians or library authorities. Keyes Metcalf, in another recently published pamphlet (*Cooperation Among Maine Libraries: a Report Prepared for the Larger Libraries of Maine*), points out that "cooperation becomes difficult if each participant is determined to profit from the project more than any other participant."

Many cooperative projects, of course, involve extra work for the participants, space problems and other difficulties, but if the project is worthwhile it is surely better to look for ways to overcome the difficulties than to abandon the project. One cooperative effort which was discontinued recently, apparently because the difficulties loomed larger than the objectives, was California's experimental Last Copy Preservation Plan. The purpose of this plan, similar to several well-established schemes in England, was excellent—to preserve cooperatively last copies of titles that might otherwise disappear. The success of the plan demanded participation by all, or nearly all of the libraries which contribute cards to the state's Union Catalog. Only 25 out of the 64 member libraries were willing to participate, so the experiment died last August despite attempts by a number of librarians to revive it.

This is, of course, only one example of what seems to be a lack of conviction about cooperation, but there are numerous others which support Mr. Eastlick's contention that "many libraries are anxious to perpetuate their isolation."

*Eric Moon*

## COOPERATE—BUT NOT TOO MUCH
May 1, 1963

"It would seem that many librarians are anxious to perpetuate their isolation," said John Eastlick two years ago in *The Sixties and After*. We quoted him in an editorial then because it seemed appropriate (*see LJ*, May 15, '61, p. 1850)—California librarians had just ditched a cooperative project to preserve last copies of titles that might otherwise disappear from library shelves. Two years further on into the sixties we quote Eastlick again. The comment is still appropriate. Only the geography is changed—we move now to the east coast.

Librarians of the Nassau (N.Y.) Library System came together in January for their fourth annual meeting. A matter of urgency on the agenda was the question of reciprocal borrowing privileges for patrons of member libraries. Nassau's provisional charter under the State plan expires next year, and the legal requirements for an Absolute Charter call for such reciprocal borrowing privileges.

A committee which had studied the problem recommended a "trial period" from July 1 to December 31, 1963. This would be long enough, the committee said, to discover any pitfalls and difficulties in a system-wide reciprocal borrowing privilege. These could then be studied and evaluated, and the system would still have time to present the best plan, some alternate solution or a possible appeal to the Commissioner of Education, *based on actual experience,* before the expiry of the system's provisional charter. The committee pointed out that 18 out of 22 systems in New York State had adopted a form of uniform borrower's card and had reported "minimum difficulties."

According to *Sum & Substance,* a monthly news-sheet published by the Nassau System, "Opponents of the plan came from both small and large libraries." The small libraries were afraid their growth would be hampered. The big ones thought their resources might be drained by invaders from surrounding communities. The trial period idea was washed out because "it is difficult to withdraw any privilege once it is granted."

So another cooperative proposal came to the point of a vote. Twenty libraries said no, ten were for it, and three abstained. Nothing was left but to set up another committee to have another look at the problem.

When are we going to play as strong a cooperative game as we talk? Walter Brahm has been trying to sell the idea of a statewide borrower's ticket to the librarians of Ohio—with much the same results. The arguments wielded against such proposals sound like echoes of the voices of reaction which have thudded dully down through all the years of what we like to call library service.

Why are the Nassua librarians afraid of a trial period? Wouldn't their fears be more realistic if they had some evidence to support them? Let's suppose for a moment that their worst fears *are* realized, and that half the patrons of library A transfer their affections to library B. Let's suppose too that the system has the courage to discontinue an experiment after six months. What then? Might not some of those patrons who have enjoyed good service for six months at library B then be prepared to go back and shout (and perhaps work) a little more vigorously for decent library service in their own community A?

We have worked in heavily urban areas where reciprocal borrowing privileges were in force. All the same hazards were present. The libraries were in quite as "close proximity" as they are in Nassau. There was the same "marked unevenness of library support." But reciprocal borrowing worked, one way or another. The librarians *made* it work, because they believed service to people more important than boundary lines—political, geographical or mental. The Nassau librarians can make it work too—if they really want to.

*Eric Moon*

## A BOOK IN HAND . . .
October 1, 1964

It is a fair estimate that the nation's libraries now buy at least $150 million worth of books a year. It is not an estimate but a fact that the individual reader still cannot, with any reasonable degree of certainty, expect to be able to obtain, easily and quickly, a copy of any book (even one published in the US) from a library somewhere within the geographical area in which he lives.

There are two probable reasons for this state of affairs. First, that a number of librarians do not believe this kind of "comprehensive" service either possible or desirable. And second, that our libraries, in the main, still operate in most essentials as isolated, individual units, despite all the talk about cooperation.

Interlibrary loan does not, and will not, alone provide a solution. British libraries discovered this after many years of operating a nationwide system of regional library bureaux designed to make interloan effective. They found that still some new books were being missed by everyone, and some old books were being discarded by everyone. There are two other major deficiencies of total reliance on an interlibrary loan system: 1) it is frequently (usually) too slow for the reader who needs an item urgently; 2) the larger libraries, already overburdened in other respects, carry the brunt of the work, responsibility, and cost.

About 15 years ago the libraries of London pioneered the first of Britain's "subject specialization" schemes. It was so successful that several other regions quickly followed suit. And within ten years, all the regional systems (12 of them, covering England, Scotland, and Wales) got together to form an inter-regional coverage scheme—a sort of national overlay on the existing local schemes.

There are two elements to these systems: 1) the acquisition of all new books published in Britain; 2) the preservation of the last copy of any older book within the defined system. And there is a third element—the mechanism that makes everything else possible—the *British National Bibliography*.

It is the classified (Dewey) arrangement and the near-total coverage of the *BNB* which have provided the framework of all these British cooperative schemes. The libraries which have decided to cooperate within a region divide responsibility for the current publishing output on the basis of specified sections of the Dewey classification. Each library then buys, for the benefit of the region, one copy (over and above its own normal needs) of every book classified within its allocated section by the *BNB*. Preservation of last copies operates on the same basis, other libraries in the region notifying the "subject specializing" library before withdrawing any books within that library's specialty section of the classification.

We have often wondered why similar systems have not emerged here. Because of the varying densities of population (and libraries) the size of the organizational areas would probably have to vary considerably, but it surely could be done, in most cases, at least on a statewide basis, and in some cases at a more local (and thus more frequent) regional level. And we have at hand a tool which, like the *BNB*, would make the system easy to operate, in the *American Book Publishing Record,* which provides a monthly, Dewey-classified, list of currently published American books (we know it sounds like a plug, but it is the nearest equivalent to *BNB* in this country).

What are the advantages of such a scheme? Most important is the potential improvement in service to the reader. He could be sure that the book he wants is available somewhere in a not too distant library, and he would have a better chance of obtaining it quickly. The library, in an urgent case, could bypass the usual interloan machinery and simply telephone the library in whose subject specialty the book falls.

The larger libraries would still, of course, have to take the largest burden, with responsibility for the most populated areas of the classification, but at least all libraries involved would share some part of the responsibility and cost. This would probably work our more equitably than present inter-library loan burdens.

The cost need not be as fierce as it looms in some imaginations. If one estimates the annual American publishing output as about 25,000 volumes, and averages these out at $5 per title, the outlay necessary to insure one copy of every book in a cooperative system is only $125,000. In many cases, the purchase of any extra copies would be unnecessary, but even if one takes the whole as a "new" cost, and imagines only 100 libraries involved in such a scheme, the average cost per library is only $1,250. Some of this cost, again, would be offset by the fact that some libraries would not need to purchase very specialized items if they could be sure they were in stock in the system.

The spectre of the space problem always looms large when one suggests a scheme of this kind, and certainly it has to be reckoned with. But once one can be sure that a last copy (or copies) of a book has been preserved, a considerable number of lesser used items stored in basements or stack areas of countless libraries can be discarded. The great weeding of duplicate deadwood from the basements of London libraries when the subject specialist schemes started there was a joy to behold. It was a substantial fringe benefit.

California started, or proposed, a last copy preservation plan (one half of what is suggested here) a few years ago. It died on the rock of some librarians' resistance to real progress through cooperation. Is anybody ready for another attack?

*Eric Moon*

## ON SCHIZOPHRENIC SERVICE
October 15, 1964

The drums are sounding strong for school and public library cooperation, and on the face of it it seems the harmony between the two institutions
gets smoother every day. But there is another facet to this relationship that
has just come to our attention. It is an ironic problem, for it is assuming new
and more complicated dimensions precisely as the public library continues
to extend itself in the present push for better education.

This is the grudgingness with which some public librarians are doing
this supplementary job—the feeling that they are being pulled into something more trivial than the function dictated by their profession, simply
because they must provide reference services to students. Their obligation,
in turn, is fostering an attitude we don't know whether to attribute to
snobbishness or to an inferiority complex: the opinion that school librarianship is a limited and comparatively unimportant segment of the profession.

These feelings were articulated for us some weeks ago by an angry
librarian. "In recent years," she wrote, "there has been a vast misconception
concerning young adult work in the public library, one that has handicapped librarians working in this field, . . . that somehow it is tied up with
schools, which is just exactly what it is not."

"No one has ever questioned the function of school libraries," she
continued. "They have been set up and financed, however inadequately, to
serve specific student groups. Granted that the public library of recent years
has literally been forced into the position of playing school library as well,
this particular function has no bearing on what is known as young adult
work. In young adult work we are trying to reach the teenager as a human
being, *not* a student, and we are hoping that exposure to books as a part of
his *recreational* life, not his school life, may possibly give him values and
widen his thinking in a way that school-assigned materials can never do. We
are showing him, not directing him; persuading him, not forcing him. What
is more, our aims do not involve education except in its very broadest
sense."

One senses the sincerity of this librarian's plaint, the wish to develop
the young adult from within, rather than help out in some global cram
course that the school is imposing on the student. One recognizes, too, some
valid administrative problems implied in his statement. Yet it serves no
purpose to widen the gap between the teaching and library professions—
and consequently, through the tug of war between school and public
librarian, in the student's interests. It is an injustice to the child or young
adult to split him into two entities, "student" and "human being," one of
whom is given "leisure," the other "required," reading.

For in the long run the "broad" and "narrow" definitions of education
are not that discrete, as the schools are coming to see. The current trend
toward individualized reading instruction (page 152) and the philosophy
behind such lists as *Books to Build World Friendship* (page 157) show the

importance of "humanizing" the curriculum and the pedagogic validity of "noncurricular" reading. In this respect the school librarian's function is identical with that of the public librarian.

At the upper levels of our library leadership this fact is well recognized. One of our most refreshing experiences this summer at ALA was to see two public librarians, Ruth Gagliardo and Audrey Biel, yield their places to the new presidents of the Children's Services Division and the Young Adult Services Division: Helen Sattley and Mildred Krohn, both supervisors in school library systems. The bibliographic projects of these divisions are certainly a help to school librarians; and the latter, in turn, can relate both these objectives and the school program to the young person's individual needs. Here the school librarian becomes an important link with public library philosophy, for it is through this liaison that the public librarian's perception of reading tastes can be conveyed to such schools as those described in the recent Educational Testing Service survey (page 146).

It was precisely to spread this kind of knowledge to school librarians that our periodical came into existence as a separate publication. With no sense of bifurcation it has attempted to meet the needs of *all* librarians who serve children and young adults, and to further the unity of these twin professions.

*Evelyn Geller*


## A MANY-SPLINTERED THING
August 1966

"Library service too long has been a many-splintered thing." The speaker was Ewald B. Nyquist, deputy commissioner of education at the State University of New York, Albany. The occasion: the President's Program during the ALA Conference in New York, another of those heart-searching sessions on inter-library cooperation.

Only a few hours before Mr. Nyquist's pronouncement, the College Libraries Section of ACRL had met across the river in Queens to discuss the results of a survey on "Community Use of Academic Libraries." There, the splinters were really showing through the skin-deep talk of cooperation.

Summarizing, E. J. Josey (Savannah State College Library), who chaired this revealing meeting, said: "It is quite evident that college and university librarians believe in community use (742 of 783 survey respondents, at least, *said* they did). But only limited community use."

In general, the college libraries meeting indicated that teachers, preachers, and a loose community group called "professionals" are okay users as far as most academic librarians are concerned, and their privileges in academic library use are fairly extensive. But not all community users are so welcome.

"The community group that appears closest to being *genuinely unwelcome* in the American college and university library is the high school student segment. *Barely restrained emotions* on the part of many respondents to our question on high school students indicates *a substantial distaste for service to this group.*" The italics are ours, but the comments are those of Richard C. Quick (Northern Arizona University), one of the panel members reporting on the College Libraries Section's survey.

Those italics are there for a purpose. The emphasized words are not a simple expression of the understandable frustrations of librarians faced with a plethora of administrative problems—insufficient bookstock, too few staff, overcrowded premises, the priority demands of their immediate clientele, etc. Administrative problems can be overcome, and the necessary support to do it can be obtained—if the professional spirit is willing, if the desire is strong enough. But Quick's summary of some attitudes among the academic library community reveals a fair measure of downright discriminatory prejudice.

The library profession in the US—through its principal organizational voice, the American Library Association—has pushed hard and far down the Freedom (of access) Road in recent years, and continues to push on in that direction. While the talk has been of access "for all the people," however, the principal objective has been to open library resources and services to minority groups, and more specifically, to Negroes.

This is, and has been, a good and valid objective to pursue. But so it would have been 50 years earlier. That the profession's pursuit of it suddenly moved into a higher gear was undoubtedly because the social ambience made it imperative. We would have had to be blind not to sense the social revolution all around us, stupid not to participate in that revolution.

Blind and stupid may be appropriate words, nevertheless, for many attitudes that still prevail in the profession in the face of another kind of social revolution. Three years ago, Ned Bryan, in his ALA presidential year, made a herculean effort to open the profession's eyes to this one: the beginning of the most massive commitment to education by any society in history. He broke down all the organizational lines and brought together the largest and most varied librarian gathering ever to concentrate for several days on one issue. The single focus of all this attention was the student reader and the collective failure of libraries, both to meet that student's needs and to grasp the opportunities with which he presented us.

Here, in New York, was an ALA conference concerned with "Libraries and the Inquiring Mind." Where, more than in the high schools, is there a larger collection of inquiring minds in this country? Minds that need and want to grow, and that need help and encouragement to do so? Yet, to what other group in American society are so many library doors—public, reference, research, academic—closed or guarded by rules and regulations?

Where, if we do not entirely accept the moral obligation to bend every cooperative effort to meet the student's needs, is the political wisdom in the present antagonism toward the student reader? Here is tomorrow's voter, tomorrow's community leader, tomorrow's power structure. If we build in him today a massive resentment against libraries, where tomorrow will libraries find the support they know they will need?

Legislated financial support for school libraries will bring some relief to the knowledge-hungry student, but it can't do the whole trick. A basic tenet in our professional gospel is that no one library can any longer hope to amass the resources to meet all the needs, even of its immediate clientele. Even with good high school libraries, the student will continue to go, as Bryan indicated, where the books (he needs) are. He cares not a fig for the artificial boundaries we hold so dear.

Two more comments from the College Libraries Section meeting in New York amply demonstrate that free access to libraries—for students—remains a major unfulfilled professional goal. Said E. J. Josey: "Library affairs are still conducted as though no one had ever heard of the recommendations of the 1963 Conference-Within-a-Conference." And Edward Howard (Evansville Public Library) commented: "We have yet to answer the basic question: what library should provide which materials to whom? Perhaps it is too late, Perhaps it should be as irrelevant to us as it is to the 'pushy' student."

Perhaps it should be irrelevant, Mr. Howard, but it is clear that there are still too many minds in our profession that envisage library service in tight little compartments, that would perpetuate the "many-splintered thing." The indications are that these attitudes are not going to remain a subject for cosy, internal, professional debate, but that they will be questioned from outside our profession and in high places.

At the College Libraries meeting, the Legislative Analyst to the Joint Legislative Committee of the California Legislature was quoted as saying in a recent report: "The university library system exists not only to serve the educational needs of [university] students but is also the major resource center in the state for research . . . for industry *and other community users.*"

And finally, questions about library splintering are looming at the highest level of all. When he signed the revised Library Services and Construction Act in July, President Johnson asked: "Are our federal efforts to assist libraries intelligently administered—or are they too fragmented among separate programs and agencies?" If he ever rephrases that and asks, "Are our *libraries* intelligently administered or are *they* too fragmented?" we had better prepare some solid justification for our present restrictions or make a convincing move in the direction of free access to libraries "for all people"—including students.

*Eric Moon*

### NEW GOALS—OR A DEAD END
December 15, 1967

At a time when public librarians are sometimes wistfully observing a reduction in the "student horde," the proposals made by Mrs. Dinah Lindauer, coordinator of programs and services for the Nassau Library

System, at the Albany conference on young adult service (see p. 15) seem to offer particular promise for the profession. It is ironic, however, that some librarians should have accepted her philosophy, but hedged at its practical implications.

What Mrs. Lindauer stressed was the need for regional, rather than systems, coordination of traditional functions, so that systems consultants could expand their services by working with youth boards and other agencies serving teens. It is a concept that has been proposed for public libraries, particularly in the wake of antipoverty efforts that depend on such liaison, and an idea that is also permeating education through the community-oriented programs launched under Titles I and III of the Elementary and Secondary Education Act. In the YA area, Mrs. Lindauer suggested, this concept of service would commit the library to tracing agencies serving youth; preparing or disseminating information not produced by commercial publishers and the government—such as directories of local organizations, and summer and part-time work opportunities for youth; and planning for joint programming. Some YA consultants in the more sophisticated systems are beginning to feel that this, rather than conventional YA work, is their job—and one that make adults, as well as teenagers, aware of the library function. The price to be paid, however, would be some surrender of local autonomy on traditional systems functions.

The operational consequences are evident from a comparison of Mrs. Lindauer's suggestions (p. 21) with the traditional YA consultant functions that Robert Ake (Spring Valley, New York) had listed earlier at the meeting (p. 16). How, a harried YA consultant asked us, could one person perform this job for dozens of understaffed and underfunded libraries? Mrs. Lindauer gave some answers that ranged from shared in-service training to the splitting up of systems reviewing by age level or subject, to be coordinated on a regional basis. Yet faced with these alternatives, some librarians persisted in justifying traditional functions on the grounds that local reviewing provided "in-service" training, motivated the librarian to read, and allowed for local adaptation. Similarly, a suggestion (made by this writer) that individual systems could each take a theme of teenage interest, develop multimedia lists and suggested activities, then combine these for an entire series of programs, met with the objection that what worked in one system might fail in another. Last, there was still confusion about whether libraries should concentrate on present clientele "or" seek new customers.

In each of these cases, it seems to us that the librarians have been posing false dilemmas. Certainly we live in a mass culture which makes an entire range of titles relevant to most libraries. Certainly, one or more national reviewing tools could be used and adapted, without the requirement that *each* review be rewritten, and *each* book reevaluated, for each system. Certainly, the remaining work load could be split up among librarians in several, rather than one system, allowing the individual librarian to work in an area of particular interest, while reading more freely in the field, and without a deadline to meet, in order to relate books to reading guidance. (What librarian worth his salt will read a book only for the glory of publication on a mimeographed sheet?) And certainly, multimedia units and programs can be intelligently adapted to local needs without making every librarian start from scratch. Meanwhile, a portion of the systems meetings, or the school-public library cooperative book selection meetings, could be devoted more fruitfully to programming and creative cooperation.

The latter move, in fact, would open up new possibilities for public and school library cooperation that would not require the public library to compete with the school in the instructional area. The school would take its place among the range of agencies the public library serves, while the great *programming* potential of YA service could be coordinated with school curricula, yet enjoy an independence in planning and selection which the more (let's face it) hidebound schools cannot match. How can librarians refuse the small sacrifices needed for these opportunities, when the future of YA service itself is at stake?

*Evelyn Geller*

# Data Processing, Automation, Information Science

## HUMOR AND HORROR
October 15, 1962

Among that curious assembly called library literature one of the most fascinating books we have stumbled on for some time is *Advanced Data Processing in the University Library,* a silver-covered tome which is otherwise produced in the normal prosaic manner of the Scarecrow Press.

Surprise preceded fascination, because we do not lightly approach books with titles like this, nor with great expectations of diversion or profit. For we must admit that we are not eager retrievers and we do not altogether dig documentation. But behind those silver covers there lurk, believe it or not, equally silver linings. Science and philosophy of librarianship, realism and dreams, and even, so help us, humor.

Read, for example, the annotations in "an annotated bibliography of readings on library mechanization." No place for an Ogden Nash, you say? We all know what annotations are: those stilted, often pedestrian and always unevaluative notes which catalogers place at the end of their entries, and which take two lines to misinform the reader. Well, *these* annotations are slightly different.

One *Journal of Cataloging and Classification* article is described unequivocally as "a somewhat tedious rehash." Of the author of a *College and Research Libraries* article, the note says: "Mr. Merryman is obviously related by blood (probably drawn) to Stephen Potter, although he will not admit it." And the animated annotator reserves for an *LJ* article by our own

Dan Melcher, the following protracted exercise in alliteration: "Mr. Melcher mentions many marvelous machines. Meaning: machines mightn't mean much."

And one last example—of a pun which even Harry Bauer would find it hard to top. An *American Documentation* article, says the annotation, "Discusses a theoretical scheme for automating a coordinate index. Seems pretty impractical but should probably be considered when the time comes as, like the boy who threw rocks at sea-gulls, we should leave no tern unstoned."

The whole book isn't like this, of course. (Do we hear a sigh of relief from the solemn?) There are facts and figures a-plenty, and some of them are shockers. Take some of the passages on cost analysis. Let's quote awhile:

"Difficult as it is to believe, a new title costing $5 costs $18.51 at UIC (that's University of Illinois, Chicago campus) by the time it gets to the shelf, and a gift book costs the UIC library over $13 to accept, check and catalog."

The reaction of most librarians to such cost figures, say the authors, "borders on the incredulous." That's understandable, and one cannot but agree with the following comment:

"Even if these UIC costs are not unreasonable when compared to other libraries of similar size and kind, it seems ridiculous to pay $8.67 to catalog one title. These cataloging costs, plus the $4.84 cost of selecting and acquiring the material in the first place, make a book almost too valuable to circulate. Also, a circulation cost of 41 cents per transaction seems to call for careful investigation of ways to cut costs."

The authors and surveyors in this study don't believe that machines have all the answers to everything. For example, they do one calculation to show that one linear search of the *Reader's Guide to Periodical Literature,* if it were put on tape, would cost $582.75, and they conclude: "Obviously putting the tools of the library on tape would make them economically impossible to use."

Nevertheless, it would be hard to disagree with one of their over-all conclusions, that "librarians actually have little choice in applying new techniques, in that something must be done to cut costs, improve efficiency, place the professional librarian in a professional position, and improve service to library users. As time is running out, this action must be taken at once if the library is to remain a dynamic force."

Studies like this one certainly help, if only to open a few eyes, ours included.

*Eric Moon*

## INFORMATION SCIENCE?
March 1, 1964

Among some (certainly not all) librarians one has sensed for some time a growing inferiority complex, induced perhaps by the propaganda of the whiz-kids of the information retrieval and data processing fields. Some eminent figures in the science-information world—for example, Walter Carlson, director of technical information at the Department of Defense— appear ready to write off "orthodox" librarians and libraries as having little to contribute to the battle with the information explosion.

There have been rumbles, however, that "information science" is not quite the science it is cracked up to be, and indications that the achievement of some of the mechanized science information centers might be summed up as a limited output at unlimited expense. Librarians may derive some consolation from what is perhaps the most telling exposé yet to appear in this area: it was published in the January 1964 issue of *College and Research Libraries*.

We draw attention to it here because the wordiness and the awful layout of a hideous five-line title—"The Scope and Operating Efficiency of Information Centers as Illustrated by the Chemical-Biological Coordination Center of the National Research Council"—may well deter all but the hardiest readers. Also, the staid, research-project style, and the "neutral" avoidance of judgments by author Richard Dougherty give no hint of the explosive content. What an Upton Sinclair or one of the other muck-raking journalists of his period could have made of this story is pleasant to contemplate. If evidence were needed that we are still far from the millennium in science information service, it is here in full in this story of the short, unhappy life of one now defunct information center.

It took about seven years, most of it spent in devising and changing minds about codes (i.e. classification schemes) and procedures, before the center reached operational status. Then, in four years, the center built up a backlog of material to be fed into the storage files equivalent to "more than one year's production."

Mr. Dougherty reveals that "accurate cost studies were never conducted," but estimates placed the cost of processing *per article* at anything from $29.46 to $50. This was for input alone. Retrieval costs were "estimated by the center variously at $60 and $150, the first figure based on unit costs, the second on overall operational costs." Again, these are costs *per article*.

Fearsome as they are, perhaps some might consider these cost figures as not too exorbitant for a red-hot, efficient service which could guarantee to produce the goods when they were needed. But the record doesn't read that way:

"A study of 1,025 requests received at the center between January 1953 and October 1956 shows that one-third of the requests were answered, one-quarter partially answered, and the remaining 45 percent unanswered . . . The time lapse between receipt of requests and sending of replies ranged from one day to more than one year. Three-fifths of the requests were handled in two weeks or less. During the latter stages of operations, a backlog of unprocessed requests accumulated, and by the middle of 1955, it amounted to almost eighty requests."

There may be worse records than this among reference libraries employing what Mr. Carlson calls "the traditional library approach," but there can't be too many. What makes the story even more ironic is that Mr.

Dougherty also investigated the "sources used in answering questions." Only one-third of the answers, he says, "were based on data originating in the center's files." Where did the rest come from?—"from conventional indexes, abstracting bulletins, bibliographies, textbooks, etc."

"Machine utilization in the retrieval process was low," says Mr. Dougherty. "Records indicated that the machines were employed in answering from three to 15 percent of the requests, and that during the latter stages the punched card files were consulted almost exclusively on a manual basis."

And so we reach the most staggering cost estimate of all. "The analysis of information requests described above showed that input costs, based on 1955 cost figures, per *successful* use of the files was approximately $1,850."

What wonders might be performed by machineless man in an orthodox reference library if libraries were reimbursed at the rate of $1,850 for every question they answered correctly and promptly, with the aid of such old-fashioned gadgets as the catalog and books!

*Eric Moon*

### FALSE FRONT
July 1964

To one scholar, "The maturity of a discipline is directly relative to the degree of standard terminology." By this definition librarianship, although chronologically middle-aged in 1964, is still in its semantical infancy. Rather than create new terms of our own, however, we are currently involved in wholesale borrowing from another discipline. Like other infant professions we are fascinated by the exterior forms of our more respected sisters in the professional world. The latest infatuation is with the language of automatic data processing.

For librarians this new language has many advantages. It is related to an area of study that has the respect, even awe, of the public. Its foundation in research is undisputed. The publicity that has accompanied its rise to fame has been far more successful than the accumulated public relations efforts of the library profession through its entire history. The new language is associated in the public mind with science, with the glamorous technological disciplines of the future, with modern space research, with the popular conception of cybernetics and the eventual supremacy of automation, and with that frightening time ahead when the machine will provide, and teach, and solve all human problems.

Best of all, the new language is obscure. To those outside the data processing ingroup it is even unintelligible. It can, to quote Russell Kirk, ". . . convert the vulgar through awe or erudition." For example, the new language defines *word* as: "A set of characters which have one addressable location and are treated as one unit"; *reader* becomes: "A device which converts information in one form of storage to information in another form of storage"; and to *read* is to: ". . . transcribe information from an input device to internal or auxiliary storage." For the uninitiated "acorn tubes," "analog channels," "random access storage," "parameters," "potentiometers," "zone bits," and "zatocoding" are as impressive as they are incomprehensible. Traditional "subject headings" (a concept still foreign to many library users) are now "uniterms" and "descriptors" although, as Theodore Stein points out (p. 2724), they are all related to the same concept.

As the new language moves into, or is taken into librarianship, and *information retrieval* replaces *reference service,* or *cataloging* and *classification* give way to some combination of *storage* and *programming,* standard terms are often lost, and with them a certain semantical maturity. Unfortunately, even with all its status advantages, the new language does not, not yet anyway, relate to what we are doing.

Changing the labels does not change the contents. This borrowing of a language is only another way of changing the labels, like the undertaker who became a mortician and is now a grief therapist, or the librarian trying to become a library scientist.

No one would suggest that precise and efficient communication is not served by the creation of words to meet technological change. One could suggest, however, that the new terms, already finding regular use in librarianship, are not yet the language of library science.

There is ample documentation of the fact that library automation is still in its infancy. The A. D. Little Corporation report of July 1963, "Centralization and Documentation," submitted to the National Science Foundation, is one excellent example of the growing doubts regarding certain machine applications. Grieg Aspnes puts it this way: "We are today very near to knowing what the problems really are."

Current proposals, and the existing applications of machines to library routines and problems clearly indicate that eventually automation will be widespread in libraries. In 1964, however, the millennium has not yet arrived. Conventional methods have not been replaced, and to replace their language with a new one is an exercise in irrelevancy. To use a new language for pedantic display at the expense of whatever terminological maturity we have attained only continues our imitation of other professions. It is another manifestation of that syndrome of librarianship variously discussed as image, or status, or professional recognition. A new language thus used is merely another false front behind which we can conveniently hide dull writing and the shallowness of much of our scholarship.

*John Berry*

### IT'S A WISE CHILD . . .
November 1, 1965

The little tyke was conceived during the fleeting affair between that somewhat shabby and passive old maid, librarianship, and the rich playboy, science. The poor kid hasn't even been named yet; in fact most of us don't even know what he looks like. Still, they were all talking about him at the FID (International Federation for Documentation) Congress in October in Washington. Some of the family felt that he ought to be reared by his mother in her flat on the outskirts of Academe. The others said that his father could give him a better life, with prestige, wealth, and status, on the best street in town. They were already calling him by his father's name, hoping he would be known as "Information Science."

In his *Reader's Guide to the Social Sciences*, Bert F. Hoselitz lists three conditions that have accompanied the birth of new disciplines. The first of these is the existence and recognition of a set of new problems which attract the attention of several investigators. The information problems probably started with movable type, were recognized with the advent of the typewriter, and attracted serious attention so long ago that the term "information explosion" is a cliché.

Hoselitz says the second condition is the collection of sufficient data to allow the promulgation of generalizations with broad enough scope to focus upon the common features of the problems under investigation. We have proceedings, reports, studies, symposia, and conferences that show how hard at work the data collectors have been. There are still very few valid generalizations, but they are trying and talking. Jesse Shera, dean of the School of Library Science at Western Reserve University, said it this way to the FID Congress: "Programs have been predicated on assumptions of what is and should be, rather than on any precise knowledge . . ."

Finally, according to Hoselitz, comes the attainment of official or institutional recognition of the new discipline. Joseph Donohue of Informatics, Inc. in Sherman Oaks, California, came to FID to deliver his paper on a study of information science (defined as the study of the properties, behavior, and flow of information) in the curricula of 34 accredited library schools. Although Donohue seemed to feel that the infant was being neglected by its mother librarianship, his data showed that five percent of the 2,950 total course hours were occupied by offerings in information science. Donohue proved a certain, if grudging, acceptance of the new discipline by library schools. The study showed that 77 percent of the accredited schools offer at least one course in information science.

We have little data on the information science offerings in other academic departments. We do know, however, that there are courses in information science or technology in the scientific and technological curricula in universities. Usually, they are more accurately defined as courses in science information, in the exploitation rather than the study of information.

In any case, the new discipline is grudgingly accepted by librarianship, and is accepted for exploitation by science, the selfish father. Hoselitz' third condition is being met: acceptance has been achieved.

We will not engage in the debate over the infant's legitimacy, attempt to decide whether "information" is a concept worthy of scientific study unrelated to applications, or try to determine whether it should be a "pure" science. Instead, we will consider who should get custody of the child. Does

"Information Science" belong in the sci-tech "club" described by Pierre Auger in his plenary address at FID, or is the parental claim of librarianship more valid?

Samuel Rothstein, of the University of British Columbia School of Librarianship, says the new discipline is really "an extension and/or specialization within librarianship." Shera, in his paper, says "Information science is rooted in librarianship." On the other side, Don Swanson, of the Graduate Library School at the University of Chicago, seems to be taking the infant back to its father, science, via the "systems planning" route.

Neither approach has achieved any great academic sophistication. The proliferation of curricula based, as Shera suggested, on assumptions rather than knowledge of what it is necessary to teach, may produce what he called a generation of "misfits" trained in a discipline without standard terminology, without any experimental foundation, and without a home in the academic world.

There is no doubt that the baby has arrived, but as yet he is unnamed and homeless.

*John Berry*


# Standards

## AN EDUCATIONAL FORCE
March 1, 1960

The outstanding event of this year's Spring season in librarianship is the publication of the ALA's *Standards for School Library Programs*. The title itself is indicative of forethought, good judgment and common sense. Standards are too often, and too easily, thought of as no more than a set of statistics or specifications, nailing down details like the height of a chair and the size of a catalog card to the nearest sixteenth of an inch.

These school library standards sensibly take a wider view. Of the three types of standards included we are firm in our opinion that the most significant are those which lay down principles of policy and practice intended to make the library program an educational force in the school. Gain this much recognition and the rest of the stated aims will follow as the night, the day. Once it is accepted that the library in any school is an indispensable element there will be far less difficulty in obtaining the proper staff, or the materials and equipment needed. Given the right staff, the principles of administration and organization that make the school library an efficient tool will also come.

There is ample evidence that the school library is a long way from being recognized as a potent force in education. The figures quoted in the *Standards* are depressing enough: 75 percent of our elementary schools without any kind of school libraries; nearly half the schools of all kinds in the United States receiving service from classroom collections only; and grossly substandard facilities in many schools which do report that they have libraries. Further evidence of a negative kind is available in the mass of books, pamphlets, and other publications which inquire and constantly lament about "what is wrong with our schools." It never seems to occur to the agonized authors that educating a child without books is an empty and futile process; and what may be most wrong with schools is the state of their libraries.

What we like most about these standards is the authority with which they announce themselves, and the obvious signs of scrupulous planning at all stages. The original meaning of standard was "a banner." Twenty varied and national associations cooperating and appearing together on the title-page presents quite a banner. There has been the widest possible consultation and gathering of advice and information from consultants and advisers, individuals and organizations.

The most encouraging feature of the planning is that it does not stop short at publication of the standards. All too often endeavors of this kind reach an early climax when years of effort have been reduced to so many words on the printed page. The resulting publication is then tossed overboard and left to swim. Such is not the case this time. Implementation programs will be getting under way almost immediately, and with pilot projects operating in nine states during the next year the standards should be away to a vigorous and practical start. The Library Services Act is perhaps the best current example that success breeds success, and a good first year could do much to ensure continued progress in improving school library services.

How great is the success will depend primarily, of course, on the school librarians themselves. It is to be hoped that there will not be too much of the negative and defeatist attitude which is common towards standards, even before they are seen. Unanimity is needed here, not the pathetic "standards may be all right for you, but you can't do that in my school" approach.

Nor should everything be left to the school librarians. They need, and deserve, the support of all librarians. There is no type of library which does not have a vested interest in better school libraries.

*Eric Moon*

## TEENAGE THEORIES
October 15, 1960

"Who are the young adults?" This question opens the first chapter of *Young Adult Services in the Public Library*, one among this year's heavy crop of publications on library standards. The neatest, if not the soundest, answer to this question might be the definition of adolescence as the "period between pigtails and cocktails." This must be about the only definition missing from the sparkling first chapter of these new standards, which concludes sadly that young adults are "persons in their teens for whom there is no adequate terminology."

This new publication has scarcely had the attention it deserves in the professional press. Certainly it would be fair to say that it has not made a big bang comparable to that which accompanied the publication of the *Standards for School Library Programs*. It is hard to understand why this should be so.

Could it be that the librarians working with young adults are less aggressive than their school library colleagues? Was their planning less thorough? In any event, if there is one area of public library work where confusion reigns, and where guidance and a great deal more thought are needed, it is in the young adult field.

We are in total agreement with the statement in these standards that "work with young adults is definitely part of *adult* work in the public library." But we part company when, in the same chapter, the standards quote, seemingly with approval, the assertion in *Public Library Service* that "all central libraries should have separate rooms or allocated space for children and young people."

Librarians in this century seem to have developed a dangerous tendency to categorize not only books but people, and then to dream up special ways of serving them. There *are* obvious cases where special services are necessary, for example to the blind and the shut-ins. But age is not necessarily an affliction, and as a basis for separation of the library public into species it seems neither logical nor practical. Which library will be the first to offer a service to the middle-aged, a neglected category if ever there was one?

A sane and firm stride in the opposite direction is that taken recently by the Brooklyn Public Library, which has abolished separate young adult departments and placed all services beyond sixth grade under the adult department.

The part of these standards which appeals least to us is that dealing with book selection. "The 'best' books for young adults," we are told, "are the books that most truly interpret to them the process of living." "Books that make life too easy or too happy" are harmful. The deadly high seriousness of these phrases and much else that has been written in this area, and the implied and reiterated objective of "improving" the young adult at all costs, of guiding his reading into all the correct channels and strata of suitability, lead us—and probably the teenager—to cry out with Swinburne: "Come down and redeem us from virtue." No young adult will become a lifetime reader unless books are fun, and the reading and choice of them a free-as-air activity. If the young adult wants to reach a bit above his head, let him, and give him Robert Browning's blessing. But save him from too many "good" books.

A British librarian some years ago wondered whether one reason why twice as many books per capita are borrowed from British libraries as compared with American is that too many Americans regard the library as "a purposive, improving institution." The young adult who sees libraries this way is not likely to adopt them as one of the loves of his life, and it may be that the soundest piece of philosophy for young adult librarians is that offered in a recent debate in *LJ*'s pages:

"Libraries should not be exclusively places of learning. They should be also, and just as importantly, places of delight."

*Eric Moon*

## STANDARDS FOR EVERYTHING
January 15, 1965

Recently, we sat in for a day as a "student" at the Rutgers library school. One teacher asked his class, "Are there standards for college libraries?" A student answered with another question: "Doesn't ALA have standards for everything?"

The student's question was far from unreasonable. One of today's favorite professional pastimes is the development of standards for—well, nearly everything. But they don't *all* come from ALA. Special Libraries Association has just issued, in reprint form, *Objectives and Standards for Special Libraries*.

Now undoubtedly a lot of people put a lot of hard work and thought into this document, but we really wonder whether it was worth it. SLA President William S. Budington says in the Preface: "The standards as here presented are not intended as a manual of operation. Neither do they set forth (except by inference) specific quantitative measures which, if followed, give automatic excellence. Following the precedent of accreditation and other similar standards, the qualities to be sought are presented instead, in a context that will point the way to their attainment. In operations of such variable parameters as special libraries, it is otherwise impossible to achieve any degree of empirical validity."

That last sentence has been put more memorably—we believe by George Bonn: "The only thing that special libraries have in common is that they are all different."

How, we still thought after reading the preface, can you possibly draft standards that will have any meaning or be applicable to such different libraries as the vast General Motors library network and the small R. R. Bowker Library? After reading through the "standards," we have to conclude that the answer is: You can't, so you draft a series of statements that are so general as to be meaningless platitudes. Examples:

"Staff Librarians should be professional librarians who can meet certain qualifications in education and experience."

"The size of a special library collection depends upon the amount of material available that is pertinent to the organization's special needs."

"The special library locates library materials and information promptly upon request."

"The special library should be located conveniently for its users."

"The budget of a special library should be based on recommendations of the special library administrator."

We have taken one quote from each of the five main sections of the "standards," to demonstrate that they have an amazing consistency throughout. The first section, entitled "Objectives," is at about the same devastating level. One sample here: "The special library serves all who have appropriate need of its services."

In case anyone should accuse us of quoting out of context, and not pointing out that these bald statements are accompanied by what is presumably intended as elucidative or explanatory text, let us requote one of the items above with "full text":

"THE SPECIAL LIBRARY SHOULD BE CONVENIENTLY LOCATED FOR ITS USERS.

"Direct contact between clients and the library is usually necessary, although other means of communication may be used effectively."

If you're looking for any more, that's all, folks!

We are perfectly willing to go along with Mr. Budington in hoping that this SLA document "will be of value to organizations considering establishment of a special library; to those reorganizing an existing facility; to professional library consultants in supporting their recommendations; to students of librarianship and information science; and to special librarians in their dialogues with executives of parent organizations." But we hope Mr. Budington and SLA will forgive us if we retain some doubts.

*Eric Moon*

## THE NEW STANDARDS
September 15, 1966

To us, the best single piece of news of the American Library Association conference was that the AASL will be revising its national school library standards with the help of a $25,000 J. Morris Jones–World Book Encyclopedia–ALA Goals for Action Award, given by Field Enterprises. The American Association of School Librarians asked for the money to develop new standards that will better reflect recent developments in school organization, curriculum, and teaching methods; include special programs for preschool, underprivileged, and exceptional youth; recognize cooperative developments in regional planning; and incorporate the impact of Federal and state legislation on libraries and education. Chairing the revision committee is Dr. Frances Henne (Columbia); consulting with it will be 25 educational and civic organizations.

For librarians still trying to make good on the 1960 *Standards for School Library Programs,* their possible tripling after only six years may come as something of a surprise. For the 1960 standards helped to seed developments which are just being felt—providing above all the ammunition for Francis Keppel, while he was U.S. Commissioner of Education, to call the state of our school libraries a "national disgrace." The gap between standards and achievements still has to be closed, even with the generous help from Washington.

Yet it has become quite clear, since Federal money started going out, that ESEA means more for libraries than Title II, which provides for their stocking, and which has doubled the school library market in a single year. With Title I money concentrating on equalizing education (often with new materials that may spread thence to the better schools) at the same time that Titles III and IV support system-wide development and experimental research on the content, organization, and use of materials, the Education Act is demanding as much as it is dishing out. What it calls for is a massive acceleration in educational thinking and development, and the result is what representative John Fogarty described at ALA: an educational whirlwind, with the library in the middle.

Libraries have already felt the impact of organizational changes in the schools: nongrading, individual study, team teaching, multiple resources. NDEA, after all, excluded textbooks, and ESEA Title II has virtually ignored them. Schools are feeling too the midcentury curriculum revolution—the "new" math, economics, English—as it is translated into materials. Looming now for libraries are concepts more radical: decentralized study areas, paperback collections, and electronic retrieval systems, that will coordinate televised texts, lectures, filmstrips, and movies. In these libraries the student may spend more than half his day with a vast range of books to call on, and a variety of materials that are still being developed by older a/v firms and new ones formed by such recent mergers as those of GE and Time, Inc., Raytheon and D. C. Heath, etc. The new learning systems, which range from "talking typewriters" to dial-a-phone TV consoles, are getting great publicity these days, and may pull the teaching machines business out of its doldrums.

These developments still have to be evaluated. Last year, Theodore Sizer, dean of Harvard's Graduate School of Education, said of the new trend in the "knowledge business": "The potential virtue of the coordination is great. Books and films and teaching machines and the rest can be related as never before." Yet "we have technical devices of great sophistication before we have clear ends, much less materials, for them. We have better learning machines than programs for them, better educational TV equipment than ideas on how to use it."

What Sizer implies, and what Jerome Bruner implied some years ago, is that we need people to serve as mediators between these materials and the teachers and students who use them, "programming" them intelligently and flexibly to individual situations, as an alternative to mass-produced "media packages." With proper staffing and approaches, it can be shown, as it was at the AASL preconference this summer, that the technological revolution can produce creativity and student innovations, and that the products of technology can also be what Gordon Ray called books: "mind-saving stations."

However, as Dr. Henne pointed out at the preconference, there are maybe 20 schools in the entire country that can run programs like those described—a fact pointing up the terrible gap, in materials, services, and especially staff to provide these services, between what we want to see in curriculum and what we can actually do. And much of the success or failure of the new programs will depend on what we expect of the materials center and the school "librarian," or whatever he comes to be called.

It will be impossible to coordinate these ventures without a thorough recasting of our ideas or organization, staff, and service to faculty and students—a qualitative overhaul that may seem remote to the little librarian still struggling with ideas a generation old. Yet with the massive expansion of Federal research and development, and our very marked commitment to what Keppel has called the second, necessary revolution in our schools: the closing of the gap between the best and worst schools, between slum and suburb, the framing of new standards and definitions seems a realistic and urgent step. The AASL deserves rich praise for having responded so promptly to the pressures fast coming from outside.

*Evelyn Geller*

## WHERE THE ACTION IS
April 1, 1967

A year and a month ago our editorial page was given over to some observations on the state of the state level of library service (*LJ*, March 1, 1966, p. 1181). The purpose of that editorial, essentially, was to underline what perhaps should be obvious: that the state level has become a focal element in the structure of library service in this country; that, in general, it is ill-equipped to fulfill this relatively new major role; and that the profession as a whole has a responsibility to see that it is noticeably and quickly strengthened.

It may be that the obvious is becoming discernible. There have been encouraging signs in recent months of an increased recognition of the state level's importance. Professional trend watchers may have noticed some of the signals going up around the ALA scene. First, at last year's ALA conference, Robert Vosper's President's Program concerned itself with statewide library development. That this impetus should come from a leading university librarian, who talked about "serious disabilities at the state level," is perhaps almost as important as that the meeting should have happened at all. Bolstering the state level should be a matter of concern for librarians from *all* types of libraries.

Secondly, the current ALA election will produce the first state librarian-president of the association in close to two decades. Either Roger Mc-Donough of New Jersey or Carma Leigh of California will be the first state librarian to be so honored since Loleta Fyan of Michigan held the office back in 1951–52.

Another recent development of some significance is the move of John Humphry from the directorship of the Brooklyn Public Library to the state librarianship of New York. A year ago we commented: "Librarianship dare not leave so much of its potential for the future hanging from some of its weakest links; it must, if necessary, reinforce them by transferring strength from other more secure parts of the chain." Apparently John Humphry agrees. It is a rare occurrence for someone to relinquish the directorship of one of the nation's largest and best-known library institutions for a state library position, but it is to be hoped that Humphry's example will persuade others of the profession's top administrators that the state level is the place where they are most needed.

Just as last year's editorial on the state scene was partially prompted by the appearance of a book—Marie Ann Long's *The State Library Consultant at Work*—so, too, is this one. Philip Monypenny's *The Library Functions of the States* (ALA, 1966) is the culmination of a long ranging effort by the American Association of State Libraries which began in 1957, produced a survey report in 1962 and then *The Standards for Library Functions at the State Level* in 1963. All the elements of this effort are important, but this latest publication, being more readable than any survey report or standards document, may reach a few more of those who have not yet adopted a statewide view.

Among other things, the Monypenny book has some important and interesting things to say about the relationships between the state library agencies and the metropolitan library services. "One of the concerns which had had the least organized attention from state library agencies," at the time of his survey, says Monypenny, "was that of improving library service in the metropolitan areas." In our February 1 issue, Sam Prentiss, former New York state librarian, warned that unless the state agencies do become more effective in this area "the federal government will bypass them and deal directly with the cities." This really would be regrettable, since there is little likelihood in most states that a truly effective statewide network of service can be built without incorporating and extending the present strength of the major city libraries.

In a sense the Humphry move has a double significance. Though it may be less applicable to New York than to some other states, "the lack of coordination between large cities and the rest of the state," to which Monypenny refers in his recent book, calls for a change in some attitudes at both state agency and large city library levels. Like a number of other people, we didn't quite believe it when we heard that Humphry was going to move to the State Library. Some of the skeptics who have not yet accepted the inevitability of the states' major role should have been listening when we asked a source very close to Humphry why he thought the Brooklyn librarian might be making this move. "Because that's where the action is now," he said.

*Eric Moon*

# The "New Media"

## NEW TECHNOLOGIES, OLD MEDIA
December 15, 1966

One of the most highly touted educational developments of the current year has been the entry of electronics firms into the school market through mergers, acquisitions, joint ventures, and other working arrangements. The moves are keynoted by caution (feedback of the first abortive teaching machine "revolution"), and the great fear, goes the story, is that some unscrupulous competitor will create a bad reputation anew for educational technology. But these careful pronouncements are countered by rather heavy publicity in the education press, which, for all the surface warning, highlights systems that cost $2000 to $3000 per student hour.

We have no gripe against educational technology as such, but wish that finer distinctions could be made among the technologies, and better note of the impact of other media on the book itself. The sensory enrichment provided by recordings and films, for example, is a far cry from the conceptual organization of programmed instruction, which is more rigidly "linear" than the book ever was; while it is no news that the augmented use of art work, photograph, document, and facsimile in printed materials has made the book a very different artifact. In his Caldecott acceptance speech last year, Beni Montresor articulately characterized the children's picture book as a medium particularly attuned to a visual or postliterate age; and his description can be applied to the remarkable combination of print and illustration that appears also in Ivor Brown's works; the *Bayeux Tapestry*; the works on DaVinci and mathematics featured in our "best books" list this month.

The familiar passage below ran in *Punch* a few years back, but seems especially pertinent to a reassessment of what is, after all, the cheapest and most accessible of the educational media.

"A new aid to rapid—almost magical—learning has made its appearance. Indications are that if it catches on all the electronic gadgets will be so much junk.

"The new device is known as Built-in-Orderly Organized Knowledge. The makers generally call it by its initials, B.O.O.K.

"Many advantages are claimed over the old-style learning and teaching aids on which most people are brought up nowadays. It has no wires, no electronic circuits to break down. No connection is needed to an electricity power point. It is made entirely without mechanical parts to go wrong or need replacement.

"Anyone can use B.O.O.K., even children, and it fits comfortably into the hands. It can be conveniently used sitting in an armchair by the fire.

"How does this revolutionary, unbelievably easy invention work? Basically B.O.O.K. consists only of a large number of paper sheets. These may run to hundreds where B.O.O.K. covers a lengthy programme of information. Each sheet bears a number in sequence, so that the sheets cannot be used in the wrong order.

"To make it even easier for the user to keep the sheets in proper order they are held firmly in place by a special locking device called a 'binding.'

"Each sheet of paper presents the user with an information sequence in the form of symbols, which he absorbs optically for automatic registration on the brain. When one sheet has been assimilated a flick of the finger turns it over and information is found on the other side.

"By using both sides of each sheet in this way a great economy is effected, thus reducing both the size and cost of B.O.O.K. No buttons need to be pressed to move from one sheet to another, to open, or close B.O.O.K. or to start it working.

"B.O.O.K. may be taken up at any time and used by merely opening it. Instantly it is ready for use. Nothing has to be connected up or switched on. The user may turn it at will to any sheet, going backwards or forwards as he pleases. A sheet is provided near the beginning as a location finder for any required information sequence.

"A small accessory, available at a trifling extra cost, is the B.O.O.K. mark. This enables the user to pick up his programme where he left off on the previous learning session. B.O.O.K.-mark is versatile and may be used in any B.O.O.K.

"The initial cost varies with the size and subject matter. Already a vast range of B.O.O.K.s is available, covering every conceivable subject and adjusted to different levels of aptitude. One B.O.O.K., small enough to be held in the hands, may contain an entire learning schedule.

"Once purchased, B.O.O.K. requires no further upkeep cost; no batteries or wires are needed since the motive power, thanks to an ingenious device patented by the makers, is supplied by the brain of the user.

"B.O.O.K.: may be stored on handy shelves and for ease of reference the programme schedule is normally indicated on the back of the binding.

"Altogether the Built-in Orderly Organised Knowledge seems to have great advantages with no drawbacks. We predict a big future for it."—*From "Learn with Book" by J. R. Heathorn.*

*Evelyn Geller*

## THE MEDIA LIBRARIAN AND A/V
April 15, 1967

We have been impressed of late by the "separate but equal" theory expressed by members of the NEA Department of Audiovisual Instruction on the roles of the media librarian and the media specialist, and what seem to be, indeed, rather small areas of functional overlapping. The recent

DAVI conference, for example, themed "implementing learning," was concerned largely with the logistics of the systems approach, the sophisticated technologies of dial-access and ITV, and the details of local film production, rather than with the evaluation of audiovisual materials (a task that is happily delegated to the librarian). And the February 1967 issue of *Audiovisual Instruction,* devoted to the "functions of the media specialist," had a similar sense of pre-established harmony, giving the librarian responsibility for evaluation and guidance with the "software," the a/v specialist or "building coordinator" administration of the "hardware."

How would the "twin" theory break down these roles? Roughly, the librarian would evaluate nonprint as well as print materials, help the student working independently, and specialize in materials purchased or stored on the building level; while the media specialist, as sort of local production man, would provide in-service training in the use of audiovisual devices (i.e., equipment), work on the local preparation of materials (slides, transparencies), and maintain, essentially, a "classroom posture." The "who's on top?" question was tactfully avoided in this discussion, or solved with the suggestion that "co-supervisors" be appointed; while the guest editorial by Richard Darling, president of the American Association of School Librarians, cheerfully pointed out that federal aid had provided enough money for both groups to expand and to settle differences.

We are glad about these attempts at cooperation, especially the efforts of AASL and DAVI to prepare jointly the new school library standards, yet we can hardly feel reassured by the picture. So careful are the media specialists to stake out separate areas of responsibility that they never have to talk to librarians—with the result that librarian and audiovisual expert conduct competing programs, while the media specialist retains a pervasive and damaging anti-book bias. (If you doubt that bias, look at the cover of the February issue of *A/V Instruction,* with its medieval monk, book in hand, receding into the background as the media he-man, that engineer without portfolio, takes over!) Perhaps more neglectful—or hypocritical— are a few systems approaches, notably some ESEA Title III "supplementary educational service" projects being developed in Nassau County (New York), Iowa, and elsewhere, that have established a direct track between the system level and the teacher in the individual school—a direct track between the a/v specialist and the teacher, ignoring the librarian; between the textbook and audiovisual materials, bypassing the riches of the trade book as it can be integrated into the entire program. A communications short-circuit indeed!

These practices, we feel, which stem from the "separate but equal" theory, are an affront not only administratively but educationally, for the anti-book bias keeps the educational technologist from recognizing that the communications revolution is keynoted not by the machine but by instant access (the world of simultaneity, as McLuhan describes it), which is coming to characterize the world of print and nonprint. The librarian's gift, after all, is for integration: of print and other media, of the library and the classroom curriculum, to form one instructional mosaic. By separating his "classroom posture" from the library's role, and the a/v program (if not collection) from the book program, the educational technologist subverts his own goals, and in the end bastardizes the purpose of the current curriculum, which is trending toward independent, not classroom, study. Last, the specious identification of "supplementary" with "audiovisual" services subverts the development of a coordinated system-wide materials program and raises serious problems of overcentralization.

We cannot believe that the twin approach will succeed at the system or building level: the loopholes are too convenient. The media librarian and the media specialist must find a way to communicate by sharing each others' literature; by planning together for an integrated program; by encouraging, not diminishing, the use of the individual library; and by coordinating their programs under the leadership of an administrator who has bridged the camps by acquiring competence in both areas.

*Evelyn Geller*

## SMALL WAYS OUT OF CHAOS
November 15, 1967

For the past three years, we have been floundering in a morass of press releases, catalogs, brochures, and photographs from the audiovisual industry, sure sign that the media revolution was upon us. And as we have watched chaos pile, we've wondered also how many school libraries across the country, faced with this inundation, could welcome these somewhat unsettling signs of their own emerging prominence. For, while we sensed that the myth of the librarian's print orientation was becoming a thing of the past, we felt that the main obstacle to better incorporation of a/v materials has been the failure to impose on them the same genius for organization that librarians, dictating their need for bibliographic control and systematic evaluation, have been able to stamp on the book industry. No pep talks for the IMC could substitute for the paramount need to provide systematic "bibliographic" and reviewing services that would keep librarians from depending on the sporadic fliers and high-pressure salesmanship of individual vendors. Above all, we felt (as our editorial last month indicated) that librarians could not permit the a/v industry to go the primrose path of the textbook field, which is not characterized by an organized reviewing structure that would make textbook selection a more rational procedure than it is today. (The result of such laxness could boomerang on a/v producers, in the end, as it already has on textbook publishers). Last, it seemed to us that in line with the approach to integrated acquisition, a subject orientation that would span the field of book and nonbook material would have to be followed.

It is this philosophy that *SLJ* has followed since it began, in January this year, to give deliberate coverage to the audiovisual field. In various issues we have explored, piece by piece, industry trends and their theoretical implications, practical problems of selection and cataloging, and have provided lists of selected films, filmstrips, and recordings to be used with children and teens in school and public library situations. We have attempted to accomplish this, moreover, not so much through special issues, but by integrating a/v coverage into our magazine as a whole. This September we supplemented these overviews with our *Screenings* column, giving monthly review coverage to two neglected a/v media: filmstrips and 8mm cartridge loop films.

With this issue, we are rounding out these efforts with a feature which we hope will enable *SLJ* to provide a full battery of services relating to a/v selection: an *Audiovisual Guide,* nonevaluative in nature, giving comprehensive coverage to current output in four important areas of media production: filmstrip and filmstrip series; 8mm cartrdige films and film series; slide series; and transparency series. Taking over the concept of the now defunct Wilson *Film* and *Filmstrip Guides,* but extending it to incorporate a cross-media approach, the new *SLJ Audiovisual Guide* is an attempt to systematize, in terms of subject area, the current output of all major producers in these fields.

In determining our review and listing coverage, as opposed to feature treatment, we have been governed by two considerations: a desire to avoid duplicating existing services; and a concern to emphasize the "small fry" of technology—the items that are purchased for the individual school or library rather than on the systems level. Both factors led to a decision to avoid, except in articles and roundups, the already massive, and extensively covered, 16mm field, and to concentrate on the developing areas that would mean more to individual librarians. Still another desire has been to establish a stronger dialogue between industry and education in emerging fields in which commercial interests have not yet become strongly entrenched, with a view to establishing the kind of professional influence that obtains in the trade book field.

Having accomplished, in the last eight issues, what we felt to be the major journalistic goals of *SLJ* with regard to media coverage, we would welcome reader reaction at this point. We should like to know your responses to our past efforts, and in particular whether our *Audiovisual Guide* will accomplish what we have planned, and what the *LJ-SLJ* book announcement issues have already done: eliminate a great deal of paper work, provide a one-glance perspective on current output, list competing products in a given subject area, provide buying information for the order of preview copies, and help you plan your budgets for building collections. We would like both this feedback and any suggestions for improvement, for we have seen the future and tried to make it work. Will it? The answer lies with you.

*Evelyn Geller*

## MEDIA MIX AT MIDPOINT
November 15, 1968

Between 1965 and 1966, when the school a/v market jumped 57 percent from $282 million to $442 million, pulling it above industry as the largest buyer of a/v materials and equipment, it became clear that "educatonal technology" was here to stay. The change has come about, moreover, despite all the warnings about an education-business establishment analogous to the Department of Defense-defense industry establishment that Eisenhower had warned about before he left the Presidency.

In the publicity generally surrounding "educational technology," one of the most frequent—and sometimes tiresome—themes is that the problems of industry-education relations can be solved through better "dialogue." This was a point made by U.S. Commissioner of Education Harold Howe II last July (not for the first time) in his address to the National Audiovisual Association. Howe distinguished the education and defense markets first, pointing out the contrast between the diffuse buying patterns and decision-making of the former and the monolithic structure of the Department of Defense, and suggested that industry advise the various organizations, particularly the new Commission on Instructional Technology, which are concerned with the media.

Despite the threat that an education-producer liaison will lead to collusion rather than altruistic cooperation (as has been the case with textbooks), a "dialogue" does seem to be the only way, at present, of coordinating market research and intuition and the actual needs of the schools. Moreover, the a/v field, being younger and able to learn from the mistakes of its predecessors selling to the schools, is in a position to make swift and constructive adjustments.

Some such moves, particularly in the direction of the emerging school library market, were made this summer by NAVA in at least two respects: first, through Dr. Richard Darling's address to its Educational Materials Producers Council (reprinted in this issue); second, in the first meeting between a small group of leading school librarians and NAVA's long-range planning committee. NAVA, of course, has had several joint committees going with the NEA Department of Audiovisual Instruction, but it had become aware of the significant buying power of the libraries and the potential of the joint DAVI-AASL *Standards for School Media Programs.* ("You have done more for us," said Ervin Nelsen, vice-president in charge of distribution for Coronet, at the meeting, "than we could ever have done for ourselves.")

The meeting was held to feel out the peculiar demands and problems librarians have, problems that have been spelled out from time to time in *SLJ:* the need for better bibliographic control, the sharp demand for more and better media cataloging, librarians' bewilderment at the lack of a jobbing structure in a/v, and their preference for individual items rather than large multimedia packages or systems from which they might want to select only certain components.

It was not in a concrete sense a fruitful meeting, but it was a fine start, marked by an air of honesty—even surprise on the part of some producers who heard the librarians' perspectives for the first time—that we sometimes find missing in the more "tea-partyish" dialogues that obtain, occasionally, between librarians and publishers. And it did lead to at least a tentative proposal for a symposium that would involve the library market and all media producers, including publishers, where these concerns could be discussed in greater detail. This move, along with NAVA's recent establishment of a task force on materials for the disadvantaged, are good and prompt steps in the right direction.

This issue of *SLJ* is, in a sense, an extension of that dialogue, outlining various problems, and centering on one of particular and basic importance—commercial cataloging of the media—whose solution is crucial if librarians are to be freed from their old stultifying tasks in order to get strong media programs off the ground. We hope, issue by issue, to center on other questions more closely, but above all invite all our readers—producers, librarians, and a/v specialists—to comment on these and other concerns, so that their dialogue can provide a continuing symposium in our pages.

*Evelyn Geller*

# Publishing

### CONCERNED WITH COPYRIGHT
April 1, 1960

"Librarians are vitally concerned with copyright, for while they may own the books they buy, they do not own their contents." That librarians were only too aware of the implications of this remark by Arthur Fisher, Register of Copyrights, at last year's Washington ALA Conference, was borne out by the attendance at the panel discussion on copyright at that conference. L. Quincy Mumford, Librarian of Congress, commented that it was probably the first time in history that such a program had played to standing room only.

Within recent years, with the adoption of the Universal Copyright Convention, Great Britain, France and Mexico have revised their copyright laws, and revision programs are under way in Germany and the Scandinavian countries. It has been evident for some time that revision of the U.S. Copyright Law of 1909, which, with only minor amendments, has governed our handling of copyrights for 50 years, is a vital necessity.

There has been a growing feeling on the part of scientists, scholars and researchers that the present law does little to promote, and indeed more frequently hinders, the spread of scientific and scholarly information. Librarians, more often than not the middlemen between the author-publisher group and the scholars and researchers, must look forward to clarification and revision of the present position with as much concern and interest as anyone in the field of communications.

Probably the area of most general interest to librarians is the photo-duplication of copyrighted material by libraries. The various and growing methods of photocopying have become indispensable to persons engaged in research, and to libraries that provide research material in their collections. In providing this valuable service, libraries receive little or no protection or guidance from the present copyright law.

There is some difference of opinion, however, as to whether a new statute should provide expressly for the photocopying of copyrighted works by libraries, or whether it would be wiser to encourage libraries, publishers, and other groups concerned to develop a working arrangement, in the nature of a code of practice, to govern photocopying by libraries.

It is interesting to note in passing that the most detailed provisions concerning photoduplication by libraries have been provided in the new United Kingdom Act, and these have been widely criticized as being too restrictive and complicated.

The basic issues, and some suggested approaches to a workable solution, are included in a study by Borge Varmer, Attorney-Advisor to the Copyright Office, titled *Photoduplication of Copyrighted Material by Libraries.*

This is one of some 28 studies in a program conducted by the Copyright Office, with the aid of an advisory panel of specialists, during the past five years. The studies themselves will afford a basis for formulating recommendations to Congress for revision of the present law, but thorough as they are, they undoubtedly do not cover all the complexities, interests and points of view in this involved field. Realizing this, the Register of Copyrights has issued an open invitation to "all persons concerned with copyright law revision" to submit written statements of their views on "any problem that they wish to have considered in a revision of the law."

We complained recently that librarians were too often "the uninvited." This time they are not. If you still have any axes to grind, now is the time to start the grindstone whirling. Mr. Fisher wants your views before April 15.

*Eric Moon*

## ARE BOOKS OVERPRICED?
May 15, 1966

Four librarians (from Detroit, Philadelphia, Washington, D.C., and Orange, N.J.) recently aired some rather serious conplaints about book publishers and wholesalers before a Senate committee. In essence, the charges were:

1) That some of the so-called "publishers' library bindings" are not worth their extra cost;

2) That librarians are nevertheless being forced to buy them because of an increasing tendency on the part of the publishers (or wholesalers) to discontinue offering alternate trade bindings;

3) That those special library editions are being "net priced" in such a way as to force all libraries—large or small—to buy on equal terms.

Unfortunately, the several charges were not clearly distinguished in the testimony thus far presented, and the distinction may be important.

Take the first charge, namely, that some "publishers' library findings" aren't worth their cost. *Of this there can be very little doubt.* One could go farther and say that *some books* aren't worth their cost. Over 175 publishers are busily producing books for the library market at prices ranging from about a cent a page to well over ten cents a page, in bindings ranging from marginal to excellent. It would be strange, indeed, if some were not better buys than others. It is not clear, however, what any Senate committee could be expected to do about this. Surely, this is a matter that can safely be left to the laws of the market place. Surely, discerning librarians will punish the publisher who overprices his books, simply by buying fewer of them—or will they?

The second charge—that publishers are allowing trade editions to go out of print—is again nothing that can be regulated except by the laws of supply and demand. It is normal for a book to have a longer life in the library market than in the bookstore market, so one would normally expect that the library edition could be kept in print longer. If it is charged that the publisher is dropping the less profitable editions in favor of the more profitable, well whoever supposed that publishing—which is a business—*wasn't* profit motivated? And a publisher who wasn't satisfied with his profit margin on any edition would always be free to raise the price.

The third charge is really the only one that warrants attention from any regulatory agency. If publishers are coercing the wholesalers into accepting more discount than they need or want, and further coercing them into keeping it and not passing any of it along to the libraries—this is illegal, and those guilty of it can and should be restrained and punished.

However, the Justice Department, after a year's investigation, found no evidence of conspiracy or coercion sufficient to warrant prosecution. Whether the Senate committee can succeed where the Justice Department failed remains to be seen.

In the meantime, however, libraries are not powerless. They can relentlessly return to the publishers any "publishers' library bindings" which they feel are unworthy of the surcharge. (Most publishers guarantee "satisfaction in service, or free replacement.") They can order prebinds in preference to publishers' library editions whenever the alternative presents itself and is favorable. They can minimize their purchases of books considered overpriced (and tell the publisher so). They can maximize their purchases of "full value" editions.

Librarians might also ask themselves whether they favor or oppose the extension of direct selling by the publishers. This is, of course, at the root of the "net price" system. Publishers who measure the success of their salesmen by the orders they bring back direct (instead of by way of the library's favorite wholesaler) are naturally going to be concerned if they are undersold on their own books by the wholesalers. If the wholesalers do not voluntarily respect the publishers "suggested net library prices," then the publisher will take whatever defensive action is legally open to him—such as cutting his discounts to the wholesalers, or even cutting *out* the wholesalers in an effort to force the libraries to deal direct.

Any suggestion that librarians "reward their friends and punish their enemies" through the book selection process is often met with cries that you must not allow commercial considerations to creep into book selection procedures. If *Winnie-the-Pooh* comes in only one binding, you are going to have to buy it whether you like the binding or the price, or not.

True. And the author and publisher of the indispensable books are perhaps well entitled to whatever rewards they exact. But of the 25,000 or more children's books in print, very few, really, are indispensable. In many, many cases a $5 book just isn't 25 percent better than a $4 book on the same subject. Price is a *legitimate* factor to consider in the book selection process. Just a little intelligent buyer-resistance to overpriced books and bindings could have a big effect in curbing any excesses.

*Daniel Melcher*

## NET PRICING AND THE SALESMAN
May 15, 1967

The obvious intent of the recently filed Justice Department civil actions involving "net" pricing of library editions is that libraries should now pay less. Presumably wholesalers who weren't doing so are to start offering greater discounts from the publishers' "net" prices, while publishers' school and library sales forces are to match, or exceed the wholesalers' discounts.

In theory, this competition should result in lower prices to libraries. In practice it could lead to almost total elimination of the very price competition which the Justice Department seeks to preserve. For once any publisher determines consistently to undersell his wholesalers, they will no longer be any competition either to him or to each other. Some publishers aim quite frankly at selling direct to all major library customers, leaving to the wholesalers only the smaller library accounts, or the smaller publishers' lines.

Recent experience shows that if a large publisher puts a sales force into the school and library field, thereby enlarging his "share of the market," (and quite possibly paying his salesmen more than he pays his authors) other publishers, inevitably, are forced to do likewise if only in self defense. Small publishers will either lose out, or perhaps club together to share cooperative sales forces. Up to now the net price system has kept most of these sales forces out of direct price competition with the wholesalers. Now that they are on notice that it is illegal to avoid price competition they must decide whether to outbid the wholesaler or be outbid by him.

In such competition, the publisher can, if he likes, give no discounts to anyone. Or he can give the same discounts to all—*i.e.*, he can sell to libraries at the very same discount at which he sells to wholesalers or booksellers, thus effectively excluding the latter from any participation in his distribution picture.

A question that all libraries must face up to is whether they favor an acceleration of the present trend toward gradual exclusion of the wholesaler from the library distribution picture. The wholesaler was not able to survive as a major factor in bookstore distribution after the publisher set up direct relations with all the larger bookstores. Is he now to be slated for gradual exclusion from library distribution as well?

Some libaries, particularly the larger ones, may see no disadvantage in a trend toward direct dealings with the publishers. It may make sense for them to deal directly with the larger publishers, and indirectly through wholesalers with the smaller publishers. It may make sense for any library to buy direct when the publisher's extra discount seems worth the added paperwork; and through wholesalers when it isn't—if indeed any wholesalers are able to survive on just the business that is too marginal to interest the publishers.

The hidden cost of the publisher's salesman, however, is another factor to consider. One informed estimate cites $20,000 as the minimum cost of keeping a salesman in the field. In some situations up to $100,000 out of each $500,000 of book buying power may be going to salesmen. In one large metropolitan library, the area salesman hangs around the buying office to the point of being a nuisance in an effort to earn the sizable commissions he draws on that library alone.

What if a library chooses *not* to buy through a salesman? Some of the larger libraries have argued rather persuasively that they should not have to pay for services they don't need, that their buying power and streamlined purchasing procedures warrant extra discounts that are not averaged in (as are the discounts on net priced books) with the cost of serving smaller or less efficient libraries. Can the argument be extended? Should libraries pay their share of supporting the salesmen even when they feel the salesman's role in book selection and distribution is not commensurate with his cost?

The individual publisher may argue that the commissions paid his library salesmen do not raise book prices, since the new business generated results in larger printings and lower costs. It is less easy, however, to see the gain for the book industry at large, or for the librarian, since other publishers are now likely to send salesmen into the field to protect and augment their own sales. A school or public library system which once operated happily without any resident salesmen may now be supporting several, all scrambling for the same pool of book money.

Is it not possible that a better basis for publisher-wholesaler coexistence could be established by shifting the salesman from commission (which forces him to a "hard sell") to salary? The arguments that salaries would destroy the salesman's incentives are questionable, for this problem seems to have been solved in many other industries, including the mass market paperback and college textbook fields. If he were on salary, he could impartially sell for either wholesalers or publishers, respecting the library's convenience and preference. If he were on salary, the time he didn't have to consume trying to get "credit" for business that was coming in anyway could be spent on generating genuinely new business. On salary, he could visit all the important accounts, not just those who bought direct. On salary he could multiply the real value of his "service" function by extending it to the library's relations with the wholesalers as well as with his company.

An adjustment of the salesman's incentives might go far to ensure that the price competition which the Justice Department is trying to preserve really works for efficiency in distribution and not against it. In the last analysis it is the librarians who will determine how this is worked out, if they methodically use their purchasing power to reward those who serve them best.

*Daniel Melcher*

### REPRINT PITFALLS
December 1, 1967

An article on a subject of considerable irritation to librarians appears in the Fall 1967 issue of the *LLA Bulletin,* journal of the Louisiana Library Association. Writing on "Pitfalls in Purchasing Reprints," James H. Hoover of the Louisiana State University Library says: "In addition to publication delays and price increases, the librarian faces the hazard of ordering announced reprints that never get published."

Hoover points out that information about cancellation of reprint projects is frequently hard to come by. "At times the only clue may be a current publisher's catalog that no longer lists a title previously announced. Publisher's replies to claim letters are often the first official word of cancelled projects. When a publisher makes it clear that unless sufficient advance orders are received for a particular title no reprint will be possible, notice of the success or failure of the venture is usually forthcoming. However, it is easy to suspect that other publicized titles depend on the same restrictions without the librarian having been made aware of the reprinter's plan."

Much of the librarian's trouble with reprint buying, Hoover notes, "can be traced to the publishers' reprint catalogs and announcements . . . all too often they fail to identify exactly which titles are readily available, in process, or merely mentioned as likely possibilities." He mentions the 1967 reprint catalog of one leading U.S. publisher and says that an exchange of letters and phone calls established that only about half the listed titles were in stock, and "only three or four more were projected for publication in the immediate future."

*LJ* has another illustration of the kind of situation about which Hoover complains with such moderation. There are two principal exhibits. The first is a 1966 catalog issued by a reprint publisher, listing some 300 titles. The cover of the catalog indicates clearly that all titles listed were or would be "ready" in the fall months of 1966.

The second item is a copy of a letter from the same reprint publisher, addressed to a major university library, and accompanied by a list of nearly 40 titles. The letter asks which of the listed titles are producing reprint editions. The significant factor here is the timing. All the titles requested from the university library appeared in the publisher's catalog as "ready" in Fall 1966, but the letter to the library is dated in late May 1967—six to nine months after the titles' readiness had been announced.

The problems, and the potential for delay, in reprint publishing are many, and it may be necessary, as Mr. Hoover does, to give the publishers the benefit of every doubt. In the case we cite, it is *possible* that the publisher had been trying to obtain copies of the titles in question for a year or more. The evidence, nevertheless, leaves the strong suspicion that these titles were announced as ready before any action or decision to obtain or reprint them had been taken. The conclusion to be drawn from this is that they were announced either to forestall competition for these titles from other reprinters, or simply as a promotional device, so that the publisher might gather orders before taking any of the economic risks of publication.

There is, of course, no reason why a publisher should not test his potential market before embarking on a reprint (or any other publishing project), but to do it in this manner is less than scrupulous. The practice may, indeed, be open to a charge of deliberately false or misleading advertising.

If this were no more than a source of administrative inconvenience or irritation to libraries, it would not perhaps be desperately serious. But such practices are damaging, both because they cast undeserved suspicion on other reputable publishers and because of their effect on library budgets. As Mr. Hoover points out, "In those cases where encumbered funds are lost if outstanding at the end of the fiscal year, the library is inconvenienced indeed!"

If steps are to be taken to counteract such malpractices, perhaps the first move should be the gathering of some solid information on the subject. *LJ* invites libraries to tell us about their experiences with reprint publishers, particularly those with whom they have had consistent problems. We would like to receive also examples of specific titles promised but never delivered, particularly any which have resulted in any library forfeiting encumbered funds.

*Eric Moon*

# Library "Literature"

## WHOSE OPINION?
April 1, 1961

The contents page of the *ALA Bulletin* carries a permanent warning that ". . . authors' opinions should be regarded as their own unless ALA endorsement is noted." This is probably a desirable precaution in a magazine which is the *official* voice of an association.

It has never seemed to us to be as necessary or as desirable in an *independent* magazine. By its very nature, such a journal is the main hope for an author holding a nonconformist view or a minority opinion, or wishing to place on record an "opposition" statement. We do not wholly subscribe to the old dictum of "publish and be damned," but we do believe that much of the vitality of a periodical depends in part on its ability to gather and willingness to publish views which argue with the parrot of conformity.

If a magazine follows this course, and is successful in its aim, it perforce publishes over a period of time a variety of conflicting opinions. Fickleness, of course, and even indecision, are to be found in editors, just as they are in librarians and other fallible human beings. But it should be obvious that a magazine which makes room for so many conflicting opinions does not necessarily agree with all that it publishes.

It should NOT be necessary, however, for the editor to footnote each article with: "We're right behind this man," or "This article is way off the beam, but remember the 'freedoms' and all that."

There are times when we may be sufficiently provoked to respond, as was the editor of the *Wilson Library Bulletin* recently, when an outrageous statement about British library efficiency understandably drew from him the comment: "Opinions advanced by *Bulletin* authors do not necessarily coincide with those of the editor, *especially sometimes*." There are times, too, when we shall feel that the issue is sufficiently vital for LIBRARY JOURNAL to take a firm and clear position. Such a position will *always* be stated on the editorial page. A recent example occurred when we published Rice Estes' article on segregated libraries: this was accompanied by an editorial on the same subject ( *LJ*, Dec. 15, '60, pp. 4418–22, 4436–7).

These thoughts on editorial attitudes are occasioned by the article in this issue ( pp. 1364–6) which advocates the ending of National Library Week. The grapevine somehow picked up the news that this was in our possession. That some people should have been disturbed about it is understandable; that they should have concluded that *LJ* was taking the position adopted by Mr. Angoff is barely credible.

We have been as strong in support of NLW as any other library periodical ever since the annual event was born. We have published articles, news stories, pictures galore—*all* in favor of NLW. We know, however, that every March or April, there are librarians who grow irate at the flamboyance of NLW publicity methods and mumble into their beards: "Why don't they stop all this nonsense?" Now one of them is out in the open, and we would like to know how many agree with him, *and* how many will feel impelled to rush to ardent defense of the book and library world's big annual occasion.

ALA has an Evaluation Committee which is at present gathering evidence on the effectiveness of NLW, and which will report at the Cleveland conference in July on the desirability of ALA's continued participation. We are sure, knowing the make-up of the committee and the determination of its chairman, that any decisions will be made as objectively as possible, but there are one or two factors which make objective decisions difficult. One is that ALA is already committed, in a sense, to National Library Week. Paragraph 8(c) of *Goals for Action* advocates "Vigorous support for, and participation in, National Library Week by all members." A second factor is that, on the admission of the chairman of the Evaluation Committee, no evidence has been obtained which has not been solicited. There must be at least a possibility that solicited evidence is not truly representative.

Where do we stand on NLW? We are *for* it, enthusiastically but not unreservedly. The original slogan, which is becoming more microscopic on the posters each year and will, we hope, soon disappear altogether, was a bad one. There *is* a degree of foolish hucksterism. But we would not agree with all of Mr. Angoff's points, even on this score. Norman H. Strouse, for example, is not *just* the head of a large advertising agency. He is also a respected bookman and has well-founded connections with libraries. It would seem to us that he was chosen to chair the Steering Committee both because he is a bookman and because his advertising experience and connections put him in a position to do something about persuading *others* to read.

NLW has its commercial and vulgar aspects—but is this such a devastating handicap? Libraries today are competing with some powerfully vulgar media, and it seems doubtful whether the dignified reserve of 19th century librarianship gives us any longer a fighting chance. Dignity, of course, is not a derogatory word, but if you stand on dignity too long or too hard, it has a tendency to get squashed into pomposity. We remember once arguing with a traditional library architect that our projected new library should be all steel and glass: he dismissed the thought as "vulgar."

There is apparently no adequate way at present to measure, as others have said before us, whether NLW has done its primary job of persuading the individual to read more, to buy or borrow more books. The Evaluation Committee has neither the funds nor the staff to undetake the kind of survey which would be needed for this purpose. But if there's a chance that ten, or 100, or 1000 books have been read which otherwise would not have been read, then NLW, in our view, has succeeded.

Apart from the national and local publicity, there is one area in which there is direct and ample evidence of the impact of NLW. Many citizens are taking part in activities connected with libraries who were not doing so before the inception of National Library Week. Such citizen participation and awareness must be to the ultimate benefit of the library. We firmly expect that the Evaluation Committee will come up with proof that some libraries have received additional support, financial and other, as a result of NLW.

There is one other direction in which National Library Week has been more than helpful. Some libraries have had for years a forceful and continuing program of publicity and public relations. This is by no means true of all, and through NLW many more libraries have sharpened up their publicity efforts and intensified their attempts to reach the man *outside* the library.

We don't need more arguments than this to be in favor of NLW, though more exist. Nevertheless, we should like to hear the other side. Blessings tend to be mixed, and criticism does the righteous no harm.

*Eric Moon*

## DULLNESS AND DUPLICATION
September 1, 1961

Library literature is in a sad state. So says Donald E. Thompson, librarian of Wabash College, Indiana, in the July–August issue of *ALA Bulletin*. His disenchantment with library literature was brought about by a check on the material published during the past 40 years on "library instruction to undergraduate . . . students."

His discoveries, in general, were that the periodicals suffered from repetition, plagiarism, superfluity, dullness and a distinct shortage of new ideas. It would be difficult to challenge these findings, but it is possible to challenge their originality. Mr. Thompson is himself open to the charge that he has been repetitious—it has all been said before, many times.

We deplore the article which is a straight re-hash as much as he does. All of us, editors and readers alike, welcome new points of view, accounts of new procedures or developments, and what Mr. Thompson calls "a slightly different twist." But there is almost no subject in library literature which has not been treated by someone, somewhere, before. We doubt that any professional periodical could survive if it set itself the aim of publishing nothing except new ideas expressed in new and vital ways.

There is, in any case, a real need for repetition and re-emphasis of the important things in librarianship, both for the benefit of the continuing stream of new librarians and the occasional revitalization of their older colleagues. The librarian or the student who will, as a matter of course, go back 50 or 60 years in the literature to see what John Cotton Dana had to say about administration or Melvil Dewey about library education is a rarity—even though he will often find more original ideas there than in some of the current issues.

What cures does Mr. Thompson prescribe for the ills he finds? There

appear to be two: "the production of stimulating and challenging manuscripts which contain new ideas and information," and a reduction in the
number of library periodicals. Admirable! We agree 100 percent. All we
need is Mr. Thompson's magic formula for bringing about these remedies.

The first can certainly be helped along by more ruthless and more
competent editing, a less easy acceptance of the second rate, and a continuing search for talent. In the final analysis, however, it depends less upon the
editors than upon the profession itself. Are the library schools encouraging
original thought and a spirit of challenge? Or is this where the re-hash
technique is largely learned? Are librarians producing a sufficient supply of
new ideas? And if so, do they know how to communicate them? Will they
work as hard at *communicating* ideas as at producing them?

One of Mr. Thompson's proposals for reducing the number of library
periodicals is that periodicals of state libraries and state library associations,
where both exist, might be combined. It is in the national and international
journals, however, that he finds most "duplication of subject matter," and
here too he proposes that some of these periodicals either put themselves
out of business or combine with competitors. Some specifics here would be
most interesting. Which periodicals does Mr. Thompson think should commit hara-kiri? Which ones should join forces, and how would Mr. Thompson
encourage such consolidation?

While we query the practicality of some of these proposals, there is only
one with which we would violently disagree. It is that "the number of
general . . . journals might be reduced by channeling more material to the
specialized journals." Specialization is a twentieth century disease which has
already bitten the library profession and its periodicals badly.

With the steady growth of divisional periodicals and journals devoted
to special interests, there is a real danger that we shall reach the point where
catalogers talk only to catalogers, reference librarians only to reference
librarians, and so on. Some general, national periodicals are needed to
present an overview of librarianship, and surprising as it may seem, there
are not very many. In fact, there are only three which have sufficiently large
circulations to ensure that a point of view or a piece of information will
reach the majority of members of the profession.

The main purpose of this editorial, however, is not to decry Mr.
Thompson's criticisms. Such criticism is necessary, and we gladly invite
other suggestions for the improvement of our professional press.

*Eric Moon*

## THE THIEF OF TIME
October 15, 1961

Some of the most interesting and useful contributions to library literature during the past ten years have often appeared in the excellent series of
*Occasional Papers* published by the University of Illinois Library School.

This fact, plus the great importance of the subject covered, led us to await the arrival of the latest paper in the series with impatient anticipation.

Paper No. 61 is entitled *Reference Service in American Public Libraries Serving Populations of 10,000 or More*. It is the report of a nationwide survey by the Public Library Reference Survey Committee of the Reference Services Division of ALA. Dated March 1961, the paper reached us in August (although it may have been available a little before that).

We endorse wholeheartedly the statement in the introduction to this report that: "Reference service in public libraries has received little research attention, has suffered from neglect in the professional literature, and has perhaps not received the attention it deserves in planning the allocation of federal funds for library development." There is no major important area of library work about which we have so little concrete information, and perhaps no area of library service which—looking at the *general* picture—is performed so inadequately.

It is these convictions which prompted our impatience and our anticipation, and which now prompt our critical reception of the report. As it turns out, the impatience was well justified, the anticipation certainly was not. Let us look at the chronology.

In May 1955, the Reference Section of the Public Libraries Division appointed a special committee to investigate existing reference services in public libraries. A pilot project had previously been completed in the spring of 1954. "Early in 1956" an eight-page questionnaire was distributed through state library agencies or state library associations. This was the questionaire on which the recently published report is based.

Now our question is: does it really take five years to distribute and analyze an eight-page questionnaire, and to produce and publish a 22-page report? And a second question: how relevant are these figures, gathered half a decade ago? Examine library statistics in any other field, and see what has happened to them between 1956 and 1961.

What is the reason for this inordinate delay? Is it the familiar curse of the committee? Or the drag of the chain of approval through committee, section, division, Association? Or is it that the people involved in the study, all volunteering their spare time and effort, had too many commitments to too many other projects?

Whatever the reasons, it is difficult to convey a sense of urgency about the need for improvement and for increased support of reference service, or hope of attracting "the attention it deserves," when the first extensive report since the Public Library Inquiry is produced so leisurely that it emerges as a piece of recent history rather than a contribution to current knowledge. Perhaps nothing *has* happened in the past five years. Perhaps the report *is* still accurate in most of the essentials. If so, we can scarcely prove it.

It is a pervasive fault of the library profession that we seem unable to undertake any research project, no matter how limited or compact, without this destructive time-stretch. An outstanding example has been the library statistics published by the Office of Education—though it must be admitted that there has been considerable improvement here. But any commercial firm which produced material of current importance at such a snail's pace would unquestionably fail. How many copies of the *American Library Directory,* for example, would the Bowker Company sell if the information it contained were five years old?

We have made no attempt to analyze what is in the report on reference service. There appears to be no hurry, and you can probably best enjoy it *at your leisure.*

*Eric Moon*

### NEWS OR COMMENTARY?
January 1, 1962

We have long felt that someone needed to take a hard look at the purpose and function of ALA's *Newsletter on Intellectual Freedom.* With a quarterly publication schedule it could scarcely be particularly effective as a news vehicle. At best it could only gather news from a number of other published sources and present a kind of digest or summary report (and it must be said that it has done this very well). But only a percentage of the matter in the *Newsletter* can really be *news* except to those who read none of the major newspapers or periodicals.

What audience does the *Newsletter* aim to reach? Is its purpose to keep librarians abreast of the censorship scene, or to persuade them that they must stand firm when the censor's hand knocks on their door? Or is there a thought that this *Newsletter* might reach outside our own professional circle (where it is to be hoped that it preaches largely to the converted) and make evident to society at large, ALA's and the library profession's clear position on all matters of intellectual freedom and its infringement?

In 1955 the *Newsletter* was attacked as being nonobjective, and its editor at that time declared that every attempt was made to keep it objective. Now, with a change in editorship has come a change in editorial attitude—one which we heartily applaud.

Donald Black of the Physics Library at UCLA took over the editorship with the September 1961 issue of the *Newsletter*. This issue, in addition to the news, includes three excellent editorials, the last of which says in part:

"We cannot entirely condone a search for absolute objectivity in a publication of this kind. First, the American Library Association has long been on record espousing the cause of intellectual freedom. We cannot laud the concept of intellectual freedom in one breath and condone censorship in the next. Second, we doubt that hard, cold, "scientific" objectivity is possible in any area involving human thoughts, spoken or written."

The *Newsletter's* function, while it remains a quarterly, should be analytical and critical. Working behind the events, it is in a good position to analyze the news as presented in other media, and then to comment and present a view that represents at least the majority opinion of the association or profession. On the basis of his first issue, Mr. Black seems well able to do this and we hope that he continues in this direction.

Both ALA and UCLA are to be complimented on providing two first-rate commentators on the current censorship scene. We now have a good double-pronged attack in the consistently excellent column by Everett Moore in the *ALA Bulletin* and in the new look Donald Black has given the *Newsletter.*

We have only two criticisms of Mr. Black's first issue. It came out dismally late—we received ours in late November—and though this may not be the editor's fault, the *Newsletter* really cannot afford this additional delay. The other point with which we wish to take issue is the last line of Mr. Black's third editorial. This reads: "Editorials will be infrequent."

Why, Mr. Black? These first three were well written, interesting and just what the doctor ordered (or at least what the patient needed). Keep 'em coming.

*Eric Moon*

## WHAT'S NEWS?
January 15, 1962

It is early December. The weather is not tropical but the questions are. The telephone shatters another train of thought. For the third time in as many days a voice at the far end of a long distance line asks: "How much information does *LJ* have about *Tropic of Cancer* and libraries?"

The police, the city manager or some other well qualified censor has moved in on yet another library. The librarian wants to know what has happened elsewhere. How have other librarians and their board of trustees dealt with the problem? Where has resistance to such pressures been successful? What were the decisive factors, the results?

Apart from the Providence stand (*LJ*, Dec. 1, pp. 4142–3), where vigilant librarian Stuart Sherman kept us (and thereby the profession) in touch with events *as they happened,* we have to admit to the voice on the telephone that our information is sparse and scattered. From other libraries under pressure we have received scarcely a word. We promise to do some digging.

Invaluable help comes to us from Roland Burdick of the American Book Publishers Council, and we top up his information with telephone calls to various parts of the country where things *seem* to be happening. After some spadework we manage to put together a three-page summary in our January 1 issue (pp. 65–68). We know that what we have is still only a small sampling from one of the most widespread campaigns against a single book in publishing history.

The point of this story is not concerned so much with the trials of the *Tropic* as with News—or rather the lack of news-consciousness in the library profession.

Libraries are a vital part of the world of communications. Of all people, librarians must know that they cannot operate effectively today in isolation. Yet news coverage remains the weakest aspect of our professional press. National news, emanating from associations like ALA or organizations like the Council on Library Resources is, in general, plentiful and prompt. But news filters through from the local scene as though the pipeline were permanently choked. It is no coincidence that, despite the many vocal critics of library periodicals, this is one aspect of library literature at which the critic's finger is seldom pointed. For the critic, the librarian himself, knows that he belongs in the dock with those he would accuse.

Much of what happens in your community, your area, your association is of interest, significance, and *help* on a wider than local scale. But time is a tough editor, and today's news has much more chance than yesterday's.

What is news? Why your bond issue succeeded or flopped, what books are giving you trouble, a small effort at cooperation, a local survey of readership or a study of costs, how to get books back without arresting people, a breakthrough in procedures or equipment, a cute piece of local public relations—news is infinite and variable.

You're still not sure? No matter, send it anyway. If there's a seed of an idea there, we'll water it. You're not sure how to present it? You don't have to, and we don't need a ten-page article. A two-line note on what is happening or may be about to happen, a clipping from the local newspaper, a telephone call (collect, if it's urgent)—any of these will do. We'll do the chasing and the writing.

But digging without a map in the vast territory of twentieth century librarianship makes looking for a needle in a haystack seem a cinch. Just put an X on where the treasure may be, and we'll look.

In some of the major cities we have some conscientious and active contacts. We need more local news-scouts and reporters who will keep their eyes and ears open, and tell us what they see and hear. What about you?

*Eric Moon*


## A DAY WITH STUDENTS
March 15, 1962

Visits to a number of library schools in the past year or two have left us, on most occasions, with an acute sense of disappointment. The qualities of vitality and enthusiasm, the inspiration which a good school should implant in those about to take off on a new career, have seldom been much in evidence. The few views expressed by most of these students have been conformist or cautious, dull or downright defeatist.

Where is the "pep" we should expect from each new generation of librarians? Well, we found an exception to the situation outlined above, during a day-long visit to the Drexel Library School a few weeks ago, and now a ray or two of hope has partially dissipated our cloud of gloomy expectations.

We had been asked to sit in on a class discussion of book selection and censorship, since the February 1 issue of *LJ* (particularly the article on "Problem Fiction") was the most current offering for dissection by the students. The discussion rocketed all the way from Henry Miller to the Hardy Boys—and back again. We began to wonder whether we were present as resource expert or victim. Our views, those of the teacher's, and some commonly accepted as gospel, were queried and challenged in forthright fashion. The discussion was invigorating and constructive. It was clear that these students had been thinking as well as studying, that they had pronounced opinions which they were not afraid to express, and that some of them, at least, were appalled by the widespread timidity and lack of conviction revealed by *LJ*'s and other studies of public library book selection.

In the evening we joined two other editors in a panel discussion of library periodical problems. The larger audience for this session ranged all the way from young students to the eminence of Emerson Greenaway, but again, in the question period the students were well to the fore.

Finding new writers was a problem given high priority by both the library periodical editors who spoke. Both expresxed a certain anguish over the apparent dearth of new voices in the library field.

Over the coffee-cups after the meeting, we were surrounded by a crowd of students. Several, the unpublished writer's gleam in their eyes, said: "You mentioned new writers. What about library schools students? Would you publish us?"

We were surprised, even impatient at the question for a moment. Wasn't it obvious, on past performance, that we would publish anyone who had something worthwhile to say? Wasn't it obvious that we made no conditions about a fifth-year degree or ten years' service in an executive position? Doesn't everyone know that these things don't ensure that a man can write, nor that he will *necessarily* have anything worth writing about.

Back at the office next day, we did a little checking, and found all this wasn't so obvious after all. An article in the June 15 *LJ* last year ("Who Writes For *LJ*," pp. 2276–7) revealed that only *one* article in a six-year period of publication had been written by a library school student. In 1961 we did better—we published at least two articles written while the authors were still students. Even so, it's a dismal showing.

So perhaps it's time to assert that our pages are not reserved for the eminent and the elderly. An article by a student, providing it has something to say and says it well, has just as much chance of acceptance as an article by Powell or Shera.

*All* the library periodicals need new writers—and the profession needs their fresh point of view. Some of the old writers are getting tired and repetitive, and scratchy as an old phonograph record. Some of them have written too much, too often. They have nothing left to say. It is always to the younger generation that we must look for new ideas, and new views on our old ideas.

But we have no magic formula for discovering the talents and abilities of those behind the library school desks. You students must help yourselves. So buckle down, write, and have the courage to send it off. But don't expect preferential treatment. Even the big boys get rejected—and so will you if what you turn in isn't good enough.

*Eric Moon*

## POPULAR OR SCHOLARLY?
June 15, 1962

Nobody loves a questionnaire—except perhaps its compiler. We send out a fair number ourselves, knowing full well that some of you must groan when they arrive. Whatever its dangers and weaknesses, the questionnaire is a useful element in communications technique. Certainly it is often one of our most effective ways of keeping in touch with library thinking and practice across this vast country, and we appreciate the willingness with which some of you respond.

If it makes anyone feel any better, it isn't all a one-way passage. We *receive* questionnaires too. One arrived the other day from Kent State University Library, Ohio, which has plans for "a guide to publications for writers on library science similar to the *Publication Guide for Literary and Linguistic Scholars* by Byrd and Goldsmith."

We hope that Kent State will forgive us if we say that some of the questions asked are naive and not designed to yield answers that will be helpful, either to those in pursuit of publication or to the library periodicals themselves.

Let us here concentrate on one question only: "Which approach do you prefer—Popular or Scholarly?"

How would you answer that? We were reminded immediately of some remarks made a few months ago by Mr. Kaye Lamb, the National Librarian of Canada. Slating historians for the dullness of much of their writing, he said:

"In some unfortunate way, dullness seems to have become associated in the academic mind with soundness. . . . The general impression seems to be that if something is readable and interesting, if it is presented with dash and style, it must be historically dubious."

Kaye Lamb was absolutely right, but he was also throwing stones from a terribly vulnerable glass house. For much of our own literature is clouded in a miasma of scholarly pretensions, where dullness and soundness are mistaken for synonyms. This is nowhere more true than in the Groves of Biblio-Academe, where the rotten grapes (not of wrath but of portentously doubtful wisdom) fall squashily into pitiful clusters of footnotes.

If the word "scholarly" is hideously misunderstood, what of "popular"?

It is a word that has come to encompass the fatuity of Jack Paar, the reading that is aimed at adults with juvenile minds, and the jazzed-up or mass approach to anything and everything.

So if the library periodical editor says, "Don't be scholarly, for God's sake, be very, very popular," then he's inviting the impression that he's editing a comic strip, and he'll quickly be engulfed with offerings of sad verse, "cute" stories and sick satire.

If, on the other hand, he plumps for the scholarly, he is inviting a product, apparently encouraged by many library schools, which can only be called "scissors and paste" research. To produce this you must ferret around in the literature of the distant past, extract the thoughts and ideas of another time, paste them together (with a plentiful supply of footnotes ad references—at least fifty are required for the library school paper that will pass), and finally present the grubby composite as your own work. No original thought, no ideas thrown out before they have fossilized—these are not required, are indeed frowned upon.

Faced with the scholarly-popular choice, then, we have to answer that we do not regard these as mutually exclusive terms. We want articles that are scholarly in that they contain—and invite on the part of the reader— thought. We want articles that are popular in that they are presented with a style and flair and vigor that invite—no, *demand*—reading. That's all.

*Eric Moon*

## A REBIRTH
September 1, 1962

Our vote for the most improved state library association periodical in the country would be awarded unhesitatingly to *The Bay State Librarian*, the quarterly bulletin of the Massachusetts Library Association.

A while back this magazine included two excellent and critical articles on public libraries, book selection and censorship—always a topic of more than passing interest in Massachusetts—by Lester Asheim and Dan Lacy. These, we understand, are to be reprinted shortly in one of the national library periodicals, so we shall say no more about them here.

Then there came an issue presenting a roundup of views on state aid for libraries, a subject of more recent topical importance in the Bay State. And in dealing with this truly sacred cow, the editor even had the temerity to present one contributor who was distinctly "agin." Charles Copeland, librarian of the Salem Public Library, didn't present a very convincing case against state aid (perhaps there isn't one to be made), but this is not the important thing. It is vastly encouraging to see an editor at the state level giving public recognition to the fact that some of our most cherished ideas have yet to be completely sold, even to the members of our own profession.

It is altogether too easy to assume that a minority view is only a crackpot opinion, and nearly as easy to conclude that what is accepted by the large majority is not only right but is accepted by all. By keeping open the door of doubt, the library periodicals can perform a real service: they can keep us healthy—and awake. But they don't do it often enough.

We have been tempted several times during the past few months to comment on this rebirth of a library periodical, but we resisted hasty judgments. We wondered if the new editor, John N. Berry, III, of Simmons College Library could keep it up. It is relatively easy to produce one, or even two, fresh and lively issues of a periodical, but to do it with consistency takes effort and imagination. Mr. Berry seems up to the challenge.

The latest issue of *The Bay State Librarian* (July) leads off with a hard hitting article by novelist Truman Nelson. "Somewhere along the line," says Mr. Nelson, "the great humanist function of the keeping and offering of books freely to the public has become a 'marketing problem.' In their attempt to remove the uncertainties of mass acceptance from their selections, the librarians have removed the surprises as well. The verb to browse has become obsolete. One no longer goes to the library to see *what* is there, he goes to see if *it* is there . . . *it* being the current book or books being touted by the book clubs, a massive advertising campaign, or by the prominence of the writer's public or private life on television or in the newspapers."

Is Mr. Nelson brash enough to offer an answer? Indeed he is. The one he offers is "that the public library accept its responsibility as the common consciousness and the continuity-keeper of the society it serves. It should provide sustenance for those people of intellectual bent who continue through adulthood to sharpen their wits, as a young cat his claws, on the rough bark of the tree of life, as reflected in fine books. It should collect and nourish, and forcibly feed if required, the works of every author who tries to write seriously, without an overriding concern about book clubs, best seller lists, and movies . . ."

If you think *all* library periodicals at the state level are as compulsively dull as yours probably is, take a look at the new *Bay State Librarian*. And ask your editor to do likewise.

*Eric Moon*


## PUBLICATIONS PERSPECTIVE
January 15, 1963

This is a tale of two publications, both emanating from ALA in the past month or so.

One is a "Reading for an Age of Change" guide (the third in the series). It is on a subject of crucial importance—*Freedom of the Mind*. It is written with deep conviction by a man who is in a place where the view of the dangers to freedom must be awfully clear, Supreme Court Justice William O. Douglas. And it is a piece of *literature*, demanding reading and re-reading by librarians and all their efforts to promote its wide reading by the general public. For this piece of valuable ammunition in the cold war with the censors, librarians should offer thanks to ALA.

The other publication is the third annual report of the Library Technology Project, covering the period July 1, 1961–June 30, 1962. Annual reports, let us concede, are probably necessary. Something must be set down for the record. Many annual reports in the library field, however, are so uninformative that one sometimes wonders.

Under a series of headings, each project is described in a general sentence or two, and nearly every one concludes "results of this study were published last year," or a report will be published next year." Throughout the year, more extensive reports from LTP appear in the *ALA Bulletin*, items appear in the news columns of most of the major and many of the minor library periodicals, and each project results, sooner or later, in a printed report. So there is little left for the annual report to tell us, and in fact, it tells us rather less than we already know. At whom, then, is it directed? What is its purpose?

We raise these questions, not only because of the contrast in content of these two publications, but also because of the contrast in their physical appearance.

The LTP report is a lavish, handsome piece of production, outshining even the annual reports of LTP's benefactor, the Council on Library Resources. Printed in two colors throughout, nicely and abundantly illustrated, and with margins like freeways (because there is so little textual content), it is a credit to the designer and a piece of print to make a librarian's heart jump.

*Freedom of the Mind* is in the standard format of the "Reading for an Age of Change" guides. It is not *un*attractive, but nobody would rate it any higher than "workmanlike." It looks just like any other throw-away pamphlet.

Let's trot out all the clichés about "clothes don't make the man" before someone else does. And let's dismiss the old books versus gadgets debate too. It is not a question of which is more important—Freedom of the Mind or freedom of book-truck casters to run on carpeted areas (a prospective LTP project)—but of impact, or if you like, perspective.

The Douglas pamphlet, *we hope,* will be distributed in many thousands, all over the country, to all kinds of people. For what select audience is the LTP report produced? And should these two publications land in the same pair of hands, what do they say to the reader of the philosophy of the body of librarians behind them?

We have no real complaints about the Douglas pamphlet's production. It will do, and there probably was insufficient finance for anything more exotic. But we do ask whether the mink-coat production of the LTP report is necessary, however much more money this project has available. The latter's balance sheet shows nearly $35,000 spent on LTP publications during the past year, with less than $7,000 returning in income from publications. The money comes from a "publications revolving fund," whatever that might be.

Perhaps ALA publication funds might be made to revolve in another way, so that the big money needle stops in the right place.

*Eric Moon*

## REPORT ON REPORTS
March 15, 1963

A pretty steady flow of annual reports from libraries crosses our desk during the course of a year. It is not unduly harsh to comment that, on the whole, these reports are uninspiring, particularly in physical appearance, but also often in content. Three came in recently, however, in a period of a few days, which gave a boost to our natural optimism. Perhaps everything does change for the better—even annual reports—if only you wait long enough.

The first jolt to preconceived boredom was delivered by the report from the Library of Hawaii, which declared that it was "Looking Over the Year 1961–62 and the Decade." The cover featured a line drawing of a quite ample Hawaiian lady stringing a lei (if that is the correct technical expression). It was the sort of cover which does its real job—to make you look inside. Once there, unfortunately, you are doomed to disappointment, for though the text is interesting, its appearance is so horrible (typewritten capitals throughout) that you would have to be passionately interested to consider pursuing the matter further. But a good cover is a start. Score one point more than most other reports.

The ample lady was followed by a pleasant patio scene adorning the cover of the report from the Mason City, Iowa, Public Library. This report is an exercise in annual concision: it consists of a single page, folded three ways vertically and once horizontally. It gives—just the facts, ma'am. What made this year's effort notable, and just a little different, is that the horizontal foldover, colored a pale green, carried a poem—"The Poet and the Bomb," by William Carlos Williams. And the poem carried these sentiments in the closing lines:

> Only the imagination is real!
> I have declared it
> time without end.

Here, one felt instinctively, was a librarian who cared about literature and about the state of the world, and cared enough to try to relate his library to both through his annual report to the people he serves.

And then there came the real startler, from the University of California at Davis. This one purported to be the "Annual Report of the Library, 1961–62 and a Little Beyond." Below this, in big bold ragged black letters was the unacademic declaration—PHYLLIS LOVES BOOKS. Who in the whatever, you are forced to ask, is Phyllis? So, inside you go. Once there, the librarian tells you in the opening paragraph:

"A large and tattered sign appeared recently on the Library's lawn. It read: 'Phyllis Loves Books.' The bookish Phyllis was running for the office of campus Queen. Her ardent admirers and campaign managers, who had erected the sign, hoped to elicit votes from other book-loving students. One can hardly imagine such a sign appearing during the era of Scott Fitzgerald and the coonskin coat. Even now such a manifestation of bookishness among students is startling. But it is a symbol, although a ludicrous one, of a real and dramatic change in student attitudes toward books and learning."

Our point in drawing attention to these three quite different reports is that here, it seems, are three librarians who realize two basic facts of publication life:

1) It isn't any good producing a report if you don't make a serious attempt to persuade people to read it.

2) Every time you produce something in print you are competing with the most massive output in world history. Every reader has more than he can cope with today, and if you want to attract some other than those already dedicated to your cause, you have to use some kind of baited hook.

We use the word "hook" deliberately. It is the term free-lance writers use for that opening paragraph or scene that so whets your interest that you just have to go on to see what the rest of the article or story is all about. It's a technique that more librarians who write, or report, could study.

We agree with Robert D. Franklin that "a library's annual report should sound more like a shot than a mumble." In a good article, "Reports on Target," which appeared in *Library Review*, Autumn 1961, he also made the point that a title helps: "We may be stuck with the unexciting categorical name . . . 'annual report,' but we don't *have* to use the phrase as a label, or in the report's first sentence. You can give the report a catchy title, and identify it as a report in small type or parenthesis."

*Eric Moon*

## A LIVING LIBRARY
April 15, 1963

We've just got back from the movies. A group of library press and public relations people were brought together in the auditorium of the Donnell Library Center, New York Public Library, by National Library Week director Beryl Reubens to see yet another library film. We were not excited when we went (you get pretty blasé after the first 20 films)—but we are now. If you except *Only Two Can Play*, which after all had Peter Sellers, this is about the best library film we have seen.

It is called *The Fifth Freedom*. Produced by the Massachusetts National Library Week State Committee, it is written and narrated by Karl Nyren, director of the Cary Memorial Library in Lexington, Mass. It's in color, runs for 15 minutes, and is intended to be used by other libraries for showing to local groups—to give them some idea how good a small town library can be. And it was all done in four days—four hard, grinding days of

15 hours solid work per day. It is a labor of love, but everything about this film is professional—the camera work, the continuity, the script, the narration, and the deceptive effortlessness.

The continuity is aided, cleverly and charmingly, by the use of a small eight-year-old girl, a gleeful, impish bundle of sheer enjoyment. The little girl is Karl Nyren's daughter—the only one, he said, he could work that hard without offending union regulations. She didn't get an Elizabeth Taylor salary (though she deserves one), but she did get a horse out of it.

The camera picks her up outside the library, heel-and-toeing along the cracks in the sidewalk. As she explodes through the front door the camera follows, and keeps on following as she skips and hops her eight-year-old curiosity around all the departments of the library. There are charming scenes where she takes both close-up and long distance views (both skeptical) of a modern abstract painting in the library's art gallery, or where she gets cheek-to-cheek with a teenage boy in the record department to hear what's coming through those big earphones he's wearing, or in the magazine reading room where she kneels on the floor for a quizzical look at the cover of a periodical an elderly man is reading.

But it isn't all cuteness and charm. The girl carries the spirit of liveliness which the producers want associated with the library, but she is also a mechanism for carrying the attention of the viewer to and through the variety of departments and activities of the library.

And quite a library it is. Mr. Nyren told us a few things about it before the film began (afterwards he didn't need to). Lexington has just over 27,000 population. Its library provides just about every service in the book. The budget is healthy, and the library is open 72 hours per week. If this film does not lie, it is an attractive, vital place which demands that the citizens of Lexington use it. And they do—this library circulates about 18 books per capita of the total population.

The film underlines the point at the end that the library is a place where even the unexpected may be expected to happen. Again, the little girl does the trick. Sitting on the floor in the Children's Department, she is reading a book about horses. Suddenly there echoes from the sound track one of the loudest and most genuine whinnies you've ever heard—it comes from the little girl.

A word must be said also for the script, which is good (i.e., not obvious) library propaganda, and for the narration which is delivered so well and so richly that Mr. Nyren bids fair to be the profession's Ed Murrow.

Before the showing, Karl Nyren said: "We have a predatory public relations policy at my library—we pick up all bets." He meant that they never miss an opportunity to publicize the library's potential, through any avenue, channel or medium.

This film is one bet Mr. Nyren should be glad he picked up. He can't lose.

*Eric Moon*

## TIPS FROM TEACHERS
November 1, 1963

"A river of quoted brilliance, dammed occasionally by a student-produced sandbar"—this is one college teacher's description of the typical high school library paper. It is quoted in a recently published report, *High School-College Articulation of English,* published by the National Council of Teachers of English (508 S. 6th Street, Champaign, Ill.; 44p. $1).

School and public librarians alike may perhaps glean some faint hope from these pages, for if the report has any impact on high school teachers it could lead to a future respite from, or at least lessening in, one kind of persistent student pressure.

In a survey of more than 100 colleges, a special NCTE committee on high school-college articulation found that *fewer than ten percent of the colleges are recommending "Library paper" assignments in high school.* Nearly a third of the colleges made the point that the time can be better spent on a number of short papers. These colleges also pointed out that high schools rarely have the library resources to support adequate research.

If a reading of this report offers some kind of hope and solace to student-inundated librarians in the field, perhaps a reflective reading of it by library school faculties might yield other results.

The description of the typical high school library paper above should ring a loud bell for those library school teachers whose ears and eyes are still open. For that college teacher's comment is also splendidly descriptive of the typical library school paper.

What has come to be mistakenly identified as the research method in many of our library schools often looks uncannily like common theft. The words, the thoughts, the ideas of others are excavated and assembled with all the paraphernalia of footnotes, references, and other tokens of "research." But there is seldom much evidence that the student is required to use the "lifted" material as a basis for thought, interpretation, analysis, and finally, some kind of personal conclusions. The present process rarely seems more creative than putting together a jig-saw puzzle.

Thankfully, the "literature survey" gets short shrift in this NCTE report, and it is to be hoped that some of our library schools will get the message before this kind of "writing" strangles and deadens our library literature altogether.

*Eric Moon*


## IN PROGRESS—BACKWARDS
September 1, 1964

When we were in England a few months ago, we sat in on a Council meeting of the Association of Assistant Librarians. One young man, obviously bitten by the "research" bug, was making an impassioned plea for the establishment, in England, of a "valuable" tool like the American *Library Research in Progress.*

Asked to comment, we were not too encouraging. We did not think an English *LiRiP*, unless it were very much better than its American model, would answer many of that young man's dreams. When we returned to New York we resolved to check our files to see whether we had been either harsh or hasty in this judgment.

Just about that time, July 15 to be precise, the latest issue of *LiRiP* landed on our desk. It was dated April 1964. By now we are so hardened to the fact that the majority of library publishing is incredibly lax, lethargic, and late that we scarcely blinked at that three month differential between publication and delivery date.

But then we started checking individual entries. There are 131 "research projects" reported in the April 1964 issue. Of these, more than 80 (about 63 percent) are projects which have already been completed and/or published, and 35 (or 26.8 percent) were finished by 1962 or earlier. Five, in fact, are already half a decade old, having been completed in 1959.

There may be value in a catalog of past research—though it might be that further research would reveal that much that is listed in *LiRiP* has previously been listed in *Library Literature* or the University Microfilms catalog. There is probably also a case to be made for listing catch-up items, but surely a publication called *Library Research in Progress* should, on balance, contain more information on items in progress than items drawn from history.

We were told in the June 1963 *LiRiP* that the publication was designed "as a clearinghouse *for projects underway*" and that thereby "duplication of effort should be minimized." *LiRiP* is clearly not fulfilling these functions, adequately at least. One example from the latest issue will serve to show that duplication is not being eliminated. Within three pages of each other, two projects are listed, each leading to a published biography of Melvil Dewey. Question: would the prospective author who started on Dewey's life in 1962 have started at all had she known earlier that another author had been working on her subject since 1955? Perhaps she would, but *LiRiP* certainly did not assist in the decision.

Let's move on from the inappropriateness of the "in progress" phrase to another doubtful word in *LiRiP*'s title. "Research" has been used so loosely by librarians and others that it has become almost as debased a word as "great" in Hollywood. Does *LiRiP* really fulfill its declared objective of stimulating library research and encouraging "scholarly communication" when it lists some of the garbage which it presently contains and dignifies it with the word "research"?

Here are a few samples: "The Rio Grande Chapter of the Special Libraries Association"; "Librarians in Who's Who in America, 1956–57"; "Report of a One Year's Internship in the Yale University Library"; or "Third Survey of Salaries Paid Professional Librarians in Texas Libraries, 1962–63." Leon Carnovsky must have had examples like these in mind when he commented recently that many of the graduate theses listed in *Library Quarterly* "qualify for inclusion only by courtesy and a very liberal interpretation of 'research'."

The professional staff of the Library Services Branch, we are told, "serves as an editorial board and considers whether contributions are significant enough . . . and whether studies . . . are sufficiently broad in scope." Based on the evidence, one must question the Library Services Branch staff's editorial judgment and vigor.

The delay factor in reporting research is not to be laid entirely at the door of the Library Services Branch. They probably could, with more effort and time devoted to the project, gather more current information, but they also deserve and require more active support from the library profession. *LiRiP* gives little evidence of real interest by those who are promoting or indulging in "research."

We agree entirely with *LiRiP*'s editorial comment that "librarians must work towards the formulation of research programs adequate to support graduate library education and library operations," but we can't feel that *LiRiP* is really acting as much of a spur to that end.

*Eric Moon*

## MICROSCOPE VS. TELESCOPE
February 1, 1966

One of the most interesting library annual reports to land on our desk for many a day comes from the Luton Public Libraries in England. The Luton Report for 1964–65 is entitled *A Year and a Day,* and the reason for the title is spelled out:

"Although this Report covers a year's work, a large part of it is devoted to one small portion of the year—a single day.

"It was thought it might be profitable and interesting for a change to analyze the work of the Library Service during a single day—to exchange the telescope for the microscope. Such a survey could provide us with more detail on our work with readers, and interest readers who do not see 'behind the scenes.' It would also give us an opportunity to look at our users and test their reactions to the Service."

Luton chose Thursday, November 26, 1964—"a typical autumn day"— to operate its microscope. On that day, all staff members were asked to keep detailed records of everything they did, and readers were given questionnaires which they could return at their convenience.

This focus on a typical day not only makes for more interesting reading than annual reports normally provide; it is uncommonly useful from two points of view.

First, it is an excellent way of showing *the public* what the library is for, what it does, the variety of demands made upon it, the numerous and different operations that library staff members perform. Some annual reports, we realize, are clearly not intended for this purpose; they are strictly administrative documents addressed to the library board, the city fathers, or some governing body. Many others, however, ostensibly directed toward the public, wear the same drab administrative cloak, and even if they enjoy the benefit of superb distributive machinery, they are still doomed to fail at their prime purpose. If they are not broadly interesting, they will not be read widely. If they are not read widely, they will not promote interest in nor support of the library service. They will be waste paper.

Luton's microscopic technique, it seems to us, gives the indiviual citizen a much clearer view of what *actually* happens in the library—both before the curtain and behind the scenes—than does the telescopic view of the year's activities. For one thing, most of us can relate to comparatively smaller figures more easily than we can to those giant annual statistics. Tell the average reader that Luton circulates two million books a year and he'll very probably shrug it off without ever realizing what this means in the daily life of the people on either side of the library service. A year's a long time; two million of anything doesn't seem very improbable. But tell him that, in a typical day, nearly 5000 people visited the Luton libraries and took out more than 9200 books, and he may begin to see the library's impact upon the community.

And if you take the breakdown further and show that reader, step by step, what happened in every branch and department as those 5000 people and 9200 books were moving in and out, he may begin to see both the individual load and how the pieces fit together. For example, if he reads that Luton had 66 library staff on duty that day, he may well think that's a pretty sizeable staff. And if you tell him that six of those bodies were occupied in the Processing Department, he'll very probably not have any idea what the department is or what they could conceivably have been doing—and thus confirm his initial thought that 66 sounds like a lot, perhaps too many. But if you show him, in detail—as this Report does— what those six Processing types actually did in one day, he may well reach another conclusion: that either the staff needs a union, or the library needs more staff!

The second value of the one-day concentration is how much the library staff—and, undoubtedly, the library board—learned about the users of the library; who they are and what are their needs, demands, and dissatisfactions with the service. The Report exhibits another virtue: a healthy and constructive attitude toward criticism. For example, "Naturally, we are looking into these deficiencies, and for this also the survey was worthwhile."

The Luton Report closes with a last paragraph whose honesty is engaging. It could be appropriate in the annual report of nearly any library, anywhere. The major lesson to be learned from this analysis of a day's work is that we are spending an undue proportion of staff time on routines . . . and not enough on systematic and detailed stock revision."

*Eric Moon*

## THE LIVING END
December 15, 1966

This issue marks the end of another period in the 92-year history of *Library Journal;* the beginning of a new one. Many months ago, we announced that *LJ,* together with *School Library Journal* and *Publishers' Weekly,* would be issued in a completely new format in 1967. The moment of change has now arrived: the next issue to fall on your desk may look unfamiliar, but we hope it will look more inviting and that it will not land with such a thud.

Many other library periodicals have been redesigned in the past few years, and most of them for the better. They have, in general, concentrated on new cover designs plus changes in varying degree in typography and layout. Few, however, have changed noticeably in size. A curious kind of unwritten code seems to have prevailed: that library periodicals should always remain the "compacts" of the magazine world, a pygmy tribe living outside the communications mainstream.

*LJ*'s last redesigning of any consequence was in 1958; its last major format change in 1920. We have concentrated for several years now on improving the magazine's content, but it has been apparent that a face-lifting was overdue. When, at last, we decided to do something about *LJ*'s appearance, we could see no good reason why the change should not be a drastic one. Nor could we see why *LJ* should not adopt the the standard size of the major general periodicals such as *Newsweek, Time, Harper's, The Atlantic, Saturday Review, The New Yorker.* Although we were not in a circulation league with these big boys, we had, with a current circulation for *LJ* and *SLJ* of over 50,000, passed many respected magazines from general, literary, or political fields, such as *Encounter, The American Scholar,* or *Commentary.* We stood, in fact, just about midway (in circulation) between *The Nation* and *The National Review.*

There were other reasons than pride for the change. First, and most obviously, *LJ,* uniquely among the periodicals of the library profession, had a weight problem—and when a man grows out of his suit (let us not even suggest that ladies ever do), he buys a new one. We knew some of the reasons for our bulk problem: that we continue to combine professional coverage with major book information and reviewing services; that we refuse to be content with some selected corner of the library field but regard the whole of librarianship as our editorial beat; and that with the awesome growth of library activity in recent years, we must grow with it. The result is that our own growth has been awesome, too. *LJ*'s total page count for 1966 (6,226) is 674 higher than last year, and 1,750 higher than five years ago.

Under this kind of pressure, type sizes in many of *LJ*'s departments had been reduced over the years, margins had been trimmed, pages had become more jammed, more difficult to read. There appeared to be only two real, and possible, solutions: move to a considerably larger page, or reduce or fragment *LJ*'s editorial coverage. When reduced to this simplicity, the alternatives did not really constitute a choice.

While we were playing with the mathematics of the problem, we took the opportunity also to think about *LJ*'s place in the library periodical field. What were our particular strengths? What should we emphasize? What could we do better than anyone else? Which departments were read first, or most—and should we rearrange them with this factor in mind?

Perhaps the major conclusion we reached during this self-analysis was that we were in a better position than any other library periodical to provide the profession with a better news service than it has had, or has sometimes seemed to want. Not only did we appear more frequently than our competitors, but we were free of institutional or association inhibitions about what news was "fit to print." And we increasingly had the capacity (and the desire) to do more than relay with the other periodicals, the same releases from the same sources, often to the same readers of the professional press.

This emphasis, then, has led to changes in the arrangement of the "new" *LJ*, bringing those departments with topical impact—the news, information about people, the editorial—out of the middle of the magazine and up front, where they can be located quickly and read first. The news emphasis, it is hoped, will grow and spread to other departments, including the articles.

But no more revelations here. We wish all our readers a Happy New Year, and hope that the new *LJ* will contribute a little to that end.

*Eric Moon*

## BETTER NEVER THAN LATE
July 1968

Library/USA—the profession's second major venture in "library exposure" at an international exposition—officially passed into printed immortality this year. The publication of *Library/USA: a Bibliographic and Descriptive Report,* released by ALA well over two years after the last gate clanged shut on the 1964–65 New York World's Fair, presumably closes the books on this experiment in exhibiting library service and automation to the masses.

Now that the report has finally appeared in all its showcase splendor (it *is* handsomely designed—pleasing typographically, attractively bound in red, white, and blue, and illustrated with an 11-page pictorial tour of the exhibit), what is its value to the profession at large and to the individual librarian in particular?

The first third of the 192-page report amasses a myriad of details about the design and layout of the exhibit; the selection of staff; the data processing training program; tabulations of the subject distribution and popularity of computer printouts; and a rather sketchy financial statement summarizing the major income and expense categories.

Three "who's whos" are also included for those interested in finding out who contributed monetarily as well as materially; who served on the various ALA advisory committees; and finally, who actually manned the exhibit—this last roster giving not only the names of librarians and their institutional affiliations, but also listing their exhibit assignments and training groups.

Running through this section of the report are evaluations of the component parts of the exhibit, its over-all impact, and the staff training program. In the opinion of the Advisory Committee, *Library/USA* "successfully fulfilled the goals set for it: (1) general public relations for all types of libraries, and demonstration of good library services; (2) exposure of professional librarians of the staff to the mysteries of data processing and electronic information storage and retrieval; and (3) recruitment for the profession." While the public relations and recruitment effect is generally rated favorably, the report states—somewhat contradictorily—that "without careful scientific opinion study and analysis, it would be impossible to make an accurate appraisal of the impact of the exhibit," and then, that there "is no scientific way to learn exactly what impact the total exhibit had on the visitors . . ." The report does note that some visitors took the trouble to write letters of praise as well as of criticism, but the latter remain unrecorded. So much for the reaction of the public.

If the report treads lightly and cautiously on the public path, it is on much firmer footing on the professional ground, extolling the virtues of the data processing training received by the staff. Through librarian feedback, we learn that the participants developed more realistic attitudes about machines in the library environment, that many subsequently became involved with the application of EDP techniques in their home libraries, and that they hoped library schools would accelerate the development of similar courses. (At this juncture, one begins to wonder whether *Library/USA* was as much an experiment in educating the public about libraries as it was in educating librarians about automation.)

The remaining two-thirds of the report is devoted to bibliographies of the books exhibited in the reference section of the Information Center and in the President's Collection, and the books and films recommended for the Children's World. Prefacing the reference list is a warning that it "does not reflect a balanced collection" since only 850 of the 1500 titles recommended by a committee of reference librarians as desirable for a "ready reference" collection were *supplied by the publishers* for the exhibit. The President's Collection, based on the James T. Babb list published in 1963, is also not complete, including only in-print titles, which were, again, *available from the publishers*. These lists, then, serve only as a display record, not as an acquisitions tool.

As the record of a professional experiment, the report undoubtedly has its place in the archives. But of what value is it to the individual librarian's professional storehouse? Might not this particular "need to know" have been more adequately served by a more timely and less elaborately produced report, perhaps summarized in the association's official journal? A profession which constantly decries the publication explosion might well look to its own publication program, already suffering from information overload and from a production time lag hitting the two-year mark, and conclude that selectivity should begin at home.

*Shirley Havens*

## A DECADE MINUS ONE
December 15, 1968

The editorial "we" has often been criticized as an artificial device. Its purpose, however, is to indicate that the editorial page speaks not for an individual but for the magazine and all that it stands for—its policies, its positions on specific issues, its overall direction and purpose. Whatever the variety of conflicting views and opinions of contributors on other pages, *this* page speaks for *LJ*.

On this one occasion, however, it speaks for no one but me. This is a personal statement, a signing-off after nine years in the editorial hot seat.

Measured some ways, nine years is a long time. A few of the measures are uncomfortable, like the harsh testimony of the mirror: the thinning hair and the thickening waistline. Others provide a statistical shock of recognition, like the 200 issues and 45,000 pages which have flowed across the presses. But images and numbers like these say little about what kind of a near-decade it has been to be editing a national periodical for U.S. libraries and librarians.

Nine years, to take another measure, is the distance from Little Rock to Ocean Hill–Brownsville; from Vice President Nixon to President Nixon. If it's a road with some impressive milestones, it is also littered with tombstones—for two Kennedys, for Martin Luther King and Malcolm X, for civil rights workers in the South and riot victims in the North.

In librarianship, nine years is the distance from the few meager millions of federal aid for rural public libraries to the current 600 million or more federal dollars for library activities and libraries of all kinds. No milestones in the library world during the sixties stand prouder or more prominently than the victories achieved by the profession's superlative legislative efforts at the federal level.

If the atmosphere of society in these years has become more explosive, less placid and self-satisfied, the change in the attitudes visible within the library profession has been no less radical. From the reluctance of many librarians even to acknowledge the necessity of the bitter struggles in the early sixties over integration of libraries and library associations, there has been movement toward a new militance in the profession, exemplified by the social responsibility movement in ALA, the aggressive professional associations in Canada and the library unions in the U.S., and the ever louder demands by younger librarians for involvement—of themselves, of libraries, and of their associations—in a relevant way, and in the real world.

Most of the crucial problems remain, but one aspect of change is that they have been brought out in the open for examination and discussion. And they are discussed with an urgency and passion that seemed to me, nine years ago, to be unhealthily and almost totally absent.

To catalog the developments of these years here is not possible; one has only to pick off a few to conjure up a dozen more for each one named—MARC and NPAC and MEDLARS; the gradual emergence of state libraries from the dark ages; the school library explosion; the information science and technology invasion; the fantastic growth of centralized cataloging and processing services, commercial and otherwise; the Brooklyn community coordinators, the outreach-experimenters at High John and Venice; the emergence of virtually new library-related industries, like reprint publishing and the consulting game.

It has, in short, been an ideal time to be editing a library periodical. When the scene is alive and turbulent, good copy flows; it does not have to be ground out painfully from inconsequentials. Old Melvil was in at the beginning of LJ and of librarianship as an organized profession, with the birth of ALA and the British Library Association. But no LJ editor since, perhaps, has had so much library activity to record and comment upon. I have been lucky in occupying this seat during what seems to me the greatest revival period in American librarianship in this century.

LJ has changed in these nine years, too—and some, at least, think for the better. If it has improved, much of the credit must go to those members of the profession who have moved librarianship so far in what, after all, is such a short time. But the main credit belongs to the editorial "we," which includes the many contributors and reviewers who have kept these pages alive, the many friends in the field who have kept us alerted to events and developments, and most particularly, all the editors and staff of this magazine, who are a team without parallel.

I thank them all, and in them, hand over to my successor an inheritance of great value.

*Eric Moon*

# School Libraries

### DREAM COME TRUE
December 15, 1962

The opportunity which the Knapp Foundation Grant brings to the cause of school libraries is like a fairy tale come true to those of us who have been working during the past years on the development and implementation of the standards. And indeed, to me it does illustrate that to achieve a worthwhile goal one must begin by dreaming.

My own participation in this work goes back about eight years when four of us—Frances Spain, Virginia Mathews, Frances Henne and I—were gathered one wintry night in a Newark restaurant to hold a post-mortem on a workshop for teachers and librarians which the Rutgers Library School had been conducting. Out of this session came an *ad hoc*, self-constituted "Fantasy Committee" through which we set ourselves the assignment of outlining all the steps we thought necessary to the achievement of the kind of library service, both school and public, which children and young people need today. My memory is that we outlined projects that came to a total of something in the neighborhood of 10 million dollars, a real fantasy even in terms of the Knapp grant.

However, the point is that since that night many of the things we listed in our plan have come true; and dreams like these, by us and by many others, have had a small part in realizing the exciting developments of the past few years—the completion and publication of the standards themselves, the grant from the Council on Library Resources, the budget allocation from Congress for a children's literature specialist at the Library of Congress and now this munificent grant from the Knapp Foundation.

It is appropriate to point out that the catalyst in this most recent development was William Nichols, editor of *This Week* magazine, who in his capacity as chairman of National Library Week called to the attention of Mr. Stouch of the Knapp Foundation the "book gap" of which three-fourths of the children in our schools are victims. Through the resources of men and women of vision like Mr. Stouch and his associates on the Knapp Foundation Board, we now have a tremendous opportunity for experimentation to improve the educational resources of our schools.

The object of the program is to demonstrate school library services to the full extent of the standards. The philosophy of the *Standards for School Library Programs* (ALA, 1960) is that the kinds of service desired in a school determine the quantitative provisions which are necessary. The Knapp grant now provides an opportunity to demonstrate what we could do if only we had the money to pay for it!

The project will: 1) demonstrate the program made possible when a school library is provided with the quantitative facilities described in the standards (personnel, materials including the cost of commercial processing, quarters if needed); 2) provide in-service education of the faculty and library staff of the demonstration school, by contract with a neighboring college or library school; 3) organize visits to each demonstration school by "teams" of librarians, educators and citizens from other communities; and 4) evaluate the effectiveness of the demonstrations. The grant also provides for the prompt production of a film on the elementary school library, which will fill a particularly serious gap in our available resources.

The tremendous lag in the development of elementary school library programs led the committee to exphasize these first. However, it was held equally important to demonstrate the excellent programs of service in secondary schools which adequate personnel and other resources could make possible. At the same time, we did not believe it would be feasible to initiate so ambitious a program in more than a few schools at a time; the approval of the grant for a five-year peroid, therefore, makes it possible to spread the project out, which we hope will make for better chance of success. It was particularly gratifying to find that the Foundation Board was as interested as the school librarians in discovering ways to decrease the lab between the trial of an educational invention and its application in practice in all schools.

As soon as possible, an announcement will be made inviting applications from schools for consideration in the experimental program for 1963–64. The line forms on the right!

*Mary V. Gaver, guest editor*

## HELP NEEDED
March 15, 1963

We remember our sixth grade teacher very well. She was tall, matronly and gracious. She was notable for her fondness for licorice which she ate at lunchtimes and for the fact that she alone of all the people we ever knew or have known since called a bicycle a "wheel."

Looking back, in the cold light of 1963, our sixth grade teacher was notable for something else: a certain kind of homework assignment. Periodically she would charge the class to look up some fact or person in the encyclopedia, adding that if there were no encyclopedia at home, the homework could be waived. It happened that our family had no encyclopedia then, and so we never had to complete these "reference" assignments, although even then, and moreso now, we felt cheated and unequal in not being able to do them.

Why, you might ask, did we not use the encyclopedia in the school library? Why indeed. There was no library in our school. And at age 10 it did not occur to us to use the public library only one mile away. Public libraries were for pleasure-books not for homework assignments when we were 10 years old. We did not learn to use the public library for work until we were in high school, and then only out of desperation for the inadequacy of our high school library.

But surely we must be talking about a country town of 50 years ago. Guess again. We are describing conditions in the city of Washington, D.C., in 1943 and up to 1950 when we left high school. A deplorable situation anywhere, but especially in the capital city of our country, which theoretically sets the pace.

The really deplorable fact is that the state of school libraries in Washington, D.C., has scarcely improved since then, nor do advances in their development seem imminent. School officials, we are quick to stress, are not to blame; neither are the city's residents who have responded heartily in book drives and cash collections by local civic groups seeking to improve Washington school libraries (*see* "The News," this issue, for one such attempt). The fault lies, rather, with a shortsighted Congress who, despite the efforts of Senator Hubert Humphrey, cannot seem to work up the votes necessary to approve the budgets requested repeatedly and in vain by the District of Columbia Board of Education and its superintendent of schools (*see SLJ* Dec. '62, p. 24; *LJ*, Dec. 15, '62, p. 4600).

We have followed the Washington story with pride in its heroes (the Washington Junior League, the Capitol Hill Community Council, the Action Committee for D. C. School Libraries, and numberless unnamed individuals) but with sinking heart; for it seems to us that nothing short of a miracle is needed there to turn the tide. To some degree we still believe in miracles. Did not the Knapp Foundation present a million-dollar miracle to the American Association of School Librarians just a few short months ago?

Phase I of the national Knapp School Libraries Project already is under way. Phase II, scheduled to begin in 1964, calls for improving library service in three elementary schools whose library facilities are inadequate but whose authorities are willing and prepared to back a library program.

We would urge individual Washington school libraries to be prepared to apply under Phase II when the time comes. The express purpose of the Knapp Project is to develop demonstration libraries that will set the example, that will stand as models of their kind. Where better a model than in Washington, D.C.; under the blunt Congressional nose.

*Ellen Rudin*

## PAPERBACK ATTACK ON POVERTY
May 15, 1964

The Federal Government should give serious thought to establishing a free book program for needy children as part of the war on poverty. Such a free book program could be patterned after the school lunch program, and could take advantage of the paperback revolution in the publishing industry.

The suggestion comes from Senate Majority Whip Hubert H. Humphrey. So do most of the words on this page, spoken during ceremonies in which the Cambridge (Minn.) Regional Library received the principal $5000 award in the annual Book-of-the-Month Club Library Awards during National Library Week.

"In planning any attack on poverty," the Senator said, "we always find the basic problem is education. And in this connection, we generally find that the most common term educators use for children of the poor is 'culturally deprived.'

"These educators believe that this cultural deprivation is one of the chief factors in the failure of these people to compete in the economic life and social life of our society.

"By cultural deprivaton, the educators always cite that the children have little or no acquaintanceship with books at home. There is little conversation and what there is is in the idiom that sounds foreign to the normal society that they find outside their homes.

"These children enter school several years behind their classmates in terms of 'cultural lag' and this lag tends to widen as they grow up. We know that the school dropout problem doesn't come merely when the child reaches his teens. It is formed early by an apathy born in a spirit of frustration because they feel they can never become a part of everyday society."

One way of helping close the cultural lag is to expand our library programs, Humphrey said. Another is to make available to children books that they are able to call their own.

"We have a great and growing paperback book industry in America," he said, "and . . . Many a drugstore bookrack today is better equipped than some of our poor libraries insofar as variety and up-to-date titles are concerned.

"We can take advantage of this revolution in the publishing industry. Back in the 1930's a Great Depression started us on a school lunch program. We still have that program today because it has proven itself to be one of the wisest investments America ever made. I believe we can do something similar to this with the free book program for needy children.

"Such a program would go beyond the needs of the normal textbooks and the reference books in the school libraries and provide needy children with paperback books of their own—novels, biographies of great men, popular books on science, history, adventure, sports and hobbies.

"I am confident that a program could be worked out that would protect the economic interest of the publishers who would cooperate with the government in such a program. I am also sure that it would spur a new interest in books that would ultimately lead to even greater sales. I also am confident it would lead to greater use of public libraries.

"During World War II an enormously popular program was operated for our servicemen. In cooperation with publishing houses, the government printed millions of books in cheap paperback form that could be fitted easily into a soldier's pocket. The shipments of these books were eagerly awaited on ships and at bases throughout the world. The books were passed from hand to hand and read until they were dog-eared and tattered beyond use.

"I believe a free book program would be greeted with the same eagerness here at home. . . . And I am confident that the seeds of learning that could be planted by these books would prove to be of incalculable benefit to this country."

Senator Humphrey's suggestion requires little comment. It has our enthusiastic support. And perhaps if it receives enough enthusiastic support from librarians, teachers, parents and publishers, it could be translated quickly into a government program along the lines suggested. There is point to the Senator's parallel with the school lunch program. If we really believe that food for the mind is as necessary as sustenance for the body, there should be no question about support for this imaginative idea.

*Eric Moon*

## "SCHOOLS WITHOUT LIBRARIES:
## OUR NATIONAL DISGRACE"

November 15, 1964

This month well over 9 million adult readers will have come across this shocking charge by Francis E. Keppel, U.S. Commissioner of Education, who in the November issue of *McCall's* magazine exposes the appalling conditions in many U.S. schools. In a national survey that included ten of our largest cities, the Commissioner reports it was found that:

Boston's public elementary schools, with more than 55,000 children, have no school libraries at all;

More than 100 of Philadelphia's elementary schools have no libraries;

Los Angeles' elementary schools have library collections but no librarians;

Three of our largest cities spend less than 15¢ per pupil for library books.

The pattern, says Commissioner Keppel, is duplicated across the country. "This," he contends, "is a national disgrace. Can we say that we are truly concerned with the ability of boys and girls to read well and with enjoyment and understanding if we do not provide school libraries for their use and librarians to guide them?"

In only two of the cities could Mr. Keppel cite positive significant steps that were being taken to establish and improve school libraries: Washington, D.C. and New York City. In Washington a citizens' group called the Action Committee for D.C. School Libraries had aroused public interest and support, and, eventually, improved library conditions in some elementary and junior high schools (see page 42). In New York City, which three years ago had no elementary school librarians and few libraries, concerted action was taken in 1962 by the United Parents Association, the N.Y.C. Board of Education, and the State Education Department. Together they succeeded in increasing appropriations to include librarians in elementary school budgets. There is still much to be done to achieve good libraries in these cities, but a promising beginning has been made through the vigorous effort of parents who are concerned.

Librarians, who have tried for years, often in baffled frustration, to convince administrators of the simple necessity for school libraries, will be thankful for the Commissioner's warm endorsement. But this is no time to rest on gratitude. Mr. Keppel's report provides the incentive for a renewed effort at mobilizing community action. The professional librarian must use it to call the attention of parents and administrators to a national emergency.

This is a job, we might add, not just for school, but for all professional librarians—particularly those who are serving adults in public libraries. For some years, public libraries have been trying bravely to handle the flood of students who come to their doors while preserving their traditional philosophy of serving all age groups and providing mainly for the leisure reading needs of the student population. This despite the fact that students often comprise well over half the total library clientele, and state as their *expressed* needs more reference, rather than leisure reading, materials. If the public library is to remain an agency serving all age levels, including the student-age group, it must do one of two things, and, hopefully, both: adapt its services to students' school-oriented requirements, as the Nioga, N.Y. Library System, not uniquely, but perhaps most originally, has done; or commit itself, deeply and pragmatically, to the school library movement.

Now the public library has another rich opportunity to carry out the current philosophy of "school-library cooperation." First, it can dramatize the Keppel article to all library users; second, it can send for the AASL literature, listed on page 40, and make it widely available to its patrons. Adults are entitled to this pamphlet as they are to the library's other resources; and this service, in turn, will help take the student drain off the public library.

A point about citizen support. Any help the school library can get through cookie sales and used book drives is all to the good, but these efforts must be regarded as interim, emergency, and at best minimal steps. Since libraries are often neglected because of pressure for other educational projects, "charity drives" will be self-defeating if they cause the school to depend on the unofficial support of the PTA. These steps must lead to provision of good school library service through budgetary appropriations, whether local, state, or Federal. As Commissioner Keppel says, "the library is a necessity, not a luxury—a central and not a side issue—in a good educational program."

*Evelyn Geller*

## WHO'S DEPRIVED?

May 15, 1965

We were planning to devote ourselves, this month, to the kind of commencement piece that seemed appropriate to this year of our novitiate, but the world spins too dizzily for us to stop and catch breath. We'd like therefore to report on some immensely important developments, and leave you with a few questions for the fall.

First: integration and what that implies in services and materials for Negroes. Hard upon the passage of the Education Act comes word from the Office of Education that a deadline has been set for school integration: fall 1967, and that integration of at least four grades is expected by this September from the 27,000 districts in this country, on pain of losing all federal aid.

At the same time, the New York City board of education has approved a plan for integrating its schools that involves their reorganization roughly along 4-4-4 lines, and is also trying to assign its more experienced teachers to slum schools, a move that the United Federation of Teachers is opposing.

Senator Robert Kennedy, supporting the move, pointed out that IQs of Harlem children drop ten points between third and sixth grade.

His comment bears on a question that educators are appraising: who is deprived, the child or the school? Schools in slum districts have been notoriously inadequate, staffed with poor teachers, few materials, and an impoverished curriculum; and while some remotivation is necessary, the provision of special education, special materials, special vocations for the "deprived" risks creating its own cultural ghetto. Negroes, after all, do not ask for this kind of solicitude; what they want is to be taken into the mainstream of our culture: they ask, very concretely, to be part of the white power structure. And while they need better representation in histories, textbooks, literature in general, they object to a literature tailored to their supposed needs, and oppose the exploitation of a "black" market. Some Negro children, librarians tell us, do love *Whistle for Willie;* others don't single it out over *Harry the Dirty Dog, Make Way for Ducklings,* or works of fantasy. And if we as a profession are committed to the idea of universality in great literature, the mater can hardly be argued. At the same time, the question of balance— between books with universal appeal and sociological relevance, between vocational education and the liberal arts—will almost immediately need careful appraisal by teachers and librarians, North and South, as the pace of integration accelerates.

*Evelyn Geller*

## FOOTNOTES TO THE FUTURE
October 15, 1967

A year ago last May, when it became apparent that government funds were creating an enormous, though possibly short-run, bull market for publishers, the American Book Publishers Council called a major conference to discuss ways of meeting the exploding school and library demand. Projections from the USOE told the industry it could expect, by 1974–1975, book expenditures of $148.5 million in public school libraries, about $246.4 million in college and university libraries, and some $109.7 million in public libraries with populations over 35,000. These were empirical projections having nothing to do with bringing collections up to ALA library standards.

The prognosis was more dubious this year at the ABPC follow-up in Washington, D.C. (see page 114). Publishers and printers had felt some leveling out of the enormous jump in sales, especially in juveniles, in 1966; but it was impossible to tell what would happen in the long pull, particularly if the Vietnam war ended.

If the Washington briefing disclosed neither this year's education budget (still in conference) nor long-term projections, it did provide some useful figures and a sense of the next decade's directions. Some library reports were illuminating. In 1966–1967:

—federal legislation had provided for a book expenditure of $326,-770,000;

—in schools, 3,368 libraries serving 1.5 million children had been set up;

—under ESEA Title II alone, some $66 million went for library books alone (a provisional figure, yet the first to isolate books from other Title II resources);

—90 cents of every ESEA Title II materials dollar had gone for school library resources, 6 cents for "other" instructional materials (i.e., books and audiovisuals not cataloged in the library), only 4 cents for texts;

—elementary schools showed an 85 percent hike in per pupil expenditure for library materials, high schools a more than 70 percent jump.

How long could the trend continue? Answers were that the figures would go up, but "not exponentially," and that other Great Society programs might need more attention than education spending. In the area of learning materials, OE officials made it clear that their competitive projects and research efforts are aimed at identifying and producing new materials that will work where traditional tools have failed, particularly with the disadvantaged. Just what is needed wasn't known yet, but publishers were encouraged to keep track of Bureau of Research programs and the ERIC information services to determine product needs, and to think of contracting to produce materials for specific target groups. High on the list of interests were the sensory assaults of the "new media" and materials for "individualizing instruction," which ranged from inexpensive teacher-made packets to computer-assisted instruction which would let the student learn on his own in a fool-proof way and take the burden of rote learning off the teacher's hands. Whether publishing, geared to a mass market, could profitably produce such highly individualized materials was moot, said the OE, but it did hold out the possibility of new sources of subsidy and the offer of a publishers-educators forum.

Despite the avid concern with innovation and a distorted McLuhanism in the insistence that print may not be the medium for everyone (have we successfully defined, to date, the level of marginal literacy that will be needed in a society dealing increasingly in information handling?), there was little prejudice against books *per se*. What has apparently disenchanted educators are the inferior materials, the concessions, the self-censorship that textbook publishers have allowed for the sake of bigger and better adoptions. Associate commissioner of education Graham Sullivan did acknowledge that in the area of trade books there "has been much more experimentation."

Moreover, Louis Bright's statement that there was no proved correlation between the number of books in a school library and the student's academic performance makes a poorly structured research project—but a perfectly valid point. We will be needing more school library money for years to come: of the school libraries found in the 1962–1963 USOE survey to be without centralized libraries, 93 percent still don't have them. But it is clear that the present methods of reporting—tallies of libraries established, books bought, clerks hired, and items processed—are hardly evidence that the library is contributing to instruction!

But it is not clear either that new materials developed under a government-business partnership, or "marriage," as it is hopefully called, will avoid the old pitfalls. Educators are reacting healthily to the potential sales power and influence of the commercial giants (described dramatically by Wayne Howell in this issue), and industry is reacting responsibly in its deference to "educational specifications." The question is, however: will this marriage work, or will it decline into a sleazy concubinage? Once the cross-movement between education and industry, which Francis Keppel suggests in our lead article, becomes habit rather than the tapping of brilliance, there is the frightening possibility that educators will be basing their decisions on what their next job will be. Public servants who act as consultants will be expected to promote given products, as they are today. If the business-education relationship is to become more intimate, a system of checks and balances will have to be created to ensure professionalism.

Second, the development of materials for a school market has no built-in defense against the procedures of textbook publishing, which is classic in its emphasis on consultants and writing to specification. The bland content of the textbook (a kind of lowest common denominator) and the marketing patterns that stress wide sales and adoptions, both result from the heavy investments required for texts, a condition that obtains in the audiovisual field. It is reasonable that similar conditions will produce similar accommodations through an understandable concern to make an investment pay.

Last, the entire process of media evaluation, especially in terms of "cost-efficiency" analyses, is fraught with ambiguity. When we discuss "individualizing instruction" do we mean a separate curriculum? A mode of communication? Or simply the pacing of identical content to individual student's needs, as occurs in computer-assisted instruction? When we talk about a "medium" do we consider the entire school environment as a "medium" or isolate a laboratory situation? If we accept the Coleman report on equal educational opportunity, which concluded that school facilities mattered less to a slum Negro's academic growth than the feeling he could control his fate, no medium will succeed in an indifferent environment that stunts motivation.

At the same time, we must acknowledge that content and quality, quite apart from "educational specifications," do function as variables in media evaluation. Assaults on the textbook, to take one case, are really criticisms of quality, not of the text as a medium that conveniently carries basic curriculum content. The producers of computer-assisted instruction insist that it's easy to "branch" a student with a special problem, but enormously difficult to prepare the remedial program for the machine—and it is on the quality of the program that its efficiency *vis-à-vis* teacher instruction will depend. How can we make some equations of quality so that a valuable textbook isn't foolishly pitted against a poor teaching machine, or vice versa?

Trade books provide another difficult example. "I'd go to the professionals," said Daniel Fader when he launched his paperback project, "who produce reading matter that has to fight for its life in the open market: newspapers, magazines, paperback books. Those men *have* to know what people will read, otherwise they'd go broke. I'd try using their products and nothing else, as teaching materials." Similarly, the ABC *Africa* documentary shown on television recently could probably hold its own against any dozen well-meaning ETV programs. What distinguishes these works is not format alone, or even subject, but the freedom, in commercial productions, from institutional coloring. The difference is that these are works students would read or watch even if they didn't have to—particularly students who don't feel the pressure to succeed academically no matter how dull the content.

Ironically, it is works like these that often have such trouble making their way into school systems—art films because school administrators think a movie is just a textbook transferred, stodgy script and all, onto the screen; books because they are too controversial. In Washington, D.C., right under the OE's nose, a junior high school teacher was forced to remove *Manchild in the Promised Land* from a highly successful remedial reading program for Negro youths. It would seem, then, that title versus title must be part of the input in media comparisons—with the result perhaps that the OE will be able to make a comment on the educational effectiveness of intellectual freedom.

If these variables, as well as aesthetic and psychological factors, can be accounted for, we see no serious danger in cost-efficiency analysis. Similar care would also have to be made, in surveys of library effectiveness, for evaluating: staffing to put library materials to effective use; a school day scheduled flexibly enough for students to be able to consult works; the quality and range of the collection. Intelligent analysis of source materials, the development of literary taste, tolerance for diverse opinions, and skepticism of the printed page would have to be included as indices of "academic achievement." So far it seems, however, that school libraries haven't generally done a good job of selling their program, which is really that of the "individualized instruction" center. There are surely alternatives, for example, to teacher-prepared photocopied "packages" that violate copyright and threaten to further restrict the publisher's ventures: classroom sets of paperbacks (more highly "individualized," since chapters are not pulled out of context and can be consulted at will), or simply bibliographic listings with multiple library copies for extended circulation periods. But to maintain a ranking position among educational priorities, school libraries will have to do a more careful job of selling these alternatives, informing teachers of already available materials, creating a climate of *directed* independent study, and choosing materials courageously to challenge the students with whom we have failed.

*Evelyn Geller*

## PRESIDENT JOHNSON AND MR. KOZOL
March 15, 1968

One of the more interesting things coming out of the spate of anti-establishment education books, including Kozol's *Death at an Early Age* (Houghton, 1967) and Kohl's *36 Children* (New American Library, 1968), is the fact that libraries are finding some of their strongest defenders in them; and that in many neglected urban schools the library is not just physically not present, but as a concept based on free inquiry and individualized instruction, is totally alien to the thinking of school administrators.

Take Kozol's experience as a case in point. He came to a school which, wallowing in money for "compensatory" programs, still had no school library, decent facilities, or up-to-date books. "The realities of America," Kozol says, "clashed with the materials I was being asked to teach in school." Of 140 biographies in the fourth grade classroom only one dealt with a Negro (George Washington Carver); the geography text did not mention a dark-skinned person; a history book, a century after the Civil War, was prissy and ambivalent on the subject of slavery. Kozol is kind about naming works, but his appended notes cite chapter and verse, and make illuminating reading for librarians.

Kozol is furious about $120,000 spent the year he was teaching on six new district superintendents. "What about 12 new genuinely qualified teachers?" he asks. "What about $100,000 worth of integrated readers, or modern histories and geography texts, or tape recorders, record players, poetry recordings, movies, slides, and prints? . . . *What about some school libraries?*" (italics ours)

Kozol did what he could: brought in *Mary Jane* (Doubleday, 1959), one of the earlier books on integration, and one of his slowest readers asked him to sell it to her; read his students a children's biography of Martin Luther King, and they asked for copies as Christmas gifts. (The school's reading teacher, incidentally, objected: "I wouldn't mind using them . . . if these were all Negro children in your room. But it would not be fair to the white children in the class to force such books on them, too.") Kozol brought in paintings by Miro and Klee, poems by Frost, and Yeats, and Langston Hughes, including what turned out to be the children's favorite, "Ballad of a Landlord." "The poem may not satisfy the taste of every critic," he says, "but the reason this poem did have so much value and meaning for me, and, I believe, for many of my students, is that it not only seems moving in obvious and immediate human ways, but that it finds emotion in something ordinary." The children asked for mimeographed copies, and on their own memorized the poem.

It was the objection to this poem on the part of *one white parent* that proved his undoing. One other reason bears comment: a school officer told him "that in addition to having made the mistake of reading the wrong poem, I also had made an error by bringing in books to school from the Cambridge Public Library. When I told her that there were no books for reading in our classroom, except for the sets of antiquated readers, and that the need of the children was for individual reading which they would be able to begin without delay, she told me that was all very well, but still this was the Boston school system and that meant you must not use a book that the Cambridge Library supplied. She also advised me in answer to my question, that any complaint from a parent means automatic dismissal of a teacher anyway."

We are reprinting at the end of this editorial the Boston school committee's defense of its action, for a public statement that can incorporate so much bigotry and self-deception ("compensatory programs," "innovation," "creative teaching") in the name of good education says more about the ironies of teaching than all of Kozol himself. It also has important implications for the evaluation of ESEA Title I and III programs, which are full of the same jargon yet lack specific criteria to distinguish word from deed, and for President Johnson's emphasis on "people" over "things" in his 1969 budget. Despite Johnson's concern with people, training, and research, the fact remains that right now there are more good materials available than good people; that the best teachers find, nevertheless, that superior materials are not *accessible* to them; and that many Title I and III projects are too notoriously elusive to permit even the tracing of components, much less evaluation, and are given to substituting federal for local support.

Yet—unless Congress is urged to restore the 1969 ESEA II and NDEA III funds to at least last year's allocations, the chances are that librarians next year will be more dependent than ever on administrators of other programs in order to buy library materials. It is not a hopeful prospect. The theoretical argument that the cutbacks still permit spending money under ESEA I and III for library materials hardly holds water. There is no *promise* of accomplishing the specific job of building libraries through *targeted* funds to backstop good teaching; no assurance that a concept of instruction pathetically late in reaching the schools has continued support; no guarantee that Title I and III will go into curriculum-building, rather than empire-building, projects.

Surely, "coordination" can be accomplished much more effectively by setting priorities *in* Title II (a portion of that money, for example, is already tagged for the handicapped). Good administrators would welcome the boost in funding to its original levels and work out patterns of coordination, while the legislation itself could ensure that money is not frittered away on useless staff and administrators, rather than concrete, and easily justified, materials investments. Meanwhile, libraries would be included in the range of *essential* "innovations" that good teachers should have without encountering the oppositions and risks that Kozol did, in a system that was smothered in funds for "compensatory" and "experimental" programs.

*Evelyn Geller*

# International

## VIEW FROM JAPAN
November 15, 1960

Librarianship in America has undoubtedly made great strides in the 20th century. Today, even the most conservative assessment would have to recognize that, over-all library service in the United States ranks with the best in the world. Our library literature nevertheless abounds with criticism and dissatisfaction with the present state of affairs and the rate of progress. It is healthy that it should. Criticism (particularly self-criticism), properly applied and considered, can and should be invigorating.

There are those, however, who do not take kindly to this hair-shirt fare, who object to the reiteration of inadequacies of buildings, bookstock, budgets and services, of the profession's inaction in censorship or social issues, librarians' timidity or failures in book selection, and their unfavorable image and lack of status. There are those who are tired of being berated by Lawrence Clark Powell and others for their concern with gadgetry rather than principles, administration rather than bookmanship. In another field, Louis Shores went so far as to suggest recently that it was time somebody took a look at what was *right* with library education.

To those who are weary of the breast-beating and the self-analysis, who feel the need for a pick-me-up, we recommend a small publication recently published by the International House of Japan. Entitled *American Libraries,* it is the report of the U.S. Field Seminar on Library Reference Services for Japanese Librarians, arising out of the visit last fall by nine Japanese librarians who toured libraries across the country and took part in seven seminars on a wide range of topics.

The book includes summary reports of the seminars and also study papers on Japanese libraries, but it is the first part of the volume with which we are concerned here, because it presents a picture of what American libraries look like to librarians from another part of the world where librarianship in its modern aspects, as understood and developed in the United States, Britain, and Scandinavia, is only just beginning to emerge.

The report records impressions of public, state, university and special libraries, the Library of Congress, library cooperation and education for librarianship. It is admitted that the number of libraries visited was "less than one percent of the thousands in the United States," but, says the Introduction, "we are confident that they were fully representative of American libraries."

A glowing picture is painted. Libraries in this country encourage greater freedom of thought and are more heavily used than in Japan. Favorable comment is made on the high proportion of adults using libraries.

American libraries are *invariably* comfortable, useful, and attractive; they are conveniently located, well promoted, and their hours geared to public convenience also. "We are of the opinion that it is the cooperation among them which keeps vitalizing blood coursing through the veins of all American libraries," adds the report.

It is this kind of comment that causes us to question whether the libraries visited *were* "fully representative." It is perhaps inevitable that these Japanese librarians should have concentrated on the larger centers, since their mission was concerned with reference services and there are few other places where they could see reference service in a well-developed state.

But we recall Lucile Morsch's recent comments (*LJ*, June 15, '60, p. 2384–5) that "It is unfortunate that most of our foreign colleagues are encouraged to follow the same circuit . . . of well-heeled libraries." We have our problems too, and it could only be helpful to our foreign colleagues for us to show them how, and with what success we are tackling these problems. Our achievements are many, but constant reiteration of the success story can be not only boring, but discouraging to those who are beginning the uphill struggle.

*Eric Moon*

## SEEING RED
February 15, 1962

*Library Journal* has been recurrently attacked during the past ten years by cheerleaders of the "far-out" right as a periodical with dangerous left-wing or "liberal" tendencies. In the words of Leon C. Hills, *LJ* "is really a major force in the mass campaign to guide American opinion in the direction of the left-wing precept." We thank him for the "major force" if for nothing else.

Those who see red at the drop of a hat will doubtless derive great satisfaction from this special "Russian" issue. They will take it as further and open proof of the subversive tendencies which we share, according to these defenders of democracy, with such other misguided or malignant publications as the New York *Times* and *Herald Tribune*, the *Saturday Review*, *Atlantic, Harper's* and the *Book Review Digest*, with wildly radical organizations like ALA, and with "comysymp" politicians like Presidents Eisenhower and Kennedy.

In case there be any librarians who react so irrationally, perhaps we should explain our reason for devoting a whole issue to Russian librarianship and Russian points of view. We happen to think there is more to be gained from trading and discussing ideas than from standing on either side of a wall or a curtain and snarling abuse at each other. It seems clear to us that, if any of us is to go on living in this world, we are going to have to learn to live with people who have ideas and beliefs which differ from our own. This is not to say that we need accept their ideas, but it is certainly safer and wiser to understand them than to ignore them.

We agree absolutely with the view expressed by Nikandr Gavrilov and Irina Bagrova in the lead article in this issue: "The personal contacts established between American and Soviet librarians as a result of the exchange of delegations can and should continue to develop. Despite the difference in their initial ideological positions, librarians of the USA and the USSR have many professional interests in common, and further mutual study of the work of each other's libraries can be of value to both sides."

We believe there is better hope for a future if we devote more attention to the things we have in common rather than to our differences, and if we concentrate more upon learning from each other than on competing.

In its technical development, and perhaps in many other ways, American librarianship has much to offer the Russians. One thing we could offer is *proof* of our expressed belief that library collections should give fair representation to all points of view and all ideologies. It is interesting to note that Gavrilov and Bagrova criticize this aspect of American public library provision just as strongly as the American librarians criticized Russian libraries for their "unrepresentative" collections.

There are things we can learn from the Soviet librarians too. Not least of these is the Soviet respect for the *power* of the book. This has resulted in tremendous support for, and development of, libraries in the USSR in the years since World War II, as that effervescent Florida trustee, Thomas Dreier, pointed out in an earlier *LJ* (January 15, '61, p. 202–3). We do not have to agree with the way that books in Soviet libraries are used as weapons in a propaganda war (indeed, we should deplore it), but both the profession and the public would surely benefit if those who hold the purse strings at all levels of American government could be imbued with the Russian respect for what Tom Dreier calls "mental capital" and the Russian belief in libraries as an effective productive source of such capital.

*Eric Moon*

## ASIAN MOTIFS
November 15, 1962

Libraries in the sense of collections of recorded knowledge or ideas are as old as Asiatic history. China built a society on the Confucian "classics" several centuries before the Christian era. The Vedas, earliest sacred books of the Hindus, were composed some time between 6,000 and 600 B.C. These were among the earliest influences in traditional Asia.

Historically Asian libraries have been storehouses of sacred and profane writings, open only to royalty, to government officials, to priests, or as in China to the scholar-gentry who attained the highest literary proficiency of their time. From these storehouses the mass of the people, illiterate, have been excluded. To the Asian the modern library with its open shelves and public service is a foreign, or as appears in the articles in this issue, a new experience.

That fact is perhaps the only true common denominator to be found in the Asian library situation. The continent is extraordinarily diverse. Stretching from the Mediterranean to Japan, it includes more than half the world's population. All the world's major religions are represented there, most of them in great and confusing force. The variety of tongues is unequalled; in India alone there are 15 major languages. As new Asian governments labor toward modernization and unity, their cultural variety, once considered a colorful resource, is seen now to be also an origin of national problems.

A selection of articles on libraries in the East can hardly be entirely representative. But perhaps from each country included here we can see a condition or a problem common in some degree to others.

Reading Dr. Leslie Kuo's article on Communist China, we may be astonished to note the number of books and libraries he has recorded. But the Communists have not only built upon Chinese literary tradition; in a drive for literacy they have opened up libraries to millions of former non-readers. Just how Chinese library service is conducted is not known, but we can gain some inkling from the government's two educational purposes: 1) indoctrination in correct political attitudes; and 2) training in a skill which will contribute to increased production. Technology and technique (and we may assume, the librarian as technician) are a fairly common objective of social change throughout the East.

The picture of the librarian as primarily a technician appears also in Taiwan. Pearl Wu mentions the new four-year undergraduate curriculum in library science at the National Taiwan University. Technical undergraduate training is in the Asian tradition. The librarian, like most other Asian professionals, misses the advantages of a liberal arts education unless he goes abroad (nor does he always receive it there).

In Korea, libraries—like other institutions—face the Cold War. North Korea looks to Soviet Russia and Communist China, and South Korea looks to the West. A strong factor in Korea, "competitive coexistence" is, in varying degrees, something of a factor almost everywhere in Asia.

In Burma, the current motif seems to be nationalistic. A few months ago American foundations, which were financing Burmese library projects, were asked to leave the country. Hereafter Burma will negotiate her aid projects directly with other governments or will finance her own. Burma's political decision may not seem to have much to do with librarianship, but such decisions are the context within which Asian library development often takes place.

Government involvement in libraries is even plainer in Indonesia. To read Winarti Partaningrat's article is to glimpse some of the incredible administrative problems facing the young island empire in developing library service. To solve its problems of communication, education, and understanding the Indonesians have not illogically called first on central government planning.

In East Pakistan James Hulbert remarks on "the large number of small private reading rooms and libraries scattered widely across the province." This is indeed a remarkable phenomenon. To date Asian libraries have developed principally in the cities. Eventually, if nations are to attain unity, they must all extend library service to the villages in the back country.

Library development has an important part to play in the modernization now taking place in the East. To foster it, we can help not only by our projects of aid, but by our encouragement and by our example of open library resources openly and democratically available.

*Paul Bixler ( guest editorial )*

## WHO CARES?
May 15, 1963

This issue includes a number of features on some current events and issues in the British library world. Because of past personal affiliations, we publish these with some pleasure, but it is not alone for our personal satisfaction that they are included.

The A. P. Herbert campaign for a Public Lending Right, which seeks to bring authors a degree of compensation for repeated use of their books, has raged in one form or another for over a decade. We have met few American librarians who seem aware of its implications and some who are not even aware that anything has been happening. The most extensive coverage of this controversy, for those who wish to fill the void, has appeared in the pages of *The Bookseller*, the British equivalent of *Publishers' Weekly*, but a reading of the Hobart Paper discussed by Mr. Harrison in "Another Battle of the Books" would be sufficient to provide some basic understanding of the situation.

Mr. Surridge's article discusses another campaign which has been waging for several years. There are those who find that the mills of Congress grind exceedingly slow, but while we on this side of the Atlantic have been enjoying notable legislative success on behalf of libraries in recent years, British librarians, in their campaign for legislation designed to improve the public library service, have been rewarded with nothing more stimulating than three government reports in less than five years. To be sure, this is more government attention than British public libraries have received in 30 years, but reports without legislative action are not much more satisfying than a catalog entry is to a reader who wants the book in his hand.

The three British government reports—the Roberts Report and the two more recent reports discussed in the Surridge article—do, however, present a better and more concise picture of the current problems of public libraries and interlibrary cooperation in Britain than perhaps anything else in print.

Five years ago, a British librarian commented in these pages: "Many American librarians, I believe, are ignorant of the kind of service being achieved in the British Isles and, equally, British librarians are ignorant, or

cannot appreciate, the problems being faced by their American colleagues"
(*LJ*, November 15, 1958, p. 3199–3202). There is no question that this is
still as true today as it was five years ago, despite the efforts of ALA's
International Relations Round Table on this side, and of some of the British
library schools on the other.

In October this year, 137 British librarians will descend on these shores.
They are coming because they want to see some of the great American
libraries of which they have heard and read, but also, presumably, because
they want to find out, through discussion with their American colleagues,
more of what is happening currently in American librarianship and what
they can take back with them for transplanting on British soil.

It would be pleasant, useful, and certainly time-saving if the forthcoming discussions between American and British librarians could start
from some base of common understanding of at least the major general
problems in each country.

The periodical output, even in librarianship, is now so huge, that it is
perhaps too much to expect that librarians will read assiduously the library
periodicals of other countries, but it is certainly not beyond reasonable
expectation that important current reports, such as those discussed in this
issue, which give a capsule picture of at least some parts of the current
scene in another country's librarianship, should be read by all who do not
consider librarianship a local parish product.

In a letter to *LJ* some years ago, Ralph Shaw said: "More important
than what we have to gain from knowing about libraries and librarianship
and library methods in other countries, I think that library services mirror
the status, the aspirations, and the knowledge of a society as few other
social institutions do. Do we need to understand the other fellow's point of
view? I do. I think the basic question is not so much what we stand to gain
personally by knowing about what libraries do in other countries but that
the question really is 'who cares about mankind?' And the answer is 'I do.'"
Do you?

*Eric Moon*

## ON THE ROAD
November 15, 1963

In an international issue which this year is otherwise devoted entirely to
Swedish librarianship, this page of thoughts British and American is not as
out of place as it might seem. Its message is the same as that of the features:
librarianship is developing everywhere and in many and different ways.
There are many problems and many solutions, but we shall all make greater
progress when we learn to look more often beyond our national horizons.

This editorial is being written just 24 hours after the departure of 137
British librarians from Idlewild International Airport for London. We spent
two weeks on the road with this group, looking at American libraries, meet-

ing and talking with American librarians, seeing such contrasting American sights as New England in its many-colored fall coat, the exquisite home of Jefferson at Monticello, and the tall-fingered jungle of Manhattan. Although almost flattened by a killing schedule, the British visitors, of course, still saw no more than a narrow selection of libraries along a narrow strip of the East Coast. They did not, could not, see either America or a fair sample of its libraries—but these, in the main, were young librarians and they made an early beginning in expanding their own horizons.

Though we traveled with the British group throughout the tour and shared hours of talk with many of them, we can do no more here than summarize a few of *our* impressions of *their* reactions.

Some of the library buildings were caviar to British librarians who have been starved of new buildings (other than branches) in postwar Britain. Contrasting libraries which were much admired included Simmons College Library, with its wild colors and experimental layout, the rich elegance of Harvard's Leverett House Library, the clean lines of the National Library of Medicine.

Cause for wonder too was the wealth of the collections in many of the libraries visited. The millions of the Library of Congress, Harvard, and the New York Public Library could be expected to impress, but there were many who commented on the strong branch reference collections, for example, in the Montgomery County Libraries in Maryland.

Less concrete were the reactions to the "atmosphere" of various libraries, from the relaxed poise of Harvard, which created perhaps the most indelible impression, to what one visitor called the "sweatshop" feeling of the Library of Congress, probably because of the volume of work going on under dismally overcrowded conditions.

Several British librarians commented that their American colleagues seemed prepared to talk about everything rather than the books in their collections. But two who visited the Pequot Library in Connecticut came back with another story, of the most incredible collection they had seen in a small library, and of a librarian hopelessly in love with his books. The two surely go together.

Despite American concentration on technical matters in recent years, few of the visiting librarians seemed unduly impressed with our technical developments and automated methods, and some commented that a few of the eleborate devices and systems they saw seemed more tedious, laborious and time-consuming than the old-fashioned hand methods. And despite our own lamentations about staff shortages, most of the visitors found our libraries better staffed than their own, and envied their American colleagues their time and their lighter loads.

Perhaps the greatest value of the tour derived from a kind of experiment in international living. Each of the 137 visitors was housed by an individual American family in each of the three cities around which the tour was arranged. Thus, they could supplement what they had seen with conversation. From the intimacy of this interchange of ideas and experiences both sides, the visitors and the hosts, must have benefitted greatly. Certainly the British librarians were loud in their admiration and praise of the many hosts, individual and institutional, who entertained them and so royally demonstrated American hospitality at its outstanding best.

If there be doubt in anyone's mind that the visitors enjoyed their trip, the evidence to the contrary is clear and concrete. Two of the group found jobs in Massachusetts public libraries, one is coming back to work in New York, and one gained a research fellowship at the Folger Library in Washington, D.C. Others took back application forms in their baggage, and still others voiced their intentions of finding exchanges or internships which would give them an opportunity to return, to see—and learn—more. Recruiters, take note.

*Eric Moon*

## THE COST OF LITERACY
April 1, 1964

A few months ago a ceremony took place in Paris. The date, December 10. The place, Unesco House. The occasion, the 15th anniversary of the adoption of the Declaration of Human Rights by the United Nations General Assembly.

One day later, December 11, across the Atlantic, the United Nations General Assembly adopted a resolution presented by 42 delegations, inviting the Secretary-General "to explore ways and means of supporting national efforts for the eradication of illiteracy through a world campaign . . ."

A tragically ironic link was forged between these two events some two months earlier, on October 18, when René Maheu, Director-General of Unesco, presented a report entitled *World Campaign for Universal Literacy* to the United Nations at a meeting of the Second Committee.

M. Maheu reminded the Committee that Article 26 of the Universal Declaration of Human Rights reads: "Everyone has the right to education." He reminded them, too, that "Fifteen years after the adoption of that declaration, there are hundreds of millions of people who cannot read this sentence in which you have acknowledged their sacred right."

The Unesco report on the world campaign for adult literacy is summarized in an article which appears in the January 1964 issue of the *Unesco Chronicle;* it makes fascinating, if rather awful and conscience-searing reading. But how many will read it, and how many will care?

At a time when most of our visits to the wailing wall at home are made because a small army of book-hungry students are surging into our libraries, or because black people want to use the same schools and libraries as white people, the Unesco report somehow shatters these limited human perspectives. Our problems in education and library provision seem like joys when seen against the backdrop of this worldwide desert of forced ignorance.

The number of totally illiterate *adults* in the world, Unesco estimates, is somewhere over 700 million—nearly four times the total population of the United States. And this figure *grows* by some 20 to 25 million each year.

These figures alone are enough to stop some of us cold in our tracks, but it is the cost figures, ridiculous in their comparative insignificance, which most vividly underline what M. Maheu calls "that inequality which divides mankind into those who make history and are opening up the road to the stars and those who endure history and whose horizons are bounded by the ancestral routine." Unesco's "rough estimate" is that "the cost of making a person literate would be from $5.25 to $7.50, depending on the region concerned." The approximate total cost of the proposed ten-year campaign, designed to make literate "two-thirds of the 500 million adult illiterates current assumed to exist in . . . Member States in Asia, Africa, and Latin America" is less than two billion dollars. This is no more than a drop in the waste bucket of this atomic, space-age world.

An inevitable minority among our readers will shrug and ask, "But what concern is this of ours?" To them, it may be futile to answer that it is the concern of all who believe in human dignity, and that librarians, if anyone, must believe that education and the ability to read contribute as much to human dignity as food and clothing and a roof overhead.

We may more profitably address ourselves to those librarians who have been subjected, in one degree or another, to anti-UN pressures. We do not know how much success those in our society have had who would like to see the United States sever its ties with the UN or, better, to see the UN abolished altogether. We must hope that not too many libraries have knuckled under to pressures not to provide or exhibit UN materials. But let us add the hope that more libraries will take a positive role and aggressively promote awareness and understanding of such basic UN programs as this worldwide war on illiteracy, which has much more in common with our domestic war on poverty than the short-sighted are capable of understanding.

Yet, as we write down those pious hopes, some cynic-realist looks over our shoulder and offers us a bet—that for every library which subscribes to, say, the *Unesco Chronicle*, there are ten which subscribe to, say, *Saturday Evening Post*. And although the library profession has made much of its social and educational functions, we still wouldn't have the courage to take that bet.

*Eric Moon*


## PREPARATION FOR WAR
February 15, 1965

We were reading recently an article on "The Library Needs of Northern Nigeria" (*Unesco Bulletin for Libraries*, November–December 1964). As we put it down, we wondered how often it might be read by those many librarians in this country who are embarking or are about to embark on that new, federally-paved highroad of service to the underprivileged and under-educated.

The *Unesco Bulletin* article is written by F. A. Sharr, the State Librarian of Western Australia who, at the request of the Northern Nigerian government, made a joint survey with his wife in 1962. The Sharrs' full report on the Nigerian library situation and their plan for its future development was published by the Ministry of Information in Kaduna in 1963.

Why on earth should American librarians who are beginning to work the newly-rich mines of poverty, be concerned with articles or reports like Sharr's on Nigeria? In a recent issue of *LJ*, Lester Asheim, ALA's International Relations Office director, emphasized that we have as much to learn as to teach in the international library world (*LJ*, November 15, 1964, p. 4465–8). Here, it seems to us, is one of the areas where we can learn plenty from abroad, or from those who have served abroad. How many of our librarians know as much about the problems of service to poor and illiterate or semiliterate people as do those librarians (and others) who have worked for Unesco or the Peace Corps or on other international assignments which have taken them into places where poverty and ignorance are much more solidly established than library services have ever been?

There is not, of course, always an absolute parallel to be drawn between the problems of library service in the underdeveloped or (depending on your tastes in euphemism) newly-emerging nations and those of service to underdeveloped or newly-emerging sections of our own country or its population. In fact, the very selectivity of poverty in an affluent society may, in some ways, make our problem of reaching the hitherto neglected the more difficult task. We do not suggest that you can pick up a how-to-do-it-in-Nigeria and find that you have the Mississippi or Appalachian problem licked. Nevertheless, there may be nuggets of informational gold in what has been written by those who have been library missionaries abroad.

For example, our meetings and literature have been full of theories lately about the kinds of books (or materials!) we need if we are adequately to serve the poor, etc. Some believe we need a deluge of really *practical* materials, written at an easy level. Others want to hang on to their belief that inspiration is still a force, that we need books, again at an easy level, which will capture the imagination of these, the unindoctrinated. But do we really *know* which we want, or, if we want both, how much of either? We know little enough about the reading, or the reading motivation, of the educated public. Do we know half as much about what makes the under-educated fail to tick?

Sharr mentions, for example, a survey of library use by Nigerians at the Kaduna Lending Library. The survey revealed, as expected, a very high nonfiction borrowing rate (74 percent), and showed that 57 percent of the titles borrowed were clearly "being used for educational purposes, including the developing of employment skills."

But Sharr turned the coin over. "On the other hand," he says, "no less than 43 percent of the titles, while predominantly purposive or 'serious' in nature, seemed to have been chosen to satisfy the readers' personal interests without any direct educational or economic motive. This appeared to be a significant finding . . . It does not support the widely held view that Nigerians will not read for pleasure, i.e., without the spur of an examination or of economic incentive, but suggests that to those who are literate reading is a serious pleasure rather than a mere pastime."

Nothing so practical there, you may say—but we didn't promise a primer on poverty. What is important—and interesting, we think—is that Sharr took hold of a widely held misconception and revealed that, if not false, it was shallow and at least partly inaccurate. More exposure to such items from poverty service points abroad might rattle the foundations of some of our "educational" clichés or, under the x-ray of experience, reveal the misshapen limbs of some of our preconceptions. And it might enable some of our knights who are riding off to do war with poverty to less resemble Don Quixote.

## HERE AND THERE
November 15, 1965

This editorial takes a rather sketchy look at some elements in the British library scene in the Sixties, with the main emphasis on what is happening in the public library world. To this observer, who used to be fairly intimate with that landscape, there appears to be considerably more movement and activity than was discernible in several earlier decades.

A number of minor differences between American and British attitudes and practices are obvious to the American observer, and Mr. Kister comments perceptively on some of these in his article in the November 15, 1965 issue of *LJ*. There is one major element of difference, however, a very simple, mundane, but crucially important one—money.

American librarianship has been very fortunate, particularly in recent years, in the enormous help it has received from two sources—foundations and the federal government. It should be added that American librarianship has fought hard for that assistance and has reaped the rewards of its persistence. In Britain, very little of either kind of fiscal assistance has been available (or has been *made* available) to the library profession, and it is becoming painfully evident that something considerably more than local funds will be necessary if British librarianship is to keep abreast of the needs of the second half of the 20th Century.

On the whole, public library service has been at least as well supported at the local level in Britain as it has been here. Mr. Gardner (p. 4898) refers to public library expenditures of $3 to $4 per capita and adds, almost apologetically, "To an American librarian . . . this may not seem a great deal." To a good many American public libraries, $4 per capita still sounds a little like Utopia.

The British local authorities have also borne virtually all the financial burden of building up a number of cooperative ventures—the regional library bureaux, the subject specialization schemes, etc.—which have given British public libraries a better machinery for comprehensive book provision than exists in most parts of the United States. But the capital costs of modernizing this machinery are clearly more than the local purse can provide.

In general, the British university libraries are even worse off and, to the academic librarian in Britain, American expenditure figures look not only impressive but downright unrealistic. Here, the necessary increase in funds will have to come from the national level.

Research in librarianship has not been very vital or inspiring here, but it does receive a considerable amount of fiscal encouragement. In Britain, library research is scarcely a meaningful term. The absence of research may be due, at least in part, to some pretty hidebound British attitudes, but the virtual absence of foundation or "federal" support has been a major contributory factor to the dearth of research.

The articles in this issue, however, left us impressed more by the similarities than by the differences in librarianship on the two sides of the Atlantic. The principal items of British library activity and present concern which seem to emerge in these articles are:

New library legislation; a higher education boom; soaring library budgets; student overcrowding of public libraries; the need for many new library buildings; special provision for the information needs of science and technology at the national level; an attempt by some librarians to come to grips with the potential and problems of automation, and a good deal of resistance by others at the local level; local government reorganization and a striving for larger units of library service; the problems created by insufficient standardization of routine procedures; efforts to improve interlibrary loan machinery and to achieve a better bibliographical aparatus; an attempt to determine priorities in book selection and provision; and efforts to modernize library education in the face of a student boom, the desire of the profession for higher academic status, and a severe recruitment problem.

Every item in that paragraph sounds uncannily familiar—for a very good reason. No general sketch of the American library situation would be accurate if it omitted any one of the factors listed. This is, of course, no very great coincidence. It only underlines, once more, the futility of parochialism. In a discipline where so many of the problems are universal, much more of our thinking about possible solutions should be shared on a wider front than is now common.

*Eric Moon*

## IDENTITY AND CONVICTION
November 15, 1966

Image and status are predominantly American preoccupations, but the big word in Canada is identity. The articles in this annual international issue may strike Americans as somewhat insistent on this score but they are, in fact, a reflection of what is virtually a national obsession "up there."

When we disclosed to one or two of our Canadian friends *LJ*'s plans to publish a special issue on Canadian libraries, the response was prompt—and predictable: "Great! It's about time. Most Americans don't know *anything's* happening up here."

The situation, of course, is not that bad, but there is some justification for the Canadian view that their American colleagues neither know nor care to know what is happening the other side of our mutual border. We have met American librarians who are no more aware of the tremendous progress that has been made in Canadian librarianship than they are of cataloging rules in Afghanistan. This issue, therefore, provides a platform for a few Canadian librarians to present a general picture of the recent and rather rapid library development which has taken place.

Despite the typical "underplaying" by most of our Canadian contributors, it is clear that not all the Canadian-American comparisons come out in favor of the US. How many of our 50 states, for example, currently provide $5 million in state aid to libraries—as the Province of Ontario now does? (Answer: one.) We have national libraries for medicine and agriculture, but nothing quite to compare with Canada's strong National Science Library, which provides services and a degree of coordination in the sciences not evident here. And a number of the current Canadian university library budgets, not to mention the rate of growth of their collections, should be matters of wonder to some of their southern neighbors.

Nevertheless, a kind of defensiveness pervades the articles in this issue, a defensiveness that is perhaps more national than professional. While some of our American readers may understand and sympathize with the Canadian quest for identity, they may also be puzzled by the fact that the "differences" about which the Canadians are so insistent are not always very clear or very well defined.

There is, for example, the Canadian tendency to point to the "massive" resources of the US and to conclude that many of Canada's library problems stem from the absence of such resources. It is unquestionably true that American libraries have more money, but it is also true that America still has large pockets of library poverty—and that many of the states do not contribute significantly more to the aid of library service than do the Canadian provinces. The real difference in recent years has been the growth of federal aid to libraries in the US, but we are not convinced that this "difference" cannot be eliminated if Canadian librarians will organize and work as hard at it as the American library profession has done in the last decade.

The real paradox is that, despite the insistent cries to the contrary, the Canadian library world often appears to be doing its damnedest to iron out rather than preserve Canadian distinctions. The American influence is everywhere to be seen—but most of it has been invited.

The Canadian library schools continue to be accredited by the American (not the Canadian) Library Association. The majority, perhaps, of Canadian library buildings these days are constructed with consultant advice from the US. Nearly every major survey, national or provincial, has been carried out by American librarians. As Basil Stuart-Stubbs puts it (p. 5530): "European consultants are unheard of. And who would think of asking a Canadian?"

Stuart-Stubbs' shot of wry contains perhaps the answer to the paradox mentioned above. US libraries have, in addition to more money, more total manpower resources than Canadian librarianship. At the organization level also, the American Library Association is a much more potent force than CLA—and the latter's lack of adequate financing is a real problem.

But at the individual level, we believe—because we have seen it—that Canada does have the top talent, the leadership, to rescue Canadian librarianship from such heavy reliance upon American advice, to preserve Canadian distinctions and philosophies, and to maintain a diversity of approach which would be healthy for Canada but healthy also for North American librarianship as a whole. The real question is whether the Canadians believe it.

*Eric Moon*

## HERE AND THERE
November 15, 1967

Take a country roughly the same size as the United States (without Alaska) but with a population less than the U.S. had in 1830 or about the same size as Pennsylvania's population. The expectation, or the easy assumption, based on this tremendous difference in density, is that the framework and organization, even the philosophy, of library service of the two countries—Australia and the U.S.—would be entirely dissimilar.

The articles put together for this issue by our guest editor, Norman Horrocks, and his contributors, however, point up as many similarities as differences in the library scenes of these two nations on opposite sides of the globe. In both one can note, for example, the dissolution of the old remoteness of academia and the increasing involvement of university libraries in the national scene; in both one can see the commitment to a graduate profession, accompanied by a serious manpower problem and a consequent increase in interest in the middle and technical ranges of personnel and their training; in both, interstate rivalry and a lurking mistrust of the federal government continue to hamper the quest for national unity. Indeed, the general current concerns of the library profession as listed by Jean Whyte sound uncannily like an American litany.

True, there are contrasts and comparisons, and some of them should serve the useful purpose of counteracting any latent tendencies toward complacency about our own progress. Our growth in recent years, certainly, has been impressive, but the Australian library development has been little short of staggering. Harrison Bryan's figures on the academic library scene, for example, reveal that university library expenditures in Australia have increased by 700 percent in the last nine years, and that his library at the University of Sydney now spends more than *all* Australian university libraries spent a decade ago. By way of contrast, in the not quite parallel period, 1959–65, American academic library expenditures just about doubled. And while academic library staffs have grown here by about 50 percent, "down under" the increase has been more like 400 percent.

One can shrug off these comparisons with the observation that, of course, the Australians are starting from a much smaller base. While this is true, it does little to detract from the picture of phenomenal Australian growth (about which our contributors appear to be almost too deprecating). American librarians who have been suffering the pangs of rapid growth in recent years are not likely to underestimate the problems inherent in a growth rate which has seen 40 percent of all Australian university libraries founded in the last decade and 60 percent of the nation's total academic library book stock added during the same period.

Even American publishers, who have scarcely been having a lean time in recent years, are likely to be impressed with the 45 percent increase in Australian publishers' revenues in the past five years, and their 48 percent increase in exports. That they are aware of it, and are acting upon it, is clear from the invasion of Australia by many important American publishers.

And can public librarians here claim, as confidently as F. A. Sharr does in this issue, that their library expenditures are increasingly "roughly 50 percent faster than the Gross National Product and significantly faster than overall social services expenditure by public authorities"? Or that "libraries are certainly getting a much larger slice of the national cake"?

There are other interesting areas of contrast in these reports from Australia. For instance, while there appears to be a growing movement in North America—with Canada taking the lead—toward strictly "professional" organizations rather than general library associations (like ALA) with somewhat loose and undefined membership requirements, Australia has moved in the opposite direction, away from the professional institute to a general association. And of interest in the interminable debate about whether the Library of Congress is or should be a national library is the example of the Australian National Library which, originally modeled on LC, has now separated its governmental and national library responsibilities.

Finally, it should be of considerable interest here to realize what a great influence some American librarians have had on the Australian library scene: Ralph Munn, Maurice Tauber, and Sara Fenwick, to name only a few of those who have had major impact. Some of the basic similarities can undoubtedly be assigned to their collective influence.

*Eric Moon*

## THE SUGAR CANE CURTAIN
May 1, 1968

In this issue, *LJ* presents a report on Cuban libraries by André Schiffrin, editor-in-chief of Pantheon Books, and one of the relatively few Americans to visit Cuba in recent years, with or without State Department blessing. Although not a librarian, Mr. Schiffrin saw and reported enough of the picture of librarianship in Cuba to confirm one's belief that, regardless of the political trappings of any people, there is a fair chance that a few of them will take it on themselves to gather together books, put them in order, and arrange for others to make use of them.

From other sources, *LJ* has received from time to time a trickle of information about librarians on this island 90 miles from our shores, but physically accessible only by an awkward Mexico City air route, and as far as exchange of information goes, more cut off from us than almost any other nation, however distant and hedged in by language barriers. Hoping like Mr. Schiffrin to stimulate a healthy desire for resumption of a more normal exchange of information with this people to the south, whose destinies have been linked so closely to ours for the last 200 years, we pass along the gleanings we have picked up about Cuban librarianship.

There were librarians before Castro, though under the Batista regime there was precious little support for librarians serving the public. Some of those librarians have left Cuba, but many, we understand, have remained; many others were among the early supporters of Castro and moved up into the higher echelons of government. Today's librarian in Cuba, though struggling with many disadvantages, has the financial support of a government which has not only wiped out illiteracy, but is following through with the creation, within a generation, of an educated populace. Books, consequently, are being published in large numbers, including many editions of American authors either pirated or imported from Western Europe and Russia.

Books are reported to be plentiful in college libraries, many being given away to students, and the collections of the Biblioteca Nacional are growing fast. Less plentiful, but still present as never before are the books in the 36 branches of the Biblioteca Nacional, where they are accessible not just to the children who have learned to read, but to the many adults who have also been taught to read in the literacy campaign.

Librarians in Cuba are predominantly women, and in short supply, as they are here; they are enthusiastic and eager for professional progress but hampered, according to one well-qualified observer, by an underdeveloped system of library education and by lack of normal contacts with North and

South American colleagues. Also against them is the tendency for librarianship in Cuba to attract too few of the young intellectuals who will be tomorrow's leaders, because of greater opportunities for advancement in other fields—university teaching, for example.

One area of definite growth is the proliferation of information centers in government agencies and in scientific and industrial establishments, where one finds documentalists as well as librarians, and the beginnings, at least, of computer applications to library problems.

And how do these Cuban librarians and documentalists feel about us? Like all Cubans, they are deeply resentful of the blockade we have imposed upon them, which makes the acquisition of library materials, like other necessities, extraordinarily difficult. Quite understandably, they just don't like us, but as librarians do elsewhere, Cuban librarians desire to see library materials flow freely in the world.

On this there should be no disagreement. As Mr. Schiffrin notes in his article, a very few United States institutions have been acquiring Cuban materials, despite the roadblocks of State Department policy. Yet some months ago, *LJ* queried a few universities which have had long-standing collections of Cuban materials, and found that almost nothing has been acquired by them in recent years.

It is time that this irrational ban on our access to Cuban books, and their access to ours, be lifted whether it be justified in terms of "know your enemy" or "build bridges of understanding." From the highest levels in recent years, Americans have been urged to increase their capacity to understand and communicate with people of other nations; within this frame of reference, it would be appropriate for the profession to inform the State Department that it is time we junked a censorship policy aimed at Americans and Cubans both.

*Karl Nyren*


## A TWO-WAY STREET

November 15, 1968

For some time now, *LJ*'s annual International issues have focused a state-of-the-art spotlight on one particular country or region of the world, with reports from librarians and other bookmen of these countries on current developments and persistent problems in library "business" abroad. This year's issue departs from that format and presents an international outlook from an American point of view. We asked a number of American librarians, some still overseas and others recently returned from foreign tours of duty, to give their impressions on the state of librarianship as they saw it and to comment on the problems inherent in a different library climate.

Believing that the international experience should be an "exchange"—

and not just a one-way street, wherein the American librarian bestows his expertise in a cultural milieu which is less well developed or developed along different lines and with different values than the American system, we also asked the contributors to this issue to consider what they had *learned* from their experiences abroad. On this point, we took as our text the words of Lester Asheim, who wrote in an earlier international issue (*LJ*, November 15, 1964): "It is frequently refreshing to librarians in other countries to find a representative of the United States who comes as much to learn as to teach and with no predisposition to impose American librarianship on other countries." Our contributors' reactions to this assignment ranged from such comments as "most foreign librarians apparently learned practically nothing useful for librarianship at home" to the statements by Everett Moore, in a letter to *LJ:* "I did indeed learn much more than I taught during my wonderful five months in Japan. If my Japanese friends wanted to, they could send me a bill for their services and I'd have to pay it."

The countries covered in this issue represent a wide spectrum of literary and library development—from nations with an ancient respect for learning and a long history of libraries, to those with no literary or library tradition at all. While some of these lands might be said to enjoy a relatively stable economy, others are rebuilding and emerging after years of political and military turmoil. Yet despite these dissimilarities, many of their library problems are strikingly similar to each other and even to those faced by American librarians. Take, for instance, the problem of locked cases and closed shelves. The foreign librarian justifies this system by citing the scarcity of books and the librarian's financial responsibility for his collection, a situation which "militates against reader service." The American librarian finds a different rationale for limited access. And even where use is no longer restricted, how much, John Harvey asks, has been done by western librarians to promote use?

Two other problems of the foreign library climate: We may deplore the philosophy which has given rise to the view that libraries are the "private preserves" of special segments of the population. And yet, librarianship in the U.S. has only recently taken its first faltering steps beyond the idea of service to a special (middle-class) clientele.

And secondly, in the area of library education, the foreign student is taken to task for being a product of an educational system which emphasizes learning by rote, with consequent failure to *apply* his learning to the local library situation. How often has our own educational system been criticized for producing the unadaptable professional who learns techniques and rules but not philosophy and principles?

American librarians might do well to take a good look at some of the accomplishments and solutions to library problems which have been developed overseas. To cite just one example: David Kaser, in his article on Korea, points out the phenomenal growth in school libraries which, in the short span of just six years, have increased by 2000 percent; staff by 750 percent; and number of library volumes by 1150 percent. Truly a herculean accomplishment and one which might provide some lessons for American librarians.

To quote again from Lester Asheim, in his award-winning book, *Librarianship in the Developing Countries:* "We must listen as well as tell, learn as well as teach, receive as well as give. It is true that we have much more material wealth than the developing nations have and that we have had more years of experience in dealing with our own library problems at a professional level. But this does not mean that we have nothing to learn from other practices, or other proposed solutions. Until we really believe that—not just say that we do—we create an unfavorable atmosphere in which to carry on the exchange from which we both might benefit so much."

*Shirley Havens*

# CHAPTER 4

# Identity of
# the Librarian

The sixties were not unique in the amount of self-examination, questioning of one's role, and pondering the values of one's calling—every decade, every era goes through this with more or less intensity, and the literature of the profession has few more important jobs than encouraging the exhaustive discussion which is necessary. A great many *LJ* editorials asked—and sometimes tried to answer such questions as the role of the library in society, the proper work of the librarian, how best to recruit and then to train the librarian, the "image" problem so painful in those years, the proper authority relations between staff and administrator, and that very hot topic of the sixties—labor unions. Finally, since almost all library periodicals are under the control of the professional associations and thus unable to take an independent editorial stand on any question on which the association staff is sensitive, *LJ* made it a point to stimulate open discussion on this most important element in professional life.

## The Library as a Social Agent

### COMMUNITY HEADQUARTERS
March 1, 1961

Two recent articles on library participation in adult education activities in Illinois and Michigan (*LJ*, Jan. 15, pp. 194–9) found many librarians in those two states uncommitted and unconvinced concerning the central role in the community that librarians can and should play. Marjorie Kroehler found "libraries in the state of Illinois . . . somewhat lax in their approaches to the community." Patrick Penland concluded that Michigan librarians "are not yet committed to (the library's) full development as a community educational institution."

It *is* undeniable that there are too many instances of librarians failing or refusing, for a variety of reasons, to gain representation for their libraries in community, educational, or bookish activities at local, regional or national levels. But there is, we optimistically believe, always a silver lining, and we have had two glittering, high-flying glimpses of it during the past year. At the mammoth White House Conference on Children and Youth almost a year ago, some 100 librarians were present and actively involved. At the smaller White House Conference on Aging a few weeks ago librarians were again present—26 of them—and they took part in a great variety of discussions, not only on the education of the aged, but also on their health and medical care, and other subjects less obviously the *direct* concern of librarians. That this active participation on the part of the librarian delegation had an impact is evident in the prominence given to libraries in three of the final statements of the conference and in dozens of preliminary statements and talks throughout the four days of meetings.

Those librarians who maintain a narrow view of library service as essentially passive, might do worse than study the remarks of a non-librarian, Dr. Edward L. Bortz, chief of medical services at the Lankenau Hospital, Philadelphia, and keynote speaker at the education session during the White House Conference on Aging. The sentiments we share, the italics we have provided, but the words are those of Dr. Bortz:

"There are certain key factors in planning a broadened education program . . . In addition to an imaginative teaching corps, there is need for wider utilization of the schools and libraries of the nation . . . The occasion is instant; *experiments are not particularly perilous,* but they do demand application, sincerity, an emotional dynamism which will uncover hidden resources that will be a joy to behold . . .

"Community libraries are a most valuable germinal center from which recent acquisitions in the form of reports, bulletins, books, magazines of all kinds can be distributed. *Libraries are a rallying headquarters for the community. Their real worth has yet to be discovered.* We can no longer fail to support them. For the public is not awakening to the need for additional information with which each citizen may reach a more enjoyable, more healthy, longer life, freed of many nuisances."

The education section at the conference took up the challenge issued by Dr. Bortz, and in its final statement and recommendations, declared: "The initial stimulation of educational programs for, about, and by the aging should be through institutions that have public responsibility for education, that in combination, have nationwide coverage and that have the confidence of all groups. These institutions are public schools, institutions of higher learning and libraries."

It is up to librarians everywhere—Illinois and Michigan included—to see that this confidence is deserved and retained.

*Eric Moon*

## RIGHT KIND OF CRITIC
October 1, 1961

"The accomplishment of reading, originally acquired to tap the store of other men's knowledge, is, in the 1960's, too precious to be frittered away. This is where the public librarian might be thought to have a social duty—to have a responsibility both to readers and to society. With universal literacy, should he not consider himself responsible for the purposes to which books are put, at least in his own establishment? Should he not be insisting that merely to read is not enough in the modern world—should he not deliberately avoid catering merely for the odd moment of leisure—should he not be proclaiming that the provision of the trivial is not within the province of the public library—should he not be insisting on the adoption of something like a literary standard? . . ."

Look around the library world with an unbiased but critical eye. If you have reason to believe that your own library is even fairly good, call in at a few neighboring institutions and you will soon realize that many of the small, and not so small libraries succeed only in making a mockery of what a library service should be. It is quite incomprehensible why so many readers, [Board] members and even librarians seem satisfied, and sometimes even proud, of the pathetic attempts to provide a service under poverty-stricken conditions—like a very poor relation showing a brave front with second-hand, threadbare clothing, and insufficient income to provide more than the barest necessities of life. . . ."

These are two extracts from a very fiery Presidential Address to the (British) Association of Assistant Librarians, delivered earlier this year by W. Howard Phillips and published in the August issue of the *Assistant Librarian.*

Mr. Phillips may be best known to librarians in this country as the author of a little yellow book entitled *A Primer of Classification,* a best-seller for many years which has helped legions of beginning students toward an understanding of this awesome subject. In years he is one of the oldest members of the young Association over which he now presides, but in spirit he remains one of the youngest, as vigorous in self-criticism as in criticism of others.

In the paper from which the above passages are quoted, he is talking, of course, to British librarians and attacking weaknesses in the British library system, but there may be librarians here who will see the relevance, not only of the above remarks but of many others, to the American library scene. We strongly recommend particularly to younger librarians and to library school students about to enter the profession, a reading of this paper, not only for its content but for its spirit. For Mr. Phillips is the kind of critic we need in librarianship, always dissatisfied with the present but full of faith and hope for the future, as the following passage from the same address shows:

"A reaffirmation of faith is urgently needed. It should be proclaimed loudly and consistently that the public library is still the University of the man-in-the-street, the College of further education of the post-graduate, the specialist and the research worker; that it stands fairly and squarely as an intermediary between the beginning of learning and its mature expression; that a comprehensive collection of good books well administered is a bank of indestructible knowledge, saving the money of the ratepayer and tax-payer alike. For no modern country, at least not an industrial democracy, can afford the wastage caused by general ignorance, by intolerance, by the lack of understanding of vital social and economic forces, by the lack of reasoning power, by a superfluity of unskilled labor and by the ill-health of its citizens. When a country stops learning—it is already dead!"

*Eric Moon*

## BACK AT THE RANCH
September 15, 1963

There is a nice irony in Dr. Beasley's statement that "Libraries are *safe* institutions, free from serious attack except in the most unusual situations" (p. 3155–60) appearing in the same issue with the story of attempted sabotage of the Ohio State Library (p. 3173–75).

But Dr. Beasley's point is fair enough in general, if his point is that libraries are usually safe because the public doesn't care enough one way or the other. He does say "Libraries are presumed to be popular democratic institutions—measured in terms of actual use, they are not." We would add, measured in terms of actual support, they are not either.

Dr. Beasley, as the outsider looking in on librarianship, is not alone in sensing something of our failure. Roy Stokes pronounces "Librarianship . . . fated unless it reflects the changing circumstances of the world around it" (*LJ*, Sept. 1, p. 3036). In the issue, Neal Harlow asks, "Why has the library, as a necessary social institution, failed to evolve like other more successful species? . . . Libraries have scored some points in recent years . . . but they stay pretty well at the bottom of the league." And Ohio state librarian Walter Brahm declares, "Some public libraries could close down without a ripple because they haven't made any measurable impact in their communities."

Deny it as some undoubtedly will, the evidence to support these somber views is all around us. The cheery New Hampshire story (p. 3169–72) illustrates, despite its breeziness, how great and arduous effort is needed to combat not just apathy but distinct opposition to libraries. There, it took 13 years of foundation building before a desperately needed state-wide system could be squeaked through.

It isn't just in the smaller states that the barriers are high. Years of frustration and failure preceded the recent success of California librarians in gaining state aid for libraries—and what they finally managed to get looks puny against the gigantic backdrop of California's vitality and expansion. Even in New York, most progressive of our states in library support at the state level, librarians have pounded in vain for several years against a wall of resistance to their plan for better reference and research resources and facilities. And forces in Ohio now seek to destroy, or emaciate, one of that state's most valuable library resources.

Our contributors present a variety of factors contributing to the lack of library support where it counts. Among them, Dr. Beasley cites the wrong kind of library board members whose interests are not representative, and the use by librarians of "exotic" data which "is completely useless in an individual city to educate people about the library program."

But each of the critics in this issue finally comes back to the librarian. Harlow declares: "Librarians themselves are more nearly at the heart of the problem . . . If libraries are to become fundamental educational institutions, they await the initiative of librarians." Says Brahm: "It is invariably librarians and trustees who want to preserve their own 'mud pies' of organization and administration . . . the consumers don't know how they are organized or administered, and very few of them care." And Beasley adds, "The Library's proper field of activity knows no limit except the competency of the individual librarian."

Now all of this is very fine, but we all know that library service can only be as good, and can only grow as fast, as the people who operate it. But why are so many members of our own profession stunted in their growth, limited in their vision?

May it not be that libraries (and the librarians who operate them) are being strangled by their history, and by their devotion to that history, of local autonomy and control?

The tight fists of local control have been pried loose from many other social services because those small hands were no longer able to hold the wild horses dragging society into the future. Libraries are too often among the few remaining captives confined to the local corral, and too many people, including too many librarians and trustees, are determined to keep them there. But the fences of that corral are buckling, and will surely fall before the growing pressure of contemporary social forces.

If librarians don't stop driving in the stakes and instead open the gate and make a dash for wider horizons, they may find themselves and their libraries buried as the 20th century pounds on over them without ever noticing that they were really there.

*Eric Moon*

### NEED AND OPPORTUNITY
May 1, 1964

A stimulating one-day symposium organized by the Alumni Association of the Rutgers library school in April left us contemplating a lot of tantalizing threads of thoughts and ideas. We don't expect to unravel them all here, but would like to pull a few of the loose ends and see where some of them lead and whether any blend into some kind of discernible pattern.

The two large threads through the center of the day's discussions were access to, and quality of library service; and for much of the day the meeting wore a city-tailored coat, with its pockets full of the problems created by a society in ferment and flux, and some of the solutions being attempted by a few major metropolitan libraries.

Ralph Shaw detonated an afternoon panel session with a paradox: the traditional "readers" are moving to the suburbs, where often they are without library service as they have known it, while the major libraries in the core cities are being left increasingly in areas populated by underprivileged people who have never acquired the habit of library use or any perspective of their potential, and whom libraries have rarely made any determined effort to reach. These libraries must now go out after a readership which will not come to them easily, and to succeed they will have to discard what Ralph Blasingame called their "obsession with a middle class ethic."

We heard what some large libraries are doing to reach this audience. Detroit's library programs and services, designed to cross color and status lines, were described by Ralph Ulveling. Janet Stevens gave a vigorous account of the ten-year record of the Pennsylvania Avenue Branch of the Enoch Pratt Free Library in establishing quality service in an underprivileged section of Baltimore. And Hardy Franklin left most people gasping with his story of life as a community coordinator (a brilliant innovation of Francis St. John's) in the Bedford-Stuyvesant area of Brooklyn. Has any librarian, we wondered, ever dived quite so deeply into the life of his community as Franklin?

Here, then, we had three examples, not just of aggressive librarianship, but of imaginative library salesmanship, and of a dedication to people as the reason for and the end of library service. But it was clear that we were not hearing about "typical" librarianship. Few libraries can back up a selling job with the resources of these three great libraries, few have the money or the staff to implement such programs, and some just plain don't have the desire.

If we didn't know that we had been on a glide above the clouds, there was always Ralph Blasingame to bump us back to hard earth. He reminded us that the large libraries and their librarians dominate our professional meetings and discussions (as they did this one), and that they also dominate and distort our reporting of the total library scene. We need, he said, to devise new ways of reporting and analyzing our statistics, so that our facts do not obscure the truth. The real truth, said Blasingame, "is awfully damned dismal."

Blasingame, prompted by his recent experience in Pennsylvania, brought us back to the realization that the need for equalization of opportunity applies everywhere, in city, suburb, and rural area alike. He cited, for example, Lowell Martin's 1958 survey of Pennsylvania public libraries, which showed the average per capita support, statewide, to be about $1. This was bad enough, but if the large metropolitan libraries were extracted, the figure would have been only about 40 cents per capita.

Blasingame spoke of the profession's refusal to discuss real issues, and offered the recent Midwinter ALA Council meeting as an example (*LJ*, Feb. 15, p. 812–816). The topic of equalization of opportunity is one, he declared, the profession must soon discuss very seriously. We are headed more and more toward increased support for library services from state and federal sources—and if we make no attempt at equalization, we deny the very basis for such support.

Certainly, with the broadening of the scope of the Library Services Act, the profession must be vigilant in remembering that its great success and acceptance thus far have been based on establishing and improving services where they are most desperately needed. The needs, the inequalities, are still in abundance, but they are forever changing shape because society is not static. Our administrations, our methods, our organizations must be as flexible as society itself. They are most likely to be so if they are defined and designed always in the context of human needs and opportunities.

*Eric Moon*


## OUR OWN POVERTY
September 15, 1964

Wilhelm Munthe saw poverty in library book collections when he noticed in 1939, ". . . the quantitative predominance of ephemeral entertainment literature—especially in the smaller and medium-sized libraries." In 1962 Dan Lacy dramatized a similar poverty by suggesting that if one percent of the people in a community of 20,000 went to the public library for information on a specific subject (Viet Nam perhaps) service would collapse after the arrival of the first dozen.

These observations, separated by more than 20 years of soul searching and painful self-analysis by librarians, are the result of two concepts that have always burdened our professional thinking. The 1939 librarian who thought that the way to public acceptance was to fill the shelves with books labelled "Romances," "Mysteries," and "Westerns," is little removed from her successor in 1962, willing to buy a maximum of two or three copies of a book undergoing great current popularity because it is timely.

It is in their acceptance of the facts that the library budget has a low ceiling, and that the library is used by only ten percent of the adult population (at most) that these two librarians are identical.

The phrases "tested usefulness" and "political neutrality" best describe this impoverished thinking and both can be used to illustrate its stranglehold on the efforts of libraries to break out of their fiscal and intellectual poverty.

"Tested usefulness" is often expressed in an *LJ* review as "recommended for large fiction collections," or in the ALA *Booklist* as "suggested for the small library." It is the basic criterion for the inclusion of books in several standard selection tools. The librarian trying to justify his rejection of a book might express the concept by saying that the book is "of limited appeal." He means that the book is of limited appeal to the small minority of people who use the library now.

The "tested usefulness" concept accepts the library's public as it stands, a miniscule and unimportant minority. By subscribing to this concept the librarian also accepts the fact that no one thinks of the public library as the source for information on Cyprus or Viet Nam, nor as the place to learn what the John Birch Society stands for, nor as where to find out about the program of the Student Nonviolent Coordinating Committee in Mississippi this summer. By accepting their minority-public librarians abrogate the selection function to that minority, build collections that are useless for those who need current information fast, and who have long since given up the prospect of getting it from the public library.

One of the reasons that the larger and more important public has given up on the public library is the profession's desire for "political neutrality." One could concede the necessity, in the early days, for the avoidance of politics. In 1964, however, nearly every professional organization has entered the political arena in one way or another. Back home in the community, librarians are still content to ride on the coattails of the school board or the department of public works when it comes to fiscal support. Few are willing to bring the free public library into the real battle for the tax dollar. In the words of Norton Long: "The price of political neutrality has been public indifference and neglect. As most public administrators have found, few programs sell themselves. Public policies, even such widely accepted—widely accepted at the level of lip service—policies as the desirability of the public library are in competition with one another for scarce public funds. The librarian . . . must fight for his share of the budget."

Because of these traditions of minimal service to a minority, and frightened aloofness from politics, the free public library, in a sense, itself exists in that impoverished "other America" to which this issue of *LJ* is devoted. Its resources, already taxed by this minority service, are in no way prepared to provide the service in depth that could make it the important agency for the whole public that it has never been. The potential public is there, indifferent and unaware that it could be served. Unless librarians are prepared to declare a "war on library poverty" as well as enlist in the war on material poverty, the role of the public library, imprisoned in those two long standing traditions, will continue to be as an impoverished cousin to richer and more vital public agencies.

*John Berry*

## STRATEGY FOR CHANGE
September 15, 1964

Not long ago, we heard a prominent and dedicated young adult librarian complain about what she considered the intrusion of the library into domains where it has no legitimate role, and no particular competence: the area of extensive social service. The librarian, she said, is a specialist in books; he is not a social worker or a therapist, and even his well-meaning attempts to assume these roles may harm those whom he is trying to help.

It is an old argument, and the lady may be right. But if she is, we feel, it is up to the library itself to do something about it—change its qualification requirements, work out better liaisons, hire specialists from other fields as part of its staff.

The reason is that the library no longer has a choice, in much the same way that the school no longer has a choice. Both professions share in origin and purpose a nineteenth-century concept of education: the democratization of society within an accepted social framework and within a fairly well defined range of services. School and library have tried to give the individual from the lower classes access to the same body of knowledge and complex of skills which more fortunate economic groups have had as their birthright.

Their aim, in other words, has been the equalization of opportunity through the standardization of background. To take a precise instance: the "deprived" child could begin his formal schooling on a level with the middle-class child through a kindergarten program which, by a variety of social and "reading readiness" activities, would provide a nucleus of concepts and attitudes. Given a basic core of knowledge, it was held, the individual would develop according to his ability. IQ and achievement tests were based on this assumption of a common background.

Twentieth-century history, for all its social fluidity, has shown the grotesque over-simplification of the concept. Culture is part of the child's weaning; it is not imposed from without. Parental indifference or discouragement, prejudice, squalid surroundings, all take their toll early. The child enters school crippled by the neglect and contempt he has already faced, stunted by his parents' illiteracy, or simply frightened by a foreign tongue. Each failure is compounded; the teacher never completely reaches the child in a group situation; the IQ test, invalidated from the start by inequality of background, becomes a weapon against him. He fails, loses his self-esteem, and accepts, in James Baldwin's words, some form of death, be it anomie, alcoholism, or crime.

Thus the life of the child is determined by forces which have lain outside the traditional province of the great democratizing institutions. It is a difficult situation, but not irreparable. In our metropolitan areas schools have instituted after-hour and summer programs, employed guidance counselors and social workers who visit the home, simply in recognition that the purpose and limits of teaching have been too narrowly defined. It does not required much greater innovation for the library to adopt the same administrative devices. The librarian, in fact, has an edge over the teacher in several ways: his one-to-one relationship with the child, the greater flexibility of his guidance function. Today these advantages impose new responsibilities upon him.

The new potential for library service may indeed, as our YA specialist feared, find librarians inadequate to fulfill their role. But to the extent that this is so, it is essential that the library profession forget its parochialism, even its struggle for recognition (which will come to it anyway, in the long run). We have reached a point where the barriers are falling not only between school and public, academic and special, library, but between adult and children's, or adult and "young adult" services. The child depends on his parents' literacy; the "young adult" is sometimes married and a parent himself. If we are to create a commensurate continuum of service, we must not only revise our definitions but bring outsiders—social workers, civic agencies, psychologists, into our ranks, as many schools have done, and as the library programs described in this issue have done. The extraordinary flexibility of library service displayed by these few systems only hints at its possibilities; and the programs themselves are not, in any broad sense, innovations. They are only part of what the library world must accept as its own "strategy for change"—the adaptation of traditional institutions and services to new conditions.

*Evelyn Geller*

## WHO'S UNDERDEVELOPED?
November 15, 1964

While this "International Issue" of *LJ* is devoted to the range of activities of several international organizations, we are impressed by a recurring theme in most of the articles. Briefly stated, that theme might read: *Libraries are a basic and integral part of a society's machinery for social change and they must be included in that society's plans for economic, social, and educational development.*

When national governments recognized this fact Earle Samarasinghe called it "The Great Step Forward" (p. 4473). The "Mission to Malagasy" (p. 4476) is a dramatic demonstration of the theme put to work. Jay Daily's contribution is as much a plea for books as the basis for development, as it is a description of the Franklin programs (p. 4483). Lev Vladimirov points with great pride to the Soviet Government's recognition that libraries are a part of the machinery for social change (p. 4469), and from our own Lester Asheim comes the view that American librarianship can learn a great deal from other nations (p. 4465).

If Asheim's view is correct, and we believe it is, one of the great lessons being offered by the developing nations of the world is that libraries have a role in the mobilization of a society for its own improvement, a role requiring that library goals, library programs, and library planning be integrated with other economic and social planning in a permanent and fundamental way.

The developing nation has, for this purpose, certain advantages. What a delight it must be to be able to build a national library system from the very beginning, unrestrained by tradition and practices that have evolved for more than a century. Consider the direction the US library development might have taken if our efforts had begun this decade, say with the 1956 standards. Think of the freedom with which we could reconstruct the whole American library edifice by starting with the Economic Opportunity Act of 1964.

The developing nation has this kind of opportunity, and if Earle Samarasinghe is right, those nations have learned a most important lesson from their more "developed" neighbors. They have, at the beginning, the same knowledge it took more than a century to acquire in our own growth, the knowledge that the library must be considered as a part of the whole apparatus for social change, not as a separate, local institution for autonomous and specific local purposes. Their library systems will be born as national systems, and as one of the central agencies or weapons in the attack on nearly all of their problems.

In this respect we in the United States are at about the same point in our library development as these new nations. It is only in the postwar years that real impetus for concerted national library programs has been forthcoming. During the period of our own "underdevelopment" in the thirties, the library, although it received government attention via WPA or the imprints survey, somehow became separated from America's "great step forward" into the twentieth century, and waited until after the war to take the step itself.

There are present indications, however, that libraries, if they have the will, can become for the United States what they are for underdeveloped lands. The great growth in state and federal aid, regional systems, and national centers is part of the evidence. Most important is recent and current federal activity, the Library Services Act which grow into LSCA, the Higher Education Facilities Act, the Vocational Education Act of 1963, and a host of others listed by Drennan, Kittel, and Winnick as "A Full Range of Weapons" (LJ, Sept. 15, '64, p. 3266–3267). At the end of the list a new opening beckons the libraries of the US in the Economic Opportunity Act of 1964 which inaugurates several programs that can utilize library service, provided libraries are willing to initiate such action. Willingness is the key.

For many reasons the United States has never had a governmental "grand design" for the "Great Society." Government here requires stimulation from the outside before action can be taken. Our lawmakers require pressure, either in the form of constructive proposals and programs, or as demands from special interest groups. This is a basic difference in the way we are governed. It may account for the fact that US libraries are only now, in the sixties, approaching the degree of integration with the society that is the distinguishing feature of the first library plans in new nations.

American librarians are now awake to this difference and have, at last, begun to press for the inclusion of libraries in national economic, social, and educational planning.

The first halting steps have been taken. If we continue our libraries will finally become an important cog in the machinery for social change; if we don't they will remain apart from that change, and as "underdeveloped" as any in the world.

*John Berry*

## CONTACT WITH THE "OUTSIDE" WORLD
May 1, 1965

Footnotes are not our favorite flowers and they rarely bloom on this page, but the long one down below is the centerpiece of this garden of words. It lists the national organizations (other than the library oriented) which were represented at a special invitational conference called at the end of March by the American Library Association.

For two days, members of these groups were isolated, with librarians, far out in the Virginia countryside at Airlie House in Warrenton. The unobtrusively planned conditions were perfect. The restfulness of the rural setting, the conviviality of the social arrangements, the programmed insistence on discussion and interchange—all were cleverly designed to lead to a loosening of tongues and attitudes.

Below, and only thinly covered by the informality and sociability, lay a serious and urgent purpose. In the letter inviting participants, ALA formally spelled out the purpose this way: "To confer with national organizations that have indicated their concern for excellence in education for all our people, in order to share knowledge and understanding, and to explore means of mutual cooperation in solving certain problems faced by people in pursuing their educational goals. These problems focus in the nation's libraries."

The last sentence of that paragraph is, of course, a statement of belief—*our*, i.e. librarians' belief—rather than a statement of purpose. The real purpose was to get some other people, who were in a position to do something about it, to believe it too. As James E. Bryan put it—and he started building the road to Airlie House when he dreamed up the 1963 Conference Within a Conference in Chicago—"Librarians have been talking too many years to themselves." To these representatives of organizations civic, governmental, and educational, he said, "We want libraries to be in *your* baliwick."

ALA president Edwin Castagna presented the problem in another aspect: "It should be safe to assume that everyone in this group has known from childhood what librarians do. But it is sometimes surprising to find big gaps between what the practitioners think they do and what the consumers think is being done."

Clearly, the Airlie House conference had one immediate purpose and a second, longer-range, corollary one. What we were after immediately was communication; what we hoped would follow was involvement. Libraries need help, support, influence, recognition: the people present at Airlie could play a big part in supplying these things—*if* they could be convinced that libraries are as central as the library profession thinks they are, and if they could be persuaded to see that what libraries are being asked to do is impossible for librarians to do alone and with the meager tools (material, human, and fiscal) they are presently given to do the job.

So how did it go? For those of us who were well-acquainted with the library scene, it must be admitted that some of the talk was tiresome and repetitive. The librarian speakers present showed the over-exhibited, grim etching of the total library scene, hung in its usual ornately ugly frame of sad statistics of unserved areas and people, under-support and lack of acceptance at the polls, shortages of staff and materials. We talked about all these, and more: the "new" library publics among the deprived and the minority groups, the student invasion, the crowded-out and the apathetic adults, the plethora or explosions, the purpose of education, the rainbowed confusion of academic disciplines, curricula planned and instituted without visible library support, automation, information retrieval, mass communications, publicity, the freedom to read, even—so help us—the "condition of man."

The "visitors" from the outside world were, in fact, taken for a fast skim across our polluted library waterfront, and were invited to conclude that it

The national organizations participating in the Airlie House conference: National Association of Broadcasters; National Educational Television; Chamber of Commerce of the USA; Office of Economic Opportunity, Executive Office of the President; National Association of Educational Broadcasters; National Urban League; American Book Publishers Council; Committee for Economic Development; Graduate School, US Department of Agriculture; American Association for the Advancement of Science; National Science Foundation; American Municipal Association; Department of Health, Education, and Welfare; American Association of University Women; National Book Committee; US Department of Agriculture Division of Home Economics; Federal Extension Service; Association of the Junior Leagues of America; National Council of Teachers of English; Council of State Governments; American Federation of Labor and Congress of Industrial Organizations; Association of State Universities and Land-Grant Colleges; American Council on Education; General Federation of Women's Clubs; League of Women Voters of the US; Association of American Colleges; US Conference of Mayors; National Association of Counties; National School Boards Association; American Association of School Administrators; Council of Chief State School Officers; and National Commission on Accrediting—and we may have missed a few at that!

could only be cleaned up with their communal help, interest, and moral and financial support.

Had this been a "library" conference, in the usual sense, the talk would have been barren and useless in its repetition. The new, the important factor this time was that the familiar voices and words were finding new ears. The reactions from the representatives of other organizations, particularly after the soft, smiling, but distinctly double-barreled blast from Wisconsin's Janice Kee in her talk on "The Current Status of Libraries," were both revealing and, we thought, encouraging. They confessed to being dismayed, disturbed, shocked, disconcerted, depressed (yes, we heard *all* those words used).

At the end of the affair, each of the workshop-type groups brought in the selective products of its deliberations. Each group was asked to define two or three major problems, to make recommendations on how to tackle them, and to specify a "first step" which might be taken immediately. Many of these group statements were awfully general (and some generally awful); few suggested anything new by way of action. But again, what will be new, if it comes about, will be the involvement of organizations representing a much wider sphere of influence and power in the kind of propaganda effort that librarians have thus far been making too often alone.

This conference will be reported (rather than, as here, editorialized upon) in our next issue. But perhaps, just for flavoring, we should give one sample of what came out of these variegated discussion groups. It is a completely untypical example, an ambitious one, and the better for that. This group defined the Number One Problem as "the achievement of a nationwide system of libraries meeting all national needs for knowledge and preserving the right to read." As a first step toward this oasis, the group recommended "The appointment by the President of the United States of a National Citizens Commission on Library Development." The conference, as you can see, did not think exclusively small.

What the conference achieved, or will achieve, is obviously impossible to calculate at this close remove. Everything, or nearly everything, will depend on the follow-up—by ALA, by the other organizations, and by the library profession individually and as a whole. One very basic achievement, however, can already be considered as part of the record.

This conference was, as Ed Castagna noted, "a first." It was, at last, tangible recognition of a number of realities: if libraries *are* a vital part of society, librarians must communicate with society at all its levels of organization and influence; if libraries *are* an integral part of the educational process, they must integrate with education at all of *its* levels of organization and influence; and if libraries are, in any sense, an important part of the governmental machinery, then officials from all levels of government must be more closely involved in our deliberations on the problems and possible solutions of the betterment of library service.

Ruth Warncke wrote the only possible end to this editorial when she said, during her conference-end summary: "These are not *our* problems;

they are the problems of the people of the United States. If nothing comes of this conference, it will be a public disgrace."

*Eric Moon*

## PRECIOUS IRRELEVANCE
June 15, 1965

Every book "symbolizes their traumatic rejection," confronts them with their own inferiority, "reinforces their deprivation and alienation," because 80 percent of the children of the poor, indeed the poor themselves, are deficient in reading skills, have some kind of reading retardation. Dr. Kenneth B. Clark made these assertions at a Conference on Librarians, Books, and the Poverty Program, held at Pratt Institute on May 15. He is a psychology professor at the College of the City of New York, the author of the recently published *Dark Ghetto,* and well-known for his leadership in civil rights and in the battle to improve educational opportunity in New York City. He must have hit the target if the explosion that followed his talk is any indication.

Clark suggested that the education of impoverished children was "criminally negligent," and that until it improved librarians would have to settle for a "precious irrelevance" to poverty programs. The audience replied, during the question period, with brief speeches in the guise of questions, attacking both the assertions Clark had made, and his research that led to them. The educationists responded with typical defensiveness, almost as if they were more concerned with their own status as experts than with the education of poor children. The librarians seemed to miss Clark's point, and couldn't accept the possibility of their irrelevance to poverty programs.

These reactions to Clark demonstrated again that enthusiasm that seems to propel the "Great Society" bandwagon as it barrels onward, never slowing down to evaluate, nor stopping to pick up the most important passengers and crew, the poor themselves.

There were a few among those present who listened to *everything* Clark said instead of reacting only to his indictment of their particular pet projects. They heard him describe with great respect and admiration a wonderfully relevant librarian named Arthur Schomburg. They heard him say that "poverty programs cannot be tied to existing social agencies," where the emphasis upon the "saturation of social services" would merely continue and increase programs that have failed for so long. "The poor themselves must be the instruments . . ." Dr. Clark said. "Poverty programs must mobilize their own latent power for social action and change." As it was with New York's Haryou project, relevant programs must be based upon ". . . persistent emphasis on social action, not on social services." A few days later, while we were planning our schedule for the ALA Conference in Detroit, we discovered that the poverty bandwagon is scheduled to make several stops there—so many, indeed, that poverty will be one of the major themes at

ALA this year. The tentative program in the May *ALA Bulletin* is loaded with titles like "The Illiteracy Equation," "Experiments in Reaching the Culturally Deprived," "Libraries, Labor, and the War on Urban Poverty," and "Libraries and Illiteracy."

It is fitting and proper that these topics come before the profession. It is important that librarians try to find a role in the most humane effort launched in our country since the thirties. They should not, however, in the fervor of their enthusiasm, overlook the warning inherent in Dr. Clark's address and echoed in so many places—in James Baldwin's or Michael Harrington's writings, or in *Roosevelt Grady* when the welfare worker's irrelevancy is so accurately described as "all snoopy and la-di-da."

When librarians go to Detroit and they hear a dozen experts or participants relate their plans and programs for the poor, we hope they will be equipped with some of Dr. Clark's questions. We hope they ask, as Dr. Clark did, whether the program being touted is relevant, or just "another cruel hoax." Most important, we hope the bandwagon will depart before the conferees get down to the real business and work of poverty. After the hoopla, the politics, and the fanfare, then the work should begin; the vital work of rebuilding a society.

The librarians in Detroit should weigh carefully Dr. Clark's statement that: "The library is another assault on their [i.e. the poor] egoes." Our society has made the poverty child incompetent; let's not create programs to remind him of that incompetence.

Clark set the stage at Pratt for a *relevant* attack, when he said: "The war on poverty cannot be waged in terms of public relations, promises, and verbal concern."

*John Berry*

## HELPING HANDS

June 1, 1967

Spring in New York City this year was heralded by a group of young men and women descending upon a block between Second and Third Avenues, armed with brooms, with the intention of spending a morning just cleaning up a little piece of their city. When not sweeping, they handed out flowers to passers-by.

A wonderful time was had by all—they even washed a police car dispatched to keep an eye on them—but the most poignant note of all was the strangely embarrassed reaction of the people who were supposed to be keeping the streets clean.

True, not all volunteer helpfulness is worth much, or is even as nice to contemplate as a group of fresh-faced kids sweeping their streets. Many good Americans keep firearms and take target practice in anticipation of shooting unruly members of minorities. But the motives in most cases are likely to be decent—people want society to work. It has taken a good many thousand years to build society, and bad as it can be, it is all we have between us and the jungle.

When society starts creaking, people *will* pitch in and try to help. The results can be creative; they can also be destructive. Librarians, as one group in charge of a social function that is becoming almost desperately necessary, might observe the experience of professional neighbors with "helping hands."

Both the Congress and the State Department have seen some of their functions taken over by other governmental and quasi-governmental groups. We look today for innovation in foreign affairs from foundations, the military, and of course the CIA, which embarrasses us all by everything but its motives, which in our hearts we know are as well-intentioned as those of volunteer street sweepers, neighbor-shooters, charity workers, and people who dash into burning buildings to save strangers. They all want society to work.

A recommendation was made recently to disband a most venerable agency—the Post Office—and turn over to a corporation the job of delivering the mail. As our giant public utilities show—unsurprisingly—a quality service can be built with something like unlimited access to the taxpayer's pocket and freedom from political control.

Librarians today are on the verge of an era in which their function will be essential to the operation of society. When a social function is recognized as essential, it attracts a great many varied people. Partly this is because it has become A Good Thing; it is also because people do want to busy themselves with recognizably important work.

So librarians can observe that already the paperback publishers have gone far toward solving a former library problem—the distribution of leisure reading. And other enterprising businessmen have come forward with plans to relieve librarians of the old problems of book selection, processing, and even cataloging. Professional consulting firms like Nelson Associates and Arthur D. Little are developing highly paid specialists in library planning and research; they do good work once librarians teach them enough, but their loyalties are first to business and profits, and second to libraries and service.

And now, businessmen are beginning to sell reference service direct to the consumer: for a nominal charge, Xerox will hunt through the titles of over 100,000 doctoral dissertations and give a researcher a listing of every one related to his inquiry. Other companies are offering varying information services that used to be thought of as burdensome library responsibilities— if rarely fulfilled ones.

Library education, as an article in this issue points out, is getting a helping hand from junior and community colleges, which are out to produce all the technicians we have been lacking. And labor unions are volunteering to provide—and enforce—long-needed changes in the personnel administration of libraries.

All these helping hands are directed toward real needs which librarians, for a variety of good reasons, have not been able to meet yet; in the process, however, these hands may help librarians right out the back door of the 20th Century. The helping hands which are still needed most of all are not those of the businessman or scientist, but those of the young. Libraries need more volunteers from the ranks of those dismayed by many aspects of our society, but willing to rescue our books from the filth of the Arno in Florence; willing both to sweep our streets and then to stroll along them, giving flowers to passers-by.

*Karl Nyren*

## SATURDAY'S CHILDREN
September 1, 1968

"The needs of vocational and technical students are not well served by general libraries . . . or school or community college libraries," said Wisconsin Representative William Steiger in the House on July 15. He went on to quote vocational school librarians and educators as saying that some 80 percent of their needs in learning materials are not normally stocked by either school or public libraries. Representative Steiger put this on the record after the House Education and Labor Committee had regretfully axed a promising library component from the Vocational Educational Amendments of 1968 "because of possible duplication with existing legislation."

The House committee *did* recognize the need which Steiger was pleading so eloquently. And so did the Senators—they put a library provision back into the bill when they ran it through their mill. It is some consolation to know that it is a lot easier today to convince lawmakers of the need for a library factor in a new or expanded educational program than it was a few years ago.

The "career" library needs of the skilled and semi-skilled person are not limited to his formal schooling period. And it is surprising that in a society so dependent upon technology, libraries have done so little to serve the craftsman and the technologist, who must continue to learn if they are to keep up with new tools, methods, and materials.

Detroit can run regular training sessions for its dealers and their mechanics, but many industries have no such capability. There is a parallel here with the need for "transfer of technology" which the new State Technical Services programs are tackling in 1200 current projects as they attempt to make available to 35,000 small and medium-sized firms the spinoff know-how being developed in such ventures as the aerospace industry.

The public library recognizes "service to labor" as a legitimate target—but this generally means service to the union movement, and this is fine, but it won't help a gasoline station attendant who wants to learn engine tune-up, or a Banbury mixer man in a rubber mill who wants to learn more about rubber compounding than he can pick up on the job.

In one area, however, librarians are making important new moves. They are seeking out easy-reading materials with real vocational content to equip the completely unskilled man and woman for a place in this industrial society. A good example is Cleveland's nascent "Books/Jobs" program. And out on Long Island, the Nassau Library System is moving toward a new role as information center for all county agencies concerned with vocational development. Significantly, Nassau's Dinah Lindauer hazards a guess that experience with the completely unskilled will open eyes to a host of unmet learning needs on higher levels of technology.

Another favorable sign is the new spirit in "adult services" which is surfacing among library leaders today. It is partly a return to the concept of "reader guidance" so popular a couple of decades back—and a reaction against a current overemphasis on materials selection such as was shown by a recent poll. The poll, conducted by the Adult Services Division of ALA, showed "knowledge of patron and community" ranking far below "materials selection" in the value scale of the average adult services librarian. It will take a while to turn these librarians around, but the "opinion makers" of ASD are determined to do just that.

While they're at it, they might make a major model change in the new version of the adult services librarian, and design him along the lines of the ideal special librarian, who is on the job to serve his boss's needs and to be as helpful as possible. Farthest from his mind is the thought that he is going to make a more admirable person out of his chemist or businessman or legislator.

There is no reason why the man with the monkey wrench should not be served as respectfully as these, whether it be through greatly improved vocational school libraries, public libraries, or community college libraries; who does the job is unimportant. As for upgrading the cultural level of patrons with less formal schooling than librarians have, and rejoicing in the truck driver who reads Plato, a cure for this impertinence is the reflection that any human task, considered deeply enough, leads one to art, morality, and philosophy. And that we are all Saturday's children, working hard for our living.

*Karl Nyren*

# The Uses of Manpower

### WHAT IS YOUR TIME WORTH?
March 15, 1960

Look at any library budget: the chances are that salaries will account for more than 60 percent of the total expenditure. By comparison, something between 15 and 18 percent will be spent on books. We have some less than tentative doubts about the perspective suggested by these figures, but it is not our prime purpose at this moment to deal with that question. What does seem odd is that it is in the very area where library expenditure is highest, in labor costs, that there often exists the most profligate waste. If administrators would devote the same probing attention to the expenditure of valuable staff hours as they do to the expenditure of dollars and cents, it is more than likely that tight library budgets could be stretched a little further.

Book ordering procedures in many libraries afford a superb illustration of the way in which man-hours are squandered. One librarian commented to us recently: "I am convinced that we are suffering from a disease that says that any amount of staff time is justified to get a half of one percent discount on a $5 book." This dickering with discounts is one aspect of the situation: another is the mountain of red tape and paper work under which some libraries contrive to get themselves buried. When LJ surveyed wholesalers for their opinions on library customers, one put his finger on both these points when he said: "As far as we are concerned the enemy is paper work. Instead of publishers by-passing wholesalers, and librarians playing off one wholesaler against another, why not all team up to get rid of needless paper work, and really cut distribution costs?"

Often buried deepest under the paper are the unfortunate government librarians, many of whom have to work through the US Treasury Department Office of Procurement and buy books under a negotiated contract with one (frequently inadequate) bidder. The resulting service is often painfully poor, and we suspect that many a government servant thinks of a book as the hard way to get a piece of information because of the delays and red tape involved in ordering one.

Book ordering is not the only area in libraries, of course, where manpower extravagance exists. It is not at all unknown for several dollars-worth of staff time to be wasted in ensuring that a ball of string or a piece of display card is not bought for 60 cents, when it could be obtained with more effort and delay from a central purchasing department for half a dollar.

Nor are all such burdens imposed upon librarians from without: some they pick up and carry willingly, and seemingly forever. Examples are those custom-bound institutions which still maintain the unholy trinity of catalog, shelf-list *and* that relic of the dark ages, an accessions register. Add too those libraries who eschew cooperative or commercial assistance with routine processing, and spend valuable man hours in attaching plastic jackets to books when they could have it done commercially for a few cents a book.

The librarian who will not delegate is one of the profession's great time-wasters and saboteurs. The check and double-check on every routine, the clearance and approval required from above for, not only every small expenditure, but every small action—these are enemies of economy, and often of efficiency too. Nothing is more likely to kill individual imagination and incentive; nothing more sure to impede a library's progress.

We wonder whether the author of *Parkinson's Law* did not have libraries and their administration somewhere in the forefront of his mind.

This book should, incidentally, be required reading for all prospective library administrators, and we look forward to its being recommended as such by one of the forward-looking library schools.

*Eric Moon*

## RUGGED STUPIDITY
September 1, 1965

"The first and most basic step toward a solution of our vast problem is, of course, a profession-wide realization that 'rugged individualism' in cataloging practices is now only rugged stupidity. If we could ever afford it, the day when we could do so has long gone . . . the relatively few members of the Association of Research Libraries are already spending $18 million a year on cataloging. I shudder to think what the full national figure would be."

We apologize for quoting from this particular source, but we knew the author wouldn't mind and these comments from a paper we gave during the ALA Conference in Detroit were the nearest at hand which seemed pertinent to the subject of this editorial. They came back to us as we examined some figures issued in June by the Dominion Bureau of Statistics in Ottawa, Canada.

Actually, there are two sets of statistics, and the story is uncovered by examining both and comparing them. The first set gives bookstock, staff, and expenditure figures for various types of libraries. It shows that, in 1963–64, university libraries in Canada had 534 full-time professional staff. It shows also that the total salaries and wages bill for Canadian university libraries that year (for professionals and others) was $7,157,852.

We turn now to the other set of statistics from the Dominion Bureau, which is concerned with technical services in Canadian academic libraries. This compilation reveals that 237 professional librarians were absorbed in this activity, also in 1963–64. There may be several reasons why a comparison of these two sets of statistics do not reveal a completely accurate picture, but they reveal enough to be profoundly disturbing. On the basis of the cold figures presented it looks as though 44.4 percent of all professional librarians in Canadian academic libraries are working in technical processes.

A glance at the salaries bill for technical processing (again, covering technical and clerical personnel as well as professionals) shows that this amounted, in 1963–64, to $2,749,327—or about 38.2 percent of the total salaries and wages cost for Canadian academic libraries.

Let us be clear: we are not knocking our northern neighbor. We take Canadian figures because these are the only fairly current ones which give this kind of breakdown. We can think of no very good reason, however, why they should be wildly different, proportionately, from American figures. If they are not—if, indeed, libraries are using dangerously close to half their professional staff in technical services—we begin to understand some of those astronomical cost figures which emerge from university library studies, such as the one from the University of Illinois at Chicago, *Advanced Data Processing in the University Library*, which revealed that a $5 book costs $18.51 by the time it gets to the shelves.

If the Canadian figures are even approximately related to the staffing situation in US libraries, we are exceptionally vulnerable to a counterpunch from some economy-minded legislator or finance officer. Our cries of short-age—last heard thunderously at Detroit when Edwin Castagna presented ALA's National Inventory of Library Needs—sound sort of hollow if it can be proven that we keep nearly half of our professionals buried back behind the woodwork, doing the same repetitive tasks in Cambridge and Los Angeles, in Michigan and Mississippi. Small wonder that we have trouble coping with the student deluge if only half of our librarians are available to serve them. The charges of Neal Harlow, among others, that we have not so much a shortage as a "wildly wasteful employment of professional staff" appear to be just when one is faced with statistics such as those from the Dominion Bureau.

The National Inventory of Library Needs produced a mountain of statistics, some of them dangerously rooted in the sandy foundation of unilaterally-compiled "standards." The US Office of Education produces figures by the barrel-load every year, for all types of libraries. Perhaps it is time that someone unearthed some relevant (national) staffing figures to reveal *how* our professional librarians are employed, and what our distribution of personnel and cost is as between service functions and supportive, behind-the-scenes operations.

*Eric Moon*

## THE LONG SIDE OF THE RECTANGLE
September 1, 1966

"But it may be that the enormous proportions to which the work has grown demand regimentation and that the old all-round craftsmanship must give way to industrial mass-production methods . . . in the huge metro-politan libraries, as the work constantly becomes more tiresome and monotonous and gives less personal satisfaction . . . Routine work has weakened their feeling of joint responsibility in the operation of the library as a whole . . ." In three brief paragraphs on the staff situation in US libraries in the late thirties, Wilhelm Munthe put his finger on the problem that was going to assume major significance 30 years later in the ALA presidential year of Mary Gaver.

As we left the banquet at which Miss Gaver gave her inaugural address in New York a colleague was saying: "I saw the two top graduates from an important library school go to work passing out books over the circulation desk, filing cards, and typing headings on cards. The whole business could have been done by a bright high school student."

Miss Gaver's rectangle of professional concern is already well-known: ". . . bounded by the topics of recruitment, instruction in the use of libraries, library education, and manpower utilization." The new ALA president had just told her inaugural audience: "It will do little good for a remodeled library education program to produce more and better qualified librarians unless the conditions of work and the nature of the career opportunities in libraries are also revolutionized, unless qualified professional staff is no longer misused on the job, unless we open our eyes to the changes which must be made in manpower utilization in order to exploit the manpower we already have."

The profession's concern about the use of professionals, telegraphed in rumblings from all over the US for the past decade, was picked up by the US Department of Labor before Miss Gaver's election to the top ALA post. Back in April, *LJ* reported a US grant to the School of Library and Information Sciences at the University of Maryland to develop a blueprint for the analysis of manpower utilization in the whole field of library and information sciences.

Salaries and the work week have replaced much of the old "library faith," dedication, and status, as motivations in job bargaining among beginning professionals. Their seeming lack of "dedication" to "the profession" stems, in part, from the fact that their jobs are not professional. Consider the recent attempts to organize a library labor union in Brooklyn. More than half of the professional librarians responded with pledges to join the union if it is organized, and librarians in Queens and Manhattan are surprising the union with their interest.

Neal Harlow, a long-time crusader for better utilization of professionals, once listed, among many others, these tasks that he feels are not the proper work of professional librarians: being on a loan desk concerned with the husbandry of books, their condition, loan, and prompt return; providing a front line of general and directional information; dealing with the business of ordering, checking, claiming, and paying; bibliographic searching for identification or to avoid duplication; the preparation of materials for cataloging, binding, or storage; proffering ready information from a hundred or so handy sources; filing pamphlets, maps, and government publications; running a loan service; doing simple descriptive cataloging; adapting printed cards; adding serial volumes; filing in the public catalog; bookplating, etc.

Most of us, especially in our first two or three jobs, have been engaged in at least a half-dozen of the activities Harlow describes. Many are still at it, five or even ten years after library school. Most beginning librarians find themselves saddled with a host of such chores, all easily within the capability of that "bright high school student."

We, therefore, applaud Mary Gaver's charge that librarians become "true commanders of knowledge, masters of the raging book." We hope, however, that the studies of library manpower utilization don't get bogged down in the meticulous methodologies of bureaucratic and academic research. A good administrator can spot the misuse of librarians by just wandering through his library, and he can take steps to change the set-up without a massive survey or a year-long study.

*John Berry*

## MEDUSA REVISITED
November 1, 1966

An uncomfortable question is slowly emerging in our minds, a monster of a doubt whose shambling toward Bethlehem has been spurred to a trot by our own two most recent *LJ* symposia. One issue brought out the library educators, the others saw the administrators airing their thoughts on the shortage of good librarians. Themes and counter themes have sounded, and their very juxtaposition has made us realize that we have precious little notion of what we are referring to when we use the word "librarian."

We are reminded of a recent and rather terrifying description of metamorphosis; when a worm becomes a butterfly, it first rots away into a little putrescent gob, losing all its original equipment. The word "librarian" is often used to describe the larval stage of an administrator, public relations specialist, personnel manager, computer pilot, social worker, or library association officer in one of the Parkinsonian structures we have reared upon the book. We have berated both educators and administrators for not equipping this larva with faster enzymes.

Many of the comments in our last two symposia have been urgent about job definition—it is important to librarians that they not be confused with clerks and typists, although they seem to be not at all worried at being mistaken for executive or any creature with "specialist" as part of his nomenclature.

We suspect that some of our most noted "librarians" couldn't handle the work in a small branch library, if they were put to that inhuman test. Yet if the great librarian, like the great doctor and the great mathematician, is not to be a projection of the bookman, and even of those marvellous and humble little bookwomen of our youth, it may be that many of the people we identify as librarians are just misguided businessmen, scientists, and teachers who have had their professional genetic code scrambled and are seeking personal evolutionary ends which have little or no relationship to librarianship. A butterfly is not a better dragonfly.

Is it possible that we have given up the original aim of librarians, that we no longer believe in the importance of the knowledge of books, and the development of their use into an art which yields personal fruition for the artist as well as edification for his fellows?

Have we instead gone far toward substituting another and insect-like or plant-like approach, by which the labor of thousands of little partial and specialized humanoids will link their bodies and minds into a colony of cells which will realize dimensions of excellence which we now despair of attaining individually?

To give the idea its due, it is appealing as well as appalling. So too, a forest is a magnificent organism, making possible life processes which no number of individually spaced trees could support. Yet few if any perfect trees live in forests, which are based on a great deal of promiscuous dying.

In our haste to escape from the stereotypes with which we feel we have been unfairly burdened, we are close to lynching the little old lady who haunts us, and burning the books she once taught us to love.

Let us turn back and face our Medusa, who first handed us a library card and walked with us to the shelf where all fiction began, as she explained, with people whose names began with "A." While we were enthralled by the metaphysical stretches this suddenly opened up, she very surely put in our hands the book she knew we would read till bedtime and bring back the next day.

Physicians, whom we envy for their "professionalism" even more than their incomes, go back to barbers, and even beyond that, surely, to a man or woman of the caves who was a little better than his fellows at dressing a painful wound. Like the librarian, the physician today needs the carapace of a large institution in order to perfect his art, yet no one confuses him with the orderlies, businessmen, and technicians who are essential to the operation of a hospital.

A recent book on aggression suggests that man is the victim of a tragic evolutionary accident that made him the only creature with an inborn desire to kill his fellows. The evolution of the librarian and his art, entrusted as it has been to our all too mortal hands, may well have already made a wrong turning, or stopped entirely in our concern with producing the auxiliaries necessary to his existence and further growth in the modern world.

*Karl Nyren*

## MYTHS AND REALITIES
June 15, 1967

Conference themes are rarely much more than frosting on the program cake. "Crisis in Library Manpower—Myth and Reality," the title of the special day-and-a-half President's Program at the San Francisco ALA conference, is, however, a good one, containing many of the right words and properly excluding others.

It does not, for example, include the words "professional" or "librarian," an indication, perhaps, that the meeting's concerns are broader than either of these words connote. It does use the word "crisis," more appropriate and more nearly accurate, certainly, than the former, ludicrously inadequate word, "shortage," applied to the manpower situation. But the keywords may well be "myth" and "reality." Unless a serious effort is made to separate these elements, all the talk and discussions are unlikely to lead anywhere.

Will the conference, for example, reaffirm the ALA diagnosis of a couple of years ago that we need 100,000 *professional* librarians? And will it do so while maintaining adherence to the Procrustean production line of the graduate library schools, which can't possibly turn out that quantity of professionals in less than 20 years, during which period the target figure will surely rise astronomically and dropouts from the profession will counteract many thousands of the number produced by the schools?

Will the conference allow us to go on believing that some neat, magical separation of professional and nonprofessional duties is anything other than a gross oversimplification which, even if it can be achieved, will leave most of the major problems unsolved?

Will it recognize that rapid social, educational, technological, and economic change will transform most libraries or library systems into vastly more complex organisms than they have traditionally been, and that these complexes will require, just as any big business does, a complicated miscellany of skills—in languages, communications, social work, personnel administration, collective bargaining, legislation, planning, not to mention increasing specialization in the literature and bibliography of ever more complicated areas of knowledge? Will the conference allow us to go on believing that all these talents and skills can be combined within our present definition of a professional librarian, or that they can all be taught, either in institutions called library schools or within the space of one academic year?

Will the conference recognize that playing with library school curricula, while perhaps helpful from a long-term point of view, contributes little to immediate solutions? Throwing an odd course or two into the library school curriculum for students who may administer automated libraries 20 years hence is somewhat like teaching a baby to read because his illiterate father can't get a job. The basic lesson here was spelled out succinctly by Roy Ash, president of the giant Litton Industries: "The manager whose education has been completed is doomed." Will we recognize that one of libarianship's urgent needs is education at the top as well as at the bottom, and place a high priority in our recommendations on establishing a formalized structure of continuing education for top administrators?

As librarians grapple in San Francisco with the complex but highly visible manpower problem, some delicate questions of status, tradition, and self-interest are sure to surface. But it will not only be librarians' attitudes and their responsiveness to change that will be on display. The Association, itself, as a mechanism for problem-solving, will in a sense be on trial.

As each chapter in a TV soap opera begins, the loyal viewer comes to the program with a list of such questions as "Will Aunt Minnie forget to take the pill?" In the course of the program, however, such cliffhangers are somehow fobbed off and the viewer arrives at the end of the show with a whole new set of burning questions.

New questions are by no means a bad thing—without them, new answers can be hard to come by. But if the ALA's grand affair in San Francisco does nothing other than raise questions, if it does not find *some* answers to old questions (such as some of those raised in this editorial), it may well be adjudged a rather badly written soap opera.

So . . . last question . . . will ALA demonstrate that it can serve as a forum within which dynamic change not only can take place but is fostered? If not, we may have another dimension of the manpower problem that thus far has not been much discussed.

*Eric Moon*

## MANPOWER: A SOVIET SOLUTION?
February 1, 1968

Last year's celebration by the U.S.S.R. of the 50th anniversary of the 1917 October Revolution produced, among other things, an abundance of articles on Russian libraries. Among these which came to our attention, the most interesting was one in the September-October issue of *Unesco Bulletin for Libraries* entitled "The Libraries of the U.S.S.R. during the Last Fifty Years," by G. Fonotov.

The article is a fascinating and heartening story of belief in libraries and of impressive progress in the face of terrible adversity. In World War II, for example, "In the largest libraries alone, over 100,000,000 books were destroyed, and 334 libraries of higher educational institutions and 82,000 school libraries were burned and destroyed. The important libraries of the Kiev and Rostov Universities as well as the Smolensk, Kalinin, Orel, Voronezh and other regional libraries were destroyed; the libraries in Stalingrad were completely wiped out, and the books in the Tolstoy Library at Yasnaya Polana were burned."

Perhaps the most interesting section of the Fonotov article, however, is neither the story of devastation nor that of the postwar library reconstruction but his account of the ways in which the reader is involved in library service in the U.S.S.R. today. "Readers of Soviet libraries," says Fonotov, "are not simply persons who use the facilities provided; they themselves take part in the circulating of books. The form of this participation has changed in the course of time, but the important point is that there has been a gradual increase in the number of people who give librarians a helping hand as well as in the influence of readers on all aspects of library activity."

The Soviet library user is apparently not only asked to help out with the routines but is also kept abreast of—and involved with—policy changes. Says Fonotov: "Every library regularly—usually once a year—reports on its activities to a meeting of its readers. After the reports have been presented and the library's work has been discussed, advisory committees are set up to take an active part in the settling of all problems ranging from the fixing of an acquisitions policy to the building or repair of library premises."

The most substantial involvement of Soviet readers in their libraries, however, "is their participation in the running of branch libraries and mobile libraries; there are now more than 300,000 of these libraries, serving many millions of people. Readers also assist in the circulation of books by working a certain number of hours in ordinary libraries; they help the full-time librarians and sometimes replace them during the librarians' non-working days or holidays. There are some regions and even republics, such as the Ukraine, where nearly every full-time public library worker has a reader to deputize for him. In many libraries, particularly scientific and technical libraries, scientists, engineers, doctors, teachers, and lawyers advise readers at certain hours or read through new acquisitions, selecting what is most important and writing abstracts and reviews."

Altogether, Fonotov says, "between 1,500,000 and 2,000,000 readers are at present taking an active part in the various forms of library work, not counting those who take part in the discussion of the libraries' activities."

Some of the above is likely to make many an American librarian shudder. Few members of the profession would welcome any large-scale return to the days of the volunteer library worker. The struggle for status and recognition is not yet unequivocally won, and even proposals of a new breed of library technicians can set off a chain reaction of nervous quivers in some parts of the profession.

If we could get past this status hang-up, however, and if the ALA figures on our library manpower shortage are really anywhere within range of reality, it might be worth considering whether something like the Soviet libraries' use of interested and able readers to augment their services might not do something to relieve the manpower situation—at least until the library schools can produce more permanent relief.

This Soviet practice seems to have potential in at least two other directions. First, it might make it possible to retain more of the library budget in the books and materials column and stop the constant escalation of the salaries column. And it might do something to bring the library closer to the readers it is supposed to be serving—a need revealed by many of today's "outreach" programs.

*Eric Moon*

## MOVEMENT IN MARYLAND
October 15, 1968

This is the first time, in this decade at least, that the entire feature article section of an issue of *LJ* has been devoted to library activity in *one* state. That the state should be Maryland, one of the smaller ones in the nation, may magnify the surprise of our readers, some of whom may consider this an undue lapse into localism on the part of a national periodical.

The emphasis on Maryland, let us make clear for those who sometimes suspect us of political motivations in everything, has no connection with the new national eminence of that state's Governor. We choose to focus this much attention on Maryland for one reason: the Maryland Library Association, or rather, its Legislative and Planning Committee, has recently issued what is clearly a revolutionary document (p. 3747), one that certainly has national implications. Another factor of some moment is that, while dissent can be expected to rage around the recommendations of this committee for some time to come, the document has the unanimous support of *all* of Maryland's 24 public library systems directors.

The most basic, and potentially most explosive, ingredient in the Maryland report—that there should be *two* professional levels within librarianship, and that the basic one should be based upon an undergraduate education—is not really all that new. The idea has been noised around in bars and corridors, and even in some committee rooms, for the past several acute years of manpower crisis in the library profession. What is new is that the Maryland committee has formalized this heresy in an official report and a set of proposals which, judging from the support that already exists in Maryland, has an excellent chance of adoption as a policy of the state's library association.

Before that happens, as Norman Finkler notes in his introductory article (p. 3745), there will be much "talk and argument and thought by able and supple minds." It is likely that other minds, less deserving of such adjectives, will also participate, both within Maryland and without. In any event, the Maryland committee has moved this topic out of the no-man's-land of endless talk, and to a stage where action, at least in one state, seems imminent.

Most encouraging in this Maryland material is the great emphasis placed upon the development of a greater number of adequately trained personnel to man the public service areas of libraries. The real victim of the prevailing defense-of-the-(professional)-realm policies in librarianship has been the library user, the reading public. Rapid expansion of library institutions (in number and size), together with an entirely inadequate increase in the production of professional (i.e., master's) librarians, and a deplorable reluctance to fill the vacuum between professional and nonprofessional, has led to a serious decline in the quality of public service at the front-desk level—a decline as obvious to the users of some major public reference libraries as to the users of local branch libraries. Charles Robinson notes (p. 3756) that Baltimore County Library is getting about the same number of beginning professionals today as it was five years ago; and those few professionals, as elsewhere, quickly move into administrative positions or other duties that take them ever further from direct service to the public.

While we applaud the motivation of the Maryland report, however, we find its numerical standards somewhat curious. We are not questioning (though others may) the validity of circulation as a more or less certain yardstick than population served, but the differing results yielded by the ALA and Maryland formulae.

Examine the table on page 3749 of this issue, for example. Using the ALA *Minimum Standards for Public Library Systems* (one staff per 2000 population, on a ratio of one professional to two clerical), the Harford library system would have 51 staff members, 17 of them professional or subprofessional. Using the Maryland formula (one master and two-three bachelor librarians per 100,000 circulation), Harford winds up with only nine, or perhaps 12 professionals. Other calculations based on this table yield the same results—fewer professionals (of either kind) under the Maryland formula than under the ALA standards.

The fault may lie in our mathematics or our understanding, but there does appear to be a gap between the expressed mission of the Maryland report (more professionals for public service) and the proposed formula.

*Eric Moon*


# Library Education

## INTERNATIONAL UNDERSTANDING IN LIBRARY EDUCATION
May 1, 1960

"Library-wise there is no international boundary." This statement by Robert Gitler in the January *News Letter* of ALA's Library Education Division referred to librarianship on the North American continent, and to the boundary as between Canada and the United States. In this context the assertion might be justifiable. But anyone who has followed during the past two years the debate (if that is not too gentle a word) between Canadian and British librarians on the subject of library education, would feel hesitant about accepting Mr. Gitler's statement. Library education-wise (to adapt Mr. Gitler's phrase) there seems to be not so much an international boundary as an iron curtain between librarians on either side of the Atlantic.

The sustained and heated controversy, which has taken place primarily in the British quarterly *Library Review* and in some of the Canadian library periodicals, bodes well, or ill—depending on your point of view—for a meeting which is being planned by the Library Education Division for the Montreal conference next month. Frances Lander Spain, President of LED, has announced that the purpose of the meeting is "to explore the possibility of evaluating different types of library training in the United Kingdom, Canada, and the United States, with attention to the problems to be considered in working for equivalencies and reciprocity."

It is to be hoped that representatives from all three countries will be present at this meeting. In this event it may well be that the American role will be that of mediator. Certainly somebody needs to inject a little sweet reason and unprejudiced thought into the arena. There has so far been small indication that the Canadians and the British are even speaking the same language.

If most of the flames up to this point have been British, most of the fuel and fanning have been supplied by Canada, in particular by Bernard Ower, who is Chairman of an international Sub-Committee on Comparative Library Education set up by the Canadian Library Association. In the time that it has been in being, this committee has produced no statement of any kind, though the same cannot be said for its Chairman, who has written voluminously, and scarcely impartially, on the subject under consideration. The subject indeed has become a little cloudy on occasions and the debate has ranged far and wide outside the field of library education to the point where British librarians have been denounced as "scabs willing to undermine the efforts of Canadian librarians to better their status and salary."

R. C. Benge, in this issue, says that it is "sufficiently obvious" that certain international standards must be worked out." We would agree wholeheartedly that there is a great and vital need for international standards and understanding in education for librarianship, but cannot agree that it is sufficiently obvious—even among those most directly concerned, the library educators themselves. And nothing that has happened in the Canadian-British argument has given any indication that it is obvious at all.

Important issues are at stake here, and they do range wider than library education only. It is imperative that they be considered with less insularity of thought than has so far been evident. We have therefore brought together in this issue a number of views on library education from librarians and library educators in various parts of the world, in the hope that these will stimulate some fresh thought on fundamental considerations before the meeting at Montreal. We would also strongly advise American librarians who will be attending the meeting, to read the past six issues of the *Library Review* so that they may be better prepared to avoid some of the crossfire.

*Eric Moon*

## PERPETUAL PROBLEMS
April 15, 1965

There are plenty of critics of library education. The *Journal of Education for Librarianship* has recently given some of them a good share of its space. Each year a new batch of critics, producing more invective and more militant dissent, is graduated from the library schools.

Few, if any, of the 600 faculty members of the accredited schools would find it difficult to produce a list of defects in this field; in fact, any librarian can, and usually will if asked, offer a set of pet gripes about library schools.

There have been conferences, articles, debates, surveys, reports, and endless private conversations on the subject. There are organized groups, too, who are concerned with the subject: ALA divisions, according agencies, even a national commission (what ever happened to that?) which is supposed to produce proposals for a "national plan." The Bonk-Galvin discussion in this issue (p. 1844) is, in a sense, an extension of this endless debate, but we hope that it may be slightly more constructive, if only because it is restricted to one specific part of "the library education problem."

More than 40 years ago, C. C. Williamson noted among other weaknesses the following defects in library school instruction: a) excessive dependence on the lecture method; b) lack of suitable textbooks and teaching materials; c) heavy demands on the instructor's time resulting from a lack of clerical assistance; and d) the part-time system of instruction.

The Williamson report came to mind when we were squirming at Wallace Bonk's reference to "the old how-to-do-it course" during our discussion at the ALA Midwinter meeting. At the same conference a recent library school graduate provided another of those off-colorful descriptions of the library school year: "It was a year of alternate gorging on bibliographic details in a multitude of forms, and puking them back on examination papers or in class." He complained, as we have, about endless hours spent typing catalog cards for "problem" books; committing to memory the noted details of some 2000 to 3000 titles; compiling list after list; dabbling with meticulous *Turabian* footnotes; and reading, reading, and rereading those few well-worn selections from "the literature."

Both descriptions, Bonk's and the recent graduate's, sound echoes from the Williamson Report. Both suggest that there is still too much dependence upon traditional teaching methods. And there are other signs and statistics to indicate that Williamson's other observations are as valid today as they were in 1923.

Some may dispute the point, but it is our opinion that there has been no great advance in either the quantity or the quality of textbooks and other teaching materials for library schools. The fact that the same few required readings are used over and over again, some in nearly every course, suggests a certain barrenness in that "professional literature" every library school student knows so well.

If you have ever joined the faculty at coffee time in a library school you have probably heard them complain about the lack of clerical help, about teaching loads and big classes. These issues continue to plague both the library school directors and faculty members. From the teacher's point of view, justified or not, there is still too little time for *teaching*.

Williamson also cited the part-time system of teaching, despite its obvious advantages, as a weakness. Forty years later, we find that 347 of the 600 faculty in the 36 accredited library schools are part-timers. And, because of research and administrative duties, a good number of the full-time faculty are also only part-time teachers. While there is, undoubtedly, some value in having a specialist from the field teach about his specialty, to have nearly 60 percent of the library school complement in this category seems excessive.

So the Williamson Report, at least the section on library school instruction, has achieved a form of permanence that few similar documents can claim: it has lasted, but for the wrong reasons. Surveys are still conducted to report on existing conditions and to recommend changes where conditions are bad—but it appears that the defects Williamson discovered have outlasted all the recommendations since. It must have been a source of amazement and frustration to Williamson to see that his observations were still as valid, in many respects, right up to the time of his death last January, as they were when they arrived, like a bombshell, on the library scene in 1923. His successors have rewritten, revised, and repeated his recommendations over and over in the intervening years, with scarcely any effect.

We are not presumptuous enough to suggest what should happen now. There are a few encouraging signs: new methods, new and young faculty, new patterns of organization in several schools, and a continued (for, lo, these many years) interest on the part of all librarians.

But an end to the debate is unlikely, because this issue, like censorship, book selection, "too many meetings," and the state of professional literature, is one of the library profession's self-perpetuating and timeless topics. Perhaps all we can suggest is that the "new critics" of library education, either those who graduate from library school or those appointed to committees to study the problems and possible solutions, will re-read Williamson, and at least save us from further repetition of the old complaints.

*John Berry*


## TOO LATE FOR THE DOCTOR
October 15, 1965

The symposium brought together by Dorothy Bendix for this issue completes our second round of discussion concerning library education and the manpower and talent shortages in librarianship. If there is one *fact* that towers indisputably above all the theory, opinion, and argument, it is that the most critical bottleneck in the professional supply line is the severe and urgent shortage of library school faculty. Until this is alleviated, the other manpower gaps can only continue to grow wider.

If one accepts this much, one strong trend in the library schools appears to be nothing short of absurd. Marie Long informs us: "Recent emphasis on the doctor's degree in all branches of higher education has probably made this the first criterion for selection of library school faculty" (*Journal of Education for Librarianship*, Spring 1965, p. 217). This was confirmed by Leroy Merritt in a letter to *LJ* (May 1, p. 2248, 50) in which he declared that the University of California School of Librarianship at Berkeley was "concerned about 'x' number vacancies," and then added, "Of course, the potential candidates must have a Doctor of Philosophy degree from a recognized institution . . ."

It is surely time to query Merritt's "of course." We hope Samuel Rothstein (p. 4884) will not accuse us of counselling expediency if we suggest—no, assert—that the profession can no longer afford this kind of precious status-seeking on the part of the schools. The "first criterion" for a teacher should be teaching ability, and the second, perhaps, some relevant background and experience. The Ph.D. might be desirable, but it certainly should not be paramount.

As Sarah Reed has noted, the emergency in library school faculty shortages was entirely predictable: "For at least 11 years library science has had a greater unfulfilled demand for teachers than any other field. In 1963, based upon the percent that demand is of supply, the index of faculty need in library science was 306 compared to 157 for the second-ranking field, general science. Ten years ago, in 1954, the index for library science was 298, compared to 187 for the second-ranking field, elementary education." ("Library Education Report," *Journal of Education for Librarianship,* Spring 1965, p. 262–65.)

Clearly, the situation is getting worse, not better. And the indications are that it will get worse yet. Marie Long points out: "The fact that at least 30 percent of the 1963 accredited library school faculty members are now over 55 years of age, and at least 45 percent over 50, indicates that retirement will take a heavy toll during the next ten to 15 years" (*JEL,* Spring '65, p. 220).

If one weighs these findings against the doctoral output, the increasing emphasis by the library schools on possession of the doctorate by their teaching faculty is at least arithmetically absurd. Only 131 doctorates in library science were awarded in the United States from 1952 through 1964. If *all* of these had decided to dedicate their professional future to the cause of library education (which is far from the actuality), the faculty shortage would scarcely have been dented. And the current doctoral output, steadily between ten and 19 per year in recent times, offers no hope of immediate or considerable aid. As Jean Ademan understates it in this issue (p. 4891): "The requirement by universities that teachers in library schools have a doctorate must be assessed and possible alternatives evaluated."

There are rumblings to indicate that some of this reassessment and searching for alternatives is already beginning in academe. There is a growing feeling that the Ph.D. trade-union card for academic promotion and tenure has driven out of teaching some who might have stayed. Now, a new degree, a sort of halfway house between the master's and the doctorate, which some have named the A.B.D. ("All But the Dissertation"), seems to be appearing.

Yale, for example, has announced a Master of Philosophy degree, which is the Ph.D. minus the dissertation. Berkeley proposes a Doctor of Arts degree, in many ways similar to Yale's M.Ph. And Michigan, with its approval of the granting of a Candidate's Certificate, seems to be moving in the same direction.

If all this indicates somewhat more flexibility in the academic world regarding how much paper qualification a teacher needs, the trend is very welcome. Certainly, a deal more flexibility will be needed before the library school crisis can be solved. There are obviously not enough doctors in the library house to effect a cure.

*Eric Moon*

## A MANPOWER MILESTONE?
May 1, 1967

The heavily-structured walls of the ALA Conference were last brought tumbling down four years ago. Then, librarians of all persuasions were drawn out of those monastic cells called type-of-library or type-of-activity divisions or round tables or whatever, and into a common cause: an attempt to come to grips with what was erroneously called "the student problem."

This year, in San Francisco, for the first time since that now famous conference-within-a-conference in Chicago in 1963, librarians will once more be brought together en masse and in a common cause. Some will wonder if the effort is worthwhile, since it is clear that "the student problem" has not been licked—perhaps not even dented—since the Chicago deliberations. But that Chicago effort should not be written off as a failure, as another airing of many pieties which led to nothing. The conference at least revealed that we had hold of the wrong problem, or perhaps just the wrong end of the problem.

It became clear that the student was only a symptom, not the disease. What was really wrong was that the library machinery was incapable of providing the kinds of services that the student, among many others, needed in today's fast-moving society. And in the years since that 1963 gathering, we have gradually focussed on one of the root problems. The focus has been made sharper by a considerable outpouring of federal funds for materials, buildings, projects, and services. While these funds have helped, they have also brought to the surface the major problem that has been growling away in the depths for many a year. And so, during the past year, we have seen the library profession harnessing its energies for a belated attack on "the manpower problem."

Even before we get to San Francisco, there are indications that a fresh breeze may be stirring in the profession's thinking on this problem. Not that anything very new is being said. What may be different is that views which once were considered heretical or the products of lunatic fringes are beginning to gather "respectable" and respected support. And, equally important, library educators and administrators are beginning to move away from adamantly polar positions and join in a serious search for solutions.

This issue of *LJ* reports two recent meetings on the manpower crisis: the one a kind of ad hoc gathering of concerned people, tired of talk and in search of positive action; the other a more formal conference involving many elements of the power structure which must be called into play if we are to take the kind of massive steps that are required.

Without question, the most revolutionary and most potentially explosive recommendation to come out of the Philadelphia gathering—and the group stressed its "solid agreement"—was that "the basic qualification for librarians be established as a bachelor's degree from a recognized four-year college." As recently as a couple of years ago, a recommendation of this kind would have been virtually unthinkable from a group which included not just library administrators but also educators and official ALA representation.

Even more significant is the fact that the more official meeting in Washington in March came up with virtually the same recommendation: that four-year undergraduate programs "be recognized as leading to the first professional level (beginning librarian)—*if* this education is liberal and not technical."

It has long seemed to us unrealistic to insist that so much that happens in a library requires nothing less than a master's level education, that many functions and services could not be perfectly adequately performed by people with an educational background equivalent to that possessed by those who teach the bulk of the nation's future adults. To talk about a "shortage" (what an inadequate word!) of 100,000 librarians while maintaining this rigidity about educational qualifications makes our whole posture on the manpower situation little short of ridiculous.

Yet there remain those hard-line educators (and others) who will maintain that recognition of programs below the master's level means undercutting the standards (that holy word) of the profession. It might be considerably more helpful if such opponents of change would open their minds to the possibility that lower-level programs might, in addition to alleviating the manpower crisis, rescue the master's programs from some of their present technical training content, enable them to become more concerned with principles and research, and add immeasurably to their prestige.

*Eric Moon*

# Recruitment

## THE HORSE'S MOUTH
May 1, 1962

In recent months we have attended two meetings on recruitment, both organized by the Library Public Relations Council. The problem was discussed at the first meeting by a panel of librarians and vocational counselors. It must have been like a thousand other inbred meetings which have been held across the country—and did not advance anyone's thinking on this subject one iota.

If there was anything to be learned, it might have been that vocational counselors are likely to be so ill-informed about librarianship that they cannot be counted upon to do us much good. They are so swamped by the pressure of 25,000 clamoring occupations that the fairy-fingered "pressure" of the library profession's recruitment effort has scarcely touched their consciousness.

At the second LPRC meeting, which was much more interesting, a dozen students—all bright, intelligent, attractive, composed and competent young people—told an audience of librarians why they had decided to become librarians and how they had been "sold."

Here are some of the common threads which ran through their remarks. *Not one* had ever been recruited by a pamphlet or a poster or a film or any other kind of "materials" propaganda. Isn't this where we spend most of our recruitment money at present? *Not one* had ever seriously thought of becoming a librarian in the pre-college years. Indeed, most of them, during their school years said they had thought of libraries as "rather dull" or "scary" places. They had had, they admitted, absolutely no idea of what a librarian does.

Nearly all these students had been recruited by *librarians,* usually college librarians, who were themselves unashamed evangelists for the profession and whose enthusiasm was infectious. Such librarians had instilled in these students, first, *knowledge* of what a library really is and does, and second, *interest* in the challenge and variety of the librarian's job. Such librarians, knowing that most college students need and want part-time jobs, had made it their business to find them jobs—in libraries. And if not in their own, in someone else's library. Once there, the students were moved around (not kept in one routine job) to give them a taste of the variety and potential of library work.

These students had not been recruited for one library, nor even for one kind of library, but for the profession. They had decided not only on librarianship but on their fields of work—special, college, school and public librarians of the future were all represented.

The point here, we think, is that these students had not been shanghaied into the profession with an unscrupulous desperation born of the "we'll get what we can" attitude. They had been hand-picked (obviously with a view to image-improvement as well as talent), but more important, they had been given understanding and a picture of library work that was not distorted or glamorized.

The students were not *dis*interested in salaries, but their remarks made it clear that salary is not the horrible hurdle that some librarians have made it. The main attractions they had found were the opportunities to use their subject specializations or interests, a certain variety in the work, the opportunity to do something for their fellow man, and challenge with involvement in a rat race. What enthused them most of all was the discovery that librarianship meant work with *people,* not just books or catalog cards or indexes.

Two of the resource experts at this meeting were Rose Sellers, who writes on college recruiting in this issue, and Hugh Behymer of C. W. Post College, New York. They disagreed pretty much about methods, but between them, these two college librarians have more than 80 students interested in a career in librarianship. If all other colleges could do half as well, recruitment would soon be far from our number one problem.

Perhaps we need more meetings like this one. Let us learn from our few successes, and get our information straight from the horse's mouth. Perhaps the recruits themselves can tell us most about what is attractive in librarianship. One lesson that was underlined in almost everything these students said is that nothing—and certainly not a mass of printed propaganda—can beat the human touch in recruitment.

*Eric Moon*

## REAL RECRUITMENT?
June 1, 1962

Could it be that the library profession has finally decided that we need to do more than *discuss* recruitment? Is there recognition at last that the sporadic efforts of enthusiastic individuals or groups on a part-time basis is not enough?

There are indeed healthy signs of emergent action, indications that all the talk of "our number one problem" may be given the financial teeth which are needed to take a healthy bite at this enormous obstacle to library progress.

On the state level, an encouraging example is set by the Pennsylvania proposal to appoint two full-time recruiters to be attached to the state's two accredited library schools. The Pennsylvania legislature, and all those who worked to convince the legislature, are to be complimented on this advance, but it is to be hoped that this will not be another one-shot or short-term deal.

The $40,000 allocated to this program will not last very long. The annual salaries of the proposed two full-time recruiters will alone eat up about $18,000 per year. Recruitment is not a problem that is likely to be solved—or even eased—in a few years. If this scheme is not to fizzle badly, as others have, funds will have to be allocated to this laudable program on a permanent basis. In the meantime, Pennsylvania has given a lead which other state libraries would do well to draw to the attention of their legislatures.

On the national level, where leadership in the recruitment effort has hitherto been at least nebulous, there are also signs of potential progress. At the Midwinter meeting of ALA, the Library Administration Division Board approved an application from the Division's Recruiting Committee for the *World Book Encyclopedia—ALA Goals Award*. More encouraging yet, the Boards of ten other divisions voted to second this proposal rather than submit competing applications.

This unanimity of purpose is admirable, and one wonders at the omission from the list of supporting divisions of the American Association of State Libraries and the American Library Trustee Association. Each of these divisions would seem to be vitally concerned.

If the Recruiting Committee's application for the award is approved by PEBCO and the ALA Executive Board at Miami Beach in June, $50,000 will be available over a period of two years for the establishment of an office for recruitment at ALA headquarters. According to the Recruiting Committee's *Newsletter,* this would provide for the services of a full-time project director, clerical assistance, travel funds, and some money for materials.

Like the Pennsylvania development, this would be a move in the right direction, but we should not like to see the continuance of a recruitment office resting solely on the tentative foundation of grants and awards. It needs the solidity and security of permanent status, and we feel that this is one place where a substantial slice of membership dues should be committed in future years.

To end these thoughts on recruitment, we'd like to draw your attention to a pamphlet put out by *Collier's Encyclopedia,* entitled *You and Your Career.* For 50 cents a copy, this analyzes 121 careers, and offers, among other tabulated information, the following thoughts about librarianship:

"*Advantages:* Excellent working conditions; important to society; immediate satisfactions in helping others; interesting colleagues; *freedom to experiment and improvise* (our italics—Ed.).

"*Disadvantages:* Some monotonous work; usually a position includes evening work; advancement opportunities somewhat limited: sedentary work."

Oh, recruitment materials help!

*Eric Moon*

## A HOLE IN THE NETWORK
February 1, 1965

At the top of the mimeographed form was the impersonal greeting, MEMORANDUM, followed by: "We are very pleased to learn of your interest in the library profession." The attractive, young, well-educated (A.M. in Medieval linguistics), editorial assistant at *LJ* was about to toss the whole package into her waste basket when she remembered that we had asked her to write to ALA for information on library careers.

She was one of four college graduates on our staff we asked to write. Each received an identical response, the memorandum, a list of accredited library schools, and the brochure *Future Unlimited.* Since August, when the first of these packets was received from ALA, our girls have had no further information from the profession.

ALA's Office for Recruitment receives more than 15,000 of these letters annually. Some are obviously from elementary and high school students completing a class assignment. Others come from guidance counselors and publishers of career materials. The rest are from "people who are seriously considering the career and who need specific information of one kind or another (most frequently relating to educational requirements, accredited schools, and scholarships)," according to Myrl Ricking, director of the Office.

Every letter is answered, some with individual replies, but the great majority get only memoranda and brochures that our girls received. Once each month the letters are sorted and sent out to each of the 50 state recruiting representatives who sort them again, "to determine which person within the state can most appropriately, in terms of library specialization and geographic location, provide additional assistance to the individual." Sometimes, according to Miss Ricking, the follow-up is more direct, the letter being sent directly to a local person, especially in cases where urgency is indicated.

The local follow-up is usually a personal letter, although it can take other forms.

The MEMORANDUM our "trial" recruits received says that a master's degree is necessary, that with it a beginning librarian can expect a salary of $6000, and that work-study arrangements can often be set up to finance the education. It offers two ALA pamphlets on financial assistance to library school students for $1.50, and makes the following promise: "We are also forwarding your inquiry to a librarian in your vicinity who will, within several weeks, be getting in touch with you to see if he can provide additional information of a more specific nature."

The brochure, *Future Unlimited,* is probably familiar to most of our readers. Its ten 3¾" × 8½" pages, plus covers, are devoted to library education; what it is, how to get it, and how to pay for it. It briefly mentions library school placement services, and in a curious juxtaposition of information, offers a two-page spread on undergraduate library education just before a single page labelled "Why an accredited library school?" We wondered about the sentence, "About half of the accredited library schools also offer undergraduate programs," since we are not aware of any accredited undergraduate programs.

Several local recruiters, all of them with more than a year of experience on the "network," said that the major problem was delay. It is normal for a letter to take six to eight weeks to reach the local recruiter from ALA. Sometimes it takes longer—once an October letter was received in June. Another recruiter decided not to answer a letter which was written December 10, 1963, and received locally for reply on September 10, 1964. These dedicated recruiters all agreed that this person-to-person communication was the most important feature of the process, even if the measurable response was one recruit in 50 letters. One said, "I was embarrassed by the dates on some of those letters. For all I know the people at the receiving end will be annoyed by another letter at that late date."

One recruiter felt that there should be a better reporting system from the local follow-up to ALA. Another said that, in his opinion, there is little attempt to contact guidance counselors in local schools, and this might decrease the number of individual inquiries. Three recruiters couldn't understand the need for distribution to the state level, rather than directly to the local network representative.

They all agreed, however, that the process, to be effective, must be faster. "By the time I get these letters, six to eight weeks later, my personal efforts are irrelevant, and most of the people have already decided." In one state the backlog reached the point where local recruiters decided, despite the promise in ALA's memorandum, not to reply at all since they were so late.

As for the response that most letters do receive, it is coldly impersonal, and because of a decision to emphasize library education, it tells nothing about the number and kinds of opportunities in librarianship, the function of libraries, what they and librarians do. To leave this basic information to be filled in at the local level seems, at best, putting the cart before the horse—if, indeed, the horse will ever show up. It is right to point out that there are educational requirements, but it seems less than encouraging to single out this particular phase of librarianship, without any other enticement to soften the blow of another year of school.

Disturbed more by the delay than anything else in the program, we telephoned Miss Ricking for more data. Her office is attempting to speed the process. She also pointed out that answering the 15,000 inquiries is only a minor part of the recruiting program.

The Office for Recruitment deserves applause for its contribution to a growing national recognition of librarianship, and for the better understanding of the profession among students and guidance people alike. A strong case could be made for the fact that the quality of recruits, and the increasing number of them is due to her efforts. Surely the quantity and quality of recruiting literature is better, and it is a vast improvement to have this material emanate from the national level, thus relieving state agencies from the complicated task of producing brochures. The ALA recruiting network has been improved, and is now manned by strong librarians at the regional, state, and local levels.

To have done all these things, and many more, with one full-time secretary and two part-time helpers, is a tribute to Miss Ricking and her staff. The Association has finally given the Office a regular budgetary allocation (this year a modest $29,557). Myrl Ricking is overwhelmed with offers of volunteer help from the profession. ALA's Executive Board and PEBCO have voiced their approval of her programs, and their view of its importance. Yet, in our opinion, the Office is under-staffed, and under-financed. The budget must take care of salaries, travel, publications, and the not insignificant bill for postage. The staff must handle meetings, projects, a tremendous correspondence, coordinate a national program, and keep the profession informed about all of these activities.

We agree with the recruiter who said, "Recruiting should be the top priority activity of the Association," at least to the degree that it should share room at the top.

We do not agree that individual inquiries should be relegated to a minor role in the recruiting program.

As another member of the recruiting network put it, "It is the single most important activity not only from the point of view of attracting new people, but as a means of bringing the library message to others who may or may not want to be librarians." Seen in this light, those marginal letters from students may be more important than we suspect. A fast reply will say a lot about the profession; a slow one will too.

As part of its third year program we suggest to the Office for Recruitment that it re-evaluate this process, and that it request sufficient funds and personnel to replace some of the mimeographed replies and pamphlets with individually typed (if not composed) letters.

Certainly some attempt to evaluate the 15,000 inquiries and responses should be made, perhaps reviving the malfunctioning report forms from local recruiters.

There is no reason for the letters to pile up for a month at ALA, and for another month at some state level office. With more staff these could be mailed at least once a week, maybe daily; and mailed directly to the local recruiter from files maintained at ALA headquarters.

We realize that there are probably other activities of importance, and we acknowledge the achievements of the Office for Recruitment—a regular reading of the recruitment column in the *ALA Bulletin* will impress one with this continuing effort. But we also feel that "a bird in the hand is worth two in the bush." In the highly competitive market for competent and outstanding personnel we can ill afford to lose by default because the machinery for communication was too slow.

If the four, highly qualified, girls we asked to write were little motivated to become librarians back in July, they are even less so now. A fast response from a dynamic local librarian, and, who knows, they might have been convinced!

*John Berry*

## THE NAMATH SYSTEM
January 1, 1966

In the football world, Joe Namath is what is known as a rookie. In librarianship, he would be called, accurately, a beginning professional. As a newcomer to professional football, he naturally earns somewhat less in salary than many of the senior professionals on his team. But he was an exceptional recruit, and to get him against all the other competition the New York Jets paid him a bonus of $400,000.

This kind of money, of course, is out of librarianship's league, despite the recent flood of federal funds. But we thought about Joe Namath recently when someone told us that one of the large city public library systems calculates that the cost of those annual library school recruiting trips comes out to about $6000 per recruit acquired. We wondered whether that library might be more successful if it took a leaf out of football's book and spent its recruiting money another way.

Suppose the library paid a small fee to an experienced person in each of the library school areas. That person would act as a "scout": his sole duty would be to find out who were the exceptional students in the library school he was assigned to cover. When the library received its scout's report, it could then offer a one-time bonus of, say, $3000–$4000 (in addition to salary) to these exceptional recruits as a "persuader" to join that particular system.

A sweetener of this size would surely benefit the library offering it, but it might have the desirable side-effect of making librarianship appear to be a pretty attractive profession in the eyes of some of the brighter college students who were still making up their minds about their future careers.

The idea, like all ideas with a certain surface glitter, has obvious snags. The most obvious one would be the attitude of some of the senior professionals who didn't get such a beginning bonus. But professional football has that problem, too, and seems not to have collapsed under its weight.

A more fundamental objection is that such an approach might sharpen the already formidable edge that the large library system has over smaller libraries in this area of recruiting. But perhaps that is not a valid objection at all. If a development of this kind had the effect also of persuading the smaller libraries that they must pool their efforts, financially and otherwise, in order to compete in recruiting with the big brothers of the library world, it might serve yet another useful purpose.

*Eric Moon*

## TALKING OF MINIMUMS
September 15, 1967

INQUIRING REPORTER: I'm doing a series on the professions and career possibilities for my paper. What's the pitch on librarianship?

LIBRARIAN: Well, according to the American Library Association, we need 100,000 professional librarians.

I. R: It sounds like a profession where a youngster with anything on the ball could move up fast.

L: Oh, it is, it is. It's a profession full of challenge and opportunity. And variety.

I. R: Yeah. Well, they all say that. But let's have some facts. What's a *professional* librarian?

L: Someone with a Master's degree from a library school accredited by ALA.

I. R: What do you pay people in that category?

L: Oh, there's a tremendous range. Salaries go up all the way to $20,000 and beyond.

I.R: Where do they start? What's the minimum?

L: There isn't a minimum exactly. Some professional librarians work for less than $4000 a year. But the average for last year's graduates was $6,765.

I. R: Did you say less than $4000? That's practically poverty level. No wonder you have a manpower crisis.

L: No, look, salaries like that are exceptional. As I said, the *average* is much higher.

I. R: But $6,765 doesn't sound high enough to be competitive with what other professions pay.

L: Remember, that's *last* year's average. This year, if the normal rate of increase applies, the average should be about $7000 or better.

I. R: Still doesn't sound very competitive to me. The College of Engineering at the University of Illinois, for example, reports that beginning salaries for engineers with *bachelor's* degrees are now at $8,676. What does your professional association say about this? Does it set any kind of minimum salary goal, or work for its adoption by those who pay librarians?

L: It depends who you listen to. *Two* salary figures were cited at the recent ALA conference in San Francisco. The president of the association told the press that beginning professional librarians ought to get a salary of at least $8,500. She pointed out that the National Education Association had named $8000 as a salary goal for beginning classroom teachers with no experience and only a *bachelor's* degree.

I. R: Sounds like a reasonable comparison. That extra year of college ought to be worth $500. So is that ALA's official position? Does your president speak for the association?

L: No, not really. At least, not in this case. I think she was trying to force the association to take some such position. ALA's now studying the matter.

I. R: You mentioned *two* salary figures. What was the other one?

L: The other was $7000. This was recommended by the Standards Committee of the Public Library Association, one of ALA's divisions.

I. R: What did the members say about that?

L: Well, someone pointed out what the president had recommended, but some of the public librarians said they'd be laughed out of court if they took a figure like $8,500 back to their library boards. So the members of PLA went along with the $7000 figure.

I. R: Sounds weird to me. Is your president way out in left field? Or does anyone else recommend anything like $8,500? Does anyone actually pay salaries like that?

L: Yes . . . oh, I don't mean the president's way out . . . I mean yes to the other questions. Lowell Martin, who's a pretty big name in the library field, surveyed public libraries in Pennsylvania recently, and he recommended an $8000 minimum. And the Library of Congress and other federal libraries can now appoint any new library school graduate, providing he finished in the top quarter of his class, on a salary grade running from $7,696 to $10,045. And these candidates don't need any previous experience.

I. R: Well, look, I've got to name some sort of figure in my story, and I guess I'll have to mention those figures cited at your conference. Suppose I put it this way: "ALA President Names $8,500 Minimum Salary for Librarians. Public Librarians Settle for $7000. This reporter concludes that, if the higher figure is to be achieved by the library profession, librarians in colleges, schools and other types of libraries will have to be paid above the recommended $8,500 minimum, to compensate for lower salaries in public libraries." How does that sound?

L: Fine, I'm a college librarian.

*Eric Moon*

## Image Problems

### THE UNINVITED
January 15, 1960

On our editorial page last August, Eleanor Smith of Brooklyn Public Library asked: "Why aren't WE consulted?" She was concerned because no librarian had been icluded among "fifty outstanding persons in various fields of thought and activity" who had been consulted by the Fund for Adult Education before a statement was issued announcing a "new venture in education for public responsibility."

Eleanor Smith's question was a pertinent one, and two recent press releases indicate that the time has come for the question to be repeated.

On December 8 the Postmaster General announced the appointment of a nine-member Citizens' Advisory Committee on Literature, to aid him in reaching decisions on the mailability of books "where questions of obscenity arise." The advisory group, it was stated, consisted of "civic and literary leaders representing a cross-section of American life."

It will be noted that the cross-section of American life includes representation from publishing, journalism, the church, and parent-teacher, youth and women's organizations. So far as the inclusions are concerned it may be an admirable list, but the omissions are cause for serious misgivings. If the phrase "civic and literary leaders" does not include librarians, it would seem to us that at least when questions about books—and particularly about what books should or should not be circulated—are being considered at a national level, librarians ought to have something in the way of knowledge and experience to offer.

The American Library Association has a Committee on Intellectual Freedom. Did it know about the Postmaster General's move? Was it consulted? Or invited? If not, why not? We are surely deeply concerned.

On December 19 the Advisory Board on the Pulitzer Prizes drew back the curtain of secrecy which has for 40 years hidden the identity of the persons who have served on the Pulitzer Prize juries since 1917. One hundred two names were announced, and as a matter of interest we analyzed the list to see from what fields these "experts" had been drawn. Way out in front were the representatives of the field of education: variously labelled as professors, educators and college presidents, they totalled 49. There were 30 authors, if you include 7 dramatists, followed by 14 editors, 8 critics and 6 historians. Down at the other end there were the miscellanea, including one music director (of a radio station) and one librarian. While we should cheer over H. M. Lydenburg's inclusion, the over-all proportions might well be taken as a sad reflection of the recognition of the status of librarians in the world of books and scholarship.

There has been much ado in the library profession in recent years about status. Perhaps too much thought and time, and too many words, have been devoted to mumbo-jumbo about certification, salaries, punched cards, and public relations techniques. If librarians cannot claim, earn, deserve, or receive recognition as experts in their own field—books—they have no right to expect greater status.

*Eric Moon*

## BOOKKEEPERS?
November 1, 1961

The reverberations from the East Orange overdues affair echo still, not through the corridors of Time, but in the pages of the *Saturday Review*, where for some weeks John Ciardi has been waxing unpoetically—even apoplectically—on the subject.

It started back in August when Mr. Ciardi, rather late in the day, apparently first became aware of what had been happening in East Orange. We could not get too stirred up about this first installment. It was a slick and sometimes silly piece of journalism, with more concern for rhetoric than facts. But no one, we felt, could too much blame a columnist for having what he thought was fun when he was faced with such an easy and obvious target. Whatever the rights or the wrongs of the case, there was no denying that the East Orange incident had, in some respects, been handled unfortunately.

It is the reaction, among librarians in particular, that interests us more than the profundities of Mr. Ciardi. Some of this appeared in a subsequent issue of *SR*, and several of the letters, naturally, came from the Orange belt of New Jersey. They included one from Learned Bulman, Coordinator of Youth Services at East Orange, which began: "Of all the stupid, asinine, idiotic twaddle I have read in some time . . ."

Now one can sympathize with a splenetic outburst of this kind from someone at the source of the trouble. It is understandable that the librarians at East Orange might be growing weary of attacks such as Mr. Ciardi's.

In a more recent column, however (*Saturday Review*, Sept. 30), Mr. Ciardi mentions a fat file of other mail he has received from librarians, who accuse him, among other things, he says, of "anarchy, encouraging the plundering of library shelves, failure to keep faith with the oppresed librarians of the world, gross cynicism, and a general assortment of deficiencies ranging largely from paranoia to schizophrenia and back again by way of communistic irresponsibility."

All this exciting correspondence persuaded Mr. Ciardi to try his hand again, with a little philosophy about librarians as people and professionals, and to indulge in that favorite librarian's pastime, classification. His classification is, as one would expect of a layman and a poet, pretty elementary. He simply dichotomizes the profession into "bookkeepers" and "keepers of books." Neat, if not profound.

The bookkeepers, by his definition, are "the fussy-minded literalists in the ranks of the librarians." The keeper of books is "the true librarian . . . (he) who lets his books into his life as well as into his clerical procedures." The true librarian, declares our polemical poet, "will keep not only his books but the idea of his library." Mr. Ciardi does not consider the possibility that this true librarian's "idea" might differ from his own.

What concerns us in all this is not Mr. Ciardi's attitude—he doesn't send our temperature soaring by even a degree—but the attitude of some of the librarians who responded to his unsubtle provocations.

The image of the librarian is, if one is to judge from the amount of discussion of it recently, a subject of some concern. But in working at improving an image, a sense of proportion and perspective are important factors in the behavior of those who wish to create a more favorable impression upon the world. It isn't enough to look happy and healthy when faced with a reader with a none too significant inquiry. The maturity and patience to ride out the comments of the uninformed and even the malicious are necessary qualities too. And if you are going to take a last ditch stand on something, it is as well to be throughly confident that you have something worth fighting for. Does everyone feel completely happy about justifying *all* the aspects of what happened at East Orange as desirable library practice?

The three librarians who could be so foolish as to write to a national magazine that they intended to take off their library shelves all of John Ciardi's books, because they didn't like the views he expressed in the *Saturday Review,* are active perpetrators of the "fussy and futile" image of the librarian which we all want to eradicate. They are indeed "bookkeepers."

*Eric Moon*

## TV AND THE OVERDUE BOOK
April 15, 1962

On March 8, the Gertrude Berg show on CBS Television was devoted to a dramatization of the problem of the overdue book—further testimony perhaps to the tidal wave of public interest created by last year's local hurricane at East Orange.

In the half hour play Mrs. G (Gertrude Berg) receives an overdue notice from her college library. Johnson and Clyde's *Social Behavior* (very apt) is more than 30 days overdue. A five-dollar fine is mentioned. Mrs. G proclaims to the world that she has been wrongly accused: she returned the book on time. A student friend is horrified by such sacrilege. Mr. Ames, the librarian, he says, "does not make mistakes." Even Mrs. G's English professor (Cedric Hardwicke) advises her to pay the fine. "You can't win," he says.

From her Uncle Nathan, however, Mrs. G has inherited not only an encyclopedic supply of platitudes but a strong sense of justice. She demands audience with the awesome Ames. The librarian is played by actor Vaughn Taylor as a hatchet-faced personification of rectitude. He browbeats Mrs. G with the information that he is the holder of a master's degree in library science and that he has worked in libraries for more than 30 years. A mistake, he says, is "inconceivable." His "quadruplicate set of cross-referenced filing records" is infallible.

Mrs. G persists persuasively. Is it not possible, she asks, that a large organization might be just as susceptible to error, if not more so than an individual? Reluctantly, Ames yields under the pressure of the waterfall of words. He is clearly aghast at the possibility of an error having crept into his "system." As Mrs. G exits, he telephones his assistant and calls "an emergency meeting in my office in one hour."

The plot develops—and Mrs. G finds the offending book under a hat in her closet. It is her turn to be aghast, but she is still motivated by virtue. "I'm going to take the book back, pay the fine and apologize to the librarian," she tells a friend. Why not just take the book back, slip it on the shelf and forget about it? says her friend, advising that this is the more common practice.

"That would be dishonest," affirms Mrs. G stoutly. Her friend looks sad. "I don't know what's happening to college students these days," he says.

Mrs. G locates Ames at the top of a ladder in the library (weeding?). She hands him the book, and with contrition written large on her face, gives him a lengthy explanation of how such an error is possible when a woman is faced with the psychological problems of her wardrobe. She hadn't worn the hat she expected to wear on the day the book should have been returned . . .

Ames interrupts the flow, and thanks her stonily. "The most important thing is that the library has its book back." Mrs. G apologizes anew for the "anguish" she has caused him, and expresses amazement that the nonreturn of one book should cause so much consternation.

Ames explains to her the disastrous consequences which can accrue from such a situation. "One book unavailable when it is needed" may cause a student to fail in the compilation of his term paper. "A library is the sum total of each of its books," pontificates the magnificent Ames.

The insistence on the infallibility of library charging systems may cause a few minor future embarrassments in some places, but so far the TV show hadn't gone too badly. The moral was overdone, but it wasn't altogether unhelpful. However, Ames, who hasn't been gilding the image too well all along, delivers the coup de grace in the conclusion.

"You are an exceptional man, Mr. Ames," says the grateful Mrs. G. Ames vigorously denies this, insisting that his job is mainly concerned with routine and "trivia." "I am the custodian of the *products* of exceptional men," he declares—"not one of them."

Recruiters, please note.

*Eric Moon*

## DEFENSIVE ABOUT THE DEFENDERS
June 1, 1963

The ratings are not analytical enough to tell us, but it's a fair guess that on the evening of March 30 there were more librarians than usual huddled around television sets. An unusual amount of advance publicity must have built up a sense of anticipation about the teleplay, "A Book for Burning," which was to dramatize for a mass audience the sensitive subject of book censorship.

Although most of us would not bet on network television treating such a subject intelligently, in this case there must have been some hope mixed with the anticipation. The play was to appear on a program called The Defenders, a series which has made a habit of tackling delicate and controversial issues with taste and courage and flair.

Now the program is over, and the judgments are beginning to come in. One of the first to be delivered appeared on the editorial page of the May issue of the *ALA Bulletin*. It is not favorable—and we should be surprised if it were. What does concern us, however, is that the *ALA Bulletin* editorial makes no attempt to discusss whether the program succeeded or failed in its central purpose, or whether the *total* effect of the play was for good or for ill. Far more important apparently, is the tired old subject of the librarian's "image."

The librarian in the play, says the *ALA Bulletin*, was "unattractive, stupid and ignorant." That she was—and we could add a few adjectives. We too would like to see the librarian get a more favorable break in some of his/her public characterizations in fiction, drama and cartoon. But we cannot think that the way to that bright new image is a sort of protest march on CBS—and for the marchers to wave the flag of the ALA Intellectual Freedom Committee is little short of ludicrous. If it is really necessary for us to declare that *all* librarians are not like this fictional librarian of Pine River, then we are in bad shape.

A while ago a number of Italian groups bellowed loudly because all the mobsters on another television series, The Untouchables, were clearly Italian. In a way, that protest worked. Now only two thirds of the gangsters are Italian. But are not viewers more conscious now of the national origin of these thugs than before the protest?

Why, asks the *ALA Bulletin*, "single out 'the librarian of Pine River' as the one most stupid, ignorant, and thoroughly unattractive witness against the book?" We cannot agree that the characterization of the librarian was the only unfavorable one. And we wonder, are the literary critics of the nation rising in wrath because the critic in this play was pictured as a braying jackass? How do the country's judges and newspaper editors react to the (mostly) cowardly behavior of their representatives (?) in this play? Or the police to the vicious ignorance of the police Chief of Pine River?

To be sure, there are the Bull Connors among our police chiefs, but they are not all like that. We regret to say it, but there are also the Miss Tuckers of Pine River among our librarians, though they too are far from representative.

The *ALA Bulletin* asks: "Why couldn't this woman have been identified as an officer of the woman's club? a school board member? a representative of one of the many volunteer censor groups? Members of these organizations—and of many others—are more likely to be identified with book censorship than are librarians."

Is *this* fair? What ever happened to the old "Do unto others . . ." philosophy? And is that last statement completely true, or just a little colored by wishful thinking? The Fiske Report identified librarians pretty clearly with censorship. And one member of the ALA staff, Lester Asheim, said, not so long ago, that while Marjorie Fiske did not claim her special sample as representative of all librarians, he thought it probably was.

We are not trying to prove that Miss Tucker was a reasonable portrayal. But we do declare that, had the librarian been pictured as a knight in shining armor, the characterization would have been no more *representative* of the profession as a whole than Miss Tucker. To suggest that one character in one play represents a whole profession is a kind of group-think a good dramatist can't afford. Nor, we suggest, can a professional association afford to react in this way. It is rather like adopting the schoolboy-howler logic that suggests that because all horses are animals, all animals are horses.

Jesse Shera, writing in the May *Wilson Library Bulletin* on this matter, "hoped the ALA would keep its corporate mouth shut." Hopes, like humans, are born to die, Jesse, and this one went fast.

*Eric Moon*

## TIPARILLOS AND HACKSAWS
May 15, 1967

Next month, several thousand librarians will gather in San Francisco to talk up, among other things, "the manpower crisis." Among the more certain topics of conversation will be the desirable levels of library education and training, recruitment, the use and misuse of professional staff, salaries, and the need for technicians. But put your money on it: present at many of the sessions will be that aged spectre, "the image of the librarian."

One may detest the word "image" or be weary of the subject, but there is no denying its relevance in any consideration of how to attract more and perhaps different kinds of people into library service. What people think, what their visual or mental images of what libraries and librarians are like, *does* matter. It is clear also that it matters deeply to many librarians who send *LJ* a fairly constant supply of complaints about the way librarians are portrayed in magazine advertisements, TV commercials, fiction, and the like.

Not all these presentations or caricatures of the librarian, however, are as grossly unflattering as the complaint stream would suggest. Indeed, one that appeared recently in *Playboy* seemed to us to carve no scars at all in the librarian's image. The ad asks: "Should a gentleman offer a Tiparillo to a librarian?" Below is pictured the kind of doll that most gentlemen would be happy to offer anything. Below also is the assertion that this "librarian" will "read anything she can get her hands on. From Medieval History to How-To-Build-a-24-Foot-Iceboat. *Loves books. Loves new ideas*" (our italics). Neither the picture nor the text, it seemed to us, could be said to deal any low blow to the librarian's "image."

Far more damaging than most of these fictional fantasies about librarians, perhaps, are the awful realities exposed when librarians themselves launch into print. Some recent examples support the possibility that this latter may be the source of some of the most irreparable damage to the "image."

*Item:* A school librarian from New York writes to *LJ* (April 1, p. 1497), protesting a recen review recommending Robert Lowell's *Near the Ocean* as "a first purchase for all libraries." The letter, with blithe unconcern, reveals that Lowell has not hitherto been represented in that school library's collection, and complains that the volume of poetry purchased as a result of the *LJ* recommendation is "eroticism," "obscene," "pornographic," a "new low," etc. The letter, of course, does not do as much damage to the profession's claims to literary judgment and standards (oft-cited in book selection statements) as if it had appeared outside the professional press. But the picture that the letter conjures up of that library's collection is not a happy one. If the collection is as miserable as the letter suggests, what does it do for the library image so far as the students of that school are concerned? Can we write off these students as possible future library recruits?

*Item:* A college librarian from South Dakota contributes to the "Idea Exchange" in the *NEA Journal* (March 1967, p. 47). Her contribution, in essence, is a short how-to-do-it course for librarians on how to use a hacksaw and other "basic equipment," to get around the problem of "budgets [which] do not include funds for binding periodicals." This presents a marvelous picture of librarians attuned to the 20th-Century age of technology. It will also undoubtedly be of great service to those academic librarians who are busily arguing with their campus colleagues that librarians deserve full faculty status and other perquisites of the professoriate.

*Item:* A (public?) librarian from California, confronted with local pressure "to remove certain volumes from my shelves," writes for advice and asks for "a strong quote . . . something suitable to show the book burners before they have a chance to strike their figurative matches." But to whom does she write? To her national or state professional library associations? To the Intellectual Freedom Committees of either of these organizations? To one of the national library periodicals? No, she writes to *Playboy* (May 1967, p. 60). The potential book burners, of course, will be persuaded by being handed the gospel according to Hugh Hefner! *Playboy,* to its lasting credit, however, referred this librarian to ALA's *Newsletter on Intellectual Freedom,* and specifically to a recently quoted and excellent policy statement by the Palisades Public Library, New York. But what kind of picture does this librarian's letter convey of the profession's competence in an area of basic library philosophy and practice?

Our case rests.

*Eric Moon*

# Library Administration

### THE CONSULTING GAME
December 1, 1963

Librarianship may not be the best paid profession around, but some of the more experienced members of the profession have found a nicely remunerative sideline in the "consultant" business. One place where there seems to be ample justification for the frequent use of consultants is in the planning of a new building.

In the early stages, at least, of such planning, the librarian should be a near-equal partner of the architect. Many architects have little experience in building libraries, and some of their architectural visions and vistas match not at all well with the functions a library is supposed to perform. The librarian coming to the planning of a new building for the first time may not be equipped for partnership with the persuasiveness of the architect and does well to ask for the assistance of an Ulveling, a Metcalf or an Ellsworth.

But the consulting game has spread far wider than the building field. It is now possible to find a librarian-consultant for just about any kind of library operation you like to dream of. And sometimes one wonders whether it is all justified.

Think a moment about how the consulting game grew up. There was a time when the librarian-administrator who wanted to institute some new development investigated the facts, built a case and presented it to his Board. If his trustees persisted in failing to see the light and refused to accept his authority, he said in desperation: "All right, if you don't take my word that this is necessary and will improve our operation, bring in an outside expert to bring you an independent and unbiased view." The Board often went along, and the librarian then found another librarian who had instituted a similar operation to come along and do the convincing. It was a reasonable process, and often successful.

Its success, in fact, may present a danger. Today a basic part of the process seems to be often omitted. In many cases we have heard of, the librarian-administrator with a problem no longer makes the attempt to investigate and propose a solution himself. Instead, he goes *first* to his Board and says: "We have this problem. I suggest we appoint a consultant to take a look at it and come up with a proposal." Is this administration? The answer is No—but it's good for the consultant business.

*Eric Moon*

## ADMINISTRATIVE DEFINITIONS
September 15, 1965

When Adlai Stevenson was offered the post as head of the United States delegation to the United Nations, he hesitated for some time before accepting the appointment because, as he told a friend, he was "not just interested in explaining or defending a policy" but wanted to be involved in the *making* of that policy. When, some time later, he was asked what job other than his UN post he would most like to have, he replied that second to the Presidency his choice would be that of the US Secretary of State, "assuming you could really be involved in making policy and not just be an administrator."

We happened upon this Stevenson story, appropriately enough, as we were putting together this special issue on library administration. We retell it here because this separatist attitude—perhaps more endemic to the statesman than the librarian—is nevertheless germane to any discussion of administrative power and responsibility.

With all due respect to Mr. Stevenson, we cannot subscribe to the theory that a sharp dichotomy exists between the policy making and administrative functions. While the administrator's power to *make* policy may be limited by a variety of pressures and vested interests, certainly it is within the province of the librarian-administrator at least to be a *shaper* of the policy he must explain and defend. Formulation of policy is assuredly a responsibility which no administrator can relinquish completely to the echelons above or below him.

In 1959, in a *Library Trends* article, E. W. McDiarmid stated that "it would be well for librarianship to associate itself more closely with discussions and research in administration generally, to the end that concepts might be more carefully defined and appraised, with the long-time objective of achieving a more definitive body of administrative theory." Since that time, library literature has turned to administrative definitions, with two award-winning volumes on the subject produced in 1962 and 1964. But, although there has been a concerted attempt at definition, much of the thinking on the subject remains fuzzy and definitions are little more than vague generalizations.

How well has public library policy been defined, let alone defended? Where is the fine line drawn between policy making and decision making?

When should trustees be involved and when not? These are some of the more obvious concepts to be defined.

If it is assumed that policy is formulated by the librarian and approved by the library board, the next obvious question is what happens when this policy comes into public question. In discussing book selection in this issue of *LJ*, Jerry Cushman notes that in mamy communities libraries have been "forced to abandon the philosophical position propounded by policy statements in the face of actualities that sometimes approach professional ignominy." It is an unusual board, he adds, that "stands up to its responsibility in terms of protecting the book selection process of the library without somehow or other compromising it." Obviously, the matter of board responsibility for policy is still not clearly defined.

"Executive posts," says another author in this issue, "are characterized by the necessity of making decisions beyond experience and record." Question: When is a decision not merely a decision but a matter of policy calling for board involvement? To be sure, the financial line is always well drawn in these matters, but there are other, less subtle, criteria. One answer comes from Philip Monypenny, in an article in the same *Library Trends* mentioned earlier. "Issues," he says, "which have become *emotionally charged* (our italics) must be classed as policy matters whatever their standing otherwise as points of technique and not of substance." Many an administrator still finds himself balancing precariously on this tightrope.

We asked a friend of ours—a brand new library school graduate—what she had learned about administration during her year at library school. Not much, she confessed. There were some personal anecdotes which, she said, were helpful in a general way but there was nothing substantive. She had concluded, however, that all professional librarians—by definition—must eventually become administrators. She said this rather sadly and to us it sounded more like a sentence than an opportunity. If she is right—and we think she is—the future librarians who are now students in library school will need a considerably more perceptive view of the administrative problem than the much-repeated phrase, "trustees make policies and the librarian carries them out."

*Shirley Havens*

### RIGHTS AND RESPONSIBILITIES
October 1, 1967

This issue includes a report on some of the recent extraordinary activities of a public library trustee who is a member of the John Birch Society. We can assume, we hope, that Carl Gorton is a far from typical trustee, but we should not perhaps also assume that he is unique.

In the area of censorship, certainly—an area on which a substantial portion of Gorton's missionary zeal is focussed—there were indications in San Francisco that a number of other trustees may be as much out of harmony with ALA's official pronouncements on intellectual freedom as Gorton is. The warm reception given by members of the American Library Trustee Association to the tirade delivered by California's Max Rafferty—who, among other things, urged librarians to become censors—should be a warning to public librarians that future discord with their boards is not only possible but probable.

Over the years, library conferences and library literature have exhibited a timid sprinkling of debate on the subject of librarian-trustee relationships; on the responsibilities, duties, rights, obligations of trustees; and on the gray question of where policy and administrative decisions divide. What the Gorton case underlines is that most of these polite discussions have failed to reach down to the nitty-gritty problems, or at least have failed to tackle them with any conviction.

Some of Gorton's actions are to be considered by courts this month, but the courts are likely only to resolve the narrow legalities of these actions: whether or not Gorton, as alleged, "stole" the *Paris Review*, and whether or not, as alleged, he "assaulted" Children's Librarian Hortensia Stoyan. The broader ethical questions are likely to remain in mid air, even after the court decisions.

The New York State Supreme Court, for example, has already ruled that while trustees have a right to examine library records, this "is not to say that the library is to remain open 24 hours a day, seven days a week, to accommodate this worthwhile objective." This ruling still leaves open the question of what kinds of records must be made available to library trustees. Although the Farmingdale board adopted a rule on August 8 to the effect that "all trustees may see all files of the library," and spelled out procedures by which they should be made available, the term "all files" seems dangerously open to many interpretations.

On this point, for example, Gorton still insists that if he wants to investigate the contents of individual staff members' desks, "I feel that it is within my rights to do so as a trustee." Some may consider this a debatable point. We do not; we regard such practice as a clear invasion of personal privacy.

Nor do we agree that an individual board member has the "right" to interview, badger, or harass members of the library staff. The board's source of information about staff or general library activities should be the library director.

But back to that matter of the library records—and to a question we raised in another context at the Ethics Committee meeting during the San Francisco conference. In a library with a computerized circulation system it is now perfectly possible to construct a complete profile of the reading or borrowing done by any or all of the library's patrons. To whom should this kind of information be available?

In the hands of the wrong person (and Gorton seems an eminently wrong person) such information could be used (or misused) to crucify publicly a library patron on the grounds of what he read. The FBI, it will be remembered, in its investigation of Oswald, checked on his reading at the New Orleans Public Library and used what it found as evidence of some prior intent because he had read books on presidential assassinations and other related subjects. Beyond the court's ruling in the Gorton case, then, some definition still seems to be necessary of what kinds of library records should be open for inspection—by trustees or anyone else.

Where does ALTA stand on such matters? It has issued no statement concerning the outrageous behavior of Gorton. And while ALA still probes away at the old problem of professional ethics, ALTA seems not to have exhibited much interest in the problem of trustee ethics. We recommend that ALTA do some hard thinking with a view to producing an official statement on the trustee's rights and responsibilities, their limitations as well as their range. The Gorton case would appear to indicate that this should be a priority project for ALTA, as the ALA division most concerned.

*Eric Moon*

## ADMINISTRATIVE INDIGESTION?
March 1, 1968

In the term "library administrator," which is the key word? A trustee complained to us recently that the librarian of the large system on whose board she served was very good on professional matters (she did not define these very clearly) but wasn't much of an administrator.

This was not the first time we have heard the suggestion that a library or a library system, once it reaches a certain size, perhaps needs a professional administrator in addition to its complement of professional librarians. Librarians usually can be counted on to react negatively and vociferously to this concept: there can only be one top man and, in a library organization, he ought to be a professional librarian. In addition to the matter of status there's the feeling that policy formulation and direction should stem from a professional librarian rather than a professional anything else—this happily ignores the fact that many lay boards of trustees think *they*, not the library administrator, set policy.

Can a case not be made, however, for a workable division of responsibility between the administrative and professional aspects of library direction? In magazine publishing—to take another field we know something about—most magazines of any real size and complexity have both a publisher and an editor-in-chief. The responsibility lines are not always crystal clear but, in general, the publisher's role is usually the business function, while the creative shaping and direction of editorial policy is usually the editor's responsibility.

Might not many librarians in very large libraries really be happier if a similar division of responsibilities could be worked out? As libraries, under the impact of federal funding in recent years, have come more and more in some cases to resemble big business operations—handling millions of dollars and involved with multijurisdictional complexities—administration, finance, and politics have become all-consuming factors in the life of some library directors.

Take the case of Stuart Sherman, who resigned a few weeks ago from the directorship of the Providence Public Library. In a letter to the board chairman he said that he had resigned because the administration of the library had become "primarily a business and financial responsibility" and that "the increasing complexity of these problems" had left him "little time to devote to the intellectual and bibliographic aspects of the institution—*factors which attracted me to librarianship*" (our italics).

Sherman's is the first statement of this kind we have seen placed on record, but we know that at least some of the many who have departed from the state level in the past year or two—both from state libraries and state school library agencies—have left for basically similar reasons. At that level the financial, administrative, and bureaucratic pressures seem likely only to escalate in the period ahead.

Nor are the library schools, as they grow larger and more complex, exempt from increasing administrative pressures. Deans, tired of administration, are returning to teaching, many faculty members are reluctant to move in the opposite direction, and at least some of the schools now seem to be finding it more difficult to locate potential deans than to recruit faculty.

The potential impact of the growth of administrative activity may well be a key element for consideration by those, like the University of Maryland, who are studying the manpower crisis in the library porfession. Is it not a waste of educational effort and time to give intensive bibliographic training to a man who will spend most of his working life on balance sheets, labor negotiations, building planning, etc.? Might not library *service* benefit if so many of the profession's best people were not forced out of bibliographic or service pursuits because the only promotional ladder that reaches very far in librarianship is now the administrative one? Might not library administration be improved—notably in such areas as costing and statistical analysis—if fully-fledged administrators were recruited to carry out such functions?

If the profession could put aside its status-nervousness and its hierarchical tendencies long enough to consider such possibilities without assuming that any move in this direction is bound to result in professional librarians becoming *subordinate* to professional administrators, the result might be some new thinking—surely desirable—about the restructuring both of library staffing and of library education and recruitment.

*Eric Moon*

## THE TRANSFER OF AUTHORITY
June 1, 1968

Firing a chief librarian is a dirty business, something like an assassination or an execution. Charges, counter charges, recriminations, and all the attendant human suffering afflict an institution when its director becomes so dysfunctional that he must be removed. It is a step not ordinarily taken except from absolute necessity; consequently, ruinous levels of incompetence are often tolerated in chief officers. General Motors, though one of the larger principalities of this world, can replace its top brass with rather less unhappiness than one generates in removing the librarian of a small town or college.

But this rather dramatic aspect of the problem of authority change in libraries may be less important in the long run than the less visible issue of authority change within the modern library staff—and specifically the need to delegate authority or freedom to the increasingly mature professionals whom library schools are attempting to produce and library directors are attempting to hire. These "new breed" librarians of whom we expect so much don't plan to punch time cards for a boss; but to work with a director who is "first among equals."

Drives for faculty status for academic librarians have been going on with varying success for years now, and in situations where open conflict arises, labor unions are being brought in to deal with the administrator as an adversary rather than as a colleague. But there are as yet few signs of creative response by administrators.

True, isolated directors have attempted to democratize their libraries or in other ways to tap staff creativity. The Brooklyn Public Library, for example, is going to try to allow greatly increased freedom to individual branch library units in order to foster a more sensitive response to local conditions. And in the ALA, a token attempt has been made to get junior members on some important committees.

But authority, once won, is hard to relinquish, and as Lear found out, it's a tricky business, for one's own freedom to act (or not to act) may well depend on others being unfree. Maybe administrators need continuing education more than anyone in libraries.

Librarians are not alone in the authority transfer plight; in the nation itself we have seen that the eight years a President can normally expect to stay in power is a long time indeed—and in the generation it may take to drag a Congressional committee into the 20th Century, irremediable harm can be done. The new groups arising in society during the McLuhan instant-tribe age, whether they be racial minorities or just a new generation, will no longer wait patiently for full citizenship, with its attendant freedom and authority; the results, everywhere in society, can be messy.

Change is in itself no news to the library administrator today. He embraces innovations in technique and equipment, sometimes even rashly; he looks forward with enthusiasm to phasing out regiments of clerks, but so far he has looked very little into the qrestion of his own possible obsolescence.

From quite different beginnings, the pendulum has swung far toward the magnification of the head librarian as chief executive, with consequent diminishing of the role of the citizen trustees who are technically his source of power, and with an inhibiting of the stature of the librarian as librarian. Trustees, except for occasional sporadic attempts to turn back the clock, continue to be quiescent in the face of this trend; but librarians are awakening and will be demanding a voice in the running of libraries.

Innovation is not necessarily a blessing, though it is generally hailed as such; the new library computer may be no more progressive than the tanks and bombers supplied to shore up a sagging dictatorship. But libraries, for the first time, have access to research funds and funds to support experiment. With this largesse available, the way is clear to question even the oldest and most respectable assumptions—among them the way in which libraries are organized and the emphasis on the library as an institution rather than on librarianship as a function which may be situated in many environments.

The administrator who experiments boldly in the decentralization of policy-making and the design of library service, to the end of fully liberating the librarians on his staff—and possibly enfranchising the library's public—will tread on uncertain ground and sleep uneasily on many a night. But in the meantime, he won't have any recruitment problems.

*Karl Nyren*

# Labor Unions, Professionalism

## HOW MANY PROFESSIONS?
November 1, 1962

What is a profession? Webster's 71-word definition notwithstanding, the question arises repeatedly. It is one which has bedeviled the individual and collective minds of the followers of many disciplines, librarianship most certainly included.

The question is usually complicated by the fact that, like many a reference inquiry, it doesn't mean exactly what it says. Those who ask it are most often the doubters and the skeptics, unsure of themselves and of their following, and what they really mean is, "Are *we* a profession?"

Let's accept for the moment that librarianship *is* a profession, recognized as such both by its practitioners and those who benefit from its services. For apparently librarianship has passed the first hurdle of self-doubt and has jumped into a new area of confusion.

Today's question might better be phrased: "How many professions are there in a profession?" Or, if you like to personalize it in the manner of the earlier question, "Is librarianship one profession—or many?"

The latest issue of the *SLA Texas Chapter Bulletin* opens with a message from that group's new president, Frank S. Wagner, Jr. Mr. Wagner, who says he is "scarcely a *librarian* and surely not much of a *special librarian*" (his italics), is disturbed at the dearth of students who signed up for an institute on the literature of science and technology offered by the

University of Texas. One reason for this situation, says Mr. Wagner, is that "the importance of *our profession—special librarianship*—has not been made sufficiently clear nor widespread enough."

The italics have been supplied this time, because that phrase, "our profession—special librarianship" is the crux of this editorial.

Is special librarianship a *separate* profession? If it is, what about university librarianship? Or children's librarianship? Or—you name it. Or are these all specialties within *one* profession?

A Special Libraries Association Subcommittee on Library Education in 1950 defined a special librarian as: "A librarian, who by virtue of special interests and talents, chooses to operate in a special discipline, and for that purpose requires a broadened and intensified knowledge of his selected field—*to which he must adapt the library techniques basic to all library practice.*"

Now, not only could this definition be applied to a host of other librarians who specialize within public or university or school libraries—as reference librarians, in cataloging or children's work, as documents librarians, or handlers of A-V materials—but the concluding phrase makes it very clear that SLA, at least, regards librarianship as something whole, and special librarianship as just a segment of the circle.

No one could logically argue against the need or the benefits of specialization within the ranks of a profession which faces the ever more complex demands of an increasingly complex society. But personally, we regret that librarianship has splintered quite as much as it has—to the point where the specialization sometimes seems to obliterate recognition of, or allegiance to any common core of interest.

The real problem, as sociology professor Everett C. Hughes noted during the 1961 Chicago Library School conference ("Seven Questions About the Profession of Librarianship," *Library Quarterly*, Oct. 1961), "is to combine some degree of specialization with some effective understanding of the whole system one operates in." If librarians don't understand the whole, what hope is there that they can communicate an understanding of librarianship to the world around them?

Ask the average layman to name a dozen professions. He'll go through the obvious ones—medicine, teaching, the law, politics, the church—but if he reaches a dozen you're lucky. And if he includes librarianship in that dozen, sing loud hosannahs, because it's a miracle. Most librarians have now reached the point where they recognize their own profession, but the gulf between that and public recognition is wide. There are still, for example, many colleges and universities where librarians are struggling for such tokens of recognition as faculty status.

Let's get one profession duly and publicly acknowledged before we subdivide into half a dozen or more smaller and less significant "professions." Otherwise recognition may be longer arriving than the real library of the twenty-first century.

*Eric Moon*

## THE BROOKLYN GAMBIT
December 1, 1966

On Friday, October 28, the professional librarians of the Brooklyn Public Library voted 188 to 62 to join a union—the AFL–CIO American Federation of State, County, and Municipal Employees. In a separate tabulation, library clerical workers voted 372 to 68 for the union. Union officials predict that in a very short time the New York Public Library and the Queens Borough Public Library, New York's other two major units, will also be organized.

So it looks as though New York will give union methods their first real test in the library world. There has been union activity in a few other cities, but nothing really conclusive has come out of the experience so far. Improvements in working conditions and salary increases are claimed here and there, but there has as yet been no convincing demonstration of the union as an effective power in radically altering the status of librarians. Consequently there has been little serious discussion of the advisability of librarians taking the union road for long-term professional objectives as well as immediate goals. Unionization in New York has two things going for it: large numbers of librarians in a relatively small geographical area, and a climate of opinion notably more favorable to union activity than in most cities.

Brooklyn librarians have already realized their first benefit: a five-hour reduction in their work week, from 40 to 35, a measure instituted not very subtly by all three city libraries shortly before the union election. The union's plans for additional gains are ambitious: across the board raises averaging $1600 for each librarian; a telescoping of the five-step salary scale to three steps, with annual raises; time and a half for overtime (they now get compensatory time off); union approval for all changes in job assignments, particularly as applied to hours worked and location of job, with a strict seniority rule to be followed in awarding "job pick"; and a schedule of additional salary benefits or wage differentials for educational qualifications.

Barring this last, the only area so far mentioned in which librarians have shown interest in the union as a means of improving library service is in keeping open all branch libraries during the summer. The possibility has been raised of fighting this battle by demonstrations, picketing, resort to mass media publicity, and even a strike as a means of keeping the libraries open. But even this concern has an immediate dollar value, as it would undoubtedly result in substantial amounts of overtime pay.

In recent years, social workers, engineers, architects, psychologists, and accountants on government payrolls have experimented with unions, as have teachers; librarians coming to this particular crossroad will not in any sense be entering undiscovered territory, but they will be making momentous decisions about the future of their profession.

Some of the stated objectives in Brooklyn seem in conflict with the ideas and aims of many library administrators. These are not necessarily the same thing, although it may be suspiciously hard to distinguish them. The extent to which behavior regulated by the Code of Ethics works to the advantage of the public and for the convenience of library officials, but at the expense of the individual librarian is a moot point. For example, professional behavior includes working 50 to 60 hours a week if the situation demands it, as we expect a physician to stay with his scalpel if an operation lasts somewhat beyond his expected working day. On the other hand, librarians are scarcely free to take off for a research project, let alone the golf course, on a quiet day.

The seniority provisions of most union arrangements will certainly conflict with administrative powers, but seniority customs which have grown up in many of our big city libraries have often been criticized as stifling the growth of new talent. As the number of independent library units decreases and libraries follow the trend to membership in large systems, the free wheeling mobility which has often made possible the rapid growth of individual careers may well become a thing of the past.

Two hard facts stand out at last: No other course of action is very likely to increase library salaries immediately and substantially; against this fact we have to point out that although truck drivers make a lot more money today than they did 30 years ago, they are still truck drivers. The question is fairly before us for debate, but it may well be answered pragmatically in Brooklyn.

*Karl Nyren*

## A MATTER OF REPUTATION
January 15, 1967

Within the last two months, the professional reputation of the public librarian of a large city, and that of the librarian of a major state university have been at stake, while their professional behavior was being tried in the courts of local opinion, often on a level little higher than gossip, or decided by an arbitrary and unexplained executive ruling. These unfortunate circumstances come all too infrequently to the attention of the people whom they most concern—the members of the library profession—except as rumor and questionable oral history at conventions.

For though librarians are reputed to be a timid breed, a fair number of them get into trouble. They run afoul of politicians, citizens with vested interests in the past, college faculty members, school superintendents, state library authorities, and of course, other librarians. In a fair number of cases, an individual is in conflict with a restrictive environment, which cannot tolerate creativity or even energy. Doubtless, there are other cases in which the librarian is guilty of poor judgment or worse. In librarianship as in other professions, the ways in which these conflicts are handled are of import to all members of the profession.

When a librarian leaves a university or a municipality under a cloud which casts its shadow ambiguously on all the principals involved, everyone must suffer. If innocent, the librarian may suffer unjust and irreparable damage to his career. The institution he leaves—and its officers—suffer from a vague stain which will affect morale and hinder recruitment at all levels, regardless of guilt or innocence on any one officer's part. The public which the library serves is the loser in the long run.

We have had proposals for the establishment of a fund and the development of a nationwide corps of legal talent which could move "advisers" swiftly into any situation threatening intellectual freedom in libraries. The proposals look even more sensible when we realize the values of extending this pattern of response to other problems. The investigation of situations involving the behavior of both librarians and the officials who hire and fire them is a highly appropriate area of activity for a professional association. It is eminently to the credit of any profession that it police its own house as well as support its own members. Two current cases in point are those of Hugh Montgomery, librarian of the University of Massachusetts, recently demoted from his position; and Guenter Jansen, who has just resigned from the New Orleans public library under a storm of abuse from one high ranking political figure.

Montgomery, after 15 years direction of the growing library facilities of the University of Massachusetts, was suddenly reassigned to a minor research job and his former authority given to an assistant professor in the philosophy department. University officials have refused to respond to Montgomery's charges of unfair and precipitous treatment, and have further refused to discuss the matter either with a staff committee, a group of librarians from neighboring institutions, the Massachusetts Library Association, or the press. We hold no brief for either Montgomery or the university, but we note that he has sought to bring the issue into the open, while the university has claimed that its actions are subject to review by no one. One cannot help but wonder what kind of librarians the university thinks it can recruit either for Montgomery's position or as replacements for those other members of the staff who are already seeking new positions elsewhere.

Guenter Jansen, director of the New Orleans public library since 1965, has just resigned after a three months trial by newspaper. During this period the president of the city council brought charges against him ranging from malfeasance in handling money to improper use of federal funds. With a board of trustees that distinguished itself frequently by intemperate behavior, alternately threatening and supporting the librarian, it is impossible to tell what the truth of the situation is in this city, which has had a singularly high rate of mortality among its library directors. Until this truth is established, the claims of two million residents to decent library service rest on the whimsical sands of chance.

An authoritative review by a blue ribbon group of library leaders could do for both New Orleans and the University of Massachusetts what they cannot seem to do for themselves. Whatever the form adopted, the creation of a professional mechanism for defense and evaluation is a proposal worth reopening.

*Karl Nyren*

### ETHICAL BONES
January 15, 1968

"Let us have done with the meaningless codes of ethics that only ponderously restate the Ten Commandments," says Samuel Rothstein in this issue (p. 156). Apply Rothstein's "test of opposites," and that statement seems to us clearly undebatable. There is little to be gained from further fire at the old *Code of Ethics for Librarians;* it is a flimsy target, already in tatters from neglect and the winds of time.

Something, however, *is* needed, and whether it be called a definition of the librarian's ethos or a new code of ethics is perhaps only a semantic quibble. What is essential is that it get to grips with realities and that some mechanism be devised for making it effective. The profession does have ethical questions to grapple with and should find a way to formulate a position on some of them.

For example, what about the librarian's relationship to the library patron? Is anything the librarian knows of the patron through their service relationship "privileged" information—as in the case of the minister and his parishioner, the doctor or lawyer and his client, the reporter and his sources?

The question becomes particularly pertinent when one considers the impact of automation and its potential for massive invasion of privacy. Not only the computer but also other charging systems in existence make it possible for the librarian now to construct a complete profile of his patron's reading habits.

This is no idle theoretical question. The FBI used what they found out about Oswald's reading at the New Orleans Public Library to help build the circumstantial evidence against him—to establish, at least, an indication of prior intent through his interest in presidential assassinations and related subjects.

To cite a different kind of example, Henry M. Wriston reveals in *Academic Procession: Reflections of a College President* (Columbia University Press, 1959, pages 133–5) that, as president of Lawrence College: "I joined with the librarian in a long and rather complex study of the books borrowed by faculty members, both in quantity and quality. . . ." He used what he found out in this manner as one way of assessing the quality of his faculty as scholars and teachers. From what he says subsequently and on the basis of his public record, it is clear that Wriston's motives were good ones. But what if a college president with bad motives, in a heat-period like the McCarthy era, used the same technique?

A quite different area in which ethical questions galore arise is the booming consultant business. One expects that a professional will devote a good deal of his time and energy to the affairs of his profession, and that his governing authority will play its part by releasing him when necessary to so participate. But to what extent do the ethical rules of the game change when the librarian is operating what in some cases is a substantial business on the side (from which he may well earn much more than his salary), for which he is inevitably going to use much of the time and creative energy for which his authority hired him and for which it pays him?

A third area, growing fast but thus far all but ignored by ALA, is the increasing influence of unions in libraries. Without making judgments about whether this is a desirable or dangerous development, it is clear that ignoring the phenomenon will not drive it away. The growth of labor unions in libraries will bring about the same kind of soul-searching that has beset teachers and other professionals in recent years, particularly in relation to the strike weapon. *Is* it ethical for librarians to strike? And if not, why not? It's another ethical bone to chew on.

A fourth area, not perhaps as significant as the others above, but relevant because of the profession's broadcast position on intellectual freedom, concerns the ethics of administrators who prevent or at least wield some kind of veto power over public expression of opinion by their staff members. This may not be too prevalent, but we *have* had contributions from people who ask that their name, position, or library not be used because the article or letter has not been "cleared." Another aspect of this latent tendency toward suppression was seen when some members of the profession wanted action taken against Daniel Gore because he had dared to speak critically of librarianship outside the walls of our association temples.

Yes, Dr. Rothstein, there are real, live ethical questions to be resolved by the library profession. The need is to get down to some specifics.

*Eric Moon*

## PROFESSIONAL POLARIZATION
April 1, 1968

As the news columns of this journal have amply demonstrated, the growth of labor unions in U.S. librarianship is accelerating rapidly. Thus far, the union movement seems to have stretched no very firm tentacles across into Canadian librarianship but an equally militant and potentially powerful movement is well under way north of the border.

There are now three professional librarians' associations in Canada: the Association of British Columbia Librarians (ABCL), the Institute of Victoria Librarians (IVL), and—the pioneer in this movement—the Institute of Professional Librarians of Ontario (IPLO). A fourth such association is brewing in Quebec, and a fifth may not be too terribly far away for the Atlantic Provinces.

Differences—some subtle, some major—exist between the U.S. library unions and the Canadian professional associations, but the similarities are striking. Both movements, for example, are blowing the bugle of "professionalism" or "professionalization" loud and clear. Eldred Smith ("Librarians and Labor Unions," *LJ*, February 15, pp. 717–20) declares that "it is through union activity alone that the professionalization of librarianship seems posible." An editorial in the journal of the Association of the British Columbia Librarians (*ABCL Newsletter,* Winter 1968, p. 2) expounds on "Polarization of Professionalism." Those who harbor the cosy belief that professional associations are likely to be less militant and absolute in their views and aims than labor unions should read Lawrence A. Leaf, editor of the *ABCL Newsletter.* Here are some of his predictions:

"Within the not too distant future progressive-minded civic administrations will turn over the entire operations of the public libraries to their chief librarians, thus eliminating the 'fifth wheel' of civic government, the local library boards, which are a carry-over from the past and whose present role has diminished to that of a civic rubber stamp . . .

"Along with the dissolution of the lay boards who, like the PTA, are finding it increasingly difficult to justify their existence, will be the gradual fading out of the non-professional library associations." Later in the column, Leaf adds that "increased reliance by library users on librarian/information specialists will automatically make the informal non-professional library associations obsolete."

Another predicted casualty is "at the provincial level, the present Public Library Commission" which "will eventually be replaced by a senior advisory group comprised solely of professional library specialists who will have a much stronger voice in initiating and guiding well-researched, carefully planned, and experimentally sound, innovative public library programmes and services throughout the province."

All of this "polarization," Leaf asserts, will lead to "the disappearance of short-sighted parochialism." It won't all happen "overnight," he says, but he does name the doomsday date: "During the 1970's a very significant number of librarians schooled in the rigid and restrictive traditionalism of the 1930's will be retiring. It is during this period that many dramatic changes will take place in the entire field of librarianship."

The process of "polarization," as described by Leaf, apparently leading to total "professional" control of library service and librarianship at virtually every level, is a highly questionable goal. There is, for one thing, no solid evidence that people who call themselves professional are *necessarily* less parochial than the rest of mankind. To hand over to one professional group the determination of society's information needs (and the degree and manner in which they shall be met) seems to us as dubious a proposition as that all civilian controls upon the military be relinquished, or that all decisions concerning the protection of the public health be left to the American Medical Association (goodbye Medicare!).

What sounds a little like extremism or power-hunger, however, may be no more than the kind of overexuberance to which young organizations are prone. These new groups—the unions in the U.S., the professional associations in Canada—seem destined to grow and multiply as long as they can cash in on the discontent with the present, traditional *library* associations. The new groups have a strong appeal for the individual professional, particularly the young and those below the administrator level, many of whom feel that the traditional associations have lost sight of the individual in their concern for the *institution* of librarianship. Whether they are right or not, unless the present library associations adjust (as they seem to show little sign of doing), at least some of Mr. Leaf's dire predictions may well come to pass. .

*Eric Moon*

## THE WASSERMAN-BUNDY ANALYSIS
April 15, 1968

It is cause for rejoicing when something new is said, and Paul Wasserman and Mary Lee Bundy have said it in the January issue of *College and Research Libraries*. Their article, "Professionalism Reconsidered," is that rare and lovely thing, a fresh synthesis of the shopworn terms with which an important but imperfectly understood problem has been worried for year after year. The Wasserman-Bundy analysis is simple and elegant, and one wonders why it took so long for someone to bring it forward.

In "Professionalism Reconsidered," the authors attack the muddled problem of how to take librarianship over the quantum jump from the status of a craft to the status of a profession, a necessary but appalling task, considering that most librarians are still at best good technicians, most library education is still designed to train technicians, and most library staffs are administered and organized on the assumption that librarians are indeed not professional people. Contributing to these unfortunate conditions, say Wasserman and Bundy, there is the American Library Association, potentially the most effective weapon for achieving professionalism, but actually in large measure an organization of administrators, to whom librarians are essentially "employees."

The Wasserman-Bundy analysis organizes these painful symptoms into a conceptual framework that is exciting both as a diagnosis and as a ground plan for intelligent debate and action. For it is the interplay of all the factors, and not any single bugbear of incompetence or ill will that must set the terms of any successful struggle to achieve professionalism for librarians and the evolution of library science into the discipline which modern society needs it to become.

Taken individually, the Wasserman-Bundy charges are neither new nor debatable. They call, not for argument, but perhaps for documentation of the facts: what librarians do; how they are educated; how they are being treated by their administrators. After a benchmark of fact is established, the logical next step should be the identification and support of the people, courses, schools, and libraries which are doing something now toward achieving professionalization. A corollary is the stern necessity of identifying and discouraging bad practice and bad practitioners in whatever exalted position they may be found.

There is the cat, one says, and there is the bell, and who is to tie one to the other? The answer, we believe, is that this is no bell-and-cat problem, no struggle of a splinter faction against an entrenched majority. For most librarians desire the evolution of their profession and share a deep disquiet at the lack of terms for a new consensus of change.

Changes themselves we have in abundance today, as Wasserman and Bundy point out—but they can lead us as easily to a further de-professionalization of librarianship as to creative evolution. Among these changes: whole new library systems are being created; information science is becoming a reality; a permanent national library commission, national library network, and national research facility are soon to be created; librarians are experimenting with unions and activist professional groups; and money is at last beginning to flow into the research that *should* create the philosophical foundations of this emerging profession.

A good place to start, whether one be administrator, librarian, educator, or student, is with the Wasserman-Bundy article. It should be read and discussed at every level and its concepts kept firmly in mind as a basic guide to what ALA should be doing, what the Division of Library Service and Educational Facilities should be doing, what the Council on Library Resources should be doing—and what one should be doing oneself.

In his acceptance speech at San Francisco last summer, ALA President Foster E. Mohrhardt deplored the use of the major national library association for an ever expanding list of specialized problem-solving chores; when librarians come together in conclave, he suggested, they should deal with matters of vital concern to *all* of them. The issue of professionalization, as redefined by Wasserman and Bundy, can provide the organizing concept within which "manpower," "standards," "ethics," "intellectual freedom," "technician training," "accreditation," and almost all the other features of the contemporary landscape of librarianship can at last be meaningfully discussed.

No new division, office, or committee is called for. This is what the American Library Association should be all about.

*Karl Nyren*


## THE UNION QUESTION
November 1, 1968

The question of the relevance of labor unions to librarians in achieving their personal and professional goals is coming closer daily. In this issue, *LJ* takes note of this pressing question in several ways: on the cover, the successfully militant ladies of the Contra Costra County Library in California; inside, the Contra Costa strike is described in one article; a second raises a strong voice against labor union affiliation of librarians (it proposes instead more militant professional associations, another current theme).

In addition, *LJ*'s news columns contain still another of the union stories which it has reported with growing frequency during 1968—a total of 12 stories, totaling 112 column inches—all adding something to the documentation of this new area.

The union question got a preliminary, if abortive, hearing at the ALA Conference in Kansas City (*LJ*, August, p. 2812); it was the subject of a survey of attitudes of library directors published in September's *ALA Bulletin;* and it will be the subject of a program at the next ALA Conference in Atlantic City. It is a question which needs all the examination it can get—an examination free from the increasingly quaint formulas of both left and right which are still being used to justify or condemn the union movement. Union membership should be debated, not in the abstract, but in the specific terms of its possible impact on libraries and librarians.

For unions are coming, all right—make no mistake about that, though it will not happen everywhere overnight, as it did in New York City, where all public library employees below a certain high supervisory level are now represented by the American Federation of State, County, and Municipal Employees—and this was brought about by the simple means of a majority vote of the city's library employees to engage AFSCME as their agency in dealing with the library administration and with the municipal fiscal authorities.

This used to be illegal, but new state laws have made it permissible in many states already for public employees to engage in collective bargaining. And the white collar unions, the fastest growing area of union power, are exploiting this whole new area of opportunity with vigor. Librarians will not be neglected.

Trends encouraged by librarians will hasten the process: the increasing numbers of nonprofessionals being developed for library service—clerks, technicians, library aides; the tendency to consolidate library agencies into large units; the impatience of the growing numbers of young graduate librarians with arthritic departmental structures of many large libraries. The union as weapon and as protection has a poignant appeal in many quarters today.

Of course, the blue collar hue of the union movement, a color which seems fast however often it is dipped in the affairs of teachers, actors, and their ilk, causes many a librarian to gag, and may for all our cerebration be the most important determinant in how librarians choose to decide on unions. Not all, fortunately, share this strange distaste; the librarian concerned with making live contact with his community would often prefer to be identified with a blue collar than with an antimacassar. For though the machinist and plumber and policeman have rather effectively moved into the middle class, it is not quite the same middle class upon which libraries have depended and which they have served. The nonuser problem in many new suburbs may be as acute as it is in the inner city, and through unions, common ground may be found with many of these owners of lawnmowers and color TV, but not books.

But there are counter-indications which should also be weighed. These

have been signs of a deepening alienation between the rank and file of labor
and the "liberal" causes with which they have traditionally been associated.
Much of Governor Wallace's strength at this writing is coming from union
members. Unions are increasingly out of sympathy with the black American
—not only on the assembly line, but rather shockingly in the schools as well.
New York City's exciting venture in restoring pride to a community by
giving it control of its schools is foundering right now because decentralization threatens the power of the United Federation of Teachers.

And this may well point to the most likely ground for the rejection of
unions—their incompatibility with social change and experiment.

*Karl Nyren*

## Associations

### POTENTIAL FOR POWER
September 1, 1960

An editorial in a midwestern newspaper some months ago welcomed
the nation's Young Democrats to the city. In doing so the editorial commented: "We not only welcome you, Young Democrats, but we also extend
to you our deepest sympathy. Why won't the Old Democrats let you grow
up? Why are you discriminated against, segregated into a perpetually
juvenile branch, kept in political short pants?"

One librarian who read this editorial said: "I've always felt this way
about ALA's Junior Members Round Table and never joined, even when I
was eligible. Nobody over 14 should want to belong to a group labeled
Junior anything."

We do not go along altogether with these comments, but must admit to
some grave misgivings about the Junior Members Round Table in its
present state. As an organization it has been in existence nearly 30 years.
What has it ever achieved?

Its declared purpose is "to help the individual member to orient himself
in the library profession and in its organization . . . to promote a greater
feeling of responsibility among younger members of the profession for the
development of library service and librarianship; and to inform young
people of the scope and potentialities of the library profession," the latter
mainly through cooperation with recruiting agencies. These objectives may
be laudable: to us they seem at once nebulous and dull. There is little in
them to stimulate the imagination or excite the enthusiasm of the young, less
that appeals for independence of thought and action, or makes demands
upon the potential energy and vitality that should be the most valuable
product our young librarians have to offer the library service and the profession.

We suspect that those who set up this organization and supported it in the beginning might have had an important and undeclared objective, or at least a hope—that the Round Table might reveal so much earlier the "coming" young men and women in the profession, the future leaders. We know that a number of senior members of the profession are disappointed that the Round Table has not fulfilled this hope to any noticeable degree.

There is, in our view, a reason for this failure, and it is perhaps best revealed by a comparison of the Round Table with the English Association of Assistant Librarians. This latter group, an official section of the (British) Library Association since 1929, and before that an independent organization, has been variously described as "an anomaly," "a ginger group," and in other less savory terms. But you would be hard put to find more than a sour minority who would dismiss the AAL as irresponsible, and there are few who would advocate its abolition.

This group is represented on all the important committees and on the Council of the parent body, and it wields tremendous influence and power. It has on occasion wielded that power by bringing together its forces (about two-thirds of the total voting strength of the Library Association) to overthrow the dictates and decisions of the elder statesmen. Sometimes it has been wrong; more often than not, it has shown greater wisdom than has been apparent on higher levels.

The weakness of the Junior Members Round Table is that it does not have the AAL's potential for power. It does not have a strong local or regional organization; it is not represented in the inner conclaves where it can have influence upon the more important activities of the association. There must be angry, or at least dissatisfied, young men (and women) in the library profession. A vital junior organization should provide avenues for the constructive use of the energy generated by that anger or dissatisfaction. It will not happen while younger librarians are herded into a "dolly" organization where they may play, but where guns are forbidden.

*Eric Moon*

## CLEVELAND TOPICS

June 15, 1961

What will 5,000-odd librarians be talking about at the Cleveland conference of ALA? The pocket being a more sensitive area than either heart or head, it is relatively certain that the hotel corridors will be steadily buzzing with comment on the proposal to increase membership dues. Despite the determined efforts in recent issues of the *ALA Bulletin* to present this proposal in a soft rose-colored light, it seems that some members see a more violent red. The meeting at which the proposal will be presented promises to be a less placid affair than usual.

We are impressed, incidentally, with the daring of the *Bulletin* editor's declaration that "every letter on this question . . . will be published." Evidently, it is not expected that a very large percentage of the 25,000 ALA members will write—if they do, the deluge will demand a special issue or a retraction.

The Midwinter meeting gave notice that the Council may expect considerable debate over the question of which divisions should be responsible for the evaluation and selection of library materials. This does seem to be something of a storm in a teacup, however, and common sense and a less proprietorial attitude on the part of some divisions should lead to some fairly simple answers.

You can expect to see small clutches of catalogers—and an occasional reference librarian—discussing, in the bars and other informal meeting places, some of the finer points of catalog code revision. Perhaps cocktail conviviality will widen these small circles to take in a stray library administrator or two, and maybe a branch librarian or school librarian to lend a certain earthiness to the proceedings.

One of the most pleasing features of the Cleveland program is the day in the sun which is being accorded to the small public library. Three large-scale meetings of the Public Library Association are to be devoted to the problems of "The Small Public Library in the Jet Age."

Last year, in our report on the Montreal conference, we said: "The platform performances left all too little time for discussion. Audience participation is valuable. It is the thing we missed most." The Resources and Technical Services Division appears to share these sentiments, and for Cleveland its Acquisitions Section has planned a meeting at which provision is made for 22 different groups to discuss acquisitions in such varied areas as microforms, paperbacks, documents, Latin-American materials, out-of-print books, etc., etc. There should be something here for everyone, including—as the program now stands—a welcome absence of prepared papers.

We shall await with great interest the report of the National Library Week Evaluation Committee. The variety of opinions expressed in many letters on National Library Week received by *LJ* since the Allan Angoff article in our April issue (*see* p. 1364), persuade us to hope for a constructively critical report which will strengthen NLW activities in the years ahead.

Although the tentative program (at the time this is written) includes no mention of the Intellectual Freedom Committee, we hope that we shall hear, or that the membership will ask for, some report on such recent events as the sit-in at the Jackson (Miss.) Public Library (*see LJ*, May 1, pp. 1750–1) and the "smut-mobile" censorship activities in Oklahoma City (*see Publishers' Weekly*, April 17, pp. 35–6).

Finally, in any conference program there are always those titles of papers which intrigue but do not inform. We admit to curiosity about a paper being delivered at a meeting of the Reference Services Division. It is entitled "The Gaiety of Library Life." That it is being given by a newspaperman only adds to the intriguing possibilities.

*Eric Moon*

## "FIRST" THOUGHTS
August 1962

More than once during the meetings at Miami Beach, senior librarians, reminiscing about their initiation into the fine art of conventioneering, remarked that their first conference had not been an entirely happy experience. Exciting and memorable, yes; but happy, no.

"No one talked to us," said one librarian. "My first library conference was such a blow, I didn't go back again for 15 years," said another. These honest confessions were meant for the aid and comfort of the 1962 crop of first-timers who were enthusiastic about attending the profession's big event of the season, but were feeling more than a little lost in the immensity of it all. Conference "blues" are suffered, it seems, by everyone at least once in his convention-going career.

How *does* the newcomer fare at his first conference? What does he expect of it? Does it live up to expectations? A first-timer ourselves, we were interested in the reactions of fellow initiates.

The junior librarian, although still very much in the minority at the annual conference, is, however, beginning to appear on the scene and to make his presence felt. And it was apparent—from the meetings held during the week—that the Association, too, has become aware of the junior librarian and is concerned about how he fares—both at his first conference and on his home ground.

One meeting, sponsored by the Junior Members Round Table in cooperation with the ALA Membership Committee, was designed to orient the first-timer and guide him through the conference maze. It was a good meeting and a helpful one for the neophyte. We hope it will become a regular part of future conference programs.

Another meeting was designed to explore the "life and times" of the junior librarian from the standpoint of the library administrator and the educator; and considered, in turn, the views of the junior librarian on library education, the library profession, and library associations. Both meetings are covered in some detail in our conference report in this issue.

The first-timers we met at Miami Beach were intense, eager, enthusiastic, attractive representatives of the profession. They considered themselves fortunate, as indeed they were, to have been sent to this big, expensive affair, and they took their responsibility to the "folks back home" with a splendid seriousness. They were also aware of a responsibility to themselves, to their own professional growth. They were concerned for the future—their own and the profession's. And they were vocal—on this and other subjects—in discussion periods and post-mortem sessions.

They were hard workers—as most seasoned convention-goers are—attending meetings on a 14-hour a day schedule. They came to listen to those at the top; to learn new methods and explore new theories; and to take a first-hand look at the men and machinery that run the association.

Did the conference live up to expectations? It was rewarding and frustrating as most conferences are. There were star-studded panels, lively business sessions, and dull program meetings. And the first-timer learns from them all. He also learns that one of the greatest things in a convention is, as Paul Dunkin once said, "not the Talks but the talk." Off-the-cuff talks in aisles and corridors, at receptions and parties—talk with new people, talk about new ideas.

And there were complaints, complaints we have heard before from hardened convention-goers. The conference is too big and the individual—especially the newcomer—is lost. The schedule of meetings is awesome and the "Great Men" are pitted one against the other like TV extravaganzas, programed at the same time but on different networks. And there is never enough time—before, after, and during meetings—for discussion.

But despite the devastating schedule and the recurring loneliness, this first-timer, like most others, was glad she came and hopes to come again next year.

*Shirley Havens*

## ONE WORLD
September 15, 1962

Most of us, though we are loathe to admit it, live in little worlds from whose snug physical and mental limits we do not often stray. From where *we* sit, for example, the universe seems to be made up of, well, libraries, revolving about, if you will, us. We are always a trifle shocked when at gatherings not related to our work we discover people talking about things other than libraries. And when, a bit nervously, we bring the conversation round to libraries just to assure ourselves that all is really right with the world, we are frequently dismayed again to find that nobody there is much equipped to discuss libraries, or even care to.

We are aware of (though not yet resigned to) the fact that most non-library-world people couldn't care less. After all, they have their own little worlds to worry about. They have their own ends. But when we see the spirit of isolation creep *within* a single group, a group that in structure and purpose has but one end—and a library group at that—we have reason to become uneasy.

We have, in fact, been justly uneasy for quite some time. For from our perhaps-lucky perch in the center of library things, we have seen that librarians, like everyone else, are disinclined to cross the borders of their own little specialty groups.

Nowhere was this sad channeling of interests more ironically pointed up than at the ALA conference in Miami Beach when some 4000 librarians gathered, presumably for the purpose of discussing librarianship together. The great eager horde amassed itself at convention headquarters, then promptly split into hundreds and hundreds of tiny groups, thus defeating the very purpose for which it had assembled. And all week long these tiny groups worked hard repeating one another, side by side (sometimes in adjacent rooms), but not together.

What an enormous waste of opportunity! What an unfortunate loss of energy and time! There is no reason, it seems to us, why, especially at ALA conventions, we cannot discuss the larger problems of librarianship *en masse*.

In our daydreams, for example, we imagine ourselves at an ALA convention. We are part of a big, general discussion group whose topic is Recruitment. In attandance are children's librarians, school librarians, college librarians, research librarians, special librarians, all conceivable kinds of librarians, and even some people who are not librarians. We are having an exceedingly fruitful discussion.

In a similar daydream, we imagine oursleves at a meeting on The Student Problem. Again all kinds of librarians are present, and again we are having a richly varied multiple view of the problem as it really exists all over. And, because we are all there to talk about it together, we are actually finding solutions!

Not only have we tended too often to cleave to our own small groups, with Donne-defying determination we sometimes cleave unto our very selves. Given the unequalled chance at an ALA convention to exchange professional views, how many of us do it?

How many of us use the opportunity to meet new people, people who are not only new to us but who (ah, the nerve!) work in a phase of librarianship that is different from our own? How many of us go to the general sessions and to the council meetings which are open to all? How many of us raise our hand in a meeting to air a grievance or make a point?

We are happy to note that new ALA president James Bryan is a man with a message that promises to make our wildest daydreams come true. In his inaugural address at Miami Beach, President Bryan said, ". . . despite the fact that we are by employment public librarians, college and university librarians, school librarians and special librarians, let us turn our attention to what in effect is the library system. . . . We are in fact a system of libraries and we must start getting used to the idea." Mr. Bryan also opined that we must begin thinking of ourselves, "not as catalogers, reference workers or children's specialists, but as *librarians*." Realist Bryan has sounded a mighty clarion call. It has a strong, sweet, compelling tone and we should all do well to heed it.

*Ellen Rudin*

## A NATIONAL ORGANIZATION OR A PRIVATE CLUB?
April 1, 1963

Ralph Ellsworth, author of the lead article in this issue, contributed a paper to *Library Quarterly* in October 1961 which purported to be a "Critique of Library Associations in America." That article spent much of its steam blasting the complex bureaucracy of ALA. By comparison with this muscle-bound giant, Ellsworth seemed to find the Association of Research Libraries (ARL) a smooth-moving and altogether productive and healthy pygmy.

"When ARL wants to work on a project, they can pick the right men, go to the problem directly, and get the job done," said Ellsworth. He tells how ARL was established years ago "because the libraries of large universities and other research libraries did not want to waste their time and efforts with the machinery of the ALA."

Despite this glowing testimonial from Ellsworth, ARL was not satisfied with itself. In a statement that same year, ARL declared that, as it was then constituted—"both because of limited membership and operational restrictions"—it could not "speak for research libraries."

As a result, we have seen within the past year the incorporation of ARL, its appointment of a full-time executive secretary and establishment of a Washington headquarters, and most recently, a considerable extension in its membership. It can now be said to have acquired the basic impedimenta of a *national* organization, and, in fact, its membership now comprises representation of most of the major library collections in the country.

In his *Library Quarterly* article, Ellsworth said that "the lure of having a small exclusive club may have been a factor" in the formation of ARL. In the *UCLA Librarian* about a year ago, Robert Vosper (now chairman of ARL) commented: "Since its founding in 1932, ARL has been in intention a philosophical discussion forum for the chief librarians of the nation's largest research libraries. In some public opinion it has been but a private club for those gentlemen."

Now, the question: "Is ARL a national organization or is it still a private club?" We believe it is the former, but it seems to lack the confidence to believe it itself, and in some ways still operates out of a private club mentality.

At Chicago we walked into the ARL meeting and asked whether the association would reconsider its customary policy of excluding the press. We did this, not because we are short of copy or because we thought we might uncover some skeletons in the ARL closet, but because we share Ellsworth's opinion that this is an organization that has done things and looks as though it may do more. And, although ARL has acted primarily on behalf of research libraries, we feel that the results of some of its work have really had a resounding effect on American librarianship as a whole.

The result of the request was that, later that night, we were advised to look in the Library of Congress *Information Bulletin* for a report on the ARL meeting. The advice was, we are sure, well-intentioned and meant to be helpful, but *anyone* should know that advising an editor to look in another publication for his copy is like holding up a red rag to a bull. We did not react with great joy, but did allow ourselves time to simmer down before writing this editorial.

We think ARL *is* a national organization. We also believe it should act like one, and allow the press to report freely on its activities. It has nothing to fear from the press while it remains as active and constructive as it has been, and if it lapses into the kind of bureaucracy which Ellsworth deplores in some other asociations, we shall have far less interest in reporting its activities anyway.

Libraries and librarians, in the twentieth century, are in the communications business. ARL has much to be proud of, but it is time it started letting the rest of the library world in on the story.

*Eric Moon*

## DYNAMIC INACTION
October 15, 1963

"To begin with, in the opinion of this committee, the American Library Association has not for some time fulfilled the objectives stated in its charter. It has not represented the profession as a whole for many years; it has not exchanged views with other associations in the field; it has not induced cooperation to any great extent." This was published in 1949, in the Music Library Association's *Notes: Supplement for Members No. 9.* Much has happened since this was written, both to the ALA and the MLA. The situation has so changed that if you reread the quotation, substituting *Music Library Association for American Library Association,* you could not arrive at a better description of the present state of the organization that so adamantly censured the ALA.

The MLA does not represent the interests of those music librarians serving in public libraries, it is not interested in representing these librarians, and it no longer even pretends to take an interest in their needs. Is this wrong? Not necessarily. It is only wrong if the rest of the library profession assumes that the MLA is more than an association of music specialists. The interests of the MLA, vital as they may be to the musicologist and the academic music librarian, do not encompass the musical needs of all libraries, or even most libraries.

Just how far removed the MLA is from the rest of the library world was brought home to me by an incident regarding their American Music History Project, which, among other things, is to include an extensive series of recordings. This important project should be of vital concern to anyone interested in American culture. In planning the *LJ* record issues, it occurred to me that the Project should be fully reported in these pages. When I suggested that the Chairman of the Project Committee prepare an article, his reply was less than lukewarm. He brought up "the matter of appropriateness," and said that "there is nothing to report except a plan, and I don't know how interesting this would be to *LJ* readers." At the moment, it seems, "the Project is in a state of what might be called dynamic inaction."

This is very sad, for it indicates that the MLA knows very little of what does interest the general library profession. The MLA does not realize that it can never achieve its aims unless it learns to communicate its ideas to other librarians. It either does not know, or does not care, that for many years we have assumed that it has been tending to our needs, when actually it has hardly been aware of our needs, or even its own potential for leadership and service.

There has always been a close association between the MLA and the staff of the Music Division of the Library of Congress. LC's Music Division staff has worked long and hard both for the Association and its publication *Notes;* but the MLA has become too much a mirror of what "music librarianship" consists of in the large research institution—it is too untypical.

One of the main tasks of a national association of music librarians should be to find ways and means of seeing that music services achieve their proper place in every library, large and small. It cannot ignore its responsibility to provide guidance to those nonspecialists working in small and medium-sized libraries throughout the land. It is through these libraries that our profession can contribute, as no other profession can, to the development of musical culture.

The isolation of the MLA has been entirely detrimental to the development of the concept of "music librarianship," and more tragic, has hindered the improvement of music services in public libraries.

*Gordon Stevenson, Guest Editor*

## CONSTITUTIONAL RITES
March 1, 1965

A very funny thing happened, not on the way to the forum, but right inside that forum known as the ALA Council, during the Midwinter ALA meeting in Washington.

A motion from the floor, which effectively changed and narrowed a resolution adopted by the membership last July, led to a disagreement, not for the first time, between the ALA president and the parliamentarian who was on the platform to see that the meeting held to rules of order.

Simply put, the argument was whether the Council could or could not overthrow a membership decision. The parliamentarian said it could not. The president asserted that the Council was the policy-making body and therefore could set what policy it liked. There was a scurry around the platform and through the Constitution and By-laws, with the net result that the president's decision seemed to be affirmed.

Some members were unhappy about this, and so were we. But we are no more habitual Constitution readers than most people, so we took a closer look at the document on our return to the office. What does it say?

Well, first it does say that "The Council . . . shall be the governing body of the Association," and that "The Council shall determine all policies of the Association, and its decisions shall be binding upon the Association, *except as provided in Section 4 (c) of this Article*" (our italics here and in subsequent paragraphs).

That Section 4 (c) declares: "Any action of the Council may be set aside by a *three-fourths vote* at any meeting of the Association, *or by a majority vote by mail* in which one-fourth of the members of the Association have voted. Such vote by mail shall be held upon petition of 200 members of the Association."

One further Section of this Article should be quoted to fill out the picture. Section 4 (a) says: "The Association by a vote at a meeting held during an annual conference may *refer* any matter to the Council *with recommendations* and may require the Council to report on such matter at any specified session of the Association."

This all presents an intriguing picture. We had thought, and we suspect others may have shared our naïveté, that a vote by a majority of the members at the annual membership meeting (the only time each year when the individual member has a direct voice in the affairs of the Association) presented the Council with an obligation to carry out their wishes.

Based on what happened at Washington and on our reading of these paragraphs of the Constitution, this is not so. What 51 percent (or even 74 percent) of the members vote for at the annual meeting can, in fact, be overturned by the 150 or so members of the Council. Then, if the Council takes the matter back to the membership, it requires 75 percent of those present at the annual meeting to reinstate what the membership asked for the first time. In other words, the original 51 percent (or even 74 percent) favoring a certain proposition can now be frustrated by a minority of 26 percent of the membership.

We are, as some of our readers may know, in favor of the utmost protection of minority rights, but we believe majorities (even simple majorities) have some rights too. The only protection afforded them by the ALA Constitution, as we read it, is the mail vote—which is very rarely used. In fact, in five years or so, we have never seen it used in ALA for other than elections. Perhaps the lesson of Washington is that members (it takes only 200 to ask for it) should use this avenue more diligently.

*Eric Moon*


## FUSION NOT FISSION
December 1, 1965

We were in the East Side Airlines Terminal a while back, waiting for a connecting bus to Kennedy Airport, when we bumped into a librarian friend of ours. He was off on a holiday to Europe and asked where we were headed. "To a library meeting," we replied. "Oh, no," he said in dismay, "not *another* library conference."

Well, it *was* another library conference, but one with a difference. Some four days, a dozen sessions, and a half dozen luncheons and dinners later,

we concluded that this microcosmic meeting was the very model of what a
library conference ought to be.

The meeting was the joint conference of the Mountain Plains Library
Association and the Pacific Northwest Library Association, held in Denver
in September. The meeting was the second such joint gathering to be held
by the two regional bodies in the past ten years.

If we had had some misgivings about the prospective regionalism of
this conference—the theme was billed as "Books in the West"—it was
dispelled by an impressive battery of speakers who covered an extensive
range of library matters.

Bob Vosper flew in from Helsinki to report on the international as well
as the national library scene. Paxton Price came from the East to bring the
word from Washington. A contingent of ALA Headquarters staff—including
Ruth Warncke, Myrl Ricking, and Dorothy Turick, among others—brought
news of Association activities. And from the West, carrying out the conference theme, that arch advocate of the Western writer—Lawrence Clark
Powell.

At our first ALA conference—some years back—we were frustrated by the
fact that the top names—all of whom we were anxious to hear—were billed
simultaneously on the program and it was impossible to cover more than a
smattering of these "performances." Not so at MPLA-PNLA. All of the "big
guns" were presented at general sessions, and these sessions totaled *eight*
in the three and a half days of the meeting. True, there was still the problem
of division-of-interest groups, and these bodies splintered off into small, con-
currently held sessions during one morning of the conference. But on the
whole, we were impressed with the number of general meetings at which
all librarians could be present.

At the end of the Conference, there was an evaluative session, at which
selected conferees toted up the credits and debits of the meeting. It was
unanimously agreed that this type of regional meeting had done much to
break down the barriers that divide librarians of disparate interests and
from discrete geographical areas.

It seemed to us that there were two lessons to be learned from this type
of meeting. First, that conference planning should provide more opportunities for all librarians to meet en masse to hear speakers on a variety of
library problems. Perhaps the most effective of these mass gatherings are the
luncheon and dinner sessions where small groups—tables of no more than
eight—can enjoy the conviviality of good conversation and discussion with
similar as well as disparate interest groups.

The second lesson is that ALA might revive the idea of regional meetings of the Association. These meetings would, of course, not be in place of
the annual meeting, but in addition to it.

As ALA continues to grow, fission not fusion (to borrow a phrase from
Bob Franklin) has resulted. The size of the annual meetings grows more
unwieldy, and the conferee is constantly faced with the decision of which
one session he *should* attend when there are half a dozen he *would like* to
attend, all going on at the same time. Some critics might argue that regional

meetings would only result in further fission not fusion, but we think not. Short of dissolving some divisions, it seems to us that the answer lies in conferences more manageable in size and scheduling, with greater profit for the individual participant.

Perhaps a step in the right direction has already been taken by ALA with the proposal that Midwinter meetings be held in various parts of the country and that these meetings include a one-day general program. But the fact remains that these are primarily business meetings, to which a large number of librarians do not go.

State library associations have been congregating in area meetings for some time now and a look into the future (1967) shows that at least four states will join forces for a regional meeting. Perhaps ALA should take a leaf from this grass-roots movement.

*Shirley Havens*

## CONFERENCE SCHEDULING
June 15, 1966

One year ago, in Detroit, the ALA membership rallied under the banner of Eli Oboler and called for action to exclude from ALA those libraries practicing racial discrimination against users. We opposed that resolution (*LJ*, Aug. '65, p. 3224), but we were (and always are) pleased to see the membership of any organization demanding action and leadership on important issues from its appointed and elected representatives.

In the matter of racial discrimination the ALA membership has been insistent and persistent for several years now, and has demonstrated that it is frequently prepared to go further and faster in this area than the association's leaders. Based on this record, it can be expected that the membership will not pass up its next opportunity, at the New York conference, to call for a full accounting of the reasons for the fate of the resolution it supported so enthusiastically in Detroit a year ago.

What has happened, in brief, is that the Detroit resolution is dead. At the Midwinter meeting in Chicago, the ALA Council found the arguments of a special committee headed by Verner Clapp more persuasive than the membership's appeal, even though the latter found surprising backing in the ALA Executive Board (*LJ*, Mar. 1, p. 1172–80).

But the Chicago events were not completely negative and two proposals for more positive action have carried forward to the New York agenda. The first is a resolution by Ernestine Grafton, which sets out to achieve what the Oboler resolution called for, but without changes in the Constitution. The Executive Board is scheduled to report to Council on this at the New York Conference.

The second item will be the report of a special committee, set up at the urging of Verner Clapp, to review action taken by ALA in fulfilling its earlier promise to "continue to promote freedom of access to libraries of all people."

We bring all this up again, not because we disagree with the actions taken since Detroit—we are, thus far, untypically in accord with the ALA Council—but because we know that a good many ALA members *are* unhappy about the events of the past year. Those members should have full opportunity in New York to debate the issue with the leadership.

In order to do so, the membership will need to be in possession of all the facts. Having taken a look at the conference program, it seems to us that the membership is unlikely to be so equipped.

The ALA Council is scheduled to meet twice during the conference week—on Tuesday, July 12, and Friday, July 15. The Membership meeting is scheduled to follow the *first* of these two Council meetings.

At that first Council meeting, the members will have an opportunity to hear the Executive Board's report on the Grafton resolution, and before the Membership meeting, will know what subsequent action the Council has taken.

But as the schedule is presently set up, the report by the Special Council Committee on Access to Libraries (the follow-up to Verner Clapp's resolution in Chicago), which is very much related, will not be presented until the Friday Council meeting—three days *after* the Membership meeting. Thus, the members will have no opportunity to consider whatever proposals this committee brings forth until a year hence in San Francisco.

The annual Membership meeting used to follow the last Council meeting of the conference week, an arrangement that made it possible for individual members to question or debate any Council actions taken during the week. There were many (including us) who did not like that arrangement because the number of members who departed the conference before the end of the week left the Membership meeting less representative than it could be if held in the middle of the week.

We still think the present practice of mid-week Membership meetings is desirable, but such an arrangement dictates that matters of great membership involvement and concern be scheduled for the first, not the second, Council meeting of the week.

We believe the ALA leadership will be buying unnecessary trouble if it does not tell the whole post-Detroit story *before* the Membership meeting. It would take only a very elementary piece of rescheduling—of one committee report from the Friday to the Tuesday Council meeting. Can't it be done?

*Eric Moon*


## BUGLES AT CREDIBILITY GAP
April 15, 1967

For years now, Americans have reeled under a series of disclosures which must have Parson Weems orbiting in Purgatory Surely no other generation has had to observe its Presidents misrepresent the truth and its heavyweight champion represent an unAmerican religion; or to realize that its official "Men from Uncle" act like the Mafia, and that the poor, the alien, and the young don't really want our guidance, but our Cadillacs, in which they will surely store their cool, rather than launder their souls.

One consolation is that we only know these things because the press, outriding our progress, has borne back across its saddle bow the many shapes of truth, ill-formed ones as compulsively as comely ones. And thus escorted through our century, our westering has taken us across the plains to a clear view of Credibility Gap.

The little troop of librarians, trekking raggedly toward the 70's, is no more eager than the rest of society for confrontations at this pretty pass—on the grounds, perhaps, that their particular quest might be endangered, thwarting (among other desires for human betterment) their understandable longing for that day when they shall be as doctors and stand at the right hand of the mint. But this reluctance for the more gamy specimens of truth sits strangely on a group which has, at all its campfires, dedicated itself, in the words of its representatives, to the free diffusion of knowledge.

Yet it could be that the problems which librarians wish least to act upon in public are those most necessary to solve. It has been revealing to see the reaction of many librarians to one of their number attacking—in a non-library periodical—what he considers faults of his colleagues: the "mismanagement of college libraries." And there are a great many such problems making their way across the plains with us to Credibility Gap.

Librarians, or their representatives, have not been spurred into action by revelations that they do not read books. But public and prompt action on this one shameful condition might do more for literacy in America than many a federal grant.

Nor has there been much beyond bemused dismay at the fact that when it comes to censorship, you've got to really go some to keep up with your local librarian. Since the Fiske study came riding in with the news, all librarians have known this, but no bugles have sounded from Fort Chicago far in the rear. No public confrontation has insisted on these librarians changing their ways. But let it be noted that the Iowa Library Association is quietly saddling up for this mission, having presumably waited long enough for action from their elected representatives at ALA.

Library education is another topic which librarians keep to themselves, limiting their protests to agonized sputters as students, and in later life doing their best to forget it. Current claims to professional status rest on feeble foundations when the "profession" includes so many members who regret their professional education. If the situation is so bad, ALA, the chosen representatives of librarians, should move against old and static schools at least as rigorously as they inspect the new ones.

In many libraries, one finds quite different stories being told by the staff and the administration. Some of the most bitter criticisms will never be heard or acted upon, because the average working librarian will get rigor mortis before he gets to ALA. But if the union movement provides these nontravelling librarians with vocal representation, one can count on an immoderate amount of public laundering.

One issue, which ALA President Mary Gaver threatens to surround and shoot up in San Francisco, is the standard pitch on the library manpower shortage. And since librarians, like imaginative pre-Columbian cartographers, have been defining implausible boundaries for years, a revision that starts out: "Would you believe 50,000 . . . ?" Will be hard to pull off gracefully. But it will be harder on the far side of Credibility Gap.

Discretion has so far taken precedence over an unseemly thirst for truth in such issues as the consultant question, the ethics of administrators and trustees, and the gap between published accounts of automation and the reality. Few issues, however, are less enthusiastically explored by the ALA, as official representatives of librarians, than one which may be the most important. Smoke signals rising over Credibility Gap ask us: Who does the ALA represent?

*Karl Nyren*


## FRAGMENTARY COMPARISONS
July 1967

The New York one (reported in this issue) was our first Special Libraries Association convention. By now an old hand on the ALA conference scene, we found ourselves, in this first direct encounter with SLA assembled, unconsciously making comparisons, noting contrasts and similarities.

The first and most obvious impression was of a general sense of disorganization, disorientation—an air of amateurism—about the SLA convention, which contrasted vividly with (whatever else one may say about it) the fairly smooth-running bureaucratic machine of ALA. The reason may be that so much is left to so many volunteer hands at SLA—and one has only to look at the sketchy, overburdened SLA headquarters staff to understand why.

What may well be the other, and shinier, side of the same coin, however, is the more relaxed atmosphere of SLA, as compared with ALA. Joseph Covino, a public librarian who spoke at one of the SLA divisional meetings, noticed it too: "I hope ALA takes note of the informality and friendliness of this group," he said. But perhaps this is wanting the cake and eating it, too. Can one have super-organization and informality—both, and together?

Most noticeable to us, perhaps because we have complained so often about the reverse at ALA, was the openness of the SLA convention. The SLA convention program is not dotted with asterisks indicating "closed" meetings—in fact, there is nary a one. And at the annual meeting, SLA members were even *encouraged* to sit in on meetings of the Board of Directors (SLA's equivalent of the ALA Executive Board), and to ask more questions. It's even in the SLA Bylaws: "Meetings of the Board, except executive sessions, shall be open to members of the Association . . ." Not only can an ALA member not get near the Executive Board in session, but it's still far from easy to gain admittance to many divisional board or committee meetings.

A similar openness, or frankness, was noticeable in the announcement of election results at the SLA annual meeting. There, the results were given in full, including the vote tallies for both the successful and the defeated (one cliffhanger even brought a gasp of interest from the audience). ALA distributes such information to those who have been candidates for election but appears to have a kind of super-sensitivity about revealing the margins of victory or defeat to its general membership.

It was apparent that there is the same inclination in SLA as in ALA to overload the platform, presenting so many speakers and papers as to eliminate time for discussion. The batting average in audience participation, however—at least in the meetings we attended—was perhaps slightly higher at SLA than at ALA.

The fragmentation into smaller and smaller interest groups is certainly more pronounced in SLA than ALA. A much smaller organization, SLA nevertheless has 21 divisions. What is worse, the divisions appear to have a completely free (uncontrolled might be a better word) rein in their conference planning. How else does one account for—to cite only a few examples—eight meetings of the Newspaper Division, seven each for the Biological Sciences and Metals/Materials Divisions, and five for Aerospace, all within the one conference week? The program is a nightmare of proliferation, more overloaded with excess fat than even the corpulent ALA program.

Having sampled a variety of the SLA meetings we came away more than ever convinced of the wastefulness and futility of librarianship being divided into so many splinter groups. We heard very little that we could not or have not heard in one or other of the ALA divisional or sectional meetings. SLA's overlapping interests with the American Documentation Institute on the one hand (witness the intense activity and interest in SLA's Documentation Division), and with ALA on the other, are pronounced and obvious. Can librarianship, looking for a larger place in whatever brave new society may be ahead, afford to divide its none too impressive strength in this way?

The fiscal rumblings during the SLA week indicated anything but strength and security, and ADI presents no outward appearance of booming progress or prosperity. Merger is a common word in the business world's vocabulary these days, and even the publishers' associations (ABPC and ATPI) are giving the idea the time of day. One suspects it may still be a vaguely dirty word in the "professional" lexicon, but it may be more necessary there than anywhere.

*Eric Moon*

## PARLIAMENTARY PRISSINESS
August 1967

"President vs. Parliamentarian": that was the title of *LJ*'s report on the ALA Council sessions at the 1965 Midwinter meeting of the Association. We quote it as a reminder that the constitutional shambles which occurred during an ALA Council meeting in San Francisco was not the first of its kind. In fact, at least three times in the past several years the ALA Council has been similarly handcuffed and hog-tied by a visiting "expert."

The first point we want to make here, unequivocally, is that ALA in future should hire no parliamentarian without first ensuring that she understands that her proper role is to help the Council do what it wants to do, by finding a way through the constitutional maze, if this is at all possible. The parliamentarians whose performances we have witnessed in recent years seem more concerned to see how many roadblocks they can create to impede the Council. This body arouses itself from torpor rarely enough; when it does, it needs to be encouraged rather than frustrated by the kind of parliamentary nonsense exhibited at San Francisco.

The point would scarcely be worth this much prominence were the matter under discussion in San Francisco not so important, and were the results of the parliamentarian's persistent blocking not so potentially harmful to the final outcome. One likely result of forcing the Council summarily to approve the move of ALA headquarters to Washington, D.C.—apparently undemocratically and without ascertaining the desires of the membership—is that it has probably already created more membership opposition than might otherwise have arisen. A similar proposal to move ALA to Washington was heavily defeated by the membership in 1957. It would be a pity, in our view, if the vote a decade later has the same result, but it will be ludicrous and shameful if the case is lost because of platform bungling in San Francisco and the pernicious efforts of a pernickety parliamentarian.

We shall deal further, in our next issue, with the merits of the proposed Washington move itself, but let us look a little more closely here at what the Council was trying to achieve out on the Coast. The ALA Council has been frequently criticized in recent years, and sometimes for contradictory reasons. There have been times when it has seemed to be reluctant to assume a leadership role. On other occasions it has been under fire for plunging ahead on controversial issues without consulting the membership. If we catch the tenor of the San Francisco debate accurately, a number of Councilors—including past president Edwin Castagna and that master politician-librarian from Rochester, Harold Hacker—were attempting to find a diplomatic path between these two hazardous alternatives. And it appeared that the sentiment of a large part of the Council was in favor of this objective.

Castagna and the others were saying, in effect: the location of ALA headquarters is a matter of concern to all members and the final decision should not be taken without their vote. The Council members, however, had

had more background information and more opportunity to consider it (and discuss it with the Executive Board) than was likely to be available to the average member before any mail vote. Those who were urging a middle mere course of action, therefore, felt that the Council should exercise leadership but not dictatorship, that it should advise the membership that the Council's best judgment was that the move to Washington should be approved.

This was what the parliamentarian said the Council could not do. As the policy-making arm of the Association, she declared, the Council, by voting to advise the membership to approve the move to Washington, would actually be resolving irretrievably to make the move.

We still believe this to be an incredible interpretation. But if it is indeed a correct one, the clear implication is that it is impossible for the Council of the American Library Association to place any matter before the Association as a whole and to offer the membership the benefit of its advice, knowledge, and experience on whatever may be the issue at hand.

If this really is the case, then it is the Constitution of ALA rather than the parliamentarian that is at fault. If we do indeed have a Constitution that shackles rather than liberates, the only way to avoid similar fiascos in the future is to amend the ALA Constitution itself.

*Eric Moon*

## MIDSTREAM OR MIDWEST?
September 1, 1967

San Francisco, 1967 and Kansas City, 1957: at each of these American Library Association conferences, exactly a decade apart, the ALA Council voted to remove the headquarters of the association from the shores of Lake Michigan and transplant it in Washington, D.C. On each occasion the Council action prompted a petition calling for a mail vote by the ALA membership.

In 1957, the membership vote overturned the Council decision by a massive majority of 5,745 to 2,199. The question now before the house is whether the climate of opinion has changed substantially in ten years, or whether the Council will once again be overthrown by the popular vote.

The arguments both for and against the proposed move are cogently and fairly presented in the report of the ALA Executive Board's Subcommittee on Space Needs, which is scheduled to appear in the September *ALA Bulletin*. Essentially, the committee's argument boils down to the fact that Washington is where the association should be because the nation's capital is where most of the action affecting the future of libraries now is, and is likely to remain. Both the Executive Board and the ALA Council concur.

But what of the arguments of those who are opposed to the move? Some new ones may yet emerge, but we shall be very surprised if they differ essentially from those raised by the petitioners for the status quo in 1957.

For example, in San Francisco the venerable and respected Kyes Metcalf said: "We don't want to become known primarily as a lobbying institution or trade union like NEA." He warned also that the infectious disease of bureaucracy was more rampant in Washington than elsewhere, and that ALA might catch it.

Compare this with a statement by the 1957 petitioners: "It is important that the membership assess the values which would be lost if ALA became identified with bureaucracy and as a lobbying body" (*LJ*, September 1, 1957, p. 1977–79).

If such fears were valid in 1957, they seem not to hold much water today. We can dismiss the trade union reference: anyone who thinks ALA even faintly resembles a trade union is relying heavily on a creative imagination and is also ignoring significant recent developments in library union activity, which are taking place entirely outside the ALA orbit—and precisely because ALA has *not* concerned itself with such activities.

The bureaucracy spectre can be counted on to rustle up a few anti-Washington votes, but it is neither a fair nor an accurate weapon. Bureaucracy is more visible in Washington, partly because there is more government per capita there than anywhere else, and partly because it is exposed more constantly and intensively to national public scrutiny. But would anyone like to defend the proposition that bureaucracy is insignificant in Mayor Daley's city—or in Mayor Yorty's or Mayor Lindsay's, for that matter?

Most interesting among these arguments are the fears about ALA becoming, or seeming to become, a lobbying body. In 1957, certainly, ALA was no great lobbying power, and the point raised by the petitioners may have had some validity. But to raise the same ghost today smacks of quaintness, since it can be clearly demonstrated that the 1957 petitioners' success in keeping ALA in the Midwest in no way prevented the association from gaining this wicked reputation for political activity.

The reality is that, of 296 organizations reporting their 1966 lobbying expenditures in the *Congressional Quarterly*'s annual lobby spending survey (*CQ Weekly Report*, July 7, 1967, p. 1161–68), ALA ranked 16th in the nation. And among the 20 professional associations listed, only the National Education Association surpassed ALA's expenditures on lobbying, which were higher even than those of the American Medical Association.

If fiscal facts are not enough, take a look at the May 15 issue of *Newsweek* (p. 70), where an article entitled "Up the Up Staircase" appears. This piece deals with the "enormous influence" of the education lobbyists in Washington and features some of the lobbying organizations and their representatives who are most influential. Well in the forefront of this group—she is one of three whose photographs appear in the article—is Germaine Krettek, ALA's gal on the Hill. Here, surely, is sufficient proof that the argument raised by Metcalf and others is sadly irrelevant. Whether ALA be located in Chicago or Washington, the association already is—and has to be—a lobbying organization.

While Washington disadvantages will be emphasized freely in the weeks to come, it is doubtful whether anyone will be able to produce any very impressive or convincing list of Chicago advantages. Some will argue (just as they will fight to retain a redundant routine because "it has always been done that way") that ALA should stay put in Chicago because "it's always been there." A slight inaccuracy may go unnoticed: ALA managed to survive elsewhere through the first 34 years of its life before moving *to* Chicago.

The most insistent point argued by the advocates of Chicago is the city's "geographic centrality." Let us not argue with a fact: Chicago is undeniably *nearer* the geographic center of the country than is Washington. But that Chicago *is* the center is just as undeniably untrue. In fact, where the center lies is very much a matter of definitions and interpretation. If one counts only the 48 conterminous states, the center of the U.S. is somewhere in Smith County, Kansas. If one includes Alaska and Hawaii—and, indeed, why not?—the center moves to Butte County, South Dakota. And if one takes into account American Samoa, the Canal Zone, Guam, Puerto Rico, and the Virgin Islands, we are unable to say, without a survey, quite where the center lands. Even more difficult to determine, if one takes into the reckoning the geographic spread of the ALA membership, is where the association's own geographic center is.

What, in any case, does this geographic centrality mean in terms of the accessibility of headquarters to the membership? Does the average member in the Deep South or the Far West really feel that an H.Q. in Chicago is like next door while one in Washington would be on the other side of the moon? Why, then, do the members of the some 1500 national organizations that have their headquarters in Washington, including most of the major educational associations, not insist on a move in the opposite direction in order to achieve this desirable geographic centrality?

As ALA has learned the hard way in recent years, "access" is not an easy word to define, but it is difficult to see in what way a Chicago headquarters is more accessible, except to those in its immediate vicinity. For the air traveler from most parts of the country, the difference in time to reach either Chicago or Washington is negligible, and anyone who travels half the country or more by rail is clearly not too concerned about time. Access by mail, the mails being what they are since the zipcode cure, is as unpredictable whether a letter be addressed next door or to Australia.

A further claim made by the 1957 petitioners which is likely to be resurrected by the 1967 opponents of Washington is that "the individual member should be the Association's first concern." The fear last time was that moving to the capital would result in increased legislative and international activity, to the detriment of this concern for the individual member. As we have already noted, remaining in Chicago did not produce the desired results: legislative activity *was* stepped up by ALA, as also were its international involvements. It is worth noting that ALA has already opened another Washington office to pursue these international interests.

The very claim about the individual member being the association's *first* concern is itself debatable. According to the ALA Constitution, Article II: "The object of the American Library Association shall be to promote library service and librarianship." It seems self-evident that this objective has been more fruitfully pursued in Washington than in Chicago during the past ten years. And it is at least arguable that the success of ALA's efforts at this level—which have led to a raising of the status, visibility, and support of library service—has contributed more to the long-term benefit of the individual librarian than might have been achieved in any other way.

Finally, we come to what may be the most potent factor raised by the anti-Washington group: an appeal to that most sensitive part of the clothed anatomy, the pocket. The letter to President Gaver which accompanied the membership petition called for "details of the proposed financing . . . and the anticipated effect it would have on membership dues."

The report of the ALA Space Needs Committee is less reassuring and convincing on this matter than on most others. It says, indeed: "Much more detail on costs will, of course, need to be assembled as soon as the basic decison on location has been made." One may well wonder about the order of the cart and horse in this case; certainly, no business would decide to relocate *before* it had fully investigated the costs involved. There is, however, one note of reassurance in the committee's report: "There is some evidence to encourage us to think that sufficient funds will be forthcoming . . . to make an appeal for membership contributions unnecessary."

Not to be forgotten, in any case, are the further points: 1) that a substantial increase in the size of ALA headquarters seems inevitable, whether the location be in Chicago or Washington; 2) that construction and property costs are about the same in both cities; and 3) that moving to Washington should enable ALA to dispense with some of the cost of maintaining seven scattered units in three different cities.

*LJ* does not find the arguments thus far produced in favor of remaining in Chicago to be persuasive, particularly when they are weighed against the substantial evidence of Washington's massive influence on the progress of library service and librarianship in the U.S. during the past decade. The evidence underlines that political centrality is more important than geographical location. We are strongly in favor of the proposed move to the nation's capital, and urge ALA members to vote for it.

*Eric Moon*


## THE GENERATION GAP
August 1968

Something happened to the old ALA in Kansas City. What was it? The following sampler may provide some faint clues for those who weren't there—or for those who were but didn't hear the rumbling:

"At times, we seem to make a virtue of our basic unconcern for the bread and butter issues that affect our members . . . It is small wonder that the unions have begun to move into a vacuum that we have, by inaction, helped to create."—*Roger McDonough, ALA president.*

"We are concerned that the ALA, in its routine functioning . . . all too infrequently addresses its talents and manpower to the major issues which affect our society, our government, and the world of 1968."—*Kenneth Duchac, ALA member.*

"I come to you to urge further action by the Association beyond anything that has so far been undertaken . . . The Association has, in effect, cut its members adrift and let them survive as best they could in rough weather. This seems, at long last, unworthy. It is time . . . to close the gap between promise and performance, to support our rhetoric with tangible aid."—*Ervin Gaines, Intellectual Freedom Committee chairman.*

"The ALA is an old organization; that is, its policies and practices are controlled by old people . . . For a considerable period of time, I believe that presidents and other officers of the Association should nominate, appoint, or otherwise involve younger persons in the affairs of ALA."—*Ralph Blasingame, Jr., retiring ALA treasurer.*

"The Membership Committee has found, in its recruiting work, that many junior members of the staffs of libraries . . . are unwilling to join ALA and pay personal dues when the Chief is getting something for nothing" (i.e., "a free ride and free votes on their Organization membership").—*Ben Custer, for the ALA Membership Committee.*

"The one relevant meeting I've been to this week was the one at which Alex Haley [ghost-writer of *The Autobiography of Malcolm X*] spoke. . . . That opening meeting [on the report of the National Advisory Commission on Libraries] was supposed to be important—I've never been to anything so dead."—*A. P. Marshall, ALA member.*

"The University Libraries Section meets ceremoniously once a year. It does nothing else. This is one of the things wrong with it. I suggested its disbandment, but the suggestion went over with a thud."—*Stuart Forth, chairman, ACRL University Libraries Section.*

"If the urban public library fails, the urban public school library fails, and the Columbia experience suggests that even the great university begins to fail as the community about it declines. Clearly, then, there ought to be a profession-wide concern about these matters."—*William Summers, Florida State Librarian.*

"We have met the enemy and they is us."—*Jack Frantz, director of the Brooklyn Public Library, quoting Pogo the Philosopher.*

A new urgency about social concerns, and the relevance of libraries and ALA to them; a swelling impatience with "the establishment" and a demand for the involvement of youth; a veritable barrage of criticism (much of it self-criticism)—in short, an insistent, rumbling awakening: that's what was happening in Kansas City.

There was much talk of a generation gap during the ALA Conference, but not all the brimstone was poured by the under-30's. All of the above remarks, in fact, were made by people on the "wrong" side of 30—and many of them are considerably over that hump. These quotations are intended to illustrate that the upsurge of concern and criticism and demand for change was broadly based, coming in some cases from high places in the ALA hierarchy. What happened cannot so easily be attributed to just another uprising of the young turks, or dismissed as irresponsible by those who seem automatically to equate youth with irresponsibility.

Yet the generation gap *was* much in evidence at this conference, and nowhere was it more clearly to be seen than in the ALA Council meetings. Anyone who attended both the Membership and the Council meetings might well have wondered whether this was the same conference or the same association. If the younger members want a priority target, the ALA Council should be number one. Change there—drastic change—is fundamentally, urgently needed. Younger members *must* get themselves nominated and elected—and some of the older members must help them do it.

*Eric Moon*

## NEWS REPORT: 1968
January 1, 1969

The news of the library world, like that of other worlds, is a steady stream of gossip and anecdote about both the inconsequential and the profoundly significant. Much of its appeal to its consumers lies in its currency and its relevance, whether to widely shared concerns (Vietnam, the inner city, student revolt) or to immediate professional interests (new methods and products, library security, automation, oral history, interloan experiments).

The amount of library news which reaches national publication each year is necessarily highly selected, but one of its more interesting properties is that its main currents and themes do vary from year to year, making it worthwhile to look back at this time and see what has been newsworthy in the past 12 months.

The approximately 150 pages of news carried by *LJ* in 1968 touch on a few dozen topics, ranging from "access" to Vietnam, and show a decided emphasis on the topics of big city public libraries, service to ghetto residents, literacy programs, the social responsibilities of libraries, new forms of library education, censorship, unions, extension of service to the handicapped and the institutionalized, new cooperative schemes, newly expanded service to business and industry, and the National Advisory Commission on Libraries. And if there is a common theme running through most of these topics, it seems to be an awareness of and a response to change.

Depending as it does on the new and the unusual, library news is hardly an accurate microcosm of librarianship or even of library literature—immensely important developments can go unnoticed once they have begun, unless they take an unusual turn, or reach some notable culmination. Yet there is a unique potential value in the report of the raw fact; it is one of the ways in which the librarian enlarges his experience, and it goes a long way toward performing for him that service which we now call "current awareness."

## The Violent Year

Sometimes no news is good news: thus we might view the lack of damage to any library in this last year during urban disturbances—though there was the usual spate of acts of God and other destructive agencies at home and abroad: three bombings, beginning with the strange attack using ice in equatorial Penang, continuing with the bombing of the USIS library in Sao Paulo, Brazil, and finally, the USIS library in Brussels. In Alaska floods took out the Fairbanks College Community Library; fire ripped through valuable collections at the Holyoke Community College in Massachusetts, the Middle River Branch of the Baltimore County Library, and worst of all, at the University of Miami's Marine Science Institute, papers representing $5 million worth of research were lost when the temporary wooden building holding them was destroyed.

Being bypassed by riots may or may not be an unmixed blessing; it could be a sign of the low silhouette of libraries in important affairs. It could also indicate that librarians are doing a good job both in the colleges and the ghettos. The student revolt has touched libraries in colleges only by chance; and the overriding issue of Vietnam has scarcely affected the operation of libraries—although in this past year, the threatened slowdown in building construction is making itself felt, as war drains away funds needed for social progress.

By the end of the year, despite much debate, the American Library Association had not laid it on the line for or against war in Vietnam, but individual librarians got involved. The year started out with a full-page antiwar ad in the *New York Times* of December 26, 1967, a move sparked by a publishers' group originally, but backed by *LJ* and signed by a large group of librarians.

At about the same time, a number of libraries found themselves crossed off the subscription list of the liberal magazine, *The Sixties*, because their universities were reported to be engaged in research on biological warfare. And in March, the next event was the involvement of a number of government librarians in a Vietnam protest petition circulated in Washington.

Librarians attending the presentation of the 19th annual National Book Awards saw one recipient of a prize, poet Robert Bly, hand over his check publicly to a representative of an antidraft group, while another, Jonathan Kozol, used his acceptance speech to denounce conditions in the ghettos.

## Blacks and Libraries

After Vietnam, the most painful symptom of the current American crisis is the condition of Negroes, Puerto Ricans, and some other less visible but disadvantaged Americans such as American Indians, Samoans, Mexican-

Americans, and Appalachian whites. Here, library response has been widespread.

A glance back over the news of 1968 shows a new attention to Negro history and related cultural materials in such varied places as the public libraries of Youngstown, Ohio; the New York Public Library, where the famous Schomburg Collection has at last won the financial support it has needed for years; Chicago, where reading and study centers are being set up in housing projects; Kalamazoo, where a Negro Heritage Fund has been established; the University of Washington, where collection development is being accelerated; and Princeton, where a major effort is being made to give library support to a big and active program of research in Negro history and related topics.

These are only the outstanding examples which have surfaced in the news of 1968; they are backed up, of course, by literally thousands of large and small library collections being developed in this country to remedy our cultural snow-blindness.

Libraries have also provided a scattering of news about efforts to get more Negroes and other minority group members into responsible positions. At the General Library of the University of California at Berkeley, a staff committee is charged with developing minority opportunities for employment and promotion; the top antipoverty post in New York City has gone to Major Owens, an ex-librarian and graduate of the Brooklyn Public Library's admired Community Coordinator program; while in Los Angeles, Mrs. Leontyne B. King has become the first Negro woman to become president of this city's public library board—and probably the first to take the top spot in any city library system in the U.S.A.

Other milestones: the publishing of an evaluation of three major library slum programs in New York City demonstrated in its frank and knowledgeable approach that inner city librarianship is indeed moving—here and there—beyond pioneer ventures to sophistication. The nervy High John project of the University of Maryland's School of Library and Information Services broke new ground—often painfully—in the *terra incognita* of education for ghetto library service. And at Case Western Reserve library science students are raising money for a scholarship to help librarians prepare for ghetto service.

### Big City Libraries

A major newsmaker in 1968 was the public library of the big city, not just for the many examples of its librarians involving themselves in Black problems, but for what just might be the first signs of a real resurgence of the city library. The city library has been an unlikely target for optimism, but there are some signs that are pretty hard to interpret as death struggles.

First, there is building, and for every library making progress toward a new building, several others are fighting hard for the financial support they need to start a building program. Just for samplers: construction has started in Birmingham, Alabama; New Haven has started the long process of building by arranging for sale of its old main library; Tampa has just brought in a $3 million-plus main building; another big one last year went up in Bethlehem, Pa.; Boston and Washington, D.C. have new construction in the works; and despite setbacks, the Los Angeles Public Library is gearing up for another big try at the bond issue it needs to have a new library building program.

The Chicago Public Library, probably one of the worst large city libraries for the last 20 years, has yet become a real front-runner in the year and a half under acting director Alex Ladenson. And while it is undergoing a massive $100,000 survey directed by Lowell Martin, it is certainly not waiting for the results before it tackles its mammoth problem of becoming relevant to its city. One high point has been the first upturn in circulation reported by Chicago, and, we believe, by any big city library in recent years. Also: a hastily-assembled but top-notch summer program brought out-of-school college students into a ghetto reading program for children.

Another really new venture has been the establishment of study and reading rooms in housing developments; stocking of jury waiting rooms with paperbacks (up to 1000 jurors sit around in various Chicago locations daily, waiting for a call to a court). And Chicago has been more determined than most of our big city public libraries to get involved in a Model Cities program. Its proposal: a string of seven neighborhood centers, located in existing branches and equipped to bring library service actively into the lives of nearby residents.

Along this line has been Chicago's experiment with a full-time social worker on the staff.

Leaving Chicago, without exhausting at all its list of impressive moves, a glance over the rest of the field shows action nearly everywhere: the Enoch Pratt Library in Baltimore opened the door to 27,000 lost borrowers—simply by cancelling the fines which they owed and which were keeping them away. The three big library systems of New York City—Brooklyn Public, New York Public, and Queens Borough Public—are quietly engaged in forging a new master plan for future cooperation in serving our biggest metropolis. From Tucson comes the encouraging word of a Model Cities Plan which will involve libraries; and from Kansas City, news of a study aimed at the present lack of relevance of a fairly expensive library effort to a great deal of its public.

The year-end reports of public libraries in places like Philadelphia and Los Angeles make unexpectedly exciting reading; while up in Toronto a reorganization of city library service is taking place which will bear watching. The city library has turned over its central collections to a new metropolitan board, and will henceforth put its efforts into developing a group of regional and branch libraries which have the unequivocal function of getting good general library service out to the public. As a contrast to the many city libraries merging with and dominating county library systems, the Toronto experiment will be particularly interesting to follow.

Another big library to watch this year will be Brooklyn. With a number of federally-supported ghetto programs having proved themselves, and with that source of financing due to dry up, director Jack Frantz is going after one of the toughest things to get in New York—a major budget boost. If the Brooklyn programs go down the drain after being proved at home and emulated elsewhere, we may well come to an ominous turning point, for most of our efforts to improve inner city service have been supported by federal funds, and under the possibly mistaken idea that the program so developed would get local funding if they worked.

Big city public libraries, as well as urban libraries of all kinds, will also be keeping an eye on the new Urban Research Center, which has been set up at Wayne State University's Center for Urban Studies to fill a real research vacuum.

## Literacy

News of literacy programs came in thick and fast in the past year, with possibly the most significant item announcing the massive reading study which has been launched by the Office of Education—to get at the scientific roots of reading problems. And along this line, from Philadelphia's Reader Development Program, comes the incidental intelligence that poor readers don't take to easy books as well as they do to hard ones which have real interest for them; Malcolm X Sí, Dick and Jane, No.

The news of literacy work rolls in: from Alaska, where Eskimo villages are getting libraries to keep school-won reading abilities from vanishing; from Philadelphia, where the Reader Development Program is racking up encouraging results, as is another one in Cleveland—the Reading Centers Program, it's called there. New Haven's Public Library, one of the few which has managed to get along with agencies like the Office of Economic Opportunity, announced last summer a grant of $17,000 from OEO for a ten-week literacy program; and from Georgia, we hear of the Flint River Regional Library, which combines a hospitable TV-viewing location for educational TV literacy programs, and follows up with individual instruction available after the viewing; the result, new library users.

## Social Responsibility

If there is one issue which has gripped librarianship at the national level it is the issue of the social responsibility of libraries and librarians. First really visible at the ALA Conference in Kansas City (1968), where it revealed the war-and-riot-exacerbated conscience of many librarians, the movement toward taking a more active posture in national affairs is threatening the first real split in ALA membership in years.

Since the flareup at Kansas City, repercussions have been heard, loud enough to tell us that the fireworks at Kansas City were not just a catharsis after which everyone would go back to his shop and go on as before. On both coasts other associations have raised their voices in favor of "social responsibility": in California, the California Library Association has moved a step ahead of ALA by immediately starting an acting committee to work on the issues so that a permanent Standing Committee on Social Responsibility can begin to function immediately upon its appointment at the next CLA meeting.

On the East Coast, that vigorous group of academic librarians with the title of Library Association of the City University of New York (LACUNY) have also come out strongly for social responsibility. And with admirable timing, Professor Kenneth Kister, of the Simmons College faculty, has published a new library textbook titled *Social Issues and Library Problems*.

The issue, be it noted, is still very vague for one which has been so hotly debated, being generally presented as the pros and cons of whether librarians *qua* librarians should take official stands, through their association, on "social issues." The Association, like the librarians themselves, has of course always taken stands on social issues, and even very recently on international issues; ALA joined with several other library associations to condemn the Russians' occupation of Czechoslovakia and their consequent harassment of the library in Prague.

ALA has not, however, come out against the American occupation of Vietnam, and that is what all the fuss is about, though in remarkably guarded terms. Beyond that, the only other implication is the question of library associations regularly making public their support of the liberal side of any social question—it being assumed that this is where librarians stand and/or that there isn't any other side to be taken anyway.

In any case, with the war stalemated or due for quiet phasing-out in the months to come, there may be more reluctance than ever among the rank and file toward taking a position that will reopen old wounds rather than—as originally intended—express a cry of disapproval of a government which was steadily escalating the war. The larger events of 1969 will undoubtedly thus have much to do with how or whether librarians take this highly debated step to which they are being urged, on the one hand, as a kind of epiphany of professionalism—and, on the other hand, urged to shun as a kind of final loss of professional virginity. It will be easier, of course, if the emphasis of "social responsibility" shifts to the issues of the ghetto and its need.

## Manpower

Making use of the term so common in 1967 and seen so rarely in 1968, we find that much has been happening as librarians go about answering the question of who is to do what work in libraries, and the accompanying question of where we are going to get them.

The past year has seen a spreading recognition of the fact that much of the work that has been done by graduate librarians can indeed be done by people with much less training—technicians, or technical assistants, or library aides—in short, the same people who have been doing the work anyway, only they won't be called librarians and they will eventually have to take courses in an appropriate institution before one hands them a glue pot or stands them behind a charging machine. The rest of the work which is not handled by the resident graduate librarian will be done by librarians-to-be, who are customarily employed for minor professional duties while earning their degrees. Acceptance of this picture is growing and will make staffing patterns easier to change.

Agreement has evidently been nearly achieved on how to look at this knotty problem of how to run libraries when we are short 650,000 librarians and unlikely to get many more in the near future. A new form of library education will be developed—not really a new one, but essentially the kind of training that Melvil Dewey introduced to solve the manpower needs of his day—only he called it librarianship and we will call it technician work.

But this breakthrough has been only a part of the rapidly developing library education story in 1968. The High John experimental library of the University of Maryland is trying to learn by doing how to train people for library service in the ghetto; government support for graduate library education continued with 499 fellowships awarded for 1968–69. New library education programs were announced: a Ph.D. program for Florida State University; ALA accreditation for Oregon and Geneseo; separate school status for the library science departments of Michigan and Kentucky; a new school of library service at Dalhousie in Halifax; a new master's program for Ball State University; two new library schools planned for Arizona, and a big drive for expansion at the University of Southern California School of Library Science.

Continuing education for librarians, increasingly recognized as a necessary future fixture, was represented in 1968 by a total of 63 institutes funded under the Higher Education Act—and also by the getting under way of a major study of the continuing education needs of librarians in 13 western states, with an eye to developing a master plan to meet those needs.

Information science seemed in 1968 to have become just a little bit more understandable as an area coterminous with librarianship; at the University of Southern California, an information science institute was run for library educators, to help them understand how best to start bringing this new area into library education. In Britain, the first information science degree course in that country was announced by the Department of Librarianship of the College of Commerce in Newcastle upon Tyne; and Syracuse University forged ahead with a grant to show library schools how to go about setting up a computer lab. Meanwhile in September, in a little-trumpeted Information Science Workshop at the University of Pittsburgh, librarians concerned with the automation in their future, library educators, and information scientists sat down to hammer out a curriculum model for the design of courses in information science and the evaluation of such courses.

One interesting new wrinkle that was proposed in library education—

for the upgrading of local hospital library personnel: use of the regional medical library videotape network to beam out courses in how to run the hospital library good.

## Service to Business

One of the stated goals for 1968 of the Public Library Association was an increase in service to business and industry. And indeed the newsletters and releases of a great many libraries, large and small, indicate that the past year has seen real attention paid to business and industry—and by these we generally, though not always, mean small business and small industry, which wouldn't be expected to have their own libraries.

Among the news items noted in this area: an intertype library network in Florida brings to businessmen in local communities the combined resources of the Orlando Public Library and the University of Florida at Gainesville.

The Tulsa Public Library announced a real red carpet service for its local business users: telephone-equipped carrels are featured; the University of Wisconsin's business service provided SDI (Selective Dissemination of Information) to 100 users; and the Connecticut State Library was using teletype to speed the loan of materials to industrial libraries.

While this escalation of service to business was going on in the U.S., the president of the (British) Library Association was questioning the whole idea of free local library service to private industry. Maybe, said T. E. Callender, they ought to pay for efficient information and research service.

## Censorship

As ever, intellectual freedom and censorship have been much in the news. ALA's *Newsletter on Intellectual Freedom* isn't getting any thinner as year by year it documents all the incidents reported in library literature and elsewhere.

With the Supreme Court decision to allow states to regulate the reading and viewing of minors, the forces of censorship throughout the land took heart and whipped out statutes, modeled on New York's, which in varying language barred young people from "obscenity." As usual the problem of the definition of obscenity is unsolved, and indeed muddied further by one conscientious attempt. A censorship law passed in Fort Lauderdale, Florida, was so specific in its terms that the *Miami Herald* declared it to be unprintable, leaving us with the interesting possibility that a law capable of holding water could itself be illegal to disseminate.

One of the more interesting, though not at all untypical, censorship stories has been developing in Richmond, California, where the "forces of decency" are locked in typical tragicomic combat with their more enlightened and liberal fellow citizens. The publication at issue is the underground newspaper, the *Berkeley Barb*, which, like *Playboy* magazine, has much wit and even substance on occasion, but is not sold or bought solely for these virtues, but rather for its rebellious tone, featuring obscenities, baiting of police and other authorities, and "personal" ads.

Richmond's librarian, John Forsman has been outspoken in his determination to maintain the kind of freedom from censorship to which most librarians pay lip service, but which few would dream of really putting into practice.

His supporters are good liberal clergymen, teachers, intellectuals, and the strong arm of the Central Labor Council of Contra Costa County. He has also received support from the California Library Association, which has laid it on the line as the first state association to pledge to come to the aid of any librarian caught in a censorship fight. It will not, however, let itself get involved in what it calls "local issues," such as attacks on the librarian for mismanagement in questions other than censorship.

This might have been wise, but was perhaps an unfortunate loss of an opportunity for an already strong association to try its hand at a game which will probably be preempted by library labor unions—defense of a member charged unfairly with unprofessional conduct or incompetence. And Richmond offers a fairly good choice of battleground, for if the librarian, John Forsman, comes on in a way to unsettle the staid, his opposite number, from newspaper accounts, and tape recorded council sessions seems almost too good to be true. This Councilman, whose latest gambit has been an invitation to library staff members to inform him of library misdeeds, is a pol right out of the funny papers, and he would be a fine opponent to take on.

And if no one comes to Forsman's aid, pressures on him and the library board will inevitably take their toll and Richmond will get the kind of librarian that its more conservative citizens want.

Regardless of how this skirmish turns out, however, it has produced a bit of oral history which can have lasting value. This is a tape of a City Council hearing, at which censorship proponents debate with anti-censorship forces in a dramatic and revealing crossfire that reveals the human failings of both sides, and might be used to help both sides understand each other in any community. The record is available for $5 from Berkeley radio station KPFA.

Winding up the censorship wars of the year, we note a new award, a question settled, and two questions raised, which is about par for the course. The award is the new Intellectual Freedom Award just created in honor of Robert B. Downs, University of Illinois dean of Library Administration; the question answered: can librarians criticize their bosses publicly without being subject to discipline? Yes, say Brooklyn boss John Frantz and Brooklyn library union officers, after a brief eyeball-to-eyeball session and a threatened strike—and yes, also seems to say a recent court decision, allowing teachers that right, though hedged somewhat by its qualifying language.

Questions raised are: what, if anything will come out of the Obscenity Commission announced in *LJ* last February, with Frederick Wagman, University of Michigan Library director, representing librarians on that body? And what will happen when the new LSCA Title IV programs take reading out to state prisons and find prisoners—and particularly Black prisoners—demanding reading materials which wardens say they can't have?

### Research

In 1968, library research continued to grow in importance and to become of wider interest. Partly this was because 1968 was the second year of substantially funded library research, with the first results of studies just now coming out, and more expected to appear momentarily.

Also, the Council on Library Resources moved into its second decade with $5 million more allotted to it by the Ford Foundation; the Illinois Library Research Center reported on its initial seven years under the direction of Guy Garrison; the Reference and Technical Services Division of ALA made a special effort to beat the bushes for new research ideas; and a new ALA group concerned with research came into being: the Library Research Round Table, provisionally chaired by James Krikelas of the University of Wisconsin.

### Surveys

In 1968 the suspicion that one could no longer overlook the library survey report in keeping up with library literature became increasingly acute. Although surveys are still appearing with the sole purpose of rubber-stamping the plans which a librarian or board want to "sell" to financial authorities, surveys are also appearing which come out with unexpected conclusions, uncomplimentary evaluations, and other surprises. And there have now been enough surveys done on enough topics so that one can occasionally observe interesting contradictions in their conclusions.

Among the more interesting surveys done or in the works are: the Lowell Martin survey of the Chicago Public Library, which is due out soon; Ralph Blasingame's Ohio survey, done last year, but of fresh interest to look at beside its offspring, the Ohio Library Development Plan. The latter, created by the Ohio Library Association and the Ohio Library Trustees Association, well repays careful reading.

A survey of four inner-city outreach programs in New York City, filling three volumes, is both a good description of new programs and a conscientious reporting of weaknesses and stresses. And the report of a study of Swarthmore College Library is interesting for its recommendation of the graduate research library as the model to follow in an undergraduate teaching library.

The kinds of surveys and studies which will be particularly worth watching in the coming year will be public library system studies such as the one coming out by Ralph Blasingame on New York's Ramapo-Catskill System; studies on processing centers, both established and projected—all processing center studies at one time assumed that central processing in itself was an unquestionably good thing. Now more and more experience is developing, and studies are saying that central processing won't help unless it serves a whole state, or region—and criticism of performance is also growing.

## Unions

The question of the relevance of library unions to libraries, professionalism, and library service is one which is slated for the attention of ALA in the coming year—as well as state associations and academic library groups. The story of public library union news this year includes two new library systems which have gone union: Youngstown, Ohio, and Los Angeles. The staffs of the Queens Borough and NYPL also officially got union representation in 1968.

There was action reported from Brooklyn, with a strike threat raised in retaliation when disciplinary action was taken against union officials who aired a letter in *LJ* which was critical of the library administration. The issue was settled amicably and evidently to everyone's satisfaction. Also early last year, the New York librarian's union presented its first salary demands to the city negotiators; they featured a beginning professional salary of $9000 and a number of raises calculated to bring the salaries of those in higher brackets in line with this base figure.

Academic librarians in 1968 were debating the pros and cons of unions rather more heatedly than most of their colleagues in the public libraries. Both in New York and in California there were spirited discussions, with union adherents claiming that only the force which a union can muster will compel administrators to treat librarians as professionals; while opponents on both coasts raised a number of objections against unions: that they might alienate academic personnel from inner city residents, many of whom now feel that labor unions are their enemies rather than their friends; and that the adversary relationship created by a union would be less effective in gaining the ends of librarians than would an organization modeled on the faculty senate and empowered by the university to work within its structure.

The national attention which will be focused on unions in 1969 by ALA is not predictable as to effect. It may stimulate the move toward unions, or encourage alternate solutions, or move professional associations into assuming some union roles, or the whole thing may fizzle out. But the last alternative seems the least likely.

## International

There has been a strong increase in the last year in news stories which reflect the interest and activities of American librarians in other countries, and a quietly growing international awareness seems to be established.

Some of the highlights of this in the past year have been news stories on the opening of a library research center in Buenos Aires; a book exchange program between a little Vermont library and one in Russia; observance of Human Rights Year in American libraries; glowing reports on the results of the overseas acquisitions program supported by Public Law 480; establishment of a Chinese Research Center by the Association of Research Libraries; closer relations between American and Japanese librarians; works on paper preservation (Russian) and compact shelving (Polish) translated and made available here; addition of Australian medical libraries to the MEDLARS system; library exchanges between schools like the University of Florida and the National University in Bogota; a study of library education abroad set for completion in 1969; and many other stories in the library news involving countries such as England, France, Botswana, Czechoslovakia, and Turkey.

Despite growing coolness in the nation for support of international activities, and continued lack of funding of the International Education Act, librarians here and abroad seem to be learning more about each other and getting together to share ideas more than ever before.

## Innovations

Reports of new ways to do things in libraries are always of interest, and this past year has had its crop. Worthy of note first, perhaps, is the establishment, in Great Britain, of an award for library inventions.

Other reports in a number of library fields include: administration: the staff of the Baltimore County Public Library got the chance to "grade" the administration in an unusual experiment conducted by director Charles Robinson; orientation: the University of Washington produced a low-cost videotape orientation tool which promises to be widely copied; collections: a North Carolina library started a circulating collection of costume patterns.

Personnel practice: the Minneapolis Public Library has started to pay staff members for good health—unused, unneeded sick leave gets paid for in cash.

Circulation: at the Copiague Memorial Library on Long Island, a tape recorder handles loan renewals after hours; a mechanized book retrieval system was demonstrated at ALA's Kansas City Conference; a book mailing service is being tested by the San Antonio Public Library; Mayfield, Ohio, like many other communities, is circulating books from a barbershop.

Copying machines: a new telecopier which can receive and record materials after library hours, and "hang up" its phone line when the message is complete; while in Wayne County, Michigan, free copying service is being tested out. Media: an 8mm film loan service has proved out successfully at the Laramie County Library in Wyoming; and *Talking Book Topics* is experimenting with phonograph records bound into each issue. The removable record contains book annotations now; in the future it may carry news, articles, and book reviews.

No survey of the innovations of the year would be complete without a nod to the library of the new Federal City College in Washington, D.C., where the intention seems to be to out-innovate the rest of the library world. Among their proposed projects: a "home library" for each student; use of the computer to integrate library materials into individual study programs; massive paperback duplication; a book catalog for every faculty member; and a current awareness program for both faculty and students.

## Library Literature

The literature of librarianship—not even to mention that of related fields—is growing and is properly the subject of the concern which prompted the calling of an important conference on the subject at the State University of New York at Albany last year. And a quick look back at the area of library periodicals alone shows how many items the well-read librarian would have to have noted in order to maintain his "current awareness" in only one area of his literature.

The three big library periodicals underwent top-level editorial change in 1968, with Gerald Shields taking over direction of the *ALA Bulletin,* and producing an immediate impact in that journal's readability and appearance; Kathleen Molz leaving the *Wilson Library Bulletin* to William Eshelman, who intends to change that publication by cutting down the number of issues devoted to specific themes and increase the number of articles by librarians. And *Library Journal,* after nearly a decade of direction by Eric Moon, takes a fresh start this month with John Berry at the helm. Since these three journals provide most of the current professional reading and information of the American librarian, these changes, occurring so close in time, can signal a whole new era in this segment of the literature.

Looking farther, however, we find a flock of new periodicals which the librarian must at least glance at and decide on as to their relevance to his needs. They include the *ERIC–CLIS Newsletter* of the Clearinghouse for Library and Information Science, which will announce the documents which the Clearinghouse is acquiring and making available to the librarian: reports, research papers, ephemera—all those publications which find their way into print but not to normal distribution channels such as the library periodical press.

Next, three new ones from abroad: *Index,* from Canada, aimed at the school and young adult librarian; the (British) Library Association's *Journal of Librarianship;* and the English-language *Scandinavian Public Library Quarterly.*

Also announced, and of potential interest to a wide audience, is the National Microfilm Association's *NMA Journal.*

Then there are the changes: the *Australian Library Journal* becomes a monthly; the Massachusetts Library Association has revived its *Bay State Librarian,* with Kenneth Kister of Simmons as new editor; while Lee Ash will edit a new bimonthly *NELA Newsletter* for the New England Library Association. And these developments, be it noted, occur in a world where there are already some 517 library and documentation journals, as reported last year by the International Federation for Documentation.

And just scratching the surface of all the rest of the literature, we find a selection of library literature is now included in *Current Contents;* a new series of publications is coming from the Graduate School of Library and Information Science at the University of Pittsburgh; *Who's Who in Library Service* is getting together a new edition; a new program has been announced for the reprinting of scarce works in library science by the College of Librarianship, Wales; and a new annual, *Advances in Librarianship,* will appear this year, to be edited by Melvin Voigt, university librarian, University of California at San Diego, and published by Academic Press as a "permanent record and digest of developments in the library field." And with a nod to the increasing pace of our times, the Public Library Association has issued its first revision of *Costs of Public Library Service 1963.*

### Forecast

As librarians read the news of their world in this journal and others, they will be looking for developments in a number of areas that will help them to chart their own professional courses. Most likely to produce news will be the following areas: the inner city; censorship; local citizen involvement in libraries; cooperation between libraries of different types; changes in library education; interdisciplinary experiments in both library schools and libraries; new services extended to the handicapped, aged, and institutionalized; and the development of information networks.

Also: library research, national, state, and local response to the "social responsibility" issue, library unions, academic status, the problems of library systems, and the wave of student unrest in the colleges.

All this seems fairly predictable, but only fairly. New developments, completely unexpected now, may well arise and become major themes in the news of 1969, while areas which look of great importance and interest now may fade almost out of sight through lack of new developments or through the continual, quiet process by which exciting and controversial issues become assimilated into the theory and practice of the profession.

*Karl Nyren*

### NEWS REPORT: 1969

January 1, 1970

The year 1969 has been one of the most eventful for librarians, and it looks as though many of the issues raised will increase in importance in the next year or two. If we could single out the topics which caught the interest of librarians most in the past year, they would lead off with intellectual freedom, closely followed by the rise of insurgent groups within library associations, groups which raise the issues of social responsibility, democracy within professional associations, and Vietnam.

Next would have to come the struggle over federal funds for education and libraries, and the relationship of this struggle to the questions of priorities.

And then come our responses to these major pressure systems in our professional weather: a ferment of change in library education; the first attempt to develop new administrative approaches, especially in the broadening of decision-making and the liberalization of hierarchial structures.

Besides all the activity within established library associations, there have been new associations cropping up which reflect both ideological concerns and the evolution of librarianship.

Skirmishing has gone on throughout the year on a number of newsfronts, with no spectacular results, but with enough action to draw our attention from time to time. The pressure for academic status for college and university librarians is one such front; the activity of labor unions in organizing library staffs is another. Libraries of all types are still moving into more or less formalized cooperative structures: systems, consortia, and networks; in the oldest of these, the systems, there is news from time to time of conflict between members and system.

The research picture has been a quiet one so far, largely because the many projects recently funded with federal money will take a while to mature. But in many areas of librarianship there has been added a steady and definite concern with research.

Library trustees made the news this year in a wide variety of ways, from vigorous lobbying in Washington to exhibitions of both good and bad handling of censorship and tenure issues; most of the new legislation or rulings that affected trustees, however, tended to restrict their power and length of their terms.

A lot of the library news was made by the public libraries of our big cities, as they attempted to respond to the evils of inequality in the society while fighting to maintain—and occasionally improve—inadequate financing.

The unrest in the society made one small and ugly subdivision of library news which we can group under "security," a term growing common today though almost never heard five years ago.

There has been little newsworthy in such things as acquisitions, cataloging and classification, circulation, reference work, administration—the traditional areas of library technology—but what there is, generally is concerned with automation. Yet here is an area where nems has been very thin indeed, although promises and projections are still being made.

### Intellectual Freedom

The year was already half over when incoming ALA president William Dix said that the primary concern of ALA for the coming year would be intellectual freedom. And ALA, thanks to its vigorous director of the Office of Intellectual Freedom, Judith Krug, did rather more along this line than ever before. Its two notable actions were a move to set up a defense fund for librarians discharged because they stood up for intellectual freedom— and a rather unexpected ruling which allowed ALA staffers time off to participate in Vietnam Moratorium activities.

It was a good year for ALA to get rolling, for the tides of censorship were rising everywhere. The book title which drew the most fire was *Portnoy's Complaint,* which made headlines in Chattanooga, Memphis, Jamestown (N.Y.), Ukiah (Calif.), and many another community. Librarians and trustees—most of the time—seemed to have shown a new militancy. Notable examples were the Chattanooga Public Library Board of Trustees and Murray L. Bob, director of the Chautauqua-Cattaraugus Library System, operating out of Jamestown, New York. Both met censorship moves head-on with articulate and vigorous statements—and both won.

Meanwhile, there were developments on the broader national and international scene. A preliminary report was filed by the Commission on Obscenity and Pornography, and a reading of its plans for action reassures one that this committee is no witch-hunt expedition, but will sponsor several valuable studies into the effect of pornography on people—since the chief reason given for banning "obscenity" or "pornography" is that they cause crime.

Shortly after, a survey taken of a large number of mental health specialists by a University of Chicago project, showed that few psychologists or psychiatrists agree that there is any serious danger in pornography.

Meanwhile, Denmark goes its way, having thrown out all its laws against pictorial or printed pornography. The results so far show a sudden boom in sale of pornographic materials, then a falling off as the forbidden fruit became common. Sex crime incidence is also reported to have dropped. And tourism is benefitting as Europeans from other less permissive nations pour in on charter flights for such events as a recent pornography fair. A British group has asked that Britain follow suit by suspending all its smut laws.

In New York, censorship of publications from "enemy" countries (Cuba, North Vietnam, and Mainland China mostly) came under legal attack by the New York Civil Liberties Union.

But as a conference sponsored by the Freedom of Information Center at the University of Missouri told Missouri librarians, censorship pressure is rising all over the country, and things will be worse before they are better. In 1969, one response of librarians was to confer the first annual Robert B. Downs Award for outstanding contribution to intellectual freedom to LeRoy Charles Merritt, a good point man for what will be a distinguished band of warriors.

The grim topic of intellectual freedom has its occasional laughs, however. One of these stemmed from the report of a religious group waging its own low-pressure war against *Portnoy's Complaint* and the ilk by slipping little religious tracts in between the pages to catch the sinner on the very brink of perdition and haul him to safety. The other incident was credited to the Farmingdale, N.Y. Trustee Carl Groton, that Birch-society dropout who is rapidly becoming a figure in library folklore. In the interests of intellectual freedom, he announced, he wanted the library to stock the *Protocols of the Elders of Zion* and *The International Jew,* both standard devotional works for anti-Semites. The library board turned him down, on the grounds of lack of demand since the books were available on interlibrary loan from the state library.

Washington, D.C. librarians put in their oar last year to criticize government crack-downs on the underground press—as did Children's Specialist Joan Bodger of the Missouri State Library, who publicly criticized the University of Missouri for the same thing. The promptness with which she was fired when the troglodytes began to growl in the local press and in the legislature provided an instructive note on the state of freedom in middle America.

Governor Lester Maddox of Georgia, patron saint and archetype of all the good, decent proponents of censorship, advised Georgians to "Burn those books"—especially books on subversive subjects like anthropology, political science, and human ecology. American Legionnaires rose up in Kingston, New York, to ask for a ban on the magazine *Ramparts;* other good Americans attacked the Inglewood, California Public Library for having records by the Beatles and the Doors, both groups, they pointed out, having advocated drug use on their records. The Inglewood trustees, to their credit, didn't give an inch.

The *Evergreen Review,* a perennial target of censors, raised a real furor in Los Angeles. Under attack from a city councilman, the library board overrode the advice of Director Harold E. Hamill and yanked the magazine issue off the shelves. They found out that turning tail didn't solve anything. They were immediately called down in public by the Los Angeles Library union, by the staff of the nearby Claremont Colleges, and shortly thereafter their director and his chief assistant resigned. *Evergreen* went back to the shelf.

Librarians were also active in defending the lesbian film *Therese and Isabelle* in Pittsburgh; Maryland librarians were prominent in attacking a state obscenity bill; and John Forsman stood up and slugged it out with the censors in Richmond, California, over the *Berkeley Barb,* an underground newspaper which he believed should be in the public library. Forsman was one of the major casualties, however, as censorship advocates prevailed in Richmond.

Intellectual freedom of another sort was invoked in the case of Ellis Hodgin, Martinsville, Virginia, library director. He is suing the city manager for firing him in retaliation for his taking part in a suit to stop illegal Bible-reading in the public schools; Hodgin hopes to prove that the firing was a violation of his constitutional right to free speech.

The saddest censorship story of the year was that of Joan Bodger and the Missouri State Library. Figuring also in the events were the Missouri

Library Association and Ralph H. Parker, the distinguished librarian of the University of Missouri. Here a valid issue of intellectual freedom was ducked and knuckling under to censorship forces was justified by denying that the Bodger case involved any issue of intellectual freedom at all. In the end, Ralph Parker squelched a move to have the case thoroughly investigated by telling the Missouri Library Association that Mrs. Bodger had been fired solely because she used "foul language." And the meeting was gavelled to a close before anyone could respond in her defense or point out what were believed to be definite inconsistencies in Parker's account of the incidents leading to Mrs. Bodger's dismissal from the State Library—by the Missouri Library Commission, of which he is a member.

Parker can lay claim to one significant advance in the means that librarians have at their command for dealing with touchy intellectual freedom cases. And that is to simply deny that the issue has anything to do with intellectual freedom at all and proceed with a clear conscience to clobber the person that the censors have fingered for retribution.

### The Insurgents

The year 1969 saw a swift rise of groups dedicated to unseating the establishment of ALA and making it an association more responsive to what they felt were their concerns. These insurgents were sparked by (mostly) young library school students and recent alumni, backed by the considerable number of ALA members who are either loudly or quietly dissident.

The insurgency move ran on a lot bigger engines than either personal ambition or grudges against the establishment. It allied itself with the great moral issues of the late sixties, issues which have almost everyone up a pole: Vietnam, black inequality, Intellectual Freedom.

Starting with ALA, the young insurgents stated their demands, asking for more democracy in the running of their association (everybody agreed that was fine); more action on intellectual freedom (that was nice, too); and so on. The crunch came when the young doves asked for resolutions against the Vietnam war and the hawks scrambled to shoot them down.

The story of the happenings at the ALA meeting in Atlantic City has been related in detail in *LJ* and elsewhere. What has not been so generally realized by all those older librarians who, somewhat paternal, somewhat conscience-stricken, went along with what could be taken for just another large public gesture—the kind of thing that associations seem particularly well equipped to provide staging for—is that Atlantic City was only the beginning, and that between Atlantic City and Detroit a year later, when the average ALA member was busy about local concerns, the new insurgents would be endlessly meeting, talking, planning.

They group themselves under a variety of banners, and the edges of the groups tend to run into each other. There are the Librarians for 321.8; the Congress for Change; the National Freedom Fund for Librarians; the National Call for Library Reform; the local chapters of the Social Responsibilities Round Table of ALA. There are new groups set up within state library associations such as California's NEWCALS group, or new Round Tables in the Ohio, New York, New Jersey, Virginia, and Illinois Library Associations or Maryland's Junior Members Round Table—a group which carries a lot more firepower than is implied by the staid name.

There is some support for these ALA-oriented groups coming from union people in libraries, but the picture is not one that is clear cut. Some union movements to date have progressive social and professional goals; others are little more than reflections of local wars between unhappy library staffs and inept library administration.

But support seems to be plentiful in other areas, which indicates that if the young insurgents can keep on providing the structure within which protest can be made in orderly and effective fashion against the heretofore-dominant group of ALA leaders, they stand an excellent chance of winning. Two tendencies will be at work, and their resolution will probably determine how the average ALA member votes when the chance comes for him to mark a ballot for or against a candidate that is committed to immediate change.

These two tendencies are illustrated by two separate meetings. One was a meeting called for the Chicago area to establish a local SRRT group. To the surprise of the sponsors, the turnout included good numbers of young public and academic library administrators—the kind of poeple who will make the final decidion on what kind of ALA we have next year.

The other tendency is demonstrated by the remarks of one older but active ALA member. She thought that the presentation of issues by the younger members at Atlantic City was a good thing, but when a similar group got the floor to bring similar issues before the annual meeting of her state library association, she said she just didn't want to "sit through all that again." How many middle-of-the-roaders will desert the young insurgents when they find that they mean business and are not making a gesture, will have a lot to do with the future of the profession.

The insurgents of 1969 found the case of Ellis Hodgin of Martinsville a natural rallying point, and they were active in starting the National Freedom Fund for Librarians on the road—long before ALA could make its ponderous move to set up machinery to make loans to librarians under attack. NFFL is now thriving.

They laid plans to submit nominations for council seats where there was no candidate for a particular seat clearly committed to change. Detailed plans were also laid to force ALA into holding a full membership meeting in Chicago, at Midwinter, to consider reorganization.

Sympathy of the insurgents for blacks was underlined by an appeal to members attending ALA midwinter in Chicago to patronize black-owned motels. And, of course, the holding of ALA-Midwinter in the city of Mayor Daley, the saint of the Opposition, was opposed.

At this writing, it seems hard to believe that these young insurgents—and their older allies—will not succeed in gaining a very potent voice in

ALA, for they are willing to do the work necessary. In the meantime, ALA is moving in their direction to minimize conflict. One such move is the Activities Committee on New Directions, for ALA, labelled the "Dix Mix," which will provide a means for liberalizing action within the present structure. The other is the effort to put on the important ballot for ALA Council a good number of librarians who are identifiably committed to progress. If successful, these "establishment" moves will allow the question of the future tenor of ALA to be settled peacefully by membership vote. If not, a lot more fireworks are in the offing.

### Protest

Like almost everyone, librarians felt in 1969 the impact of a lot of things generally lumped under the heading of "protest," not including their own protest movement just discussed.

Five years ago, had 90 percent of the staff of a major city's public library stayed home one day to protest their lack of a parking lot, it would have made front pages, plus a lot of cute remarks about mice roaring. This year, it was scarcely noticed—except by the library administration and the library patrons—when this happened at the Los Angeles Public Library.

And it seemed a normal thing for University of Nebraska students to dramatize their need for better library facilities with a good-natured "protest" action that featured a little jerry-built "library" display booth.

Parochial school students descended on the Morton Grove Library in Illinois with their mass protest against some library practices that they felt to be unfair. Chicago Public Library pages put out their own manifesto— surely the first time the library profession's coolie class has got up the nerve to do anything about their lot.

In England, students at Manchester College and Salford College held a sit-down strike to protest their lack of proper library facilities. And the subject of protest seemed important enough at Cornell for the library to embark on a project to document recent disturbances on the campus by oral history techniques.

"Protest" once again is the theme of a new bibliographical service being launched by students at Carlton College in Minnesota, who are about to bring out the first index to the "alternative press," a guide to articles in some 200 publications.

When federal funds for education and libraries—especially libraries— were slashed in Washington last year, the dimensions of the resultant protest, mounted by library associations, library trustees, and publishing firms, all joined in a consortium of everyone else concerned with education, were truly astounding. And threatened budget cuts in cities like New York and Newark, which would have crippled public library service, were the subject of massive and fiery protest meetings and demonstrations.

But the thing at the root of so much of everyone's troubles, the Vietnam war, was the hottest issue, and one which divided librarians severely. Many felt that no library association or institution had any business in expressing a point of view on Vietnam. Others felt as strongly that their associations, their institutions, even their profession meant little unless they tangled with the issue.

The Vietnam Moratorium days, October 15, and November 13 and 14, brought the matter to a point where decisions had to be made—even if it were to be a decision to perch securely on a fence.

To almost everyone's surprise, ALA's David Clift made a quiet but decisive move, important because it had not waited on a bandwagon. ALA employees were notified that they could take off October 15 without loss of pay if they wished to observe the first Moratorium day. This coverage will go to press before any news can be reported of either the November or December happenings, but as of early November, a sizable "Librarians for Peace" contingent was signed up to march on Washington.

Many librarians, acting as individual citizens, observed the October 15 Moratorium by taking to the streets. Many others felt that their duty lay in keeping their libraries open to give people access to materials and programs dealing with Vietnam, and to make discussion areas available. Most institutions which did anything to observe the day put out pro-and-con displays on the war; only one to our knowledge acted to protest Vietnam without equivocation: the Oshkosh Public Library, where librarian Leonard B. Archer took the flag down to half mast, displayed anti-war materials, and marched in the local peace parade with his children. And, as one might expect, he made a date with a hot carpet by doing so.

### The Budget Cuts

We started out the year with a new administration in the White House, an unknown quantity in every way. The new secretary of Health, Education, and Welfare, Robert Finch, was a straw to grasp at, for in his political career in California he had not only been a booster of libraries, but he had refused to go along with the pro-censorship views of many in his party.

After a long wait, the new Commissioner of Education, James Allen, announced a reorganization of the Office of Education that promised a chance at least of upgrading the Division of Library Programs, which had built up a good, talented staff under director Ray Fry, but had been severely hampered by its slot in the OE organization. This situation found it under a Vocational Education administrator. This was changed, and the DLP wound up in harness with something called "Educational Technology." Two more higher administrators were programmed into the structure between the Division and the Commissioner's Office, but to date these slots have not been filled and, indeed, no one seems to know what sort of bedfellow the DLP is to have in the unknown quantity labeled "Educational Technology."

The first real blow on the Washington front came with the Nixon budget, which cut library programs unmercifully—harder, indeed, than most other education programs. Secretary Finch was quoted as saying he felt library programs were very important, but they did not rank as high as many others in the top priority criterion of doing something about poverty.

A quick survey of state library agencies by *LJ* revealed that the effect of the cuts would be to wipe out almost all library activities aimed at the poor. And the next most severely hit would be the purchasing of books and other library materials.

Another survey revealed that most legislators were strongly opposed to library program cuts. Trustees marched on Washington to collar their legislators, and to these trustees, and the skilled efforts of ALA and other associations, has to go the credit for letting legislators know that if they bucked the White House on the educational section of the budget, they would have the backing of a lot of very angry people.

The House revolted with the now-famous Joelson Amendment; and at this writing it will be only a matter of time before the fate of a joint House-Senate Resolution is known. Prospects are good for an overthrow of the Nixon cuts, but failure is still possible; also possible is the carrying out of a Nixon threat to freeze the money and not allow it to be spent no matter what Congress does. But the big news out of all this is that library forces, in coordination with all the other (and bigger) forces with a stake in education, can now field a lobbying pressure that until recently was reserved for the makers of war materials and the builders of highways.

Similar actions brought against local authorities for threats to cut library funds brought vigorous action—sometimes with results, sometimes not. Newark and New York staved off—not cuts in budget increases, but cuts back below what they already had. Detroit was running libraries on shortened hours; the town of Farmingdale, on Long Island, closed the main library for several weeks to make ends meet; and the pinch was felt in many another community. The only big library to get good financial news (I believe) was the Chicago Public Library, which won new state legislation which would allow it a much higher income.

### The Cities

Chicago—home of Mayor Daley—was also planning actively to add a big new piece of main library building to its old structure, and as announced an architectural competition. CPL has also put out a call for a superman to run their big, scary mess of a library system—the job will pay $35,000, say the trustees.

In other big cities: the Victoria, British Columbia Public Library cut out almost all its book funds for the coming year. Los Angeles lost its director and his chief assistant after the library commission fumbled its job once too often, but a boost of $100,000 in new money from Mayor Yorty enabled branch hours to be greatly extended. Oakland, California is batten-

ing down the hatches for a severe budgetary storm; cutbacks in book purchasing are slated for the big Baltimore County Public Library, and the St.
Paul Public Library, faced with a slash of $140,000 has cut its hours of
service. Detroit has cut back on evening hours, staff, and book purchase in
order to make ends meet.


## Library Education

It looks as though 1969 will go down as the year in which a lot of
interesting new things began to happen in library education, after a good
many years of a dialogue that consisted largely of gripes and defenses
against gripes. Partly the changes have been made possible by new money
to work with; partly they seem to be the initiative of library educators
responding to student and alumni criticism and calls for help from practitioners needing more and better librarians.

A rundown of some of the high spots shows newly accredited programs
at Western Ontario, University of Missouri, University of Montreal, and San
Jose State College. New library schools opened at the University of Puerto
Rico and the University of Arizona, and another is in the cards for Ohio
State.

Upgrading of the potentials of another group of schools shows in the
new Ph.D. programs at the University of Minnesota, the University of
Texas, and the University of Oklahoma, while a new Master's program is
announced for the University of Wisconsin at Oshkosh.

Educational innovation is high-lighted by the University of Michigan's
computer-assisted reference course; new computers for Berkeley library
science students to work with; and the ambitious Syracuse LEEP computer
laboratory experiments. The University of Southern California announced
an impressive new group of censorship courses, following ground broken the
year before at Simmons, and at the University of Pittsburgh, the library
school has been reorganized into a two-department structure—one for traditional library science, one for information and communication science.
Southern California is also pioneering with a plan to let undergraduates take
heretofore graduate-only courses.

Little has happened yet, but much is forecast for the active involvement
of students in the planning of their education in library science. So far we
note the resolution passed at the New York Library Association, which
would urge all library schools to give equal representation on curriculum-
planning bodies to students, alumni, and teachers. At the University of
Michigan a plan was reported early in 1969 to choose the next dean from a
list of candidates submitted by a board composed of faculty and students.
And at Columbia University, a tough evaluation of all courses by students
set a model for similar action elsewhere.

Little action has yet been reported in an area where all educators know
they will have to move: continuing education. Maryland, however, ran for a

second year a Library Administrators Development Program and studies are starting to come in on just what is wanted and needed.

The education of the library technician or library technical assistant seems to have proved that it is no flash in the pan, though as a concept it is far from achieving full acceptance. A big step was taken with the release of the new standards for education of technicians by ALA's Library Education Division. The University of Kentucky has taken on its shoulders responsibility for providing what guidance it can to the programs developing in the community colleges of the state. A number of new programs were announced, among them an associate degree program at the Vocational Technical Institute of Southern Illinois University, and a two-year program at the Wilson Campus of Chicago City College. And a technician program scuttled last year at Brigham Young University, in Provo, Utah, was reconstituted and is rolling again.

All this activity bears a real relationship to the focus brought to bear on manpower problems by ALA three years ago. And while education is the main approach right now in meeting manpower needs, a nod is deserved by the New York Public Library, which waved a wand and turned some 20-odd professional positions into "Information Assistant" positions to be filled by people with a bachelor's degree working in subjects for which they have the intellectual background, although they may have no library experience.

And strange as it may seem, manpower shortages may not necessarily be always with us. In Great Britain this last year, a quick counting of heads and tallying of positions revealed that if librarians are turned out any faster than at present, England will shortly have a surplus of this valuable commodity. Incidentally, if they do, it won't help U.S. libraries unless the decade-long project to do something about figuring equivalencies for foreign library education gets off dead center and does something.

### Academic Status

The question of academic status got heated up a little in 1969. Improved, if not perfect changes in status were reported at colleges like Bucknell and Penn State. And out in California, where state college librarians have been waiting with surprising patience for the state to come through on promises which it made long ago, sanctions were voted by the California Library Association. Librarians were advised to leave the state colleges if possible, and libraries elsewhere in the state were urged to try to help the refugees find suitable new positions.

### Unions

It was a relatively quiet year for library union activity, but more librarians than ever were seriously considering the merits of collective bargaining, and many an association meeting heard speakers pro and con. In January, college and university librarians meeting at Columbia heard an often acrimonious debate on the subject, learning, among other things, that unions attract a fair number of people who like to holler.

At ALA, a hospitality suite was set up by an AFL-CIO group, and a lot of librarians stopped by in search of enlightenment.

Meanwhile, in more than one community, trustees and administrators were getting pointers from professional union foes on how to keep the union away from the door—or how to keep it from biting once it got in.

In Richmond, California, library union members spoke out firmly against threatened censorship; in Los Angeles, they even took their own Library Commission to task for folding up on a similar issue. And in Oakland, the union made what seems to be the first intelligent new suggestion in ages on what to do about censorship—beyond fighting the censors. They suggested a procedure for negotiating differences, and if it works, they will have made a real breakthrough in communications between the librarian and his public.

## Cooperation

Hardly a library today of any type is not involved in some formal kind of cooperative scheme, be it a system, a consortium, a network, or whatever. The past year saw an increasing number of announcements of new consortia formed by academic institutions. They ranged from the actual sharing of a new library building by neighboring institutions to creation of a central pool of reference materials or sharing of specialized materials. Little has been heard from any of these arrangements, but as experience is gained, one can expect to learn a lot about the mechanics and the advantages and difficulties of these consortia—into which many institutions seem to have leaped with not too much planning, but a determination to qualify for federal funds.

Public library systems, on the other hand, are by comparison venerable institutions, yet we are beginning to learn much about them that has been concealed by rosy public relations work. Systems librarians are only now beginning to realize that they have their hands on machines for which no one has written the manual, and what may be gospel in the administration of a city branch system or an individual library may be of the highest irrelevance to the new task of system administrator. One result of this in New York State has been the formation of an association of system directors to share knowledge and create a means of communication that otherwise does not exist. Alert library educators can be expected to explore this ground in the future—with the blessing of aministrators.

Three news stories point up the need for knowing more about this area than we do now. One told of the dissolution of Minnesota's first public library system—one which had not by any means been a lemon, but was noted for breaking a lot of new ground.

A second related the secession from its Canadian system of the Penticton Public Library—and indicated some of the political stresses that brought this about. And a third noted the strong protest brought by the Buena Park, California Public Library against what its trustees felt to be policies which discouraged rather than rewarded vigorous local initiatives in library development. There were others, and too frequently they revealed stresses which had not been suspected when this particular answer to the ideal of "library cooperation" took its first shape.

One study looks as if it could be a landmark, or at the very least a valuable direction guide. This was *The Regional Library Center in the Mid-1970's: a Concept Paper* by Thomas Minder, published by the Graduate School of Library and Information Science of the University of Pittsburgh. The picture it sketched in of the role of the central facility, which must exist in some form for any cooperative venture of magnitude, departs from the idea—or ideal—of the necessity of a system center to have line authority in order to effect its services to the member institutions. Increasingly relevant debate on this subject can be expected in 1970, and indeed is badly needed.

In the area of cooperation, a number of other news stories have more than passing interest. Two Iowa university libraries are coordinating the automation plans, starting with what seems an admirable item: sharing the coordinator. The District of Columbia area libraries are forming an inter-state interloan system which will embrace eight public library systems, the National Library of Medicine, and four university libraries. In Wisconsin, the ideal of intertype library service moves a little closer to reality with the opening up of the state library reference and loan services to public, school, and academic libraries. And the Southern California Answer Network (SCAN) will link the Los Angeles Public, several large library systems, the state library, and the Library of Congress.

A new departure in New York is the chartering of a county reference library to serve the huge Nassau County Library System, which has got along to date without a real core collection of reference materials. The new library, an ambitious one, will also serve several academic and special libraries in the booming Long Island area—and could set an organizational model of great interest to many regions of the nation.

One of the most promising schemes for central processing got into actual operation at the University of Colorado, where, with National Science Foundation funding, a year's trial run will test the merits of an advanced system through the processing of some 60,000 books.

### Research

Undoubtedly one of the areas of librarianship suffering most from the lack of "packaging" to make it really accessible to the working librarian is research, which is just beginning to proliferate in the often-cryptic listings from the ERIC operation—not that these are to be denigrated by any means. But too often the only way to find the tiny kernel of knowledge in a huge report is to read the whole thing, at unconscionable expenditure of time. Abstracts rarely give more than a general idea of the area dealt with, especially if written by the author of the research study.

The function of rendering the fat of a really important report into English is largely just not being performed, and no listing of contents pages, or compilation of abstracts, or publishing of lists will really help very much. The best that can be offered at this time is a skimming of some of the more general news about the whole library research effort as it flowers under the guidance—and watering—of the federal funds now available to augment what has been going on under foundation support and self-supported work by students in doctoral programs.

Some straws in the wind are hereby offered: a new Library Research Center is announced for the University of Toledo, while the one already going strong at Kent State announces that it has the talent and will research for any institution which can pay the freight. British library research, we hear, has increased in quantity by 30 percent.

The Office of Education has been leaning toward research projects which will yield evaluations useful for policy decisions, and one such will evaluate library programs serving the urban poor in 15 cities.

A little-noted user study done for the Los Angeles Public Library would seem to be freighted with importance, if for nothing else than consideration of the implications behind one of its findings: that people come to the central library, not to take advantage of specialized staff service, but for books. Bit of heresy there?

Some kind of painful turning point is signalled by the statement of the Connecticut State Library that it will no longer fill out long, time-consuming questionnaires—free.

And a reading of the annual report of the Council on Library Resources has been particularly rewarding this year. Usually it is frustrating, because like many organizations, the Council tends to put into every annual report everything it has ever done, giving to the unpracticed eye the illusion that a truly marvelous year of activity has just passed by.

CLR, however, is edging into a second decade and testing the water carefully. With a lot of research money available to libraries from other sources, it will need to be more selective if it is to have its greatest effect. The report issued in 1969 gives a glimpse of some of the soul searching that is going on at CLR.

Automation, it concedes, is not just around the corner. It is going to cost an awful lot of money just to achieve automation—but to keep the monster running is going to be even more expensive. CLR sounds pessimistic for the first time, but it says that it is still going to back what look like really sound projects working toward library automation.

Returning to the thought at the beginning of this section on research, we recall the statement reportedly made by Dean Swanson of the University of Chicago Graduate Library School in a 1969 speech. Talking about the publication and information explosion, he said that there would have to be some kind of packing down or implosion of information. And a similar thought was voiced by iconoclast Harrison Bryan in an *Australian Library Journal* article. The publications explosion, he said, is more talked about than real, since a great deal of research is published in several repetitive forms, and much of the publication going on is not intended for the transfer of information. Which brings us back to the need for repackaging, and thence to the topic of library literature.

## The Literature

Among the major circulation library periodicals, *LJ* can claim the dubious distinction of suffering the greatest changes in personnel, with Eric Moon leaving to head up Scarecrow Press and Margaret Cooley retiring from the editorship of the Book Review section. Fortunately, in both cases, replacements were found among *LJ* alumni: John Berry was recaptured from the Bowker Book Division, which had gotten him away in 1966; and Judith Serebnick, formerly on the staff of the Book Review and seasoned with terms in acquisitions work at Northwestern University and later at Princeton, was brought back to take Margaret Cooley's place. Eric Moon, be it noted, has not left the field of library literature; Scarecrow, which has developed into a formidable source of books related to librarianship—among other things—will expand its publishing program.

A notable change has taken place at *Special Libraries*, with Frank McKenna taking over the full-time editorship. The results are already happily apparent to *SL* readers. But still ahead of us at this writing is the promised revamping of the venerable *ALA Bulletin*, which has been hailed more than once this last year as the most improved library periodical going—under the editorship of Gerry Shields. A new size, new design, and lots of color are promised.

Other Good Things: the reformatting of the *New York Library Bulletin* to newsletter style—something we wish almost every state association would do to keep their news and information from becoming history before they ever reach a public.

Also new this year are periodicals or newsletters emanating from the social responsibility groups which are springing up around the nation—although it is to be hoped that as the young insurgents in the library world begin to make themselves heard, they will also contribute to the pages of their state and national periodicals; a group of them did recently in *Maryland Libraries*, where they gave one of the more frank evaluations of a library association meeting that we have seen.

## Miscellaneous

Looking back on a year of library news, after I have sorted out the big matters, I still have left a mixed bag of things I am not quite sure what to do with. Of such is the large and growing number of reports which have to do with library "security." The Buffalo and Erie County Library is planning to get four walkie-talkie sets to help its big guard force control troublesome people. Two libraries which installed TV people-watchers have had to put up with a certain amount of flak from some readers, but a lot of people like to see a crackdown on misbehavior. At the University of California in Berkeley, they felt it necessary to give the staff detailed instructions on tear gas treatment. Brooklyn had to close a branch library in a slum area after vandalism and violence made it untenable for the librarians staffing it. A library used largely by black children was burned out in Hartford; arson hit the library of Indiana University twice; apprehensive University of Washington librarians were microfilming the card catalog; a Molotov cocktail hit the Bronx campus library of NYU; a bomb hit West Berlin's American Memorial Library; vandals at Beloit flooded the library; $50,000 damage was done to the card catalog of the University of Illinois; two Molotov cocktails hit the USIS library in Frankfurt; and the University of Washington suffered $100,000 damage, mostly in glass breakage, when a bomb was set off outside it.

These are not all the examples of damage willfully caused, nor all the stories noted in the library press about security measures and programs to defend libraries against one or another danger. They are, without question, more numerous than ever before, and take their meaning from their numbers.

Looking back on this brief account of one year's library news, I am struck by the logical extension of this last observation. All the things which happen in a year gain a great deal of their significance from other, often apparently unrelated events, that occupied the same world at the same time.

*Karl Nyren*

## DATE DUE

| | |
|---|---|
| | |
| | |
| | |
| | |
| | |
| | |
| | |
| | |
| | |
| | |
| | |
| | |
| | |
| | |